THE
SLANG OF
SIN

By Tom Dalzell

THE SLANG OF SIN

By Tom Dalzell

Illustrations by Istvan Banyai

Merriam-Webster, Incorporated
Springfield, Massachusetts

Copyright © 1998 Tom Dalzell

Library of Congress Cataloging-in-Publication Data

Dalzell, Tom 1951-
    The slang of sin / by Tom Dalzell
        p.   cm.
    Includes bibliographical references (p.   ) and index
    ISBN 0-87779-356-5 (hardcover : alk. paper) — ISBN 0-87779-627-0
(pbk. : alk. paper)
        1. English language—United States—Slang—Dictionaries.
    2. English language—United States—Etymology. 3. Vice—
    Terminology. 4. Sin—Terminology. 5. Americanisms. I. Title
    PE2846.D35 1998

    427'.973—dc21   98-26827
                                                        CIP

Printed and bound in the United States of America

123456RRD009998

For Mother, who aced the final.
And, for Jake and Julia—we remember Karleen.
As ever, for Dick—I can hear your voice as you read
"Oh father, dear father, come home with me now. . . ."

Contents

Acknowledgments

ALTHOUGH I REALIZE the potentially dubious honor of being recognized for one's contribution to a book about sin, I thank the following people for their help: Paul Dickson and Madeline Kripke, slang mentors of the ages. Paul is a great American in every sense of the words, and Madeline has forgotten more about the literature of slang than any of the rest of us will ever know. Archie Green, a scholar and humanist whose eyes are always on the prize and who demands that my eyes stay there.

John Morse of Merriam-Webster, whose appreciation of slang as a legitimate voice made this book possible.

Alicia diLeo of Merriam-Webster, who gave me a big "thumbs up" whenever I needed support.

Also at Merriam-Webster: Jennifer N. Cislo, who did most excellent copyediting; E. Ward Gilman, who brought erudition and humor to his reading of the manuscript; Sarah E. LeSure, who contributed citation research; Kara L. Noble, for her awesome help indexing; and Thomas F. Pitoniak, whose grasp of lexicography and popular culture enhanced the final edit of the manuscript and who coordinated production of the book. Rebecca B. Bryer, Deanna M. Chiasson, Donna L. Rickerby, Michael D. Roundy, Karen L. Wilkinson, and Linda Picard Wood also helped with proofreading and indexing.

Bob Ciano of the Encyclopaedia Britannica Art Department, and Joseph Paschke, who created and carried out the design of the book.

Randy Roberts, who until last year was the principal archivist working with the Peter Tamony Collection at the Western Historical Manuscript Collection at the University of Missouri, Columbia, for his scholarly and inspired mastery of Tamony's life work. This book was drawn in no small part from the Tamony Collection, and Randy's help was invaluable.

Language writers Reinhold Aman, who is a brave pioneer, Barry Popik, Robert Chapman, Gerald Cohen, Trevor Cralle, Jim Crotty, Connie Eble, Jonathan Lighter, Pamela Munro, Judi "Da Bomb" Sanders, and Jesse Sheidlower, all of whom helped one way or another to breathe life into *The Slang of Sin*.

Shawn Berlinn, who was there for the birth of *Sin* and whose comments polished it along the way.

Lynn Faris and Mark Cromer for their leads, Kathy Zingaro who shared from her collection, and Frank Potestrio who guided.

And not least, the book dealers who helped stock the sin section of the Slang Library—most notably James Musser of Skyline Books; Patterson Smith; Donnis de Camp and Marc Selvaggio of Schoyer Books; C. J. Scheiner; and Jean Kapp Van Fleet and Daryl Van Fleet of Bibliomania.

INTRODUCTION

LOOKING AT THE PICTURES AND turning the pages of American history, one is struck by the fact that our past is filled both with sin and with those who have been eager, too eager at times, to denounce sin in all of its manifestations— smoking, drinking, horse racing, gambling, cockfighting, enjoying oneself on the Sabbath, playing pinball or shooting pool, the popular election of judges, celebrating Christmas, and so on. We are a culture of shame; we are ever ashamed of our lust, our desires, and our sinful nature. We are, though, also a culture of selective denial. We denounce a sin (such as gambling), yet create an exception (such as bingo). Pious on the Sabbath, on Saturday night we find ourselves in the haunts of the low and vile, in dance halls or saloons or casinos, where bleary-eyed men and faded women drink, smoke, engage in vulgar conduct, sing obscene songs, and say and do everything to heap upon ourselves degradation after degradation, rejoicing in licentiousness, debauchery, pollution, loathsome disease, dissipation, misery, profanity, and blasphemy.

Whatever this book may be, it is not a theological or philosophical treatise on sin, morality, or virtue. Ten years of an Episcopalian education which ended almost 30 years ago, in which the subject of sin was glossed over once a month in the general confession ("I have done those things which I ought not to have done and left undone those things which I ought to have done"), did not prepare me anywhere near adequately for a religion-based discussion of morality and immorality. I have made a conscious effort to avoid the dogmatic whenever possible. I respect those who are sincere on all sides of the religion fence, and I neither mock those who believe nor condemn those who transgress. Throughout, I use the terms "sin" and "sinner" quite loosely, referring to conduct that is generally considered to be on the vice side of the scales. Do I truly believe that those who play pinball, shoot pool, or drink coffee are sinners? Hardly. I simply recognize that these activities, and those included as sins here, have been at times considered by society to be vices.

Our willingness to sin and our shame at having sinned are secondary concerns here though. Of primary interest is the language that we use when we break the rules, when we do that which society, driven by religious and/or secular tenets, deems that we ought not do. Sin and the seedy, vice and venery, the underworld and the underside of life all produce one of the richest bodies of slang in the English language. It is no accident that many of the early slang dictionaries dealt heavily, if not exclusively, with the slang and cant of criminals, lowlifes, and patrons of the sins.

Why is it that we are so inventive in our language when we set out to sin? How is it possible that even those who are engaged in horribly destructive conduct develop, acquire, and use such innovative and resourceful slang? Why is the language of the sinner so much cooler than the language of the saint?

Some believe that those who break the law develop a private language to mask the meaning of what they are discussing from all but fellow sinners, and especially from the secular authorities with uniforms, badges, and the power of arrest. This may have been true at one time, but with several notable exceptions (the use of coded slang by con grifters and the use of slangy jargon by pornographers) it is not true today. The slang of sin is not spoken in front of the uninitiated, but rather with fellow initiates. In most instances, the police are among the first to pick up new slang of sin; they may sound goofy when they use the slang, but they definitely understand it. For these related reasons, the desire to conceal the meaning of what is said is most often not the motivation for the use of slang by sinners.

Another theory that I don't find particularly convincing is that the slang of sin is developed to name techniques, equipment, people, things, and experiences that are not adequately named in standard English. Again, this may be true in limited circumstances, such as the development, discovery, or arrival of a new drug, but it does not fully explain the constant renaming that goes on in the slang of sin. If all we needed was a name, "marijuana cigarette" would have sufficed, or perhaps one slang synonym, **twist**. If we had **twist**, why did we need **reefer**? If we had **reefer**, why did we need **joint**? If we had **joint**, why did we need **doobie**? Occasionally a single word establishes and maintains a monopoly in the field, but as a rule, the generation of new slang continues as the sin continues, undercutting the theory that the use of slang in sin is driven by a need to name the unnamed.

An explanation that rings true to me is that the slang of sin fulfills the same function as the slang of youth, to establish a group identity, and a cool identity at that. By using a specialized nonstandard vocabulary when we sin, we are expressing our identity as a subculture or counterculture. If I can talk the talk of the bar, blackjack table, drug subculture, racetrack, strip joint, pool hall, or pinball arcade, I can probably walk the walk. Most sinners do not proclaim their sinning status to the world at large, although the Hells Angels do leap to mind as a striking exception. By using the slang of the sin, however, we can build an identity and we can establish our cool status as fellow cool sinners without necessarily revealing ourselves to the non-sinning, uncool public at large. Slang becomes a lingua franca, the language used by all those seated around the blackjack table or at the racetrack, melding regional and cultural differences into a common language.

A final reason for the abundance of the slang of sin is the pure joy of being a wordsmith. As a species and as a culture we have a strong creative streak that is at times revealed in language; if Elbert Hubbard were alive today, he would neutralize the gender in a comment from *Concerning Slang and Other Droll Stories* (East Aurora, N.Y.: The Roycrofters, 1920) and say that "slang was not made for people ["man"], but people for slang." On top of our natural tendency to slang, sin in all of its manifestations excites linguistic creativity. When we stray from the straight and narrow, we lose our inhibitions, moral, sexual, emotional, and rhetorical. New and clever words and expressions—or new and clever meanings attached to old words and expressions—come to mind and are articulated. The few that are the most popular and, usually, the most clever, survive to fend off newcomers as long as they can until they are themselves deposed and supplanted. Freed from the inhibitions and restraints of societal norms, creativity blossoms, fueled by the thrill of transgression.

Humor and striking images characterize much of the slang of sin, often making the sin sound more glamorous and fun than it really is.

Even in the darkest corners of the human experience and the deepest and most destructive sins, one finds glimmers of the creative spirit in the slang. There is nothing arguably good about delirium tremens, about heroin or crack cocaine addiction, or about life in a maximum security prison, yet the slang of each is vibrant, witty, and powerfully evocative of the experience.

There is some truth in the sentiment that the more nice the vice, the less spectacular the vernacular; put otherwise with a continuing tip of the hat to Johnny Cochran, if the sin is tame, the slang is lame. On the not-nice end of the sin spectrum, over there huddled with the tattooed, convicted felons working out with the weights and with the heroin addicts with their hollow cheeks and darting eyes in search of their next fix, one certainly finds lively language, while at the nice end, at the neighborhood bar, one finds a relatively harmless body of slang. The most spirited gambling slang comes from illegal street crap games, while the ubiquitous and legal lottery games found in much of America have generated no slang, lively or moribund. Sure, bingo players have a cute little idiom, but for a slang vocabulary, give me a meth tweak any day. The illegal status of a sin adds a dimension to its slang not found in most legal sins, and definitely not found in the language of virtue.

In that respect, a startling number of slang-of-sin terms and expressions have found their way into colloquial American English. We decry the fascination of today's youth with the grim and violent urban realities portrayed by gangster rap, yet as a nation we have always had a deep fascination with crime, vice, sin, and decadence. In large part because of exploitation of the slang of sin in fiction, movies, and popular song, we know or think we know how sinners talk or used to talk. The slang of sin creeps into everyday vernacular, at first with a daring and naughty edge, but soon devoid of its original association with sin.

In the chapters that follow, I have tried for a self-explanatory style. Words set in bold face constitute the main entries of this book, be they in an A-Z sequence or set within text. At the end of each chapter is a list of the principal references relied on in the writing of that chapter. Many of the Tamony clippings that are used are from San Francisco newspapers. Reference sources that are referred to and were relied on throughout the book are listed in the Bibliography that appears at the back of the book.

All of this talk of sinning and slanging and still no sin or slang? It's time for a little pick-me-up, an eye-opener—some of that antifogmatic, Balm of Gilead, social lubricant, Dutch courage—it's time to flusterate. Name your poison—it's on the house—shaken or stirred? Bust out those bones and ivories and rocks and stones and tiles and cubes—cut for the deal, run me down, deal me in, paper plays! Shoot the bones, Mr. Jones 'cause you've got a wager, major, bet a chunk and win a hunk—low man feeds! Let's hit the pipe and blow a pill, let's go meet that funny reefer man! Just give me some weed, whites, and wine, and let's slam and bang, jab and jolt, let's get stupid! Are you rolling? Are you experienced? They're at the post . . . they're off . . . it's a sure thing . . . can do! "Hello honey," she says to us, "Would you like some company? Wanna party? Do you want me to get nasty?" Let's sin!

Chapter One:

ALCOHOL

My father is a drunkard, my mother she is dead
And I am just an orphan child, no place to lay my head . . .
We all were once so happy and had a happy home
Till dad he went to drinking rum and then he gambled some.
He left my darling mother; she died of a broken heart,
And as I tell my story, I see your teardrops start.
—*Anonymous 19th-century anti-liquor verse*

ORE THAN ANY OTHER VICE or sin, alcohol has from the earliest Colonial days divided America into a shrill and righteous few who accept the Bible's unreserved disapproval of all alcohol consumption (wine is a "mocker," stronger drink is "raging," and whoever is deceived by alcohol is "not wise") and a tolerant or sinful many who consider alcohol a mild social evil at worst.

From the start, we have had a mixed mind on alcohol—the Puritans who sailed from England to Massachusetts did so with three times as much beer as water, yet as early as 1629 the new colonists began attempts to control excessive consumption and the unseemly if not outright dangerous behavior of those whose consumption was immoderate.

Since our earliest days, we have been unable not to sin, yet we also have been unable not to condemn ourselves for sinning, banding into the Sons of Temperance, the Women's Christian Temperance Union, the Anti-Saloon League, and the Woman's Crusade, crying out for abstinence, rejoicing in the legally dry years of Prohibition, and then fading away, almost silent in the face of the zealous assaults on drug use in the 1980s, still knowing that alcohol is a much greater problem than illegal drugs are or will be, yet jaded after the failure of the Noble Experiment.

Here—sit at the Bemelman's Bar in the Carlisle Hotel on the Upper East Side in Manhattan, sip a cocktail, and with Cole Porter on the piano get used to the dim light and appreciate the hand-painted Madeline-inspired wallpaper, and now listen to the competing voices swirl over the century—the WCTU singing proudly "Forward! to Enforce the Constitution!" as they pass out leaflets telling us that "Alcohol Inflames the Passions, thus making the temptations to sex-sin unusually strong"—*Here she goes! Here's down the hatch! Here's hoping!*—Congressman Richmond P. Hobson of Alabama on the floor of the House of Representatives on December 22, 1914, thundering "Science has thus demonstrated that alcohol is a protoplasmic poison, poisoning all living things; that alcohol is a habit-forming drug that shackles millions of our citizens and maintains slavery in our midst. . . ."—*Here's lookin'! Here's looking atcha! Here's mud in yer eye! Here's the go!*—an advertisement placed by the Ohio Prohibition Campaign shrieking that the saloon's "prosperity depends on the number of victims it entraps

. . . . They ask you to approve temptation of your son to become a drunkard" as the church bells ring in Xenia, Ohio, because the Shades of Death Saloon has surrendered, and in the street there is running a half barrel of blackberry brandy, a barrel of high wine, a few kegs of beer, and bottles of ale and whiskey producing "a rank offense that smelt to heaven" amid the shouts of the enthusiastic multitude—*Here's to you! Here's to your health! Here's how!*— with the WCTU band and choir now launching into "Work for Enforcement Where You Are / Warfare is not over, shout the slogan near and far / Work for enforcement where you are!" *drowned out though by the Kingston Trio's gentle "Scotch and Soda" which gives way to Willie Nelson's joyous "Whiskey River"* . . . .

The voices of drinking are rich with slang. No concept in the English language has generated more slang synonyms than the state of intoxication; drinkers over the decades have churned out literally thousands of slang terms and expressions to use instead of the pedestrian "drunk." Types of alcohol and types of drinks demand slang names, as do bartenders, bars, drinking, and the slang idiom happily complies, providing a largely jocular, moderately clever vocabulary.

Drinking is as social a sin as there is, and this fact accounts for the breadth of the glossary. As alcohol lexicographer Ernest Abel observed, if the number of words associated with a subject reflect the importance of that subject, "alcohol ranks almost supreme in the minds of English-speaking people."

What alcohol slang lacks, though, is that clever, biting, sardonic edge usually found in slang and especially in the slang of sin. Most adults drink, and drinking is not in and of itself illegal, which means that the forces that shape most slang of sin are not present with the slang of alcohol; those who drink escape for the most part any degree of oppression or repression, ostracism or isolation. Slang produced and used by the many is far less sharp than slang produced by a few who are conscious of the fact that they are a few.

American society as a rule makes light of drinking, and so does much of the slang of drinking. Except for the idiom of the moonshiner and the bootlegger, there is no sense of being outside the law found in the slang of drink, and the group using the slang is much too large to develop an in-group identification to be reinforced through an in-group slang.

Despite its breadth, then, the slang of drinking is not particularly deep, not particularly sharp, and not particularly fun. There are exceptions, of course, and some of the brighter little pieces of drinking slang have worked their way as metaphors or loan words to colloquial English.

All this talking makes one thirsty, though. Hey bartender, please don't be so slow—let's **decorate the mahogany** and get down to the serious business of drinking words.

absorb To drink

Act of Congress Beer. *The British version is Act of Parliament.*

Adam's ale, Adam's wine Water

admiral of the blue A tavern keeper

admiral of the narrow seas A drunk who vomits into the lap of another. *A quaint naval term.*

admiral of the red A drunkard

after-dinner man A heavy night drinker

afternoon man A heavy afternoon drinker

ah-so A two-pronged wine opener. *If you've ever tried to work one of these, you'll love this trade name.*

alchy, alki, alky 1. Alcohol 2. An alcoholic

alcoholiday A binge

ale passion A beer hangover

Alkie Hall Alcohol. *This is one of those slang personifications that is much more clever and funny when intoxicated than when not.*

alley juice Pure methyl alcohol

allowance A drink

ammunition Alcohol

angel foam Champagne

angel's share The whiskey that evaporates during the aging process

angel tit High-quality whiskey

Another acrobat! Another drink!

antifogmatic The first drink of the morning

antifreeze Alcohol

appetizer A drink consumed before a meal

apron A bartender

arid Feeling the urge to drink

attitude adjustment hour A several-hour period after work when bars serve drinks at a reduced price in order to attract business

auctioneer A bar patron who talks too much

awakener The first drink of the morning

Baby A quarter bottle of liquor

back Any drink that is served in a separate glass and accompanies alcohol served without ice, as in "I'll have a shot of whiskey with a beer back."

bad corn Home-brewed alcohol

bald face Whiskey

ball A drink

balloon A bar

balm Alcohol

bane Brandy

bank Bar money provided to servers to make change for customer sales

baptized Diluted with water

barbecue An unlicensed, illegal bar

barfly A frequent customer at a bar

barhop To visit one bar after another

barkeep Bartender. *Barkeep was the term used for "bartender" prior to the latter's coining in the 1800s.*

barker A bartender. *A term coined by Damon Runyon.*

barley, barley broth Beer

barley cap A heavy drinker

barrel goods Alcohol

barrel house A bar

barrel stiff An alcoholic

beast, the Alcohol. *This term was later applied to LSD.*

beat To leave a bar without paying the bill

beer boy A bartender

beer emporium A bar

beer jerk, beer jerker A bartender. *Cousins to the cracking-wise soda jerk and soda jerker.*

beertorium A bar

beevo Beer

belly up To drink at a bar

bellywash Poor-quality alcohol

belt the grape To drink heavily

bench The shelf behind the bar on which the bartender uses his tools

bend the elbow To drink

bender   An extended period of drinking

bezzler   A heavy drinker

B-girl   See Word History, page 20.

bib   To take a drink

bibber   A drunkard

bilgewater   Low-quality beer

binge   An extended period of drinking. *Some have pointed to the 19th-century tonic medicine containing alcohol—brand name "Binge"—for the source of this word, but it is well-attested that* **binge** *is derived from the English dialect* "binge," *meaning "to soak."*

bingo   Brandy

bingo boy   An alcoholic

bivvy   Beer

Black Betsy   Whiskey

blacksmith and his helper   A shot of whiskey followed by a glass of beer

blind   An alcohol binge, used in the phrase "on a blind"

bloody shame   A nonalcoholic drink made with tomato juice. *A great little pun at the expense of the bloody Mary.*

blow-out   A party with heavy drinking

blue pig   Whiskey

blue ribbon   Gin

blue ruin   Gin, usually low quality

blue sky   Gin

blue stone   Low-quality gin

blue tape   Gin

boar's nest   A bar

bock beer   Very dark, very strong beer

boilermaker   A shot of whiskey followed by a glass of beer

boiler room   A bar

booster   The first drink of the morning

bootleg   See Word History, page 22.

Drunk, intoxicated, smashed, etc.

More slang synonyms may be found to describe the state of alcohol intoxication than any other word in the English language. Benjamin Franklin was so struck with this fact that in 1733 he published a *Drinker's Dictionary* which included 228 terms and expressions for "intoxicated." Others have made their mark along the way, but language writer Paul Dickson has compiled the mother of all drunk lists. When last published, in *Dickson's Word Treasury* (New York: Wiley, 1992), it contained 2,231 entries. Dickson has added several hundred since and no doubt it will be published again in its growing glory soon.

Sticking with the most commonly used and most likely to be recognized, instead of simply saying that someone is "drunk," one might resort to slang and say that their alcoholized friend is **annihilated, beery, blasted, blotto, bombed, buzzed, croaked, done, embalmed, feeling no pain, fossilized, four sheets to the wind, fucked up, gone, had a few too many, hammered, illuminated, in the bag, juiced, lit, loaded, looped, lubricated, oiled, ossified, pie-eyed, pissed, plastered, plowed, polluted, pounded, ripe, sauced, schnockered, shellacked, shit-faced, smashed, soused, stinko, stoned, tanked, tight, wasted, well,** or **whipped.**

booze *See Word History, page 23.*

booze bazarre A bar

boozer A heavy drinker

boozery A bar

bottle baby An alcoholic

bottle nose A large, red nose that is caused by heavy drinking

bounce Cherry brandy

bracer A drink consumed to regain one's calm

branch Water

brandy blossom A red nose that is caused by heavy drinking of brandy

brave-maker 1. Whiskey 2. Alcohol

breakage The amount of alcohol used during a shift at a bar

breathe a prayer To take a drink

brew, brew dogger, brewhah, brewage, brewski Beer

Brigham Young cocktail Very strong whiskey

brown cow A barrel of beer

bubbly, bubbly water, bubble water Champagne

buck beer Very dark, very strong beer

bucket A double old-fashioned glass

bucket of blood A bar

bucket of suds A glass of beer

bug juice Alcohol

build To prepare a layered drink

bull pen 1. An enclosure with a high fence located next to a bar's rear exit, into which drunk and rowdy customers are thrown until they sober up and calm down 2. The area next to a courtroom where those charged with being drunk can sober up before being tried

bump A drink

bum's rush The rapid ejection of an annoying customer

buster An alcohol binge

button house, button job A union bar

buzz A mild intoxication felt after moderate drinking

cage The service bar

calabash A bottle of liquor. *Calabash is discussed in the booze Word History at the end of this chapter (see page 24).*

call A request by a customer for a specific brand of liquor

candle's end To drain a glass in a toast

canned heat Strong, cheap liquor

Cape Horn Rainwater Rum

cat lap Weak liquor or a nonalcoholic beverage

cat's water Gin

chain lightning Bad whiskey

chase the duck To drink to excess

chaser Any drink that is served in a separate glass and accompanies alcohol served without ice

cheer Alcohol

chilly Beer

chimney A zombie glass

chow bev To drink beer

chuck horrors The craving of food during alcohol detoxification

chug, chugalug To drink hastily

clear crystal Gin

clip joint A bar that cheats customers

cobra head, cobra gun The nozzle on an automated mix system

cocktail *See Word History, page 25.*

coffin varnish Strong, poor-quality whiskey

cold cream Gin

cold tea Brandy

comb An instrument used to scrape suds from freshly poured beer

combo Mixed liquor

comp A drink given by the bar free of charge

concoctail A cocktail

constitutional The first drink of the morning

conversation fluid Whiskey

cop's bottle A bottle of cheap liquor, usually the worst in the bar. *Police are often given free* drinks, served from the cheaper brands.

courage Liquor

cowboy cool Room temperature (said of beer)

crapulate To drink heavily. Related terms include **crap** *(the dregs in a barrel)*, **crapula** *(a hangover)*, **crapulous** *(hungover)*, **crapulence** *(excessive drinking)*, and **crapulent** *(hungover)*.

craw rot Low-quality whiskey

crazy water Liquor

cream of the valley Gin

crib A bar

crimson dawn Cheap red wine

crook an elbow To drink

Croton cocktail A glass of water. *The Croton River is the main source of water for New York City.*

crying jag Intoxication accompanied by crying

cuff Credit given at a bar, usually used in the phrase "on the cuff"

curse of Scotland Whiskey

cut the wolf loose To drink liquor

cutter A liquid used to adulterate liquor

Dago red Cheap Italian red wine

damper A bar's cash register

dandy A small glass of whiskey

daylight The space between the top of the liquid and the top of the glass

deadeye Gin

dead-head stretch it A large, empty glass. *Sounds like it belongs more at a soda fountain than in a bar, but it was recorded by the Federal Writers' Project in 1938.*

dead man, dead Marine, dead soldier An empty liquor or beer bottle

decorate the mahogany 1. To put drinks on the bar 2. To pay for drinks that have been placed on the bar

dehorn Nonbeverage alcohol, consumed by the most destitute of alcoholics

depth charge A shot of whiskey in a glass of beer that is chugged after the drinker announces "Depth charge!" *This combination is also known as a* **submarine.**

derail Illegal liquor

dew drink, dew drop The first drink of a morning

dingle The back room in an illegal bar

dishwater Low-quality, cheap liquor

ditch Water

dive A no-frills bar. *Believe it or not, this term comes from the days of Pro-*

hibition. *(See Slang of the 18th Amendment, pages 8-9.)*

doctor 1. Bartender 2. To adulterate a drink

dog juice Cheap wine

Don't bruise it! Don't stir that drink so much!

dope To adulterate alcohol

double A cocktail using twice the amount of alcohol usually called for

down A cocktail prepared without alcohol that is served to entertainers who must remain sober

drag A drink

dragon's milk Strong ale

drain To drink

drain pipe A drunkard

drap the bead To add concentrated alcohol to increase the proof of a beverage

draw one down To pour a small glass of beer

draw one up To pour a large glass of beer

drench To drink to the point of intoxication

drinker A bar

dry tank A jail cell holding prisoners picked up for drunk driving

duke Gin

dummy An empty liquor bottle

dunk the beak To drink liquor

dusty cutter Whiskey

Dutch courage 1. False courage imparted by

liquor **2.** Liquor *This is just one of several drinking terms derogatory to the Dutch. The vile treatment received by the Dutch in colloquial English is a fascinating bit of linguistic chauvinism, addressed by Paul Dickson in* What's in a Name? (Merriam-Webster, 1997).

Dutch feast A party where the host gets drunk before his guests

Dutch mild, Dutch suds Beer

dynamite Whiskey

eighty-six **1.** Out of a product **2.** To eject a customer from the premises. *Rhyming slang for "nix."*

elevener A drinker who waits until at least 11:00 a.m. before drinking

eye opener The first drink of the morning

eye wash, eye water Gin

facer A glass of whiskey punch

faithful A drunkard

fall off the wagon To start drinking again after a period of abstinence

family disturbance Whiskey

fancy smile A drink

far and near Beer. *Rhyming slang.*

fast house A bar where most of the business con-

sists of mixed drinks

fighting jag Intoxication accompanied by belligerent behavior

filling station A liquor store

firewater Alcohol

fish bowl A large schooner of beer

fizzical culture The art of mixing cocktails

flag A combination of garnishes on a toothpick

flash of lightning

flak shack A bar

flash of lightning A drink of gin

flat dead-head stretch it A small, empty glass. *This is the opposite of dead-head stretch it, also recorded by the Federal Writers' Project in 1938.*

flicker To drink

float Any liquid that is used

to top a drink

flush To drink

fluster, flusterate To drink to the point of intoxication

flying on one wing Having had one drink

fog-cutter The first drink of the morning

foot bath A large glass of beer

fortify To add liquor to wine

forty-rod lightning Strong liquor

forty-two caliber Strong liquor

four fingers A stiff drink

fourteen feathers Thunderbird wine

free pour To pour a drink without using a measuring device

French lace Brandy

frosty Beer

full hand Five beers

gage, gauge Cheap whiskey. *Also a slang term for marijuana.*

gas hound A person who drinks denatured alcohol or Sterno

gas up To drink heavily

gawk An inexperienced bartender

Get it on the line! Drink up!

gin and fog Hoarseness produced by heavy drinking

gin blossom A large, red nose caused by heavy drinking

gin hound A heavy drinker of gin

gin joint A bar. *Humphrey Bogart immortalized this phrase in* Casablanca, *with his musing about all the gin joints in the world.*

gin mill A bar

gin trap The mouth

gin up To drink hard liquor

Slang of the 18th Amendment

ONLY IN AMERICA—a constitutional amendment with its own slang vocabulary! Whatever its considerable failings may have been as social policy, the 18th Amendment was a linguistic success, producing as it did a cheerful and inventive body of slang. Even leaving aside the abundant slang that was produced by organized crime which came into being and power thanks to Prohibition, the slang of Prohibition has much more in common with its cousin the **moonshiner** than it does with its legitimate cousins in the field of legal alcohol. It is inventive, clever, and bright, thanks to the criminal and underground status conferred upon drinking by the United States Constitution between 1919 and 1932.

The Prohibition Era was known variously as the **Noble Experiment** (thank you President Hoover), the **Great Drought**, the **Lost Cause**, and—with humor—the **Prohibition Error.** With a touch of hyperbole of its own, the repeal movement that flourished in the late 1920s and early 1930s was known as **Newer Freedom.**

The vehement Prohibitionist was commonly known as a **teetotaler**, a term which grew up in an 1830s temperance pledge (said variously to be English in origin, born in Hector, New York, or again in Lainsburg, Michigan) to indicate a total abstainer, as distinguished from a person who did not pledge to give up milder forms of alcohol, such as beer and ale. Drawing on the **dry** label of the Prohibitionist (which spun off into **bone dry**, **cracker dry**, and **Drymedary**), the average citizen who opposed Prohibition was known as **dampish**, **moist**, **wet**, **soaking wet**, or **wet as the Atlantic Ocean**. And then there was the **scofflaw**, he or she who defied the Constitution and continued drinking. In 1923, Delcevare King, a millionaire from Massachusetts, staked $200 of his own fortune as prize money for the best new word to describe those who ignored Prohibition. The prize went to two different people, who independent of each other had coined the synthetic slang term **scofflaw**, which survives to this day to describe persons who do not pay their parking tickets. The dual coining is, incidentally, of great interest to slang etymolo-

give a Chinaman a music lesson   To take a drink
glow worm   A heavy drinker
glue   Liquor
go-down   A swallow of liquor
gold   Gold tequila
golden nectar   Beer
good-natured alcohol

Denatured alcohol
good stuff   High-quality liquor. *A term used during Prohibition.*
goon   Beer
go to town   To indulge in an alcohol binge
grease the gills   To drink
grog   Beer
grog hound   An alcoholic

grog up   To take a drink
growler   A can of beer
Guinea red   Cheap Italian red wine
gullet wash   Liquor
gum tickler   A strong drink
gut-warmer   Alcohol
hair of the dog that bit you   The first drink of

gists, supporting at least in an anecdotal fashion the theory that there is often no single source for a catchy slang word or expression.

Passage of the 18th Amendment did nothing to slacken the nation's thirst for liquor. Into the breach stepped the **bootlegger**, whose slang titles included **booter**, **bootician**, **bootie**, **booze hister**, **booze legger**, **duck**, **gob** (especially applied to a smuggler), **legger**, **moonlighter**, **pint peddler**, **porter** (he who actually smuggled flasks of liquor ashore), **puller**, **rat** (applied to a small-time retailer who carried the liquor to be sold on his or her person), **rumrunner** (a term which also was applied to a boat, car, or truck involved in smuggling liquor), and **shell**. The **batman** was the armed guard who made the entire operation safe.

Euphemism was the favored style when it came to describe an entire load of illegal liquor (itself known as **run goods**) being transported—it was **freight**, **goods**, or **hardware**, **stinkibus** if ruined by immersion in the sea. Liquor was most easily purchased at an illegal bar, known most

commonly as a **speakeasy** or a **speak** (a term first found in Pennsylvania in the 1880s) but also known as a **barbecue**, **barrel house**, **blind pig** or **blind tiger**, **creep joint**, **dive**, **half-way house**, **moonlight inn**, **red nugget**, **red onion**, or **sample room**.

In the alternative, one could, and many did, ferment, distill, brew, or otherwise concoct liquor at home; the generic product was known as **home-brew** or **jack ass**. Common homegrown concoctions included **bathtub gin** (alcohol mixed with oil of juniper, which imparted something like the taste of gin), **Jersey lightning** (applejack), **red ink** (homemade red wine), and **Who Shot John?** (a mixed drink of questionable lineage). There was always **near beer**, a legal product that contained less than 1% alcohol. The quite-clever dismissal of **near beer** captured in "The guy who called that near beer is a bad judge of distance" has been variously attributed to cartoonist Thomas A. Dorgan ("TAD"), to Phlander Johnson in *Shooting Stars*, and to Luke McLuke, a columnist for the *Cincinnati Enquirer.*

the morning, said to cure a hangover

hair-raiser   A strong drink

Hallelujah syrup   Whiskey

handshaken   Shaken by hand in a mixing can instead of being mixed in a blender

hang one on   To drink to the point of intoxication

happy hour   A several-hour period after work when bars serve drinks at a reduced price to attract business

happy wet   Stout

head   The layer of foam on top of a poured beer

headache   1. An annoying customer 2. Liquor

heart's ease   Gin

heater and cooler   A shot of liquor followed by a glass of beer

hell around   To indulge in an alcohol binge

hellbender   A binge

hell broth   Alcohol

helper   Hard liquor added to a glass of beer

highball   *See Word History, page 28.*

high voltage   Strong liquor

hoist one   To take a drink

hit the bottle, hit the hooch, hit the sauce   To drink heavily

hog wash   Beer

hollow leg   The capacity for drinking large amounts of alcohol

home brew   Alcohol brewed at home

homespun   Alcohol brewed at home

hooch   *See Word History, page 22.*

hooley   An extended drinking session

horny man   An agent of the Federal Treasury Alcohol Tax Unit

horse's neck   1. Ginger ale 2. A nonalcoholic drink

house   The bar, tavern, lounge, or establishment that one works for

hummer   A drinking spree

hush house   An illegal bar

I'll have one more!   I intend to get very, very intoxicated!

ignite oil   Whiskey

imbibe   To drink. *When used with mock formality, this completely standard English word is rendered informal.*

indoor tan   A red complexion produced by excessive drinking

injay   Gin. *Pig latin.*

in the rough   Served over ice

invigorator   Alcohol

Iowa champagne   Spiked beer

Irish cocktail   A drink containing drops of chloral hydrate

Irish wine   Whiskey

irrigate   To take a drink

jag   An extended period of drinking

jake hound   A heavy drinker

jig juice   Alcohol

Jinny   An illegal bar

John Barleycorn   Whiskey

John W. Lumberman   A shot of whiskey followed by a glass of beer

jolly up   To go on a drinking spree

jolt   A drink

jug up   To take a drink

juice   Beer

juice head   An alcoholic

juice joint   A bar

juicer   A heavy drinker

jungle juice   Home-brewed alcohol

juniper, juniper juice   Gin

keep the sails up   To remain sober

Kentucky corn   Corn whiskey

kick in the gut   Liquor

kick up the devil   To indulge in an alcohol binge

kill   To finish a glass or bottle of liquor

kill a Marine   To finish a bottle of liquor

kill-devil   Rum. *The first name by which rum was known. It evolved into Rumbullion (meaning "a great tumult") and then was clipped to simply "rum."*

kiss the baby   To drink

knock-down   Strong beer

knock-out drops   Chloral hydrate, drops of which are added to alcohol to induce unconsciousness

lace   To add liquor to a nonalcoholic beverage

Lady May   A gallon of whiskey

lamp oil   Whiskey

laughing water   Champagne

leave out the garbage   To refrain from adding garnishes such as olives or onions to a mixed drink

life preserver   A pocket flask of liquor

likker   Liquor

liquor head   An alcoholic

little church around the corner   A nearby bar

live Marine   A bottle of alcohol

livener   Alcohol, perceived as a stimulant

lone eagle   Someone who drinks alone

long   A drink served in a tall glass. *Now used as slang in espresso shops to refer to a large-size coffee.*

lost memory   Cheap wine

lost weekend   A drinking spree that lasts an entire weekend

low-country soldier   A heavy drinker

lush   A chronic drunkard

lusher   An alcoholic

Madam Geneva   Gin

make a night of it   To indulge in an alcohol binge

make the rounds   To visit one bar after another

March beer   Bock beer

Marine   A bottle of liquor

mechanic   A skilled bartender

Michael   A hip flask

Mickey Finn   A drink containing a strong sedative, usually chloral hydrate

milk   **1.** Beer **2.** A mixed drink of milk and Scotch, favored by drinkers with ulcers

misery   Gin

Misery Mile   The district within a city where cheap bars and destitute drunkards are found

Mississippi   A glass of water

mist   Liquor served over shaved ice

mixing job   A bar where most of the business consists of mixed drinks

mixologist   A bartender who is adept at making mixed drinks. *Not just a bartender but a "doctor of mixology."*

mokus   Liquor

moonshine   *See Word History, page 22.*

monkey   A rum cask

monkey juice   Cheap wine

mop   A drunkard

morning rouser   The first drink of the morning

morning's morning   The first drink of the morning

mother's milk   Gin

motorman's glove   Potent whiskey

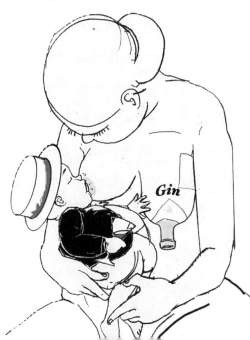

Mr. Haig   Scotch whiskey

M.T.   An empty bottle of liquor

muddler   A round piece of wood used to grind up sugar

mule   Whiskey made from corn

mung rag   An old towel or other piece of cloth used to wipe up beer spilled during beer drinking games

Muskadoo   Muscatel wine

Name your poison!   What would you like to drink?

neat   Served without ice. *This expression dates back to the 16th century when it was used to describe unadulterated wine or ale.*

neighborhood job   A bar patronized by local residents

never fear   Beer

nightcap   The last drink at night

nip   A small amount of alcohol. *Technically, a nip is 1/6 of a quartern, 32 to a standard bottle.*

nipper   A drinker who takes small drinks all day long

no bung in his barrel   Immoderate in one's drinking (said of a heavy drinker)

no daylight   A glass filled to the top with beer

nockum stiff   Bourbon

nose paint   Liquor

nurse   1. To drink slowly   2. A bar waitress

oasis   A bar

off the stuff   Not drinking

oh-be-joyful   Liquor. *A British expression which migrated to the United States in the early 1800s and which became a favorite piece of slang during the Civil War.*

old Tom   Gin

on a bum   On a drinking spree

one for the road   A final drink before leaving a bar

one up and one down   A large and a small beer combined in a single order

on the house   A drink paid for by the bar

on the rocks   Served over ice

on the wagon   Not drinking. *Clipped from the fuller on the water wagon.*

other half, the   The second of two drinks

out cold   Passed out from drinking

out for the count   Passed out from drinking

over-pour   To pour too much alcohol in a drink

packie   A liquor store

packie run   A trip to a liquor store to purchase alcohol

pain killer   Liquor

paint   To drink

paint remover   Strong alcohol

pale   Near beer

panther   Gin

pay the freight   To pay for one's own drinks

phlegm-cutter   1. First drink of morning   2. Strong liquor

pigeon   An alcoholic

pine top   Cheap whiskey

pink wine   Champagne

pizen   Inferior whiskey. *A jocular play with the Southern dialect pronunciation of "poison." The metaphor of death is not infrequently used when describing inferior alcoholic products; take for instance the Anglo-Irish "kill-the-beggar" for inferior whiskey.*

plain   Without alcohol

plank   The bar

play the Greek   To drink to excess

pledge   A vow of abstinence from drinking, used in the phrase "take the pledge"

poison   Low-quality whiskey

polish off   To drink

pony   1. A cordial glass   2. An eight-ounce bottle of beer

poor boy   A small glass of whiskey

pop   Beer

Pop Wallah   An abstainer

potate To drink

pound, pound down To drink

pounder Beer

prairie dew Whiskey

protein Any food

prune juice Potent alcohol

pub crawl To visit one bar after another

punch in the mouth A strong drink

put on the bag To drink

quencher A drink of whiskey

quick one A drink consumed in a hurry

rag water Gin

rammer A drink intended for quick consumption between other drinks

reaches Vomiting resulting from extended drinking without eating

real, real McCoy, real stuff, real thing Liquor bottled in bond

red Cheap red wine

red ruin Strong whiskey

reeb Beer. *Cute backwards slang.*

refresher A drink

reposer A final drink of the night

rescue station A liquor store

revelation A drink of liquor

reverent Potent

reviver Alcohol

ribbon Gin

ride the train To refrain from drinking

rinse A glass of water or soda water used to chase away the taste of a straight shot

rip A drinking spree

roadies Beer

rocks Ice cubes

rosin Liquor given musicians at a party where they are performing

rotgut 1. Wood alcohol 2. Poor-quality, inexpensive alcohol

rough Over ice

royal poverty Gin

rubbydub Nonbeverage alcohol, consumed by the most destitute of alcoholics

ruin Inferior gin

rum-dum, rum dumb The lowest form of drunkard

rum mill A bar

Saint Margaret's ale Water

Saint Patrick Whiskey

sample A drink of liquor

sap Alcohol

satin Gin

sauce Alcohol

scatter An illegal bar

schooner of suds A large glass of beer

scrap iron A bootleg drink containing alcohol and mothballs

scuds Beer

see a man To drink at a bar

sentiment Sediment

service wine Wine made from mountain ash berries

set 'em up 1. To buy a drink 2. To pour a drink

set out A free lunch set out on the bar

settler The final drink of a night

shaken not stirred Mixed by a shaking action, not by a stirring action. *James Bond's classic admonition to bartenders as he ordered a martini, this is one piece of alcohol lore and language that is embedded in our cultural consciousness. Bond specified that the bartender mix three measures of Gordon's gin, one measure of vodka, and half a measure of Kina Willet vermouth in a deep champagne glass, shake it very well until it's ice cold, and then add a large, thin slice of lemon peel. The bartender was always pleased with the precision of the order.*

shake tail A mixed drink or cocktail

shake up A cocktail

sheepherder's delight Cheap whiskey

shellac Cheap liquor

shellac your tonsils To take a drink

shoemaker A clumsy bartender

shoe polish Whiskey

shoot To drink a can of beer by punching a hole in the bottom of the can which has the effect of propelling the beer out of the top of the can when it is turned upside down and opened

shooter A drink intended for quick consumption between other drinks

short Unadulterated

short one A small drink of liquor

shot One ounce

shot in the arm A drink of liquor

shrub Any alcoholic drink made with fruit juice

shut off To stop serving any more drinks to a customer at a bar

side Any drink that is served in a separate glass and accompanies alcohol served without ice

simon pure Liquor bottled in bond

siphon To take a drink of liquor

sissy beer Beer that has low alcohol content

sixer A six-pack of beer

skate A drinking spree

skee Liquor

skit Beer

sky Whiskey

sling 1. A type of cold mixed spirits drink 2. A drink made with gin, water, ice, and bitters

slop Liquor

slops Inferior beer

sluice your bolt To take a drink

slush Weak liquor

smilo Alcoholic cider

smoke Solvents that drunkards drink when nothing else is available

snake Whiskey

snake head whiskey Cheap whiskey

snake water Whiskey

snarf To expel beer through one's nose in a failed attempt to chug a beer

sneaky Pete Cheap alcohol favored by skid row drunks

sniff the cork To take a drink

soak An alcohol binge

sober as a buck shad, church, deacon, judge, or **shoemaker** Completely, undeniably sober

sober side of the bar The bartender's side of the bar

social lubricant Liquor

soother Liquor

sop A drunkard

S.O.T. A heavy drinker—a Son of Temperance. *A*

play on the old and not slang term "sot" for drunkard.

spacer A nonalcoholic drink that is served between drinks to pace one's alcohol intake

sparkle Champagne

sparrow Cheap whiskey

speedball A glass of wine that has been adulterated

spike To add alcohol to another beverage

splash A small amount of mix added to a drink

sponge A heavy drinker

spree An alcohol binge

spring beer Bock beer

squirt gun A seltzer siphon

staff naked Gin

staggerer A drunkard

stand To pay for drinks for everyone at a bar

starter The first drink of the morning

stew Beer

stewie A drunkard

stick 1. The handle of a beer spigot at a bar 2. A bar

stiff blade A heavy drinker

stone sober, stone cold sober Completely, absolutely sober

straight up Served without ice

strip-me-naked Gin

strong water Alcohol

suck To drink

suds   Beer

suds jerker   A bartender. *A cute little play on "soda jerk."*

sundowner   The last drink of the night

swamper   A bartender

swicky   Whiskey. *Tongue-tied drunk dialect.*

swig   1. A drink   2. To drink quickly

swill   1. Alcohol   2. Beer

swizzle stick   A stick used in mixing drinks

table Zamboni   An old towel or other piece of cloth used to wipe up beer spilled during beer drinking games. *"Zamboni"is a trade name for a machine that smoothes the surface of an ice rink.*

take a drop, jolt, nip, oath, pull, shot, shot in the arm, shove in the guts, shove in the mouth, slug, smell, sneak, some cheer, snifter, snort, or **wet**   To take a drink of alcohol

talking jag   Intoxication accompanied by verbosity

tall   Any highball that is served in a 9-ounce tall glass

tank up   To drink

tap the admiral   To take a drink

tear   An alcohol binge

temperance drink   A nonalcoholic beverage

third rail   Strong whiskey

tie one on   To drink to intoxication

tin roof   A drink paid for by the house

tipple   To sip alcohol

toby   Beer

tonsil varnish, tonsil toot   An alcohol binge

toot   1. A drink   2. An alcohol binge

top off   To drink what remains in a glass

torpedo juice   Home-brewed alcohol

toss   To drink

touch   A small amount of mix added to a drink

true blue   A heavy drinker

tub   A double old-fash-ioned glass

12-ounce curl, do a   To drink

twist   A piece of a lemon peel used as a garnish

two fingers   A moderately strong drink

up   Prepared in the mixing glass and served in a stemmed cocktail glass

up and over   Prepared in the blender and served over ice

usual, the   The drink reg-ularly ordered by a cus-tomer at a bar, who sim-ply asks for "the usual."

valley tan   Whiskey

virgin   Without alcohol.

Thus the **Virgin Mary** *is a Bloody Mary with-out vodka.*

warmer   Liquor

wash   Any drink that is served in a separate glass and accompanies alcohol served without ice

water bottle   Someone who abstains from all alcohol

watering hole   A bar that one frequents often

wedge   A slice or section of lime used to garnish a drink

well   The brands poured by the house unless the customer requests a brand by name

wet the clay   To take a drink

wet your whistle   To take a drink

wheel   A slice of lemon or lime cut into a wheel shape and served on the rim of a glass

whiskey mill   A bar

whisper   An illegal bar

white eye   Whiskey

white horse   Whiskey

whoopie water   Liquor

wild cat   Illegal liquor

with the feathers on   Whiskey served straight

wood   A barrel containing beer, wine, or whiskey

workshop, workhouse   A busy bar

Moonshine

I know a place 'bout a mile down the road
Where you lay down a dollar or two.

If you hush up your mug, they will slip you a jug
Of that good old mountain dew.

They call it that good old mountain dew
And them that refuse it are few

You may go 'round the bend
But you'll come back again

For that good old mountain dew.

—*"Mountain Dew"*

THE **MOONSHINER**—the illegal distiller of whiskey—holds a special and curious place in the heart of American culture. Although a criminal, the aura and mythology surrounding the moonshiner is for the most part favorable. The crime of which he or she is guilty is against neither person nor property—it is a crime against the law, and as a people we seem to find some solace in knowing that there are outlaws among us who will risk the wrath of the law and defy it.

In stark contrast to the rather bland slang associated with alcohol, the language of the **moonshiner** is rich and expressive, for several reasons. The criminal nature of the distillation business produces a certain edge to the slang used by **moonshiners**, an edge which is missing with most alcohol slang. This tone is intensified by the fact that the natural enemy of the **moonshiner** is most often not local law enforcement, but outsiders, in a culture that is for many reasons wary of any outsiders. In addition to this us-and-them dynamic, the language of the rural, Southern Appalachian society in which **moonshining** flourishes is ironic and spirited, and it serves as a friendly host to a subculture's language.

Starting with the players, a producer of illegal whiskey is known as a **stiller** or a **blockader**, and the distinctive black felt hat that is worn is known affectionately as a **bootleg bonnet**. Transporting the moonshine from still to dealer or customers is the **hauler**, **runner**, or **tripper**, who drives a **crash car** (an old car that can be abandoned in a pinch) or a **weed monkey** (a truck).

Working the other side of the street is law enforcement, known amiably as **the big fellow**, **Johnny Law**, or disparagingly as **Revenoo** or a **Revenooer**; local law enforcement is usually not the problem, either because of sympathy for the cause or because of a **granny fee** or bribe paid to avoid investigation. Upon the approach of a revenue agent who is trying to **find the sign** by discovering physical evidence leading to a still, neighbors will give a signal of danger borrowed from the coal mines to the **moonshiners** at their stills with a resounding shout of **Fire in the hole!** If arrested, the **moonshiner** usually **gets probate** (is sentenced to probation) instead of actual jail time.

The **moonshiner's** still is known generically as a **boiler**, **kitchen**, **kitchen boiler**, **mess**, or **rig**; a still with large tubs is known as a **submarine**; a **coffin still** is a small **rig** that fits over two burners of a stove; a **groundhog** is a still dug into the side of a hill; and a **mountain teapot** is a small still that produces for one family or at most two families. The names for most of the parts of a still are joyless jargon, with the notable exception of the **money piece** (the part of the still where the whiskey emerges) and the **worm** (copper condensing coil inside the still). During the distilling process, the **moonshiner** might use a straw to sample the distillate, known as a **quill** (a word among cocaine users to describe a rolled up piece of paper used for snorting the drug) or a **thief**. Whiskey that is poured into soft drink bottles is known as **soda-pop moon**; a **can** is a half-gallon fruit jar, while a **jar** is any container for the whiskey, regardless of size of material.

Each cycle of distilling is known as a **run**, and **piggy-backing** or **rabbit-footing** is distilling the liquor more than once. During the distilling process, a **dog head** is a large bubble that appears in the cap of a still; **puke** (lovely!) is material that boils over from the still into the connections; **beads** are small bubbles that form in liquor; and **frog eyes** are large beads in

clear distillate, free of **puke**. To reduce the chance of contamination, the **moonshiner** might **lime** the still, or whitewash the inside of the fermenters.

The ethics of **moonshining** frowns on adulteration of the product, but it is not unheard of. By adding chips to moonshine (**pickling** or **quick aging**), it is possible to give young liquor the appearance of aged whiskey. **Beading oil** can also be added to low-proof liquor to make it appear stronger, and **kick** or **kicker** can be added to the mash to increase the yield.

What of the product? The first liquid to come through the still is undrinkable, known as the **alkihol, first shots, foreshots, heads,** or **high wine. Beer** is not beer but is fermented mash that is the product of the first stage of whiskey production, and **singlings** refers to liquor that does not have enough alcohol to be deemed whiskey. The low-proof distillate near the end of a **run** is **backings, faints,** or **tailings.** The waste from the distillation of the **beer** is **off-falls** or **slop,** while **doggins** is the liquor obtained by **bull dogging** or **barrel dogging,** leaching absorbed whiskey from whiskey barrels by placing them next to a fire.

The finished product is known variously as **alky, Balm of Gilead** (a lovely and lyrical

12-Step Slang

RECENT DECADES HAVE seen a proliferation of 12-step programs such as Alcoholics Anonymous, Narcotics Anonymous, and Al-Anon, self-help groups that assist members in establishing a personal wellness program to overcome their addiction to alcohol, their addiction to drugs, or to understand the ways in which family members or associates **enable** an alcoholic or drug addict by supporting directly or indirectly the addict's behavior.

The language of 12-step programs is heavily coded and is high-context language at its best; a single word is used as shorthand to speak of a whole set of concepts that serve as the vernacular of the group. While much of the language consists of acronyms and slogans, there is a definite slangy ring to many of the terms and expressions used.

Starting with the membership, a **baby** or

pigeon is a new-comer to the program, an **old-timer** is a veteran (who is usually a stickler for the program's rules), and a **winner** is an **old-timer** who has not only stayed **C&S** (clean and sober) but who has found a measure of happiness and contentment in life. A large number of program participants are **CIA**—Catholic, Irish, and alcoholic. The vast population that does not participate in a 12-step program is known as **citizens, civilians,** or **Earth people**. On the extreme end of things is the **wet brain**, someone whose drinking has produced severe brain damage.

The basic tenets of 12-step programs may be found in the **big book**, known to **civilians** as *Alcoholics Anonymous*. A smaller book, known as **ODAT** (*One Day at a Time*), contains shorter, inspirational readings—a participant might say "I carry my **ODAT** wherever I go so I've always got

biblical allusion), **blockade likker, bottled-in-barn, bust-head, cannonball swig, corn, dead man's dram, donk, embalmer's special, fighting soup, fox head, good corn, horse blanket whiskey** (so called because a blanket may be used to collect the distillate), **ignorant oil, joy juice, Kentucky fire, kickapoo joy juice, King Kong, moon, moose milk, mountain dew** (an odd borrowing for the name of a soft drink, no?), **panther breath** or **piss** or **sweat** (young, wild, biting whiskey), **pop-skull, red eye, shine, splo, squirrel, stump likker, stump liquor, sugarhead** (with a high sugar content), **sweet lightning** (sweetened), **white lightning** (mentioned by Merle Haggard as "the greatest thrill" of his salt-of-the-earth heroes in his classic "Okie from Muskogee"), and **white mule**. These synonyms for moonshine were gathered from primary sources. Richard A. Spears in his fine *The Slang and Jargon of Drugs and Drink* collected another 40 or so terms, the most colorful of which include **A-bomb juice, bald face, barrel goods, blackstrap alchy, boilermaker's delight, brush whiskey, choke dog, devil's eye water, goat hair, hog wash, snake juice, snake water, tiger's milk,** and **Who shot John?**

a **meeting in my pocket** if I need it."

When participants give detailed reminiscences of their personal drunken behavior, they are said to be giving a **drunkalogue**; in talking with the group, members are urged to **get off the pity pot** (to stop feeling sorry for themselves) and to stop looking for someone to **co-sign for their bullshit** (enable their behavior). Some groups do not allow **crosstalk**, prohibiting commentary on what others have said. Program participants are encouraged to change their friends and the places they visit to help break their old habits, or to **change playmates, playgrounds, and playthings** (or **people, places, and things**).

The first step in recovery is to stop being **in denial** and recognize one's drinking problem. This realization often comes when one **hits bottom** or reaches the lowest point in one's personal life, often losing a job or a spouse as a result of the addiction. One strives to get in touch with a **higher power** (for many a traditional Christian God) and to **Let go, let God—** stop trying to have control over everything and instead have faith in the **higher power**.

Participation in a group is no guarantee against recidivism; the first period of sobriety upon first joining a group is with some irony called a **honeymoon,** and a relapse and return to drinking or drug use is known as a **slip** or, with a bit of sarcasm, as **doing research** or being **out on maneuvers**. When old memories and old coping mechanisms surface, a participant is said to be **playing old tapes** or engaging in **stinking thinking**, predictors of a relapse. Success is measured by continued group participation, with each anniversary marked as a **birthday**.

WORD HISTORY

B-GIRL

HELLO HONEY, WANNA buy me a drink? The **B-girl** is that most special of sinners; she straddled the two sins of alcohol and sex, and in so straddling she managed to create a sting-the-sinner sin within the sin, encouraging with sexual teasing those al-

ready engaged in the sin of drinking to drink more than they had planned to drink while paying whiskey prices for her to drink colored water or tea.

The earliest recorded use of **B-girl** was in an advertisement in the *San Francisco News* on July 31, 1936, promising that at the bar in question there were "NO B GIRLS buzzing around you here to sip tea you think is a highball.

No hostesses...." She continued to grab headlines for two decades, culminating in California in the mid-1950s with legislative and regulatory action against the poor **B-girl.**

On the linguistic front, **B-girl** quickly crowded out her competition, and over the years when a new term developed to challenge **B-girl** it did not last long—**mixer, taxi drinker,**

Name Your Poison: From Angel Teat to Zombie

Over the years, creative bartenders and curious drinkers have invented thousands of different drinks. Our culture may no longer appreciate the art of mixing drinks and drinking well-mixed drinks, but the names linger. The names given drinks are often poetic, at times clever, and at their best slangy. Good examples of the use of slang in the naming of mixed drinks include the following:

angel teat Heavy cream, creme de cacao, and a cherry

B and B Benedictine and brandy

B and S Brandy and soda

baby titty Anisette, creme Yvette, whipped cream, and a cherry

black and tan Stout and ale

black velvet Champagne and stout

blackjack Kirschwasser, brandy, and coffee. *The popular notion is that this drink was named because of its powerful knockout effect.*

blood and thunder Port wine and brandy

blue blazer Whiskey and hot water. *The whiskey is set fire, hence the blazes.*

dirty martini Gin and olive juice. *A martini made with olive juice instead of dry vermouth.*

dog's nose Beer and gin

ess and ess Scotch and soda

flesh and blood Port wine and brandy

flip A drink made with some liquor, an egg, spices, and sugar

fruit salad Whiskey, Angostura, water, sugar, lemon peel; an "old-fashioned whiskey"

G and T Gin and tonic

gin and it Gin and Italian vermouth

half and half Beer and ale, or dark beer and light beer. *This is primarily a British choice, and there it is often pronounced with a decided Cockney lilt—"arf an' arf." The expression*

percentage girl, house girl, drink hustler, seagull, hostess, and **entertainer** came and went, but **B-girl** lived on. The first recorded use is agreed upon, but the term's origin is not. There are at least three explanations of the etymology of **B-girl**, each with its logic and its supporters.

Wentworth and Flexner accepted without question the easy and logical route, pronouncing unequivocally that **B-girl** was a shortened form of **bar girl**, a term which one finds used at least as early as 1857. Support for this theory came early and from the heart of tabloid America, the December 1938 issue of *True Story*, which clearly and simply told us that **B-girl** is "just short for bar girls." Likewise, Arthur "Bugs" Baer, in his "Biographies of a Bug" column in the *San Francisco Examiner* on September 10, 1939, wrote that the **B-girl** was already a thing of the past, and in so writing he submitted that "The monogram 'B' is an abbreviation for 'bar.'" The **bar girl** theory may have a strong appeal to the modern mind because of the resurgence of **bar girls,** referred to by journalists as **B-girls,** in early 1966 in Vietnam and then throughout Southeast Asia; these were young hostesses who mixed prostitution with solicitations of Americans to buy them "Saigon tea."

Peter Tamony rejected the bar girl association. In his "Origin of Words" column in the *San Francisco Wasp and Newsletter* (February 24, 1939) and a privately printed monograph in May 1965, Tamony took **B-girl** back one step in evolution to **bee drinker**, a term included by A. J. Pollock in *The Underworld Speaks* (1935) to mean "female entertainers in nightclubs, who drink cold tea camouflaged as liquor, for which customers pay full prices." While the term **bee drinker** may not sound familiar to most, it was still in use on Bourbon Street in 1962, recorded in an article "Night Spot Cleanup Attempt Flops in New Orleans" in the *San Francisco News Call-Bulletin* (November 19, 1962). Focusing on **B** as a corrupted **bee,** Tamony went back even further to a 1911 reference in *The Social Evil in Chicago* to a **"B" gin-**

has also migrated into sexual slang, referring to a combination of oral and vaginal sex.

hemorrhage   Beer with tomato juice. *Sometimes ordered in the hope that it will cure a hangover.*

hop toad   Jamaican rum, apricot brandy, and lime juice

lawyer's revenge   Port wine, sugar, orange peel, and water

Long Island ice tea   Vodka, gin, tequila, rum, a splash of triple sec, lemon juice, and Coca-Cola. *A devastating cocktail made with all the clear hard liquors at the bar.*

red-eye sour   Whiskey and lemon

shake-em-up   White wine and lemon juice

smash   Any of several drinks made with a liquor base, mint, water, sugar, and ice. *The term "smash" as slang for a tremendous success is the origin of this term.*

snowball   Rum, ginger ale, egg white, and sugar

stinger   Whiskey and soda

Tom and Jerry   A highly-spiced gin-based punch

whispers of the frost   Whiskey, sherry, port wine, and sugar

zombie   A haphazard mix of many different types of alcohol

ger ale highball which was "colored water made in imitation of" a real highball.

Based on these pieces of evidence, Tamony argued that **B** or **bee** was a shortened **beading oil**, a substance used to give weak alcohol or a nonalcoholic beverage the appearance of high-quality whiskey. A **B-girl** or **bee drinker** drank **B drinks** from **B bottles** of iced tea or perhaps root beer extract containing beading oil.

A third association is suggested by the **bee drinker** route taken by Tamony. In the early 20th century, to **put the bee** on someone was to ask for money or to swindle someone, while to **buzz** someone was to chat or flirt with someone. Add to that the sense of a **buzz** as mild intoxication and there is a case to be made for a **bee-buzz** connection, one enforced by the 1936 first usage of **B-girl**—"NO B GIRLS buzzing around you...."

B-girl took on a new life in the late 1970s with the birth of hip-hop culture. In *The Rap Attack: African Jive to New York Hip-Hop* (1984), David Toop wrote: "In 1979 the b boys and b girls (as they had come to be known) were in for a shock. From seemingly nowhere, two singles were released to send hip hop public." The **b** in the new **b-girl** came either from "breakdancing" or "break," the part of a tune where the drums take over.

WORD HISTORIES

BOOTLEG, MOONSHINE, AND HOOCH

ALTHOUGH THE PRACTICES of bootlegging and moonshining are closely related, the terms have different lineages, with **moonshine** stretching back to the 18th century and **bootleg** popping up only in the late 19th century. **Hooch,** that which is produced by the moonshiner and smuggled by the bootlegger, is also a late-19th-century coining.

The earliest recorded usage of **bootleg** in the sense of illegal alcoholic liquor was in 1889. Although Maine (*American Mercury,* June 1926), Kansas (Herbert Asbury in *Carry Nation,* 1929), and Oklahoma (the *San Francisco Examiner,* August 1, 1946) all claim **bootleg** as their own, the concept is the same in each claim–the **bootlegger** concealed a flask or several flasks of illegally produced liquor in the leg of his heavy boots.

The term was catchy and has been applied to a number of products other than alcohol, implying that the product was illegally produced or distributed; products to which **bootleg** has been applied include: babies (1928), barbiturates (1946), books (1925), candy (1936), cars (1954), cattle (1927), censored books (1931), coal (1940), coffee (1895), cream (1932), ducks

(1940), food (1919), houses (1931), immigrants (1925), lemons (1944), meat (1943), phonograph records (1952), produce (1925), watches (1953), and wheat (1928). In the 1970s, **bootleg** was a major concept in the music industry; **bootleg tapes** and **bootleg records** abounded, offering recordings that were not intended for release.

Despite its authentic Appalachian sound, **moonshine** is a British import. In 1785, Captain Francis Grose wrote that "the white brandy smuggled on the coasts of Kent and Sussex, and the gin in the north of Yorkshire, are also called moonshine." It was recorded in America in the late 1820s; Bartlett (1877) and Farmer (1889) both include **moonshine** in their dictionaries of Americanisms, and by the final decades of the 19th century it was firmly ensconced in American slang. Farmer wrote that **moonshine** was probably of Scottish or Irish origin, while H. L. Mencken suggested that the term immigrated along with professional criminals who left London in response to Sir Robert Peel's crackdown on the criminal element starting in 1829. Unlike **bootleg,** though, **moonshine** has not left the confines of illegal alcohol and it is not applied to any other illicit endeavors.

The etymology of **hooch** is an exception to the rule of murky etymology in slang, for its origins are clear–**hooch** is shortened from *Hoochinoo*, a small tribe of Tlingit Indians in Alaska with a reputation for drunkenness. Its use was confined to molasses-based liquor distilled by the Hoochinoo until it surfaced as a popular term for alcohol during Prohibition.

The *Oxford English Dictionary* places the first recorded usage of **hooch** in 1897. **Hooch** proper may have first been used in 1897, but the full **hoocheno** was certainly used earlier. Mitford Mathews in the *Dictionary of Americanisms* has an 1877 hit on **hoocheno** from the *Puget Sound Argus* in Port Townsend, Washington, suggesting that **hoocheno** found its way south through the Chinook trading jargon of northwest Indians. In July 1960, Wallace Stegner steered Peter Tamony to a piece by Clarence Gohdes, "American Liquor Lingo" in the *Georgia Review* (Spring 1959), and in that article Gohdes cites an 1878 article from the *San Francisco Chronicle* using **hoocheno,** which was also used in the *Report on Population of Alaska, 11th Census* (1893). Even the 1897 dating of **hooch** may be soft, for in *Gambler's Wife: The Life of Matilda Jenkins,* there is a reference to an incident that occurred in Dawson, Yukon Territory, in 1896—"all the home-made stuff was called

hooch in them days, just like now."

As a general term for alcohol, **hooch** dates from at least the 1920s. The earliest use in the general sense which I have found is in the Tamony Collection, a cartoon by Thomas Dorgan ("TAD") that ran on December 15, 1915, in which a character says, "Listen, dummy, I'm off the hooch for good."

Hooch derivatives over the years have included **hooch fest, hooch graft, hooch hister, hooch hound, hooch house, hooch humps, hooched, hoocher,** and **hoocherie**. In the 1970s, **hooch** was applied to marijuana and, according to one source, to cough syrup used as an intoxicant. During the conflict in Vietnam, another **hooch** came into the language; it applied to a hut or dwelling, and was derived from the Japanese *uchi* for house. A **hooch girl** or **hooch maid** was a Vietnamese woman who cleaned American dwellings at base camps.

WORD HISTORY
BOOZE

LIKE HER SISTER-IN-SIN "hooker," the universally understood slang term **booze** has two pedigrees. One is ancient and scholarly and the other relatively modern and commercial; without the newer, commerce-driven impetus, **booze** would probably be a bit

player in the slang of alcohol, not the patriarch that it is.

The venerable and scholarly **booze** traces its origins in two directions. The first is Germanic—the Middle Low German *busen* or *buzen* (to drink deeply), which passed into Old English as *bouse* or *bouze,* recorded early in the 14th century. Sometime in the 16th century it slipped into the cant of thieves, and from there into slang; it is recorded in its slang sense with variant spellings in the standard slang dictionaries, including "B.E., Gent" (1698-99), Grose (1785), Barrére and Leland (1899-90), and Farmer and Henley (1890-1904). The second old-money ancestor of **booze** is the archaic Persian or Turkish *bosa* or *buza,* an alcoholic beverage made from millet, barley, or rice. From the Persian or Turkish, the term migrated throughout Asia, Europe, and North Africa, into Russian as *buza,* into Czech and Polish as *buza,* into Bulgarian as *boza,* into Rumanian as *bouza,* into Albanian as *boze,* into Magyar as *boza,* into Hindustani as *buza,* and Arabic as *buze.*

The multi-lingual heritage is impressive, but probably less important in the long run in America than one E. G. Booz, a Philadelphia purveyor of spirits who in the 1840s began selling whiskey in a cabin-shaped bottle inspired by William Harrison's successful campaign for president, which used the log cabin as a campaign symbol of Harrison's humble roots. The bottle was inscribed with "E.G. Booz's Old Cabin Whiskey" on the side, and soon **booz** or **booze** became synonymous with whiskey, and then alcohol in general. It was Booz that gave *bouse* a second wind which brought us the **booze** that we enjoy today. As a historical afterthought, E. G. Booz Kentucky straight bourbon whiskey in a Booz bottle was still for sale at least as late as November 1961, when it was identified as "a name so famous it has become part of the English language" in an advertisement for The Emporium department store in the *San Francisco Shopping News*.

While in the names-of-liquor-bottles vein, Ernest Abel points out that another 19th-century whiskey bottle of some fame was the **calabash**, an oval whiskey bottle with a long neck, imprinted with portraits of national heroes, presidents, and popular entertainers such as Jenny "Swedish Nightingale" Lind. In the second half of the 19th century, Americans often kept a

calabash in their home as decorative art; among the most popular was that depicting Jenny Lind. Manufactured by the Fislerville Glass Works around 1850 and then the Ravenna Ohio Glassworks around 1857 (and reproduced by a manufacturer in Czechoslovakia in the 1920s), the Jenny Lind bottle was one of the most

popular **calabash** bottles of all time. Abel suggests—without much hard evidence—that Jimmy Durante was alluding to the whiskey bottle with the portrait of Jenny Lind when he coined his standard closing line, "Good night, Mrs. Calabash,

wherever you are." Other theories are that Mrs. Calabash was the nickname of a hat check girl at the Brown Derby restaurant in Hollywood, that she was named after a card game that Durante played with Joe Pasternak, that she was dreamed up by a press agent, that she was a long-lost love, that she was his mother, that

she was a boarding house keeper in Illinois, that she was the widowed mother of a small boy who listened to Durante's radio show, that she was a racehorse, that she was named after a little town outside Chicago, that she was named after a pipe, or that she was Durante's deceased first wife.

WORD HISTORY

COCKTAIL

BAR NONE, **COCKTAIL** is the Big Kahuna of multiple etymologies within the slang of sin. Saints and sinners all agree that the

is supposed to be an excellent electioneering potion, inasmuch as it renders the heart stout and bold, at the same time that it fuddles the head." The **cocktail** is as American as apple pie, and at its peak in the 1920s and 1930s it attracted an almost religious following.

Competing explanations of the word's origin have swirled

published seven that he considered "plausible." Of the less than 40 etymologies that I have encountered, those with identified sponsors, plausible or not, include:

Old-time English trainers of fighting cocks prepared a bread for their fowl, using a blend of liquors in the dough. In the process, one intrepid trainer sampled the blend and found it fortifying for humans as well as fowl. It became known as "cock bread ale," which was shortened to "cock ale." Somehow a "T" ended up in the mix and you had a **cocktail**. (*American Mercury*, May 1929)

In the 18th century, "cock ale" referred to superior quality ale which, Captain Grose wrote in 1785, was a "provocative drink," one that aroused a man's sexual appetite, hence the "cock." (Repeated by Farmer and Henley, 1891)

word **cocktail** was first recorded in a publication, *The Balance*, in Hudson, New York, on May 13, 1806: it described the **cocktail** as "a stimulating liquor composed of spirits of any kind, sugar, water, and bitters—it is vulgarly called bittered sling and

around **cocktail** since 1806, most apocryphal at best, but each with its advocates and sponsors. H. L. Mencken claimed that he had more than 40 etymologies in his archives, but he considered most of them "no more than baloney" and he only

During the 17th and 18th centuries, a drink called "cock ale" was popular in England, made by flavoring a cask of new ale with an old red cock that had been pounded to a pulp and seeped in spices.

(Peter Tamony, "Origin of Words: Cocktail" in the *San Francisco Wasp and Newsletter,* August 4, 1939)

Cocktail was derived from the French *coquetel,* a drink from the Bordeaux region of France, popular during the time of the French Revolution (*Baltimore Evening Sun,* February 11, 1926). A variation on the theme accepts the Bordeaux connection, but identifies a *coquetel* as a wine cup brought to America by Lafayette's volunteers.

The daughter of King Axolotl VIII of Mexico, named Xochitl or Coctel, invented the mixture, which then took her name (Harry Craddock's *The Savoy Cocktail Book* [1930] and Alfred E. Holt's *Phrase Origins,* 1936). A variant has the maiden Xochitl winning the heart of the king of Mexico with a liquor discovered by her father. (*New York World,* 1891)

In the Yorkshire dialect, a **cocktail** was a fresh and foaming glass of beer. (Joseph Wright's *English Dialect Dictionary,* 1905)

Mistress Peggy Van Eyck, daughter of inn owner William Van Eyck, was preparing a mixed drink for her fiance at the Philips Manor House in what is now Yonkers, New York, when a tail feather of the champion fighting cock Lightning fluttered into her lap. She saw the feather as an omen—"Lightning names this drink!" and urged her fiance to drink the **cocktail** in hopes of success with her father. (*American Mercury,* October 1926)

Betsy Flanagan, the owner and operator of a tavern near Yonkers at the time of the Revolution, decorated each bottle and jar in her tavern with the tail feathers of roasted male fowl cooked for American officers. When a guest called for a "glass of the **cocktail,**" Flanagan prepared a mixed drink which she stirred with the tail of a cock pheasant. James Fenimore Cooper promoted Betsy Flanagan as having invented the drink, if not the word, in *The Spy.* (Promotional literature published by the Roosevelt Hotel, New York, 1937)

The tail of a cocktailed horse (well-docked) flounces out gaily, giving it the appearance of vivacity." Hence a **cocktail** ought to be so-called because it gives you the jolly feeling of a horse with its tail up." (*Journals of Arnold Bennett 1919-1929,* published in 1954)

The mixed drink was named after mixed breeds of racing horses, **cocktails,** that are not full-blooded like thoroughbreds. (*New York Herald Tribune,* December 23, 1925)

Like the fighting cock, a **cocktail** is bright, spirited, and cheerful—a projection of the fowl's character. (*San Francisco News Call-Bulletin,* August 4, 1965)

Cocktail may have moved into English from the Krio of Sierra Leone, where a *kaketel* is a creature with a sting in its tail. (J. L. Dillard, *American Talk,* 1976)

The **cocktail** was invented by a New Orleans apothecary, Antoine (or Amédée, or Anthony Amédée) Peychaud, who served the mixed drink of cognac and bitters in an egg cup, a *coquetier* in French, which gave the drink its name (*American Guide Series: Louisiana,* 1941). Mencken favored this etymology as "the most plausible."

In cock fights, spectators would toast the cock with the most feathers left in its tail with drinks made with the same number of ingredients as there were tail feathers left in the cock. (Attributed by Mencken to an English attorney, Thomas Bagley, in 1937)

An anonymous bartender in an anonymous early American

bar emptied the last ounce or so of all liquor bottles into a common bottle, the cork of which was decorated with a rooster's tail feather, which gave the blend its name (*American Speech*, April 1945). Mencken credited a close relative of this theory to one William S. Gleim of Rohrerstown, Pennsylvania, in 1938; Mr. Gleim paired cock as a valve or spigot with *tailings* as dregs or leavings, to produce "cock-tailings," shortened in turn to **cocktail.**

In the 19th century, the **cocktail** was consumed in the morning and just before dinner. Its association with the cock's crow gave it the name **cocktail.** (William Terrington's *Cooling Cups and Dainty Drinks*, 1869, and *Patsy McDonough's Bar-keeper's Guide*, 1883)

All of this would have been sufficient, but there are more. In *The World of Drinks and Drinking* (1971), John Droxat presented without identifying sources three more possible etymologies for **cocktail:**

The daughter of a patriotic tavern-keeper during the American Revolution, flustered by her father giving her hand to her intended when he returned a lost prize fighting cock, could not concentrate as she mixed drinks for the betrothal banquet. The crowd loved the mixed drinks, and in honor of the fighting cock that led to the marriage bestowed the name **cocktail** on the drink.

British sailors visiting Campeche in the Gulf of Mexico drank local mixed punches stirred with a wooden spoon. At one bar, the drinks were stirred with a root named after its shape—*cola* (tail) *de* (of) *gallo* (rooster, or cock). *Voilà*.

Gamblers traveling on steamboats on the Mississippi River preferred drinks mixed with every liquor in the bar, mixed with a stirrer that resembled a cock's tail feathers.

Joseph Lanza included two additional etymologies in *The Cocktail* (1995), neither of which is cited with a source:

In standing up to Great Britain, George Washington acted with the same courage and defiance that characterizes a good fighting cock. One evening during the Revolution, Washington and his officers were in the midst of a drinking binge. Searching for a new toast, an officer spied Washington's feathered cap and blurted, "A toast to the cock's tail!"

Served a wine laced with gin by his friend Boswell, Sam Johnson proclaimed that the drink was a "veritable cocktail of a drink," referring to a mixed breed horse with a bobbed tail being passed off as a thoroughbred.

However questionable its parentage, cocktail has not been shy in spawning progeny—**cocktail bar** (1929)**, cocktail barmaid** (1949)**, cocktail belt** (1950s)**, cocktail buffet** (1952)**, cocktail cabinet** (1933)**, cocktail chair** (1955)**, cocktail chatter** (1952)**, cocktail circuit** (1953)**, cocktail conversation** (1953)**, cocktail date** (1945)**, cocktail drama** (1926)**, cocktail dress** (1935)**, cocktail glass** (1907)**, cocktail gown** (1935)**, cocktail hour** (1927)**, cocktail lounge** (1939)**, cocktail mixer** (1904)**, cocktail music** (1953)**, cocktail napkin** (1943)**, cocktail onions** (1951)**, cocktail party** (1928)**, cocktail pianist** (1962)**, cocktail piano** (1952)**, cocktail rocker** (1953)**, cocktail room** (1944)**, cocktail route** (1910)**, cocktail sausages** (1939)**, cocktail set** (1926 in the sense of a mixer and glasses, 1945 in the sense of a group)**, cocktail shaker** (1868)**, cocktail stick** (1937)**, cocktail suit** (1950)**, cocktail suite** (1953)**, cocktail table** (1946)**, cocktail time** (1914)**, cocktail tray** (1958), and **cocktail waitress** (1971). In the meantime, **cocktail** picked up another slang association (the butt of a marijuana cigarette smoked in a tobacco cigarette from which the tobacco has been shaken) and a slang cousin, the **Molotov cocktail,** a crude incendiary device fashioned with a flammable liquid and a glass bottle. Lastly, in the *Economist* in 1986, **cocktail** makes its first appearance as the catchall term for a combination of drugs used in the treatment of AIDS and the HIV virus.

WORD HISTORY

HIGHBALL

THE **HIGHBALL**—whiskey and soda served with ice in a tall glass—has been a fixture of American alcohol life since the turn of the century; the *Oxford English Dictionary* dates the term to 1898, but Merriam-Webster's citation files contain an earlier usage ("a high ball to compose his nerves") from the *New Orleans Times-Democrat* of November 1, 1896. It's a straightforward term, yet there is no single accepted explanation of its etymology. **Highball** is no "cocktail" when it comes to multiple etymologies, but it's no slouch either.

The explanation which has probably attracted the greatest support is that **highball** was borrowed from the lexicon of railroaders, the theory embraced by Mitford Mathews in his *Dictionary of Americanisms* and by an article

in the *New York Journal* on September 16, 1898. In the late 19th century, railroaders used a ball on a high pole as a type of semaphore to signal to an engineer to speed up. Railroad workers, who were always on a tight schedule, had time only for a quick drink, usually whiskey and water—thus **highball.** H. L. Mencken rejected this theory on philosophical grounds, reasoning that any railroader who detected a bartender diluting his whiskey with water would have "butchered him on the spot."

The next most popular theory is that **ball** was bar slang for a glass and that the tall glass needed for whiskey and soda was taller than the glass needed for straight whiskey, and thus it was a tall glass, or **high ball**. This explanation was favored by the *Literary Digest* (July 15, 1933), the historians of the Waldorf-Astoria bar (1935), and Mencken.

There are several other far-reaching accounts of the origin of **highball**—it was borrowed as a metaphor from baseball because enough "hits" in succession will affect one's "batting average" (Waldorf-Astoria, 1935), it was derived from the cry "high bowl" signifying that a customer wanted another drink dipped from a bowl of whiskey (*New York Sun*, July 26, 1902), or it evolved from the term "ball" for horse medicine—a stimulant became a "ball," and the seltzer water made the "ball" a

high ball (*New York Sun*, July 27 and 29, 1902).

SOURCES AND REFERENCES

MAJOR WORKS WHICH I have drawn upon for my exploration of the border behavior of drinking include *Alcohol: Wordlore and Folklore* by Ernest L. Abel (Buffalo: Prometheus, 1987); *Dictionary of Alcohol Use and Abuse: Slang Terms, and Terminology*, compiled by Ernest L. Abel (Westport, Conn.: Greenwood, 1985); *From Beer to Eternity: Everything You Always Wanted to Know about Beer* by Will Anderson (Lexington, Mass.: Stephen Greene, 1987); *The View from Nowhere: The Only Bar Guide You'll Ever Want—or Need* by Jim Atkinson (New York: Harper and Row, 1987); *Pour Man's Friend: A Guide and Reference for Bar Personnel* by John C. Burton (Santa Rosa, Calif.: Aperitifs, 1978, 1990); *The Complete Book of Drink* by T. E. Carling (New York: Philosophical Library, 1952); *The Second Oldest Profession: An Informal History of Moonshine in America* by Jess Carr (Englewood Cliffs, N.J.: Prentice-Hall, 1972); *The Old Waldorf-Astoria Bar Book* by Albert Stevens Crockett (New York: A. S. Crockett, 1935); *Mountain Spirits: A Chronicle of Corn Whiskey* by Joseph Earl Dabney (New York: Scribner's, 1974); *The World of Drinks and Drinking* by John Doxat (New York: Drake, 1971); *A Treatise on Lager Beers* by Fred Eckhardt (Portland, Ore.: Hobby Winemaker,

1970); *The Well-Tempered Lyre: Songs & Verse of the Temperance Movement* by George W. Ewing (Dallas: SMU Press, 1977); *The Association of Brewers' Dictionary of Beer and Brewing*, compiled by Carl Forget (Boulder, Colo.: Brewers, 1988); *The Complete Book of Beer Drinking Games* by Andy Griscom, Ben Rand, and Scott Johnston (Memphis: Mustang, 1984, 1989); *Ardent Spirits: The Rise and Fall of Prohibition* by John Kobler (New York: Putnam, 1973); *Kentucky Moonshine* by David Maurer (Lexington: University Press of Kentucky, 1974); *The Dictionary of Drink and Drinking* by Oscar A. Mendelsohn (New York: Hawthorn, 1965); *A Dictionary of Words about Alcohol* by Mark Keller, Mairi McCormick and Vera Efron (New Brunswick, N.J.: Rutgers Center of Alcohol Studies, 1968, 1982); "The Vocabulary of the Drinking Chamber" in *The American Scene: A Reader* by H. L. Mencken (New York: Knopf, 1965); *Bluff Your Way In Whisky* by David Milsted (Horsham, West Sussex, Great Britain: Ravette, 1991); *A Treasury of Cocktail Humor*, edited by James E. Myers (Springfield, Ill.: Lincoln-Herndon, 1994); *The Faber Book of Drink, Drinkers and Drinking*, edited by Simon Rae (London: Faber and Faber, 1991); *The Great American Beer Book* by James D. Robertson (Ottawa: Caroline House, 1978); *W.C.T.U. Songs* (Evanston, Ill.: National Woman's Christian Temperance

Union, 1928); and *The Official Harvard Student Agencies Bartending Course*, edited by Eric Witt and Geoff Rodkey (New York: St. Martin's, 1995).

Newspaper and magazine articles on this subject, almost all of which can be found in the Tamony Collection at the University of Missouri, include "Two 'Prohis' Are Taken as Drunk" in the *San Francisco Examiner* (November 14, 1927); "Volstead English" by Achsah Hardin in *American Speech*, Vol. 7 (December 1931); "The Drinker's Dictionary" by Cedric Larson in *American Speech* (April 1937); "Stiller's Argot" by Fred Hamann in *American Speech*, Vol. 21 (October 1946); "American Drinking Language" in *Bohemian Life*, published by the Bohemian Distributing Company (May 1947); "Drinking Lingo" in *Bohemian Life* (June, 1947); "Drinking Slang" in *Bohemian Life* (May 1951); "No Relief for Booze Hounds" in the *Examiner* (February 23, 1966); "Firewater With a Past" in the *San Francisco Chronicle* (July 31, 1966); "More Americans Boozing It Up" in the *Examiner* (November 7, 1968); "A Badge of Disgrace: Court Strikes Drunk Law" in the *Examiner* (January 19, 1971); "Bars and Their Extensions" by Philip C. Kolin in *American Speech*, Vol. 49 (Spring-Summer 1974); "Barroom Slang, on the Rocks" by William Safire in the *San Francisco Examiner and Chronicle* (March 29, 1981); "Passing the Wet Bar Exam" by

William Safire in the *Examiner and Chronicle* (May 17, 1981); and "Last Bastion of Temperance" in *Downeast* (November 1995). Additionally, I drew upon an October 5, 1965 letter and extended word list sent to Peter Tamony by Robin Room, identified as a Research Assistant for the Drinking Practices Study of Berkeley, California.

For my peek inside the **calabash**, I drew on the following articles from the University of Missouri: "On the Side" by E. V. Durling in the *San Francisco Examiner* (March 20, 1953); "Durante Rides Again" by Billy Rose in the *Examiner* (July 5, 1954); "Who Is Mrs. Calabash" in *Fortnight* (September 1, 1954); "Durante's Mum About Mrs. Calabash" by Vernon Scott in the *San Francisco News* (October 23, 1954); "Day and Night with Radio and Television" by Dwight Newton in the *Examiner* (January 10, 1956); Ann Landers' column in the *San Francisco Call-Bulletin* (August 13, 1956); Mike Connolly's column in the *San Francisco News-Call Bulletin* (October 31, 1959); "Who is Mrs. Calabash?" by Joe McCarthy in the *American Weekly* (July 30, 1961); "The Answer Column" in the *News-Call Bulletin* (March 30, 1965); "At Last He Tells: Durante and Calabash" in the *Examiner and Chronicle* (March 20, 1966); and "The Grab Bag" by L. M. Boyd in the *Examiner and Chronicle* (January 22, 1978).

Chapter Two:

GAMBLING

Oh once in the saddle I used to go dashin'
And once in the saddle I used to go gay
But I first took to drinkin', an' then to card playin'
An' then I got shot, so I'm dying today.
—*The Cowboy's Lament*

EAFING THROUGH OUR NATIONAL scrapbook, one can't help but be struck by the many familiar images showing us gambling—the intense colors of the neon-lit Strip in Las Vegas on a desert summer night—the cigars clenched in teeth around a Norman Rockwellian green felt poker table littered with beer bottles, potato chips, and pretzels—the Mississippi riverboat rambling-gambling man (nickname: "Diamond Jim") with an elegant vest, elegant cufflinks, and the clear, twinkling eyes of a hustler—the crap game in a back alley of New Orleans with the sound track of *Porgy and Bess* and the shooter's shout of "Come on six, come on six, baby needs a new shirt—children are cryin' for bread!"—the Western saloon, sawdust on the floor, rotgut whiskey, the faro layout, and danger never far away.

As a nation, we love to gamble. As a nation, we also love to hate gambling. Both the love and the hate run as themes through American history, from the arrival of the first Europeans to the present day. Hedonist one moment, Calvinist the next, we exhibit a startling lack of consistency in our views on gambling.

This ambiguity can perhaps be explained by the fact that the Bible does not speak directly on the subject of gambling. Like the codes of Hammurabi and Solon as well as Mosaic law, the Bible does not explicitly condemn gambling. In the Old Testament, tough choices were made by lot, a decision-making process that was seen as specifically sanctioned and commanded by God. Likewise, in the New Testament, Matthias was chosen over Justus to replace Judas in the body of disciples by lot.

Ever vigilant, though, Christians have not let the absence of specific scripture on the subject stand in the way of a carefully constructed denunciation of gambling as sinful—it is motivated by greed, covetousness, and selfishness; it violates the golden rule; it destroys the work ethic; it is contrary to good stewardship; it enslaves and thus violates the First Commandment; and it creates a trust in material things and chance rather than God's will and care. Lest there be any doubt as to the degree to which gambling was seen as a sin, in a sermon preached at Bologna in 1423, Saint Bernardino of Siena traced the origin of playing cards to the Devil himself.

With no bright line in theology, it is not surprising to find the split in secular views towards gambling. From the start, we have condemned gambling. In 1624 legislation directed at ministers, the Virginia Assembly forbade "playing at dice, cards, or any unlawful game." The great Puritan moralist Cotton Mather noted the role of lots in the Bible as "acknowledgment of God sitting in judgment," and by extension wrote that games of chance "cannot be made the tools

NICKEL A $5 gambling token

and parts of our common sports without, at least, such an appearance of evil as is forbidden in the word of God." The Massachusetts legislature in 1670 banned cards and dice as a "great dishonor of God," while the Connecticut blue laws banned playing cards (and observing Christmas) as sinful and illegal. A century later, in 1774, the Continental Congress outlawed "every species of extravagance and dissipation, especially . . . all kinds of gaming."

It cannot be said, however, that the early European settlers were entirely successful in their efforts to stamp out gambling. In fact, were it not for lotteries—as blatant a game of chance as ever there was—there would have been no New World. In 1612, King James I granted permission for a lottery "in special favor for the present plantation of English Colonies in Virginia." Virtually every major university founded in America was built on the strength of funds raised through lotteries, which were also used to capitalize a number of private manufacturing and agricultural ventures. In 1776, the same Continental Congress that two years earlier had legislated against "all kinds of gaming" resolved "that a sum of money be raised by way of a lottery, to be drawn in Philadelphia." Thomas Jefferson was a skilled gambler who meticulously recorded his winnings and losses as he drafted the Declaration of Independence, while Benjamin Franklin waxed eloquent on the joys of gambling.

Gambling was deeply rooted in our national character as we charged into the 19th century. Henry Clay is said to have been one of the sharpest poker players of all time, and Andrew Jackson bet $200—a tremendous sum of money—on a single roll of the dice. From the cities of the East to the riverboats of the Mississippi River, gambling had a firm grip on the country. For a moment it even appeared as if we might become a land of, for, and by the gamblers, when in June 1835, a planned uprising in the Mississippi and Ohio valleys by a group of Southern gamblers, the Clan of the Mystic Confederacy, was thwarted.

Even with the dark side of gambling, there was, it must be conceded, a curious unifying and cohesive effect to it. Men with widely differing political views and from different classes fraternized around the faro or euchre table. Gambling is, after all, ultimately egalitarian, and in its own way it served to fuse disparate elements of the society.

The second half of the 19th century saw the rise of a fervent anti-gambling reform movement. Gambling, alcohol, and white slavery were the targets of a movement supported by prigs, zealots, and honest reformers. In the 1840s, America was captivated by Jonathan "The Reformed Gambler" Green, lecturer and author of *An Exposure of the Arts and Mysteries of Gambling*. Vigilance societies, societies for the prevention of crime, and societies for the suppression of vice sprung up in every major city, and ministers thundered from their pulpits:

> *Gambling houses flourish in New York as thick as roses in Sharon. They are eating into the character of some of what we are accustomed to think of as our best and most promising men. They are a sly and constant menace to all that is choicest and more vigorous in a moral way in the generation that is now moving onto the field of action.*
> (Dr. Charles Henry Parkhurst, Madison Square Presbyterian Church, March 14, 1892)

As the country moved into the 20th century, the Calvinist within us seemed to win the day. John Philip Quinn leapt to the forefront of the battle against gambling, writing in *Gambling and Gambling Devices* (Canton, Ohio: J. P. Quinn, 1912) as follows:

*Of all the vices which have enslaved mankind, none can reckon among its victims so
many as gambling. Not even the baneful habit of drink has blighted so many lives or des-
olated so many homes. Its fascination is insidious and terrible, and its power is all the
more to be dreaded in that it appeals to a latent instinct in nearly every human breast.*

Prohibition was the ultimate success of reformers, but that noble experiment ultimately
failed. With the repeal of Prohibition, though, the country lurched away from the Calvinistic
spirit towards the libertine within us. Legalized gambling in Las Vegas and Reno boomed after
World War II, with a glitz and mobbed-up edge that unmistakably cried out "SIN!" As the 20th
century moves to a close, Americans seem more than ever at ease with our sinful gambling
ways. Legalized gambling has spread dramatically from the friendly confines of Nevada and
Atlantic City, back to the Mississippi River, the Indian casinos, and the state-sanctioned lotteries
from sea to shining sea. In a breathtaking display of a sin undergoing cosmetic surgery, hiring
a press agent, and reinventing itself, Las Vegas is now portrayed as a great destination for
family fun, with gambling receiving the same naughty wink that prostitution did in *Irma la
Douce.*

John Philip Quinn exhorted us to "rise up, shake off this dark enchantment—dash down
the dice, shred the cards into the flames—pass out into the pure air." We have instead embraced this dark enchantment and rejoiced in the heavy chains that Quinn and his ilk urged us
to cast off. To borrow from Conrad, we have in the destructive element immersed ourselves.
Dash down the dice? Never! Shred the cards into the flames? Never! *Rien ne va plus*, babe—
Viva Las Vegas!

The Language of Gambling

AS IS THE CASE with most sins, gambling has produced an abundant and lively body of slang,
about which several observations may be made.

Much of the slang of gambling has a slightly archaic ring to it. Several words and expressions used by gamblers may be traced back to the profligate sporting gentlemen gamblers of
19th-century England. Many more, though, were conceived, delivered, and nurtured in the
1920s and 1930s, and there is something slightly old hat about them.

There is a strong underworld influence on the slang of gambling. Given the illegal nature of
most gambling, it is not surprising to find that a wide selection of criminal argot worked its
way into gambling slang, giving it a decidedly tough guy, con man, Damon Runyon character.
Aside from the direct borrowings from the guys and dolls of the 1930s, the slang of gambling
is definitely cynical; as befits the facets of human nature most in play when humans gamble,
the language is jaded and, at times, quite humorous.

Within the slang of gambling there is some degree of cross-pollination, with words from
card games working their way into dice games, words from cribbage popping up in dominoes,
a backgammon term appearing in golf betting, and so on.

Gambling is deeply ingrained in our national character, and so it is only logical that many
gambling expressions have crossed the slang barrier into standard informal speech. The

expressions **according to Hoyle, ace in the hole, ace up his sleeve, all bets are off, bet the ranch, blue chip, crap shoot, fifty-fifty, follow suit, long shot, new deal, pass the buck, play it close to the vest, roll of the dice, square deal, stand pat, strong suit, wild card,** and **work both ends against the middle** all have a gambling birthright and all are heard in everyday conversation.

ace deuce To sustain heavy losses. *The expression is probably derived from the boxing slang of a "one-two punch."*

aces around In pinochle, one ace from each of the four suits

action The total amount that a gambler will bet

action player A gambler who bets heavily and, often, unwisely

advertise To make a bluff with the intention of being exposed

Africans Gambling tokens worth $100. *Most $100 gambling tokens are black, hence the continental/racial reference.*

age The player to the dealer's immediate left, who receives cards first

alien card A card not belonging to the deck in play

The Boneyard Patois

DOMINO GAMES ARE PLAYED both for recreation and for wagers, bringing them into the domain of sin. They are played in clubs (*Life* magazine reported in 1966 that as much as $100,000 changed hands in domino games during lunch at the San Francisco Commercial Lunch Club) and on city stoops, recently glorified by Ice Cube in the hip-hop song "It Was A Good Day," by 4-Tay in "Player's Club," and a number of other rap songs. The domino pieces have a feel, look, and sound, all of which are an integral part of the ambiance of the game. Along with the click of the pieces as they are played there is within the subculture of domino players an unpretentious body of slang.

The dominoes themselves are known as **bones, ivories, rocks, stones,** or **tiles,** with the markings denoting numbers referred to as **dots, pips,** or **spots.** The set of dominoes is a **deck** or the **stock.** The

dominoes not in use at a given moment are referred to collectively as the **boneyard** (a term used at least as early as 1897); a tile in the **boneyard** is a **sleeper.** In bidding games, the dominoes left after the players have drawn their hands are **widows.** A **stinker** is one who forces another player overboard (the player must draw from the **boneyard**), sometimes eliciting the comment, **"Man overboard!"**

After mixing up the dominoes (**washing the bones** or **getting your hands dirty**), most games begin with deciding who will go first by lot, drawing a single domino from the pile. The first domino played in a hand is the **down, lead,** or **set;** the matched dominoes in play are a chain or leg.

As is the case with dice players and card players, domino players have their own counting system. Any domino with a blank is known as a **repeater,** while **count**

all-in Betting all of one's chips

All jokes, no tokes. There is a lot of banter at the gambling table but not much tipping of the dealer.

all out Betting up to the house limit

all the way in one play A bet of all of one's chips

ammunition Gambling tokens

apron The cloth band worn by dealers around their waist. *A theft deterrent, the* ***apron*** *prevents easy access to pockets.*

army odds The correct odds, as opposed to the adjusted casino odds which favor the house

backer A gambler who finances a game without playing himself

backstrap A telephone hookup used by bookies to relay calls and avoid traces

bad rack A gambler who does not pay his debts to a casino

baggage A person who stands near a game but does not gamble

bait To make a bluff with the intention of being exposed for later strategic advantage

bananas Yellow $20 gambling tokens used in baccarat

bang up To close a game or table

barber pole A bet made up

---

dominoes are any pieces whose **pips** add up to five or ten. Other slang names for domino pieces are:

0-0 **Blanks, zeroes, whites, pales, bar of soap, Ivory soap,** or **Saturday night**

1-1 **Snake eyes, double ace,** or **grandma's peepers**

2-2 **Double deuce**

3-2 **Banker's set**

3-3 **Poison ivy** or **Spanish curse**

4-4 **Scorpion**

5-0 **Idiot's delight**

5-5 **Gold nuggets**

5-_ **Dancing girls** or a **kicker**. Names for a 5 in any combination.

6-1 **Kicker**

6-6 **Hairy belly** or **jaws**

A good hand is a **sweet count**, and in bidding games any domino which has not been played and is the highest in its suit is the **walker** and any domino that is not trump and not a double is **off**.

Points have their slang values—a **nick** is five points; a **dime, tension,** or **tennis shoes** is ten points; a **nadine** or **fidene** is fifteen points; **twimps** or **19 hoes and a pimp** is twenty points; and **hoes and some** or **a quarter** is 25 points.

Once play begins a **spinner** is a double played on both sides, which thus may be played off of on both ends. In addition to the main wager, there are several possible side bets, including the **hickey**, a side bet on a bid for tricks. Any score of one point is a **cheap play**, while to **lock up** is to play the domino that leaves the game or a **leg** of the **chain** closed. A game in which no player can play a domino and the **boneyard** is empty is **blocked, closed,** or **locked up,** and may earn the complaint, "Aw, why'd you lock the game again!"

Words of the Asian Games

THE ASIAN INFLUENCE on gambling in America is not insignificant. Most of the illegal gambling houses which operated in every town in the western United States before World War II were run by Chinese, and several of the games which have captured our gambling fancy in the 20th century are Asian. These games bring with them an Asian idiom, some of which is lost along the way, some of which is translated into English, and some of which is supplanted with English jargon or slang.

Mah jongg was a fad to end all fads between 1922 and 1925, and was glorified by Eddie Cantor in his hit song, "Since Ma is Playing Mah Jongg." Americans, mostly women, were fascinated with the beautiful Asian tiles, the exotic words that were imported with the games, and the thrill of even modest gambling. It was not just the housewife who loved mah jongg—according to Babe Ruth, legendary baseball manager Connie Mack banned the game from the Philadelphia Athletics' clubhouse because of the intense interest it generated among the players.

Several expressions used in mah jongg are lyrical, verbatim translations from the Chinese—**fish from the bottom of the river** (to go out with the last discarded tile), **moon from the bottom of the sea** (to go out with the last tile of the **wall**), and **nine gates** (a concealed winning hand, all of one suit, which scores the limit) are three examples. The deference shown the dealer, known as the **chief**, **elder hand**, **leader**, or **parent**, is distinctly Asian.

Moving to the game, like the dice and dominoes, there are **bones** in mah jongg, a set of sticks that are given point values and used like gambling tokens. After mixing the pieces, or **washing the tiles**, the tiles are arranged in rows around the table stacked two-high, known as the **wall** or **pile**, and hands are drawn. The **dead wall** is the last 14 tiles on the **wall**, which are usually not used in the game. A **fall** is a tile that is thrown and declared. Possible house or table rules include **garbage** (tiles may be exchanged) and **kitty** (a bonus collected for all players). When there is betting, a **pie** is the pre-determined amount that any player can lose.

There are many exotic names associated with the different tiles, none particularly slangy, and then there are the **simples,** the suit tiles, excepting the ones and nines. Hands have names—a **dead hand** is one in which a set or sets are incorrect, a **ready** is one that lacks one tile of being a winning hand, **one before ready** is a hand that lacks two tiles of being a winning hand, and **waiting** is a hand whose incomplete set is a serial pair.

Kong is a big word in mah jongg, referring to a set of four tiles. **Kong on kong** is a limit hand, while **to rob a kong** is to win a hand by taking a tile just added to a melded triplet by another player who wishes to make a four-tile set.

Keno has shown considerably more endurance than mah jongg, having worked its way up from a game played only by Chinese immigrant laborers in the 19th-century western United States to an established fixture in all casinos. It was targeted by law enforcement in the 1930s, subjected to jingoistic attacks during World War II ("BUY VICTORY BONDS INSTEAD OF ILLEGAL ORIENTAL CHINESE LOTTERY TICKETS!"), but it has endured and survived, now a tame fixture in casino gambling.

Keno is in essence an 80-number lottery game, with individual games (**races**) played several times an hour. A casino employee, the **writer**, writes the bet on a ticket, takes the money bet, and gives the gambler a duplicate of the ticket (the **outside ticket**), keeping for the casino an **inside copy** or **master copy**. The gambler otherwise occupied need not stop what he or she is doing and go place the keno bet in person, for a **runner** will do it for them. In the days before computers, the **writer** might have used a **banger** or **puncher** to punch the numbers bet onto a

keno ticket. If the bet has been placed, the ticket is a **booked ticket**; if marked incorrectly, it is a **dead ticket**.

After the announcement of **Last call!** is made and betting has been closed, numbers, perhaps painted on a small ball known as a **pea** siphoned through a **goose neck** or **rabbit ears**, are drawn and announced by the **caller**. The entire operation is overseen by the **first man**, who is assisted by the—yes—**second man**.

Before the days of computerized keno, a master copy of a ticket with the winning numbers was then produced; known as a **draw** or **punch out**, it was used to compare with gamblers' tickets. To **catch** a number is to have a bet-upon number drawn as a winning number, also known as the noun **catch**; to **make a hit** is to win a keno bet. A particularly impressive win is a **wall ticket**, one which the casino is likely to post on the wall as evidence of the great possibilities of winning. A **cheat sheet** shows all or some of the possible payouts on a game.

An individual number chosen by a gambler is a **king**; a **hit** of all the numbers on a basic ticket is a **solid hit**. A ticket with three or more groups of equal numbers is a **way ticket**, a block (such as a 1, 2, 3, 11, 12, and 13) is a **solid six**, and an **around the world** bet is one on all eight corners (the numbers 1, 10, 31, 40, 41, 50, 71, and 80). A **catchall** is a bet which is won only when all numbers selected by the player are drawn; conversely, a **catchzero** is won when none of the numbers selected by the player are drawn.

of tokens of different value and color

bare run In pinochle, a run without an extra king or queen

barracuda A cheater

bean A gambling token

bear A frugal gambler

beard A person who places a bet for a cheat

beat To win money by cheating

beef A complaint lodged by a gambler against a casino employee. *Though a part*

B–I–N–G–O—Here it is!

IF ALL GAMBLING IS A SIN, and bingo is gambling, that would seemingly leave bingo a sin. Apparently not, though, for since its earliest days bingo has been a favorite fund-raising technique for church groups, and no self-respecting, sin-hating, Bible-believing, God-fearing church would tolerate open and notorious sinning in the name of fund-raising.

Only a year after toy salesman Edwin Lowe launched bingo in 1930, a priest from Wilkes-Barre, Pennsylvania contacted Lowe; intrigued by the fund-raising potential for the game, the priest was troubled by the fact that the cards which Lowe was selling permitted multiple winners in a game, causing turmoil among the parishioners. Sensing a huge opportunity, Lowe spent a considerable amount of money hiring a professor from Columbia University to design 6,000 bingo cards with non-repeating number groups. With that design feature straightened out, bingo boomed.

In the 1930s, bingo prospered on parallel paths, in churches and in commercial bingo halls like the bingo parlor run by Bill Harrah in Venice, California; bingo parlors ran from the bargain **two-for-a-nickel joints** to the plusher **two-for-a-dime joints**. When Harrah opened one of the first casinos in Reno in the 1940s, bingo was a major attraction. Over the years, the commercial applications of bingo ebbed, although the 1980s saw a boom in high-stakes bingo games on Indian reservations.

The culture of bingo is rich and vibrant, if a tad tacky. Men call women "darlin'" and other men "friend," while women call everybody "darlin'," cars in the church or VFW or Moose Lodge parking lot are plastered with bumper stickers reading "I've got a hunch I'll win a bunch" or "Get out of my way, I'm on my way to play bingo," and each player has his or her own superstition-laced rituals leading up to the announcement that the game is about to start—**Eyes down!**

Much of the cultural creativity in bingo seems consumed with naming patterns on the bingo board, but there is a modest slang idiom used by bingo players. Bingo cards that are made of a durable material and covered with markers (or **chips**) are known as **hard cards**, **marker cards**, or **all night boards**; a **shutter card** is usually made of plastic and has individual shutters that cover each space. Some bingo games use cards printed on newspaper stock (referred to colloquially as a **flimsy**, **special**, or **throwaway**) which are marked with a crayon or **dauber** (a small bottle of ink with a sponge applicator) and thrown away after one game.

*of general slang, **beef** is a minute-to-minute player in the language of games and gambling.*
Benji *A $100 bill. A por-*

trait of Benjamin Franklin graces the front of the $100 bill.
bet blind *To bet without seeing one's cards*

Big Bertha A huge slot machine with many reels and an oversized handle, usually placed near the entrance to a casino

There are dozens of different games, based on the patterns needed to win. A **blackout** or **coverall** is a game in which the winner must cover all the numbers on a card; in a **Texas blackout** game, the player must cover all the odd or all the even numbers on the card; and in **South of the Border**, all numbers in the third, fourth, and fifth rows must be covered. **Maggie and Jiggs**, a game played with a **wild ball** (each number on the card with the same last digit is covered—a 17 is good for 7, 17, 27, 37, etc.) on **hard cards**, is one of several with exotic names. In a **Tom, Dick, and Harry** game the winner must have three bingos on three separate cards, while **Four Musketeers** requires one straight-line bingo on four different cards. Some games are based on **crazy** patterns, meaning that the pattern can be made in any direction on the card; others require that the bingo be made the **hard way**, five numbers in a row without using the **free space** (the center square on the bingo card, traditionally free). A **sliding** bingo is one that can be made by sliding one of the lines up or down, as in a "Sliding T." Some bingo halls feature lottery games on the side, known as **break-opens**, **jar tickets**, **pickles**, and **pull-tabs**. A **housewives special** is a daytime bingo session, which

strangely enough is aimed at housewives.

Bingo players are sensitive to streaks, and will say that a number is **running** if it is called frequently during a session. A **run** on a number might elicit a shout of **Shake your balls!** from a player (urging the caller to mix up the number balls used for the drawing); another bingoism with sexual overtones is the use of **sex** for the number six. If the caller is announcing numbers too fast, players might say **The caller has a promise**, suggesting that the caller is in a hurry to leave the game for a date. A game that proceeds slowly is **slow death**.

A **wait** is the number one needs to win, and a **wait for a wait** refers to the two numbers one needs to win. **Sit on it!** is a common cry of exasperation when a **wait** is not called or when a **shirttail** is called, a **wait** discovered after another player wins. A **sleeper** is a bingo discovered after the caller has moved on to the next number, and in most games it does not count as a winner. In some high-stakes games today, a prize is paid for a **bullet** (a win made after a minimum number of possible calls).

The traditional way of announcing a win is to shout "BINGO," although variations abound, including **Full house!**, **Here!**, **Here it is!**, or **That's it!**

Big Six   An upright wheel-of-fortune gambling device, usually placed near the entrance to a casino

bird   1. A sucker   2. A 25¢ gambling token. *In this sense, "uncap the birds" means to permit gambling with 25 ¢ tokens.*

bitch   In playing cards, a queen

bite   The casino tax on a bet

black   A $100 gambling token. *Most casinos follow a uniform color code for their gambling tokens, under which a $100 token is black.*

black action   A situation where a gambler is betting heavily with $100 gambling tokens

black book   A list of persons who are barred from casinos, including cheats and card counters

Black Maria   In hearts, the queen of spades

bleed   To win a lot in small increments

blind   Extra cards left over after the deal, usually going to the high bidder

blitz   A gin game where one player fails to score at all

block   In gin, to hold a card that an opponent needs

blocker   In a slot machine stealing team, the person who obscures the actions of his confederate working on the machine from cameras or security guards

blow back   To lose all or most of one's winnings

boat   The box that holds unused dice

boat people   Gamblers arriving at a casino on a bus excursion. *This*

expression is not without its racist overtones, as many excursions cater to Asian-Americans, and hence the reference to Asian refugees.

bone   1. In playing cards, an ace   2. A $1 gambling token

bookie   A person who establishes odds and accepts bets on events

books   Playing cards

book the action   To accept a bet

boy   A jack

break the deck   To stop play and reshuffle because of a perceived irregularity in the game

break-in dealer   A new, inexperienced dealer

break-in joint   A casino that hires inexperienced dealers

broad tosser   The dealer in three-card monte. *Three-card monte was immensely popular in the 19th century. It was almost without exception a confidence game played by professional cheats who took advantage of unsuspecting pigeons.*

broke money   A small amount of money given by a casino to a gambler who has lost his entire bankroll

brush man   A hawker at a

casino poker game

bubble peek A technique by which a dealer can see the value of a card before dealing it by squeezing the card between his little finger and the heel of his hand

buck the game To bet against the house

bug A device placed on a mechanical slot machine that prevents the reel from stopping at a particular symbol. *This cheating device used by crooked slot machine operators is euphemistically referred to as an "odds adjuster."*

bull An ace

bullet 1. An ace 2. A $1 gambling token

bump To pay off a player's bet by placing a large pile of chips next to the player's bet and leveling it off to leave a second pile of equal size

bundle A substantial amount of money

bunny An eight

buried Losing badly

burn To remove a card from play

bury To place a card

Rien ne va plus . . .

THE MOST POPULAR GAME in European casinos, roulette is a fixture in American casinos and classier illegal gambling joints, not to mention church fund-raising Monte Carlo nights. Roulette is deeply rooted in European tradition, and much of the language of roulette is French. The calls of *"Mesdames, messieurs, faites votre jeu—rouge ou noir"* and *"Rien ne va plus"* have a decidedly classy ring to them, elevating them somehow from the gutter of carny hawker to James Bondian sophistication and decadence.

That said, there is some English colloquial idiom associated with roulette, describing the equipment, personnel, and betting schemes. The roulette wheel is nested in a wooden **bowl**, fastened to the hub by a metal finial known as a **spindle**. **Frets** (a musical borrowing) divide the compartments (**canoes** or **pockets**), colored and numbered at the boot (the **pads**). The "0" and "00" are the **knotholes**. The **mucker** assists the dealer (the **keeper**), placing the **dolly** (a glass marker) on the winning number, collecting bets, and chasing errant balls which spin over the **shield** around the wheel, leading to calls of **Ball out!** Assuming for the sake of argument that cheating is possible in roulette, a **mule's ear** is a hidden device for controlling the roulette wheel.

Roulette is a **crank game**, one in which bets are won or lost based on a single event. Bets include the **low bet** (a bet on the numbers 1-18) and **high bet** (a bet on the numbers 19-26), the **red bet** (a bet on all numbers backed by red) and the **black bet** (likewise, but black, as in the "Black 17" favored by James Bond), **column play** (a bet on the 12 numbers in one of the three columns), and bets on the **dozens** (bets on 1-12, 13-24, or 25-36). More complicated bets include bets on the **finals** (the last digit of the winning number), the **Mickey Mouse** (two corner numbers and a single number or **straight-up** bet), a **street bet**, **street play**, or **trio** (a bet on three numbers), and a bet on four different numbers, known as a **corner bet**, **quarter bet**, and **square bet** or simply **square**. A **basket bet** is a bet on the 0, 00 (**double dot**), and 2; if a player has bet on either odd or even and the ball lands on 0, it is neither a win nor a loss and he or she is said to be **in prison**.

in the middle of a deck of playing cards

bust-out joint A casino that cheats gamblers

cage The area in a casino where the cashier is located

California bible A deck of playing cards

call bet A bet made without producing cash or chips, a privilege reserved for only the most preferred customers

cap A gambling token of one denomination placed on top of a stack of gambling tokens of another denomination

cap a bet To add tokens to an existing bet, usually illegally

carousel An area in a casino with a group of slot machines

carpet joint A casino that caters to big-spending gamblers

cartwheel A silver dollar

case bill, case money One's last money. *This term is drawn from faro,*

where the case card was the fourth and final card of a denomination.

catch To draw a card

century A $100 bill

change Money. *When gambling, money is stake; otherwise it is change.*

chase a bet To increase one's bet in order to make up for losses, usually with disastrous results

check A gambling token

chill To lose interest in a game

chip A gambling token

A Lover's Leap to Comfort Station: The

BACKGAMMON—THE GAME on the other side of the chess/checker board that is folded up in the game closet—goes with gambling like soup goes with sandwich. It was a favorite game of Thomas Jefferson, who fastidiously recorded his backgammon winnings and losses for the three weeks during which he drafted the Declaration of Independence.

An essential part of the game is the **doubling cube**, a die marked 2, 4, 8, 16, 32, and 64, rolled before each game to determine the game's stake. Still in the world of betting, **automatic** is an optional rule under which the game stake is doubled if both players throw the same number when rolling for the first move. A player can **double** (offer to double the game stake), or under the **beaver** rule, a player who has been doubled may demand that the stakes be quadrupled.

Aside from betting, the slang of backgammon is strategy-oriented, slightly militaristic, and not particularly humorous. Beginning with the equipment, the game is played with playing pieces known primarily as **men** but also as **checkers**, **counters**, **stones**, and **tiles** which travel around the board, from **pip** to **pip**. The center of the board, from which the playing pieces **come in**, is known as the **bar** or the **rail**; a sailor's version of backgammon, **acey-deucey**, has all pieces enter the game from the **bar**. A single playing piece on a space, referred to as a **blot**, is subject to attack; if **hit** or **knocked off** it is taken out of play and must start its journey around the board again. Moving a second playing piece (a **builder**) onto a spot is to **cover a blot** or to create a **safety**. If there is more than one playing piece on a spot it is known as a **block**. A **blockade** is a series of contigu-

Chip change! An announcement by a dealer that a gambler is trading smaller denomination gambling tokens for larger denominations

chip copper A person who steals gambling tokens from other gamblers

chippy A sucker

choppy game A game where neither the casino nor the gamblers have been winning consistently

chump A sucker

chunk To bet heavily

claim artist A gambler who tries to cheat by claiming that he or she intended to make a certain bet after the fact, counting on the casino's desire to placate gamblers

claw machine A mechanical contraption which pushes quarters dropped into the machine towards a ledge; a player wins all the quarters that fall off the ledge when he or she plays a quarter. *Usually no quarters fall off the ledge.*

clerk An excellent dealer

clock To keep track of a game. *This gambling term has worked its way into the language of urban drug dealers, who employ groups of clockers to watch out for potential customers and the police.*

clumping The sticking together of card denominations when shuffled

coin snatcher A slot machine

cold Unfavorable to the gambler

Strategic Slang of Backgammon

ous **blocks** which impede the opponent's movement; six consecutive spots occupied by one player are a **prime** and prevent the movement of an opposing playing piece trapped behind the **prime**. If a player's pieces are all in positions that are not exposed to being **hit**, he or she is **safe**.

The first six spaces on the board are the **home board**, and the two men that start the game on the 1-point of the opponent's **home board** are known as the **back men** or **runners**. The **bar-point** is the 7th spot, one of the key blocking spots; the **comfort station** is the opponent's 12th spot. A **lover's leap** is the move of a **runner** from the opponent's 1-point to the 12-point (the **comfort station**) by rolling a 6-5. A move from opponent's side of the board to one's own side of the board is **around the corner**.

After both players have moved past the opponent's **blockades** and are focused solely on reaching home as quickly as possible, they are engaged in a **straight race**. The final stage of the game, removing **men** from the board, is **bearing off**.

Strategies include the **blocking game** or **back game** (an ultra-defensive strategy where a player tries to impede his opponent's pieces), **staying back** (a moderately defensive strategy, keeping some men in one's opponent's exiting quadrant), the **running game** or **race** (an offensive strategy where a player tries to moves his men home as quickly as possible), and **wipeout** (an ultra-aggressive strategy in which a player hits **blots** and races for home as if there were no tomorrow, keeping his opponent off balance). An absence of strategy or poorly executed strategy which produces a poor relation of the **back game** and the **bearing off** is known, appropriately, as a **nothing game**.

color for color In the same denomination as a bet. *A $25 bet made with five $5 tokens would be paid off with five $5*

tokens, not a single $25 token.
color up To exchange tokens of one denomination for tokens of a higher

denomination
comp Complimentary hotel services
count down To make small stacks of tokens,

Dart Words

ALTHOUGH THE GAME of darts is primarily associated with Great Britain and more specifically her pubs, it is not without its enthusiastic supporters in the United States and her bars. You don't have to be a beer drinker to play darts, but it helps; the two activities have enjoyed a close historical relationship, one which happily continues. Add to beer and darts the third leg of the trinity—betting—and you have a neat little package of sin.

The language of darts is decidedly British English, with a strong contribution from Cockney slang, and much of the dart slang used in American bars is a direct borrowing from British pubs.

Darts themselves are known as **arrows**. Heavy darts are **bombers** or **cannons**, while light, thin ones are **nails**. The dart board is the **clock**, and the bull's-eye is referred to as the **bull, bung, bunghole, button, cork** (probably the most commonly used slang synonym in the United States), **dead bull, dosser, little Audrey,** or **pug**. The segments (**beds**) of the **island** or **turf** (the actual playing surface of the dart board) include **downstairs** (the lower half of the board), the **married man's side** (the left side of the board), and **upstairs** (the top half of the dart board); a dart that completely misses the playing surface is said to **hit the woodwork** or be **off the**

island. The **spider** (more appropriately but less commonly called the **spider web**) is the metal web that delineates segments of the board; to bounce a dart off the **spider** is to **wire one**.

Players stand behind a line known as the **hockey**; if a player strays over the line, he or she is said to have **wet feet** or **one foot in the water**, and other players might call out **Blacking back!** or **Father's boots!**

The game usually starts with **three up**, or three practices tosses. To **cane** an opponent is to defeat him soundly; if one wins without one's opponent scoring, one has **given them the brush**. A **dry wipe, tin hat,** or **whitewash** is a win of the first two **legs** (one of the three complete games that make up a match) of a three-leg game, thus shutting one's opponent out. One might expect a **dry wipe** when playing a **chucker** (an inexperienced or mediocre player), who is likely to throw a **sloppy sailor** (a dart that bounces or falls off the board).

On the other hand, evenly matched players might find themselves **in the front room** (a close game), known also as **level pegging** (an expression on loan from the game of cribbage). There the game might come down to a difficult shot where a certain point must be made, a **crack, rip,** or **split**; a precise hit of the desired number makes it **dead**, as in a **dead 12**, while in a

easily counted by the pit boss from a distance, from taller stacks

cousin A gambler who does not tip or tips poorly

cover the bet To accept a bet

cowboy 1. A reckless, free-spending gambler 2. A king

crack the nut To win enough money gambling to meet one's expenses

cradle The part of a slot machine where coins that

---

cracked toss one hits the single not the aimed-at double. The final victory-clinching throw is known as the **game shot**, after which one calls out **bingo!**, **Domino!**, **House!**, **Office!**, or **Old Lady!**

A great deal of dart slang revolves around the numbers on the dart board. The following is only a partial list of a seemingly endless string of numerical ter-minology:

0: **Oxo**
1: **Annie's room, up in Annie's room, Kelly's eye, Bill Taylor, wagon and horses**
9: **Doctor's favorite**
10: **Downing Street**
11: **Legs**
20: **Top of the house, top of the shop, tops** (usually a double 20)
21: **Key to the door**
22: **Swans on the lake, dinkey doo, fish shop, fried fish, two little ducks**
26: **Half a crown, bread and break fast, brewer, Style & Winch**
33: **Feathers, fevvers, bull calf**
42: **Weaver's donkey**
45: **Bag o'nuts**
57: **Heinz, varieties**
66: **Clickety click**
76: **Trombones**

77: **Sunset Strip, umbrellas**
88: **Garden gates, Golden Gates, Connaught Rangers**
100: **A ton, Bill Harvey**
111: **Lord Nelson**
222: **Double Nelson**

Three darts in the same number are known as **three in bed**, while a dart that is stuck in the shaft of another is known fittingly as a **Robin Hood** or mildly lewdly as **humpin'**.

Darts is a game which is rich in ritual, and with it ritualistic expressions—**Come out!** or **No practicing!** (said when one's opponent should stop throwing because he or she has scored too many points), **Game on!** (a plea for a little less noise, please), **Good darts!** (a compliment on a good throw), **Hard cheddar!** (too bad), **Hops!** or **Cat's on the counter!** (a reminder to the player who has just lost that he or she is obliged to buy a round of drinks), **Muggs away!** (said to the loser of a game, who will go first in the next game), **On your knees!** (said to a player who has to shoot a double 3, very low on the board), **You're sufferin'!** (said when one's oppo-nent has a very difficult shot to make), **You've been!** (said when one's opponent has had a chance and not taken advantage of it), and **Wrong bed!** (said when a dart has gone astray).

have just been played land and are assessed as valid or not

crank game Any game where the bet is won or lost based on a single event

cross A maneuver designed to outsmart a cheat. *Cheats know the famous little maxim, "Every **gaff** has its **cross**."*

crossroader A traveling casino cheat

cry act To pretend to lose

cucumber A sucker

cushion A gambler's bankroll reserve

cut checks To hold a stack of gambling tokens in one hand and use the index

Words of the Sports Book

BETTING ON SPORTS EVENTS is endemic in the United States, in office **pools** on the Super Bowl, **over-under** bets at the stadium, licensed **sports books** in Nevada, bookies who operate in virtually every town in the country (making bookies "the mob's cash cow" even in 1997, according to Charles Hynes, the District Attorney of Brooklyn), and the Oregon Lottery. The Black Sox scandal of the 1919 World Series and the hue and cry surrounding Pete Rose's compulsive gambling are two shining examples of the widespread existence of—and widespread public denunciation of—sports betting in America.

On a given day, there are a number of events or games for which wagers are accepted, known collectively as the **board**. **Run me down!** is a request that the bookie or clerk give the caller the odds on all upcoming games. **The chalk** is the favored team or player, while **the dog** is the underdog, leading to the expressions **chalk player**, **dog player**, and **road dog** (the team favored to lose, playing away from home). To attract bets on **the dog**, bookies or sports books will **set a price**, either by **laying odds** or by **laying points** on **the dog**, creating a **point spread** or **spread**,

in essence by giving the underdog a fixed number of points; a bet on Dallas by **three and a hook** means that Dallas must win by at least 3.5 points for the **chalk** bettor to win. If Dallas wins by three points, the **chalk player** is **hooked**. One might bet on the underdog because of the odds offered (**to take the odds**) or because of the **spread** offered (**to take the points**). A game with even odds where neither team is favored is a **pick** or **pick 'em**.

Within the family of sports bettors there is many a species—the **blind bettor** (the gambler who wagers without having complete information on the sporting event), the **client** (a regular bettor whose credit is good), the **cold customer** (a gambler who picks his own bets without regard to where big-time gamblers are betting their money), the **everyday action** or **everyday Eddie** (a regular, compulsive bettor), the **mover and shaker** (someone who bets so much that his or her bet affects the odds), the **scalper** (a bettor who **swaps**, or bets on opposing teams with different bookies offering different odds, thereby gaining an advantage), a **shortstop** (small bettor), the **shouter** (big bettor), and the **sport player** (a bettor who only bets wagers likely to win). The placing of large

finger to create a series of equal stacks

cut into To pay off a player's bet by placing a large pile of chips next to the player's bet and leveling it off to leave a second pile

of equal size

cut tokes To divide tips between casino employees

dame A queen

dead fish A gambler who places small bets

dead head A nonplayer

dead wood **1.** A nonplayer **2.** In gin, unmatched cards in a hand

deal around To leave a player out of a deal deliberately

dean An astute gambler

money bets by a syndicate of big-money gamblers is known as a **banana game**. Worst of all are the **result player**, the gambler with 20-20 hindsight on what bets should have been made, and the **pick mooch**, a bettor who won't do his or her own handicapping, won't pay a handicapper, and who tries to wheedle information from bettors who do.

When it comes to **getting down** (making a wager), the simplest wager is a **flat bet**, a single wager on a single game; the terms and details of the wager are known as the **proposition**. Bets on more than one event or game are known as **cards** or **teasers**, while a **BB** or **back-to-back** is two consecutive wagers. Each game has a cutoff point for betting, known as the **limit**; the total amount of bets made with a bookie or book on an event or a day is the **handle** or **write**. At the end of the day the bookie or book does **homework**, settling accounts. A bookie **knocks down the play** when he or she beats the **action** that has been bet into him. On an unusually large bet, the bookie will probably **play faces**, or only accept bets from known customers.

Events and betting patterns can affect the odds which the bookie or book is willing to give. Some bookies or books will release an

outlaw line, a tentative handicapping which is given to preferred customers whose reaction will help adjust the odds or points given. The **morning line** is a handicapper's first assessment of a game or event, which will affect the odds later in the day, the **late line** (an adjusted assessment, usually made after bets have been placed). The **official line** is set by several books in Las Vegas, but books and bookies will often deviate from the official line based on local betting patterns. The least reliable line is the **newspaper line**, which is often inaccurate.

A game is **sided** or **steamed** when more money is bet on one team than the other, moving the betting line and perhaps creating a distortion or **crease** which the diligent bettor who has **clocked** the event (monitored the teams and game carefully) can exploit.

With sports gambling comes the danger of fixed games or events that are **in the bag**. A bribe is known as an **envelope**, which might motivate a player or players to **shave points**, miss or make points in an effort to manipulate the final score of a game to favor a bet on the game, or even to **tank** the game (a **bucket job**) or event by losing deliberately. Say it ain't so, Joe.

with a grasp of odds

deece In pinochle, the nine of trump, worth ten (*dix* in French) points

devil's bedpost The four of clubs

devil's bible, devil's book, devil's picture, devil's playbook A deck of cards

dirty Mixed in denominations (said of gambling tokens)

dirty Dora In hearts, the queen of spades

dolt The past tense of "deal"

down a bet To separate a bet made with tokens of different denominations into separate stacks of a single denomination

down to the cloth Down to one's last money or gambling tokens

drag To take back all or part of a bet

drop The amount of money that a player uses to purchase gambling tokens at a casino table

drop box The box at a blackjack table where currency is placed

drown To lose heavily

dry Depleted of money

dump 1. To lose a lot of money quickly. *This expression is most often applied to gamblers, but it can apply to the casino. For example, a slot machine that is "dumping" is paying off at a rate higher than one would expect based on the machine's settings.* 2. In pinochle, to give the dealer the bid because all other players pass

Dutch No percentage in

Numbers Words

THE **NUMBERS RACKET**, known also as **digits**, the **Kentucky lottery**, or the **policy racket**, is not as pervasive today as it was 40 years ago, but it is still an integral part of the daily life of America's working poor. The concept is simple—bets are placed on a three-digit number; at the end of the day, several numbers are drawn as winners, usually determined by a fixed system such as the final three digits of the closing Dow Jones average.

Bets are gathered from gamblers by a **runner** (or **sheet artist** or **sheet writer**), who calls the numbers and amounts bet in to the **controller** or **pick-up**, in essence the area manager for the local **policy king** who runs the game. The headquarters of the local numbers racket is the **bank** or **big drop**. In the rare

exception to this three-layer organization, a **spot controller** will operate alone, without **runners**, handling a select group of bettors directly.

The simplest bet, a bet on a three-digit number, is a **head bet**, **head number**, or **straight number**; a **catch** or **hit** on that number pays 500 to 1. In some circles, this was also known as a **flat gig** because only suckers, or **flats**, would make the bet. Many players worked off a basic three-digit number, which they would then **box**, or rearrange in every possible combination of the three digits. Some players took the number a step further, using a **rundown** (usually either the **1-1-1 minus** or the **1-2-3 plus**) to build off the basic number.

A **day number**, which paid at approximately 5 to 1, refers to a bet on any num-

favor of the bookie or operator

Dutch honors The 10 and 9 of trumps in whist

Dutching play Crossing the suit in euchre

earing Currency not completely inserted in the drop box, subject to theft by the dealer

early out An early dismissal from work at a casino on a slow night

edge The advantage in a game

eighty-six, 86 To ban a gambler from a casino

eye in the sky The area above the casino floor where gambling is observed through mirrors or by cameras

fast company Experienced, seasoned gamblers

fire To bet aggressively

fish 1. A sucker 2. In gin, to discard tactically to lure a card from an opponent

fish hook A seven or a jack

flash To show a card, either intentionally or not

flat A sucker

flat bet A bet that is the same amount from one

hand to another

flats Cards

flea A small-time bettor, on the prowl for **comps**

flush the john To play slot machines

foreign checks Gambling tokens from another casino

free bet A bet where the casino pays true odds. *A rare event.*

frenchy A gambler who is for the most part honest, resorting to cheating only rarely

friendly game Social gambling, where players bet

ber from 1 to 78 which can appear anywhere on the list of winning numbers. Paying 7 to 1 is a **single action** bet, a wager that a certain digit will appear in a certain place in the winning number. To play **on the nose** is to bet on the same three numbers regularly. Several numbers command their own name, such as the **fancy gall roll**, **magic gig**, or **washerwoman's gig** (4, 11, 44), the **gall roll** (5, 9, 55), the **moving roll** (9, 12, 29), and the **white policeman roll** (13, 37, 70).

Moving up into the higher odds is the **saddle** (two numbers bet to appear anywhere on the winning list, paying 32 to 1) and the **station number** (one number bet to appear at a specified place on the list, paying 60 to 1). Moving even further away from rational wagering is the **gig** (a bet on

three numbers that can appear anywhere on the winning list, paying 200 to 1), the **station saddle** (a bet on two numbers that must appear at specified places on the list, paying 800 to 1), and the **horse** (a bet on four numbers).

Numbers are most often bet on hunches or rumors; a **hot number** is one that is rumored to be a winner on a given day; if a lot of money is bet on a single number, the **policy king** might insure against a big loss, or **edge off**. Some bettors wager based on patterns in the number, such as betting on **triples**, or numbers with all three digits the same. Others resort to a **dream book**, a pamphlet which explains to the truly astute bettor how dreams can be interpreted to predict winning numbers, from abbey (bet on 306) to Zulu (bet on 764).

against each other

fruit machine A slot machine using pictures of fruit for the symbols on the reels

full pencil The unrestricted right to issue complimentary services to players

funbook A collection of discount coupons given by casinos to guests

gaff A cheating technique

George A gambler who tips generously

ghost A blank symbol on the reel of a slot machine

girl A queen

go To receive tips, as in "What did we go last night?"

goose A poor player

go south To put money or gambling tokens into one's pockets

gravy Winnings

greenie An inexperienced gambler

greens $25 gambling tokens

grind A gambler who places small bets

grind down To win all of a player's money over a period of time, due to the advantage that the casino has on most bets

grind joint A casino that caters to small bettors

gut card In gin, a card that completes a broken sequence

Hand in! A dealer's an-

Bingle-bangle-bungle—Golf Bets

TO THE DEVOUT CHRISTIAN, any wager is an attempt to gain something from one's neighbor without giving that person a fair service in return; in the words of Martin Luther, "gambling is always contrary to love and is motivated by greed because a man seeks to the harm of another, what does not belong to him." Accepting this proposition, golf wagers are a sin.

Even if one does not embrace the premise that all wagers are sinful, it is difficult not to recognize that the language which has sprung from the practice of playing golf "for a little something" is humorous and inventive. The slang of golf betting is driven by two subjects—the rules of the game and the nature of the bets.

In the betting game **gruesome**, each player hits two balls on each shot and his opponent picks which will count, leading to an aptly named game of worst-case scenarios. **Hawk** or **the boss** is a distant relation to the bar dice game of the same name, and involves players rotating driving first and picking a partner or playing against all three other players on that hole. **Ransom**, **six**, or **six and six** is a game in which different rules apply on the first six, middle six, and final six holes, in an attempt to equalize playing skills. **Reject** or **wipeout** is a rule that can be invoked in any game on the first tee, under the terms of which each player can force his or her opponent to replay four shots.

Bets covering the entire game include **honest Johns** (all players pay every other player for every stroke taken), **Nassau** (the most common wager, with a payout to the winner of the front nine, the winner of the back nine and the entire game), and **skins**, **scats**, or **skats** (won by the player with the low score on a hole, with a tie carried over to the next hole, known as **carryovers**). Each hole is played for a set amount in **backgammon** or **double**; like

nouncement to his super-
visors that a gambler is
giving him a tip directly,
rather than playing a hand
for him

handle slammer A slot
machine thief who engi-
neers payouts by manipu-
lating the handle of an
older model slot machine

hanger Currency not completely inserted in the
drop box, subject to theft
by the dealer

hawker A casino employee
who encourages gamblers
to join a game

heel To place one **marker**
token on top of another,
angled in the direction of
the player

helps' hall An employee
cafeteria in the casino

high roller A gambler who
bets heavily. *Many* **high
rollers** *prefer the eu-
phemism "preferred cus-
tomer."*

hit and run To leave a
game immediately after
winning

hold The actual amount that
the casino takes from its
games

hook A jack

hooker A queen

hot Favorable to the player,
as in "hot dice" or "hot
deck"

hot and stuck Losing
badly

house A casino

the board game, at any point during the
game, either side may double the bet,
which the opposition must accept or else
concede the hole. Another doubling bet is
carpets or **wall-to-wall**, where the
amount wagered is doubled if one player
or one team wins every par-three hole;
similarly, the player who is losing can
increase the bet by **pressing** (the most
common term) or by **bumping**, **pushing**,
rolling the drums, or making a **checkers bet**. In the wonderfully alliterative
bingle-bangle-bungle, each hole is
played for three wagers—the first player
onto the green, the closest to the hole once
on the green, and the first into the hole.

Side bets—collectively known as an
umbrella or **garbage**—are also colorful-
ly named. Bets named after professional
golfers include the **Arnie** (won if a player
never has his or her ball in the fairway yet
still scores at least a par), the **Hogan**
(won if a player's ball never leaves the fair-

way), the **Nicklaus** (won by the player
with the longest drive in the fairway on
each hole), and the **Watson** (won by a
player who sinks a shot from off the
green).

A player who hits a tree yet still scores at
least a par wins a wager in **barkies**, while
a **flaggy** is won if a shot lands within flagstick distance of a par-three hole, a bet
which is quite similar to the **k.p.**, a bet
won by the player closest to the flagstick.
Bongo is won by the player making the
longest putt, **greenies** are won by the player closest to the hole after one shot on a
par-three hole, **moles** are paid by a player
who leaves his ball in a bunker after one
shot, and **sandies** are won by a golfer who
gets up and down in two shots for at least a
par from a bunker. A **bridge** or **contract**
bet is based on a prediction of the final
score of the match, while a **hedge bet**
refers to a bet made on a hole after a player has lost a bet on the previous hole.

house person A dealer who enjoys watching players lose

hunch A bet placed on impulse or intuition rather than an appreciation of the odds

hustler A dealer who solicits tips from players, sometimes cheating the house in their favor in return

Jackson five Five $20 bills. *So named because Andrew Jackson is pictured on the $20 bill and reinforced by the Jackson Five musical group.*

Jake A jack

jammer A dealer who can perform with any level of betting

J-boy A jack

jimbroni A dealer who is not completely proficient

job A card protruding slightly from a deck of cards

joint A casino

juice The casino tax on a bet

juice joint A casino that cheats

Language in the Pit

COCKFIGHTS ARE A deadly and brutal thing. Needles, called **gaffs** or **blades**, are strapped to the spurs of a specially trained cock; a well-aimed kick by the cock can decapitate its opponent. George Washington and Thomas Jefferson both raised fighting cocks, and Andrew Jackson loved to bet on them. Cockfights are now illegal in most states, and even where legal are convincingly sinful and a vice. Their most recent moment in the national spotlight came in 1980, when then presidential candidate Ronald Reagan asked reporters "How do you tell the Polish fellow at the cockfight?"

As hideous a spectacle as cockfighting may be, it is not without its flashes of linguistic creativity. A breeder of fighting cocks is known as a **feeder**, while the man who actually readies the cock for the fight and places him in the pit is the **handler**. Still in the person department, a **customer** bets on the underdog.

When a cock is trimmed before a fight, it is said to be **in trim**; if trimmed well, it is **clean cut**. If the cock's flesh is pink, it is deemed healthy, **in the pink**. Cocks are fitted with knives on their spurs, or **heeled** with **gaffs**. A cock showing particular courage and fighting spunk is **game**, **cocky**, or **plucky**.

A **hack** is a single match; a **main** is a set of fights; and a **portable main** is a set of fights at everchanging locations. In a **derby** the prize money is pooled and awarded to the bird with the most victories. Another cockfighting term that is found in mainstream English is **battle royal**, which refers to a fight in which a number of birds are placed in the ring and which continues until only one bird is alive.

Before the fight the **handlers** will **bill the birds**, letting them peck at each other to activate their animosity. At the cry of **Pit your birds!**, the birds are **set to** or placed in the ring. During a fight, a cock that rises over an opponent is said to be a **high flyer**. If during a fight a cock appears to have given up, it is placed **breast to breast** with its opponent in an effort to make it fight.

junket A trip bringing gamblers to a casino with some subsidized services

k-boy A king

key man A slot machine mechanic

kitty Extra cards left over after the deal, usually going to the higher bidder

lace To mix the cards after the shuffle in baccarat

lady A queen

lamb A victim

lammer A small disc used to indicate the value of a token or loan

let it ride To leave the winnings from one hand as a bet on the next

live one A gambler who tips generously

lobster A sucker

local joint A casino that caters to the local population

loose Liberal in pay-off percentages (said of slot machines)

lucky bucks Casino coupons

lumber A nonplayer

lump A poor dealer

mallard A $100 bill

mama A queen

mark A sucker. *This little piece of slang is widely used by swindlers as well as gamblers and others.*

marker A loan extended to a gambler with a line of credit at the casino

marker button A button with the amount of the marker on it

Marker down! The marker has been repaid!

mark off To separate gambling tokens in the rack into regulation **stacks**

marriage In pinochle, a king and queen of the same suit

mason A gambler who does not spend freely

mechanic A casino employee who sets the slot machines for their payout

Michigan bankroll A single high-denomination bill folded around a wad of $1 bills, giving the appearance of a large amount of money. *At least one source includes* **Philadelphia bankroll** *as a variation on this theme. As a more or less native Philadelphian, I deeply resent this more or less slur.*

Money plays! A call to the supervisor that paper money is being bet

monkey A gambler who thinks that he or she knows what he or she is doing but doesn't

mooch A customer who angles for complimentary hotel services

mortal cinch A bet that is, one is told, certain to win

move A sleight of hand

mystery payoff A payoff on a slot machine on unposted, mysterious alignments of the symbols on the reels

nail To catch someone cheating

name player A heavy spending gambler known to the casino

nickel A $5 gambling token

office A signal to another gambler

oil wells Aces

one-armed bandit A slot machine. *The term came into general usage in the 1930s. The metaphor was materialized in slot machines built into man-sized cast iron figures in Nevada in the 1940s.*

on the cuff Made without tokens or currency actually placed on the table (said of a wager). *A privilege accorded only the most preferred cutomers.*

on the edge Broke

on the rail Observing a game without playing

on the rim Playing on credit

on the wood Being adjusted at a casino cashier, said of a **marker**

on tilt Upset by losing. *This comes from pinball slang discussed in Chapter Six (page 241).*

out in front Winning

paddle The tool used to push paper money into the **drop box**

paint A face card

Paper plays! A call to the supervisor that paper money is being bet

parlay To bet the amount of the original bet, plus the winnings of that bet

patsy A sucker

pepper A sucker

perspiration pennies Money that a gambler cannot afford to lose

pheasant A sucker

pigeon A sucker or victim

piker A gambler who bets small amounts against a gambler who bets large amounts, believing that the bank almost always beats big-spending bettors

pinch To remove gambling tokens from one's bet after losing the bet

pinch and press To add money to a bet when holding a good hand and remove money from a bet when holding a bad hand

pit An area within a casino with a number of gambling tables

pit boss The most senior casino official in a **pit**

pizza To mix cards before shuffling in baccarat

play close to the chest, play close to the vest To gamble conservatively

ploppy A gambler who plays his or her own system which he or she explains to the annoyance of fellow gamblers

plunger A gambler who bets heavily and compulsively

pot hooks In cards, nines

Pot up! In the game acey-deucey, to make your bet

power of the pen The right to issue complimentary services to players. *A variation on this expression gives the casino employee full pencil.*

press To increase the next bet

producer A gambler who loses often and big, producing profits for the casino

professor An astute gambler with a grasp of odds

prop Someone who works for the casino, gambling with casino money to generate interest in a game

pump up To lose steadily

punter The shooter or player in baccarat and chemin-de-fer

push A tie

put the horns on To try to change one's luck by changing seats, crossing one's fingers, etc.

quarter A $25 gambling token

rabbit A sucker

rail bird A thief who steals gambling tokens from gamblers when they are not looking

railroad bible A deck of cards. *Also known as a California bible and* *a devil's bible or a devil's book.*

rainbow A bet made up of tokens of different value and color

rake A croupier's stick

reds $5 gambling tokens

reducer In gin, a low card picked up or held to reduce the **deadwood** count in one's hand

RFB Room, food and beverages—the complimentary services which a casino can offer guests

rhythm player A slot machine cheat who places the reels into play and then locks them into place when a winning combination appears

ride To leave the winnings on the table with the original bet as a new, increased bet

riffle A shuffle of the cards. Several **riffles** make up a shuffle.

rock A conservative gambler

rough it up To bet heavily

round robin In pinochle, a meld consisting of a marriage in each of the four suits

rug joint A casino that caters to big-spending gamblers

rule rap An explanation of the rules of a game by a dealer to an inexperienced gambler

runner A casino employee who transports tokens from the cashier to the tables

running bad Losing badly

running good Winning nicely

rush A better than normal run of luck

salesman In gin, a card discarded to lure an opponent into discarding a wanted card

salty Unlucky at drawing cards

sawdust joint A casino totally lacking in pretensions

scan To peruse quickly the cards that have been played

scared money Money that a gambler cannot afford to lose

Schneider A gin game where one player fails to score at all

score A better-than-average night for tips

seed An ace in playing cards

send out a salesman In gin, to discard a card tactically to lure a wanted card from an opponent

shark A cheat

sharp A cheat in card games. *Because a sucker is a flat, the combination of cheat and sucker, sharp and flat, makes a lovely musical metaphor.*

sheep A sucker or poor player

shill Someone who works for the casino, gambling with casino money to generate interest in a game. *General slang but frequently used in casinos.*

shimmy Chemin-de-fer

shop A casino

shot An illegal move by a gambler

shuffle up To stop play and reshuffle because of a perceived irregularity in the game

sign A signal to another gambler

silent partner A confederate in cheating

silver Silver dollars or $1 tokens

single-0 A cheat who works alone

skill button A button on the side of slot machines that was supposed to regulate the movement of the reels, but in fact had no effect whatsoever on the machine's operation

skinner A cheater

sleeper A bet that a player has forgotten

slicker A professional gambler

slots Slot machines

spike An ace

spook A superstitious gambler

spoon To insert a spoon-shaped object into the payout mechanism of a slot machine in order to trigger a payout

spot An ace

spotter A casino employee who watches for cheats and misconduct by casino employees

spread the deck To spread all of the cards at a table in an arc in the middle of the table, turn one's hands upward, and clap lightly. *This is a part of blackjack protocol when dealers are changed at a table.*

square up To form the deck of cards into a neat packet after the shuffle

squeeze The control device that operates a cheating mechanism

stack A column of 20 gambling tokens or silver dollars

stake Money. *When gambling, money is* **stake***; otherwise it is* **change***.*

steam To bet progressively higher after losing

steerer A person working for a crooked casino who is paid for bringing in customers

steer joint A crooked casino

stick A casino employee who gambles with the casino's money to drum up business

stiff A gambler who does not tip well

stonewall, Stonewall Jackson A gambler who does not tip well

store A casino

storm A seeming deviation from the law of averages

straight slots Slot machines whose payoffs are defined and do not vary

strangers In gin, unrelated cards in a hand

stringing A cheating technique used on slot machines, in which the coin is lowered into the machine on the end of a string and then retrieved for another play

sucker bet A bet with strong odds against the bettor

swabs, swabbers Face cards in whist

sweat To gamble nervously and carefully

sweater A dealer who cheats gamblers

swing To steal from the casino

take down a bet To remove a bet before the next hand

Tap City Money given to a gambler who has lost all of his or her money. *The protocol is that the money may not be used for further gambling and that it must be repaid before those who give it will play with the gambler who got it.*

tapped out Without money to gamble, having lost one's entire bankroll

tell An unconscious signal given by a player or dealer, revealing something about their hand

There goes the ax! The casino is taking its cut.

throw a party To lose heavily

thumb cut To use one's thumb to equalize a series of stacks of gambling tokens

ticket A card

tight 1. Not favorable to the bettor. *A* **tight** *slot machine pays out infrequently.* 2. A conservative style of play

toilet A shoddy casino

toke A tip. *From a clipped "token."*

Tom A poor tipper

tough money Money that a gambler cannot afford to lose

trap A casino that cheats gamblers. *The late 19th and early 20th century had a number of synonyms for crooked casinos, including* **bird house, brace house, brace room, deadfall, snap house,** *and* **wolf trap***.*

treasure hunt Looking around a casino for someone from whom to borrow money

trim   To cheat

turkey   A gambler who is not familiar with the etiquette of the game or gambling

twofer   A $2.50 gambling token

U-boat commander   An incompetent dealer

valet   A jack

velvet   Money won from the casino, as in "After that run at blackjack we played on the velvet all night."

vic   A sucker

vig, vigorish   The casino

tax on a bet

walk   **1.** To leave a gambling table **2.** In pinochle, to win a trick with a card that one expects to lose. *Will it walk? Can I make it walk?*

wash   One bet that cancels another

well   The metal tray at the bottom of slot machines where payout coins drop

whore   A queen

wide open   An abandoned, loose style of gambling

widow   Extra cards left over

after the deal, usually going to the high bidder

wire   A signal to another gambler

wise guy   A sophisticated gambler who knows the game, knows the odds, and plays carefully

wood   A nonplayer

yard   One hundred dollars

yuck   A sucker

zero   A loser

zuke   A tip

I raised, I saw, I called—Poker Slang

POKER IS QUINTESSENTIALLY AMERICAN, as much a cultural fixture as baseball. It knows no boundaries, no class or race or sex lines. It is equally at home in the country club or the casino, the firehouse or the White House, the college dormitory or the penitentiary, the living room or the card room. It can exist as a game with buddies on Thursday night, as a "friendly game" with strangers, as a high-stakes tournament game, and as a casino game.

Poker's parentage defies precise identification. It is clearly related to a number of bluffing-oriented card games popular between 1600 and 1800, including *as-nas* in Persia, *pochen* or *pochspiel* in Germany, *poque* in France, *primero* in Italy, and *brag* in England. The game which would evolve into poker as we know it today originated in Louisiana in about 1800, and quickly worked its way up the Mississippi River. Jonathan "The Reformed Gambler" Green wrote of an early form of poker in 1834, a bluffing game played with 20 cards (ten through ace of each suit).

Sometime in the middle of the 19th century, Mississippi River gamblers began playing poker with a full 52-card deck, and there has been no turning back. The game's rules were a blend of rules from other games, and the name was simply the poorly pronounced French *poque*. Far from ostracism as a vice, poker has been eulogized in intelligent, thoughtful, and articulate terms as a tonic for our society. When Warren G. Harding was chosen as the Republican nominee in smoke-filled room 404 of the Hotel Blackstone in 1920 to break an all-night deadlock at the convention, he told reporters "We drew to a pair of deuces and filled," and we knew what he meant. Harding went on to appoint a "poker cabinet," bringing to the game the blessing of the highest office in the land.

To understand the slang of poker, one must first have a basic grasp of the game. As far as the rules of the game go, poker is fairly simple—it is a card game for two or more players, in

Pockets of Slang: Hold 'em Names

HOLD 'EM IS A FAMILY of poker games, the basic premise of which is that hands are formed by combining cards dealt facedown (the **pocket**) to each player with cards dealt faceup on the table, known as **boardcards** or the **flop**. For some reason, there exists an entire lexicon of slang names for various combinations found in the **pocket**. Among the slangiest and most clever are the following:

Ace, ace:	**Snake eyes** (on loan from craps), **rockets, pocket rockets,** and **American Airlines**
Ace, jack:	**Ajax,** or **the foamy cleanser**
King, king:	**Cowboys**
King, jack (off suit):	**Bachelor**
King, 7:	**King salmon**
Queen, queen:	**San Francisco marriage, mop squeezers**
Queen, 3:	**Gay waiter.** *A queen with a trey. Get it?*
Jack, 5:	**Motown.** *With a nod to the Jackson Five.*
10, 10:	**Boxcars.** *On loan from craps, but applied to two 10s, not two 6s.*
10, 5:	**Woolworth's, dimestore,** or **Barbara Hutton.** *All play on 5 and 10, with a reference to the chain, the common generic name, and the heiress.*
10, 4:	**Broderick Crawford.** *A cultural allusion to the 1950s television show "Highway Patrol." Every episode featured the star Broderick Crawford using police ten codes, including "ten-four."*
9, 6:	**Breakfast of champions, chew for two,** or **dinner for two.** *A 9-6 combination is also a 6-9 combination, hence the allusions to mutual oral sex.*
9, 3:	**Jack Benny.** *A 9-3 combination is also a 3-9 combination, bringing to mind Jack Benny's claimed age of 39.*
8, 8:	**Two fat ladies, the mighty Wurlitzer.** *88 keys, right?*
8, 6:	**Oldsmobile,** or **Eubie.** *The Eubie is probably a play on the sentiment, "You be broke if you be playing this hand."*
8, 3:	**Raquel Welch.** *An 8-3 combination is also a 3-8 combination, which suggested to someone Raquel Welch's bust measurement.*
7, 7:	**Sunset Strip**
7, 6:	**Union Oil,** or **The Sign of the Finest.** *The latter was a Union 76 slogan, a clever advertising association.*
6, 4:	**The Question.** *A quiz show reference, to the "$64 Question."*
4, 2:	**Lumberman's hand.** *The allusion is to a 2 by 4 piece of lumber.*
2, 2:	**Two little ducks**

which each player makes one or more bets that his or her hand ranks higher than those of all other players. **Draw** is a form of poker in which five cards are dealt facedown; players who bet rather than withdraw from the hand on the basis of the five cards originally dealt may replace one or more cards in their hand before betting continues. **Stud** is a form of poker in which cards are dealt both facedown (known as **hole cards**) and faceup.

Other species of games mentioned in the word list that follows are **lowball** (a five-card **draw** game in which the lowest hand wins), **high low** (in which the pot is split between the highest and lowest hands), **hold 'em** (in which two cards are dealt facedown and five community cards are dealt faceup), and **omaha** (a variant of **hold 'em** in which players must use two down cards and three of the community cards to form their hand). In any game it is possible to designate a card as **wild**, meaning that it can be used as any card in the deck.

With its friends in high places, poker often escapes classification as a sin or vice. We need look no farther, though, than the ever-vigilant John Philip Quinn to remind us that, yes, poker is a sin and vice:

> *Whatever argument may be advanced against any form of gambling, may be urged with equal force against poker; and that this game sanctioned as it practically is, by the countenance of the reputable men who never set foot within a gambling house, has done more to weaken the moral sense of the country at large as to the general question of gambling than any other single agency. Its growing popularity and increasing prevalence constitute a menace by no means to be ignored to the prosperity, the morals, even the perpetuity of the people.*

Regardless of poker's standing in the circles of hell, it is without dispute a fertile breeding ground of colloquial American English. It is a highly social game, and as such it is a game with its own culture and vocabulary. While perhaps not as popular in casinos as blackjack or craps, poker easily boasts the most magnificent American slang idiom of any game of chance.

ABC 1. In low games, A-2-3 2. To play predictably

ace high A hand with no pairs and an ace as the high card in the hand

ace in the hole In stud games, an ace as a down card. *The term came to mean any secret reserve; in the West, it came to mean a shoulder holster.*

ace out To win a hand bluffing with an **ace high** hand

aces and spaces A hand made up of two aces and three worthless cards

A-game The game with the highest stakes in a card room or casino

aggressive Bold when one has a good hand, as opposed to **loose**, which refers to boldness regardless of the hand

All the way! An announcement by a dealer that all players still in the hand have bet all their money and that the remaining

cards will be dealt without betting intervals

angle A stratagem that is nearly illegal and definitely unethical

angle shooter A poker player who uses unethical, unfair stratagems

ante The amount that must be put into the pot to be dealt a hand

apple The highest stake game in a card room or casino

Arkansas flush Four

Hey Pilgrim—Hello Professor
Player Types

THE ESSENTIAL ELEMENTS of a poker game are the players, the cards, and betting. A vivid slang idiom has developed to describe different types of players, often known generically as **laddies**.

A **card rack** is a player who seems to end up with many good hands, while a **professor** is a smart player, perhaps too smart for his own good. The **radar Charlie** at the table has a good intuitive sense about what cards others are holding and what cards will be drawn. Sounds bad but is good—the **zombie** is an expert player who shows the same lack of emotion whether winning or losing, whether holding an **immortal** or **rags**. Sounds outlaw but is good—a **Jesse James** wins more than his share of hands by bluffing.

On the losing side of the scale is the all-around poor player, happily referred to by others as a **drib**, **duffer**, **goose**, **heel**, **live one**, or **palooka**. There is also the **architect** (a player whose heavy betting builds pots), the **feather merchant** (a timid player), the **flinger** (an undisciplined, careless player), the **last-card Louie** (a player who stays with a hand up to the last card that can be drawn, even if good sense dictates an early fold), the **pay station** (a player who rarely folds and often loses), the **pilgrim** (a novice), the **provider** (a player whose losing ways make the game profitable for other players), the **rabbit**

(a timid player, likely to fold), the **ribbon clerk** (a player who cannot keep up with the pace or level of betting in the game), the **shoe clerk** (a small-time bettor), the **table captain** (the self-appointed authority on rules and etiquette found in every game), and the **table cop** (a player who calls any player whom he or she thinks is bluffing).

A player's playing and betting style produces slang descriptions. On the **loose** side is the **bulldozer** (the player who bets and raises heavily whether his hand is good or not), the **driller** or **driver** (the player who bets and raises aggressively), the **piranha** (a player who bets aggressively), and the **Stone wall** (a player with a poor hand who calls at every turn to the end of a pot).

On the more conservative side is the player who actively pursues a pot only when he or she holds a very good hand, known as a **drummer**, **drummer boy**, **hard rock**, **locksmith**, and **milker**. A table full of **tight** players is a **rock garden**, conjuring up a great little image.

Unpredictability is a plus in poker, but it has its limits. **Corkers** play inconsistently in general, while the **calling station** or **telephone booth** calls hands frequently and is thus difficult to bluff. Fittingly, a **maniac** raises, bluffs, and bets in a fanatic fashion, and fittingly a **minnow** plays over his or her head.

cards in one suit and the fifth in another

assault rifle Hole cards of A-K-4-7 in omaha

ax The percentage of a pot kept by the card room or casino

babies In lowball, cards below 6

back door To make a hand that one is not playing for, such as a four of a kind when one is drawing for a full house

back in To enter the betting after having checked earlier in the hand

backline 1. An agreement between two or more players to divide their collective earnings 2. A stack of chips behind the chips used in play

back peek A cheating technique by which the dealer sees the face of the top card on the deck

back seat The last player to act in a particular situation

back-to-back A pair formed by the down card and first up card

bait A small bet made to encourage a raise

bang up To close a game

bay and a gray A bet of red chips and a single white chip

Beast, the Any hand with three 6s. *In the book of Revelation, 666 is the Mark of the Beast, which Satan will demand everyone wear as a sign of allegiance to him during his temporary reign on Earth.*

Beats me! Your hand is

better than mine!

beat the board To hold a hand that can beat any exposed cards

beggar In high games, a hand with no pairs and no card higher than 10

behind a log Far ahead in a game, so playing only premium hands

belly buster A card that

makes an inside straight

belly hit To draw cards that fill an inside straight

berry patch A game that is easy to beat

best hand A cheating stratagem where confederates signal to each other and the best hand is played

bet into To bet before another player who seemingly has a better hand

B-game The game with the second highest stakes in a card room or casino

bicycle In lowball, an ace to 5 hand, the best possible hand

big bobtail A special hand sometimes recognized in private games, four cards that form a straight flush

big cat A special hand, made up of king-high, 8-low, no pairs

big dog A special hand, made up of ace-high, 9-low, no pairs

big eight Four 2s. *An apparent direct borrowing from craps.*

big hand A good hand

big tiger A special hand, made up of king-high, 8-low, no pairs

blank A card that does not appear to help any player

blind A mandatory bet, usually by the player to the dealer's left made without looking at the cards

blood game A game for high stakes

blooker, blook The joker

board The showing cards

bolt To fold

boost To raise

boxed Facing up (said of a card in a deck)

break To win all of somebody's **stake**

breakers Openers

breathe To pass when one first has the chance to bet, to **check**

brick In omaha, a useless card. *Perhaps related to "brick" as a poor shot with little chance of going in the basket in* *playground basketball.*

bring in the hand To open the first round of betting

brother-in-law poker Poker played with friends

brush An employee of the card room responsible for the seating list

buck A marker used to indicate the deal position. *See Word History, page 90.*

buddy poker An arrangement avoiding betting against a friend

bug The joker when used as a wild card in some situations but not others in cer-

tain poker game variations

bull a game To play aggressively in betting and bluffing

bump To raise

busy card Any card that completes a hand

button The marker used to indicate the deal position

buy To receive a card or cards on a draw

buy a pot To bet heavily in the hope of driving out other players

buy-in The amount of chips that a player must buy to join a game

By me! "I pass."

Cap the raises To take the

From Rags to Immortals: The Slang of Poker

THERE IS A SEEMINGLY endless body of poker slang to describe hands, good or bad, straight, flush or full.

Immortal—What a cool word! **Loaded for bear**—What an expression! Both describe a nearly unbeatable hand, as do the slang nouns the **berries**, **brass Brazilians**, **Brazilians**, a **chalk**, the **golyoonies**, **iron duke**, a **lock**, a **monster**, a **no-brainer**, the **nuts**, a **powerhouse**, the **pure nuts**, **rock crusher**, **Royal Brazilians**, a **woolly bear**, or the **world's fair**, and the slang adjectives **boss**, **clutch**, and **ironclad**. Good but beatable is the **major hand** (a hand consisting of a straight or better), and likely to win but not quite unbeatable is the **summertime hand**.

A truly terrible hand is referred to as a **blivit**, a **dog**, **garbage**, **Mickey Mouse**, a **piece of cheese**, **rags**, or **trash**. A mediocre hand that is not likely to develop into a winning hand is a **chasing hand.**

When a very good hand is beaten or **cracked** by an even better hand, the defeat is known as a **bad beat**, and many of these defeats produce **bad beat stories**. Sometimes a player with a poor hand will win a pot from players with better hands, **snapping off** the win.

The full house (three of a kind combined with a pair) can be described by any number of slang expressions, including **barn**, **boat**, **crowded cabin**, **flying** (meaning "holding a full house"), **full barn**, **full**

final raise permitted in a round

card wrench An imaginary device used to pry cards apart so that the card one has drawn will fit the hand

cards speak The rule in hi-lo that players are not required to declare which way their hands are to be considered, high or low

case The final card of a denomination in a deck. *This expression is a direct loan from faro.*

cat flush A special hand, consisting of a **big cat** or **little cat** all of the same suit

catbird seat A position where the player who declares last can assure himself of half of the pot. *This expression is better understood in colloquial English than in poker, thanks in large part to James Thurber and baseball announcer Red Barber, both of whom popularized the expression.*

catch, catch perfect To draw the card that one needs

catch a fish To lure another player into calling or raising when one has a good hand and has made a small bet

catch someone speeding To call a bluff and win

ceiling bet The largest bet permitted in a game

C-game A low-stakes game

change gears To alter the pace at which one is playing

change-in The amount of chips that a player must buy to join a game

chase To stay in a pot when it is necessary to improve one's hand

check To remain an active player without betting, reserving the right in his

Hands

boat, **full tub**, **no room**, **packed house**, **Philadelphia**, **shanty**, and **shed**.

A hand that consists of all face cards is a **blaze**, and so a full house made of all face cards is a **blazes full**. A hand of face cards and aces is the **Holy City** or **Jerusalem**. A full house made with three 6s is a **house of hell**. A **waiter's delight** (from the poker slang **treys full**, an expansion on **trey** as "three") is a full house made with three 3s and a pair.

A flush (five cards of the same suit) made up of spades or clubs is **all black** or **all blue**, while **all pink** or **all red** is a heart or diamond flush. With apologies to natives of Arkansas, a four-card flush— which is worth nothing—is an **Arkansas**

flush, one meaningless step above a three-card flush, or **monkey flush**.

Straights, made up of cards in sequence without regard to suit, have their own language—a **broadway** (a straight ending with an ace as the highest card), **from here to there**, **here to there**, **here to there without a pair**, **like an arrow**, **office hours** (a straight running from 9 to 5 or from 8 to 4), a **run**, a **stretch**, a **string**, or a **stringer**. With apologies to the natives of Holland, a sequence of every other card (for example, a 2-4-6-8-10)— which is worth nothing—is a **Dutch straight**.

Put them together and you get a straight flush, or a **quint**.

or her next turn to bet, call, raise, or fold

check and raise To check a possible winning hand and then raise any subsequent bet in the same round

chip along To stay in a pot without raising and with making the smallest bet allowed

chop 1. To return the blinds to the player who posted them and move on to the next hand 2. To

play briefly in several different games and to cash out after winning

class A game in which one player endlessly analyzes the correct play of each hand

clinic A game in which one player endlessly analyzes the correct play of each hand

close To call for a showdown

closed cards Cards that are dealt facedown and

seen only by the player to whom they are dealt

coaxer A small raise of an opponent's raise, made with the hope of soliciting a further raise

coffee-house To attempt to mislead opponents about one's hand by one's speech or behavior

cold call To call more than one bet at a time

cold turkey A pair of kings as the first two cards in five-card stud

come hand A hand that relies on drawn cards

connectors Consecutive cards which might make a straight in hold 'em or omaha

counterfeit To turn a leading hand into a loser

coup A brilliant play

covered with horseshoes, covered with roses Very lucky in drawing cards

crank To deal

crazy Wild

cripple the deck To hold most or all of the cards that somebody would want to have with the current **board**

crying call A call by a player who is virtually certain that he or she will not win the pot

customer An opponent who calls one's hand

dance every set To play

Oh those poker puns . . .

OH THOSE CLEVER POKER PLAYERS! In the why-use-jargon-if-you-can-make-a-pun department, poker players have a clever little lexicon of sound-derived puns. Like most puns or verbal mannerisms, a little bit goes a long way with these, and any player who relies too heavily on this type of word play is bound to wear out his welcome sooner than later:

Alcohol ya "I'll call your bet."
Capitola "The betting is capped."
Cappuccino "The betting is capped."
Dewey! "Two cards please."
El Paso "I'll pass."
Holie olie A hold card, or a card dealt facedown
Pasadena "I pass."
Raisin bread "I raise your bet."
Stew! or **Stu!** "Two cards please."
Tapioca "I'm tapping out and betting all my chips!"
Up scope! "I raise your bet."
Up the slope! "I raise your bet."
Up the slope with the antelope! "I raise your bet."

Get them? Got them? Good.

every hand

dark   Without looking at one's hand (said of a bet)

dead   Played, as in "The 6s are dead."

dead man's hand   A pair of aces and a pair of 8s, all black. *This is said to have been the hand that Wild Bill Hickok held when he was shot in the back and killed in the Mann-Lewis Saloon, Deadwood, Dakota Territory, by Jack McCall on August 2, 1876.*

devil's boat   A full house made with three 6s

dig   To replenish one's stake while the play of a hand is in progress

dinner for four   A pair of 9s and a pair of 6s. *If one arranges the hand as 6-9 6-9, the crude reference to oral sex involving two couples is understood.*

Doctor Pepper   A wild-card game, with 10s, 4s, and 2s wild

dog it   To play a good hand cautiously so as not to drive other players out of the pot

doghouse cut   1. A cut of the cards that leaves the deck in more than two stacks   2. A cut of the deck which leaves cards on the bottom of the deck unchanged

door card   The first up

card dealt to each player in any stud game

down and dirty   The final card in seven-card stud, which often changes the course of the hand

down the river   Seven-card stud

drag   1. To separate money from a pot to show the amount owed by a player who is **light**   2. Take chips out of the pot as change

draw   A form of poker in which five cards are dealt facedown after which players bet or fold and players who remain in the game may replace one or more cards

draw dead   To draw a card when it turns out that you would lose even if you drew the card you needed

drawer   An imaginary card magnet which enables a player to draw the cards he or she needs

drum   To play conservatively

duke   A hand of cards

eight, skate, and donate   A no-limit game with a minimum bet of $8

fall   The order that cards are dealt

family pot   A hand in which all the players have stayed through the first round of betting

fancy buy   A draw made with the hope of drawing

an unlikely combination of cards

fast play   Aggressive betting of a good hand

fatten   To increase the size of the pot

feed   To set aside a percentage of each pot to defray the expenses of the game

feeler   A small bet made to find out the strength of other players' hands

fifth street   The round of betting that takes place after the fifth card has been dealt to each player in stud poker

fill   To draw cards and complete any specified hand

finger poker   A game run on credit

fire   To make the first bet in a betting round

first jack deals   A common method of selecting the dealer, by dealing cards one at a time until a jack is dealt

fivezies   A pair of 5s

flat call   A call that emphasizes the fact that the player did not raise

flicker, flicker   Five-card stud high-low

floor   A card room employee who manages the play

flop   The first three community cards dealt in games such as hold 'em and omaha that use five community cards

Counting Words

CONSIDERED BY CASINOS TO BE UNDESIRABLES in the same league as cheats, card counters and card-counting teams—**card mobs**—capitalize upon their well-honed card-counting abilities and a profound appreciation of probability in their efforts to beat the house in blackjack. Playing with a greater level of skill than the average blackjack player, they slightly increase their potential player advantage, creating a small long-run benefit. They are legally sanctioned yet often barred from casino play.

The general modus operandi of card-counting teams is to play throughout a casino, **bopping** from one table to another, searching for and converging upon momentary windows of opportunity, perhaps consisting of only several hands when the card count is favorable to the card-counting player.

As card counters play blackjack, they often adapt a personality and playing style to disguise their expertise, known as an **act**, **camouflage**, or **cover**. In that vein, a **cover bet** is an ill-advised bet made by a card counter to disguise the fact that he or she is counting. To gain more information about the deck in play, a card counter might **eat cards**, or play multiple hands (a.k.a. **spreading**) or take ill-advised **hits** while betting small amounts.

There are dozens of counting systems and an oppressive technical jargon that comes with them. Several of the slangier entries are the **back count** (counting cards while not playing, waiting for a favorable count to play), **bombing for a jack** (one method for determining an above-average chance for being dealt a blackjack), **depth charging** (a single-deck strategy using the depth of the deal to gain an advantage), or estimating **penetration** (the amount of the deck or shoe that has been dealt). Some counters rely on plus and minus systems, often using **my** as an abbreviation for "minus." Counting is most effective during **end play**, the last few hands of a deck or shoe.

When a member of the counting team who has **cased the deck** at a table ascertains that the deck is ripe for a player advantage, he or she signals to a team member, the **relay**, who in turn conveys signals to other team members. They then move to the table (**bopping**, **hitting and running**, or **table hopping**), and based on signals from the counter (**call plays**) place their bets. The original counter at the table might signal that the deck is **poor** or **rich** in aces or tens and face cards (having a lower or higher than normal percentage of a card value present in the deck), or he or she might simply signal the bet. A team member who places large bets for the team without counting cards himself, looking instead to a confederate for a signal on how to bet, is known as a **big player**, **BP**, or **take-off man**. If he or she has to reach onto the table and place a bet on another player's betting square, he or she is **backlining** or **piggybacking**.

At the end of the night's work, the team will **break the bank**, or distribute the proceeds won by the team, unless, of course, they are spotted by a **catcher-dog**, a casino employee hired to spot counters.

flush To draw in hopes of building a flush

flying To hold a full house

foot A poor hand

foul hand A hand having the wrong number of cards

fourth street The round of betting that takes place after the fourth card has been dealt to each player in stud poker

freak A wild card

freak hand A nonstandard poker hand, such as blazes, Dutch straights, kilters, or skeets

free ride Playing without paying

freewheeler A player who is allowed to play without betting until he or she wins a pot

freeze-out A game in which each player is forced to drop out as soon as his or her entire bankroll is lost with all the stakes thus going to the last remaining player

freezer A short call; a call for less than the amount bet in table stakes

friend A card that improves one's hand

fuzz To mix the cards by continuously stripping off the top and bottom cards

gadget Any special rule in effect in a wild-card game

gallery Spectators who are not playing

gang cheating Cheating accomplished by several confederates

garbage hand A hand that is not worth playing

Gardena miracle To make a good hand with an improbable draw. *Gardena is the capital of legal card rooms in southern California.*

George Very good (said of a game)

get one's feet wet To get into a pot

get the cards in the air To start dealing in a poker tournament

ghost hand A hand that reappears on the next deal because the deck has not been properly shuffled

give it yeast To raise a bet

go better To raise a bet

go cow To pay half a player's buy-in to a game, and to share his winnings half and half

going home hand A hand on which the player has bet the last of his or her chips. *He or she will go home if he or she loses.*

Good hand! The hand that you just showed me in the showdown is better than mine!

gorilla A bouncer in a poker room

go upstairs To raise a bet

gunshot draw To draw for an inside straight, where only one denomination will complete the straight

guts, guts to open Draw poker with no opening requirements

hand from hell Any hand with three 6s. *In the book of Revelation, 666 is the Mark of the Beast, which Satan will demand everyone wear as a sign of allegiance to him during his temporary reign on Earth.*

Hart, Schaffner, and Marx Three jacks

hay Money

heavy Having too much money present (said of a pot)

hedge bet A side bet made with the hope of limiting potential losses on the main bet

heel A poor player

heeler An extra card held with a pair or three of a kind to give the impression of having a better hand than one actually does

high society, high society chips Chips of the highest denomination in a card room or casino

hit A drawn card that improves one's hand

hitchhiker An unexpected participant in a pot

hog To announce or win

Bridge Banter

BRIDGE A SIN? It's admittedly something of a reach, but at times there is wagering involved and if one believes that playing cards were invented by the Devil then any card game is by definition a sin. San Franciscans were reminded that bridge is a sin and vice on January 14, 1997, when seven members of the vice squad raided the San Francisco Bridge Club and cited 14 senior citizen bridge players who were playing for the princely sum of a penny a point. Go Vice Squad!

Bridge is as complex and graceful a game as any, yet most of the language used by bridge players is weighty and joyless technical jargon. Buried in the jargon, though, are some slang gems. In *Adventures in Duplicate Bridge,* Edith McMullin of the American Contract Bridge League strung together this bright necklace of bridge patter—"He was gin for six hearts, but when he converted to six no-trump I cracked it and he rewound. It seems that his partner's cue bid had been a void, *not* the Ace! He lost the first six tricks and went for a telephone number."

A **pajama game** is a hand with all **tops and bottoms** (high cards and low cards) and no mid-range cards (**body**). To be **bare** or **stiff** in a suit is to have only one card in that suit, while a player who has only two cards in a suit, say the ten and four of clubs, would say "a ten **and one**" or "ten-four **tight.**" Borrowing a slang term from the game of whist, a **Yarborough** is a hand with no card above 9.

The slang of bridge is full of militaristic metaphors—a **coup** is any unusual tactical move; a **guard** or **stopper** is a card that stops the opponents from winning a suit; a **submarine squeeze** is a maneuver by which a player determines the right timing to force an opponent to throw away winners or cards that protect winners; to **blitz**

both high and low

Hollywood   Acting, as in "Quit the Hollywood."

horse   **1.** To pass a small amount of money to another player after winning a pot **2.** Someone playing with your money on your behalf

house cut   The amount of each pot taken for the house

house rules   Special rules, usually about betting, agreed upon by the players before a game

idiot end, ignorant end   The low end of a straight in hold 'em

idle card   A card that adds nothing to a hand

in   Remaining in the pot, as in "I'm in."

in the bag   Crooked

in the breach   The first player to act in a given situation

in the hole   Dealt facedown (said of cards)

in the middle   Between two players who are raising the bets

in the mouth   First to act. *This is said of a player in a given situation who is sitting usually but not always to the left of the dealer.*

jack up   To raise a bet

jacks to open   A rule that a pair of jacks or higher is required to open

or **pound** is to score all the matchpoints on a round; to **crack**, **hit**, **punish**, or **strike** is to double for penalties; and to **force** or **tap** is to make a player trump to lose trump control.

Bidding is a critical element of bridge; within the world of bids there is the **psychic bid**, one made primarily to interfere with the opponents' bidding. Similarly, to **swing** is to make an unusual bid, also called **the movies** (as in, "*That* could only happen in the movies"). Bidding results in a contract; if the contract is **cold**, **gin**, or **icy**, it is a **laydown** or a **spread**, a contract which is sure to be made.

Once the contract is made and play begun, it is sometimes advisable to **duck**, or to concede an early trick in a suit for tactical reasons. To **echo** or **peter** is to play high-low as a signal in defense. If one has two or more worthless cards in a suit,

the high card is known as **the top of nothing**, a clever little sobriquet. Loitering for a moment in the loser's bracket, poor or unplanned play in general is known as **family bridge**, while a **loser-on-loser** is playing a losing card on a losing trick.

Clearing a suit is driving out the opposition's high cards in a suit, **rewinding** is redoubling, and **cutting** or **ruffing** is playing a trump card. If a player is **light** he or she has fewer points than advertised; also in the trouble department, an **ambulance service**, **pull**, or **rescue** is a move to save one's partner from a large penalty in a doomed bid. A **menace** is a card that an opponent must protect.

And, returning to McMullin's charming little necklace, there is the **telephone number**. Inexplicably to the uninitiated, a **telephone number** or **zip code** is doubled and down a lot.

Hit me! Paint me! Oh no—to the farm! Basic Blackjack

POKER MAY REIGN as America's sinful card game of choice, but blackjack is the most popular card game played in casinos. It is deceptively simple: the object is to draw cards whose values total 21, or closer to 21 than the dealer's. More of a casino game than a private game, blackjack's slang idiom cannot compare with the voluminous vocabulary of poker, but it has its clever and saucy moments.

Casino blackjack rules vary from casino to casino, with a casino with favorable blackjack rules and games known as a **candy store**. Some casinos pay a bonus for a **five-card Charlie** (a five-card hand that totals 21 or less) or a **Royal 21** (a 21 made with three 7s). The casino's rule on **soft 17s** (which are explained below) produces two slang labels, an **H-17** being a game where the dealer must hit a **soft** 17 and an **S-17** being a game where the dealer stands on a **soft** 17. **Caddy blackjack** is a private game played without a bank, where the deal is rotated among players.

The positions occupied by gamblers at a blackjack table all have slang names. The player to the dealer's immediate left, who receives the first card and the first opportunity to augment his hand or pass, is known as **first base, shotgun**, or the **eldest hand**; it is often preferred because one's play is not affected by idiotic decisions made by other gamblers. The seat to the dealer's immediate right, favored by some but shunned by others as the inevitable victim of poor play by other gamblers, is known as the **anchor** or **third**

base, with the player known as the **anchorman**. Continuing the baseball metaphor, a player sitting between **first base** and **third base** is known as—yes—**second base** or **center field**.

Before dealing, the dealer offers one of the gamblers the **sweat card**, a plastic card used to cut the deck or decks before the deal. The deck or decks are placed in a **shoe** with a plastic card, the **flash card**, inserted near the bottom of the **shoe** to signal when the shoe is nearly finished, and the game begins. The first card in a deck or **shoe**, which is removed from play, is the **burn card**; the first hand dealt from the deck or **shoe** is **off the top**. Bets are placed in **spots**, a designated area in front of each playing station.

The dealer deals two cards to each player and two cards to himself, one of which, the **up card**, is dealt faceup, driving a calculation of odds by the players who compare their hands with what they know about the dealer's hand and the cards remaining in the deck or **shoe**. Further assessment of the dealer's hand is possible if he or she is a **flasher** (a dealer who intentionally shows his facedown or **hole card** as he or she deals) or a **frontloader** (a dealer who unintentionally shows a **hole card** while dealing), or by an analysis of **tell play** (body language) to determine whether he or she has a good or weak hand, looking for and understanding any **leak** (weakness). A player who tries to see the dealer's **hole card** is a **peek freak**; to take things a step further,

spooking is a blackjack cheating scheme involving a confederate who plays at a table behind the dealer, observes the dealer's **hole card** by looking through the space between the dealer's body and left upper arm (the **window**) and signals that information to the cheat at the table.

Leaving aside hands where the two cards dealt add up to 21 (a **natural** or **snapper**) which are paid at **time and a half** (a payout of one and one-half times the amount of the bet), a hand is generally either a **pat** (potentially winning hands between 17 and 21) or a **stiff** (a potentially losing hand between 12 and 16). Esoteric slang names for other hands include the **California blackjack** (an ace and a 9), the **Chinese blackjack** (a dealer's hand consisting of a 10 **up card** and a 4 **hole card**), a **cold turkey** (a hand with two face cards), a **red snapper** (a blackjack formed with two red cards), or a **wired** hand (a very good hand).

Each player who does not have a **natural** must decide whether to play with the hand as dealt (**stand** or **stay**) or to have the dealer deal additional cards (**hit**); a **scratch** is a sweeping motion made with the cards on the table signifying that the gambler wants a **hit**. If the player has a card count of 11 and could thus achieve a perfect count with a face card, he or she might say **Paint me!**, thereby asking for a **paint**, or face card. An ace can count for either 1 point or 11 points; using it as a 1 leads to a **soft** point count—a **soft 17** would be an ace and a 6, which could total either 7 or 17. A **hard 17** would be one made without using an ace as 11 points. Some players simply follow the rules followed by dealers in terms of when

they will hit, a technique known as **mimic the dealer**.

In certain situations, the exact nature of which differ from casino to casino, players can double their bets, known as **doubling down**, and take one more **hit**. A decision on whether to **double down** would be easy if one knew what card was about to be dealt; at times a dealer sympathetic to the player will intentionally show the next card in the deck to the player, a move called a **double down flash**.

If in the hitting process the player's point count exceeds 21, he or she **breaks** or **busts**, going **over** or **to the farm**. If the dealer's first two cards produce a hand between 12 and 16, the player might make a **bustout bet**, betting that the dealer, who must draw another card, will **bust**.

In blackjack, a table with no players is a **dead table**, and the dealer assigned to the table is said to be **holding up a dead table**. A game between a single player and a dealer, which is most favorable for the serious player whether or not he or she counts cards, is a **head-up** game. A solid, dependable blackjack dealer is a **clerk**; if a dealer talks too much with the gamblers, the pit boss might yell out, **Dummy up and deal!**

Still within the specialized lexicon of the blackjack dealer, **Card down!** is the dealer's signal to his supervisors that a card has gone off the table. Dealers check players' hands and pay or collect either all at once (**lay and pay**) or player by player (**pick and pay**). When it is time to close a table down, the dealer **puts the lid on**, literally putting a locking mechanism over the chip rack, and announces **Table down!**

jam To bet or raise the maximum

jammed pot A pot with multiple raises

Judge Bean, Judge Duffy

Three 10s. *This expression is probably derived from the popular belief that a sentence of "thirty dollars or thirty days" was com-*

monly handed down by judges to gamblers in the 1930s. Eric Partridge reports **Judge Davis** *as a British cousin.*

Cribber Slang

CRIBBAGE IS THE CHILD of Sir John Suckling (1609-42), a wealthy English poet, playwright, soldier, general-purpose adventurer, and gambler who was known as the best card player in Britain, if not all Europe, during his short but intensely lived life. Because cribbage was a gambling game, the rules were carefully recorded and preserved, appearing in *The Compleat Gamester* in 1674.

It is a deliberate game, as different as possible in pace from the high-adrenaline instant-gratification world of craps. There is little bluffing involved, a great deal of strategy, and no strong demands on memory or card-counting; a knowledge of odds comes in handy, as does an appreciation of a considerable body of etiquette and a modest body of slang idiom.

Cribbage is played with a standard deck of cards and is scored by **pegging** a board with 121 holes. Holes 1 through 30 are known as **first street**, holes 31 through 60 as **second street**, holes 61 through 90 as **third street**, and holes 91 through 120 as—you guessed!—**fourth street**. The slang-slinging **cribber** or **pegger** (cribbage player) refers to the 120th hole as the **dead hole**, **mud hole**, or the **stink hole** (all derogatory because one's opponent often **pegs out** or wins if one's turn ends

in the 120th hole) and to the 121st or winning hole as the **game hole, home hole**, or **win hole**.

Before starting the game, players agree if **Muggins** is in effect—a rule penalizing players who miscount the points in their hand; a **Muggins** penalty involving a fair number of points is punningly known as **Major Muggins**. After the cards are cut by the **pone** (a term not specific to cribbage, referring to the player to the dealer's right if there are more than two players, the other player if there are only two), each player is dealt six cards. On the first hand, the **pone** is under some rules given an allotment of three points, known as **three for the last**, to compensate for the advantage of dealing.

The best possible hand in cribbage is worth 29 points; a hand with no points is known as a **bust hand** or a **nineteen** (an ironic allusion to the fact that it is impossible to have a hand worth 19, 25, 26, or 27 points).

In cribbage, the player who has dealt the hand in play is given an extra hand of four cards which is known formally as the crib, informally as the **box, cat, kitty**, or **stock**. The crib is built from discards **laid away** by the players. The dealer will try to **salt the crib**, or discard into the crib with the

juicy An easy game or
player
kick To raise a bet
kicker An extra card held
with a pair or three of a

kind to give the impres-
sion of having a better
hand than one actually
does
kill game A game in which

a player may place an ex-
tra bet, thus exceeding the
betting limits for one
game. *The player is the*
killer, *the pot is a* ***kill***

---

thought of maximizing the potential value of
the crib hand; one way to do this is to discard **close cards**, or cards whose values
are near each other and thus likely to be
built into a **run** (at least three cards of successive rank). The dealer's opponent, on
the other hand, will try to **balk** or **bilk the
crib**, discarding cards which will not help
the dealer's crib hand; just as the dealer
might discard **close cards** into the crib,
the opponent will tend to discard **wide
cards**. These are cards whose values are
far apart and thus not conducive to building
a **run**.

After the crib has been built, the **pone**
cuts the cards and the dealer turns over the
top card on the bottom half of the cut; this
card, known as the **starter** or **turnup**, is
melded, or played as part of each player's
hand. If the **turnup** is a jack, the dealer is
awarded two points and the jack is known
as **His Heels** ("Two for His Heels!" is
called out) or, less commonly, **High Heels**.
If the card is not a jack, the jack of the
same suit as the **turnup** is known as the
right jack, **His Nob** or **His Nobs** (cribbage evolved from an earlier game,
"Noddy," in which a jack in the crib was
known as **Knave Noddy**, and later as **His
Nobs**), **His Nibs**, or the **Jack of Nobs**,
and is worth one point.

After the hand is dealt, the **crib** built,
and the **turnup** has been cut, the players
play cards in succession, counting the
cumulative point value. This portion of the
game is known as the **count**. When all
cards have been played, players add up the
value of their hand and this part of the
game is known as the **show**.

When cribbage is played as a betting
game, the typical bet is both on the points
by which the winner wins and the game. A
victory when the opponent has not passed
hole 90 is known as a **lurck**, **lurch** (from
a French game "Lourche" popular at the
time cribbage was developed, and from
which the everyday idiom "in the lurch"
was coined), or, most commonly, a **skunk**,
and the payoff is doubled; if the opponent
has not passed hole 60, he or she is **double skunked**, and the payoff is quadrupled. One other betting technique is known
as the **Q-Pool**, used in tournament situations; players can bet on their own success, with the entire pool of bets being
divided among those players who qualify
for the championship round of play. The
one cheating term peculiar to cribbage
which I have encountered is **walking the
peg**, which refers to the cheat's practice of
moving the scoring peg more spaces than
the points actually scored on a hand.

pot, *and the player is said to have* **killed the pot**.

kilter A special hand consisting of no pair, no four-flush or straight, and no card as high as a 10

Ku Klux Klan Three kings

knock To pass on a bet by rapping the table

lalapolooza A **freak hand** allowed to win once a session

lame Lacking the funds to meet a bet and thus **light**

leak To lose part or all of one's winnings through other gambling habits

leather ass Patience

lid The top card or the only card of one-card draw

light Playing on credit, as in "I'm a dime light." *Said when a player borrows from the pot.*

limp, limp in To call an opening, forced bet in a fashion that emphasizes the fact that the player did not raise

limping Lacking the funds to meet a bet

little bobtail A special hand consisting of a three-card straight flush

little cat A special hand, 8-

high, 3-low, no pair

little dog A special hand, 7-high, 2-low, no pair

lock them up To play an unbeatable hand slowly and well

look To call another player's bet

look down one's throat To have an unbeatable hand

loose Displaying boldness regardless of the hand

made hand A hand that cannot be improved upon

major league game A game with high stakes

make the pack To shuffle

Cribbage Inc.

THE SUBCULTURES THAT produce and support slang can be large or small, regional or institutional, racial, or occupational. Even relatively small subcultures can generate slang, at times at a prolific rate. One such tiny subculture that has spawned a vital slang vocabulary calls itself "Cribbage Inc." In the early 1990s, cribbage-playing students at the Earl Haig High School in North York, Ontario developed a rich, private slang vernacular which they used with each other and with opponents at the university level as they have moved into the world.

The slang of Cribbage Inc. screams with the exuberance of youth. A few examples as compiled by Daniel Goldlist are:

all What all respectable Cribbage Inc. players play for

classic run A shorthand way to identify a point count in cribbage. *Purists insist on a thorough recitation of point counts; a double run of three would be scored as "A double run of three for six and a pair for two makes eight." Using Cribbage Inc. shorthand, one would say, "A classic run of three for eight."*

crib-lebe A book-learned cribbage player with no practical experience at the game

d'oh Two points

dragon flush A *faux* flush with the cards being the same color but not the same suit, worth nothing, sometimes counted by Cribbage Inc. players as "a dragon flush for zero."

for zero Worth no points. *A common*

and cut the cards before dealing

mate A card that makes a pair

meet To call a bet

mess A draw that fails to improve a hand

Mexican standoff The end of a game with two hands at the same value

middle To trap a player between raises and further raises

midget Any poker game with less than five cards per hand

milk To mix the cards by continuously stripping off

the top and bottom cards

minnie A perfect hand in lowball. *A 5, 4, 3, 2, and an ace.*

minor league game A game with small stakes

miss To fail to draw a helpful card

mitt A hand of cards

moo To share the cost of the buy-in and the profits

moon A hand that wins both the high and low halves of a game

mouth bet A verbal bet not backed by cash

muck The pile of discarded cards

murder Difficult to beat

natural A hand made without any wild cards

needle To insult another player in an attempt to disrupt his thinking

nickel-dime A game with small stakes

nigger bet An unusual bet, such as $4 instead of $5. *The language of craps is full of racially offensive terms and expressions. With several notable exceptions, such as this, the language of poker is not particularly offensive.*

---

and potentially annoying Cribbage Inc. quirkiness, identifying card combinations in their hand that are worth no points.

galloping off into the sunset Winning a game with a **mega hand o' doom** when one is already leading

go for all To make a reckless discard to the crib hoping for a certain cut card to build a **mega hand o' doom**

honor point A tie-breaking score. *An esoteric, Cribbage-Inc.-only rule brought into play to decide a game that is interrupted.*

mega hand o' doom A hand with substantially more points than the average.

punt into the cellar To pass an opposing player

purist cribbage Cribbage played by its normal rules

quintessential card The eight of diamonds. *There is, of course, a story behind this expression. A Cribbage Inc. member retrieved many decks of cards from the Ho-Chunk Casino in Wisconsin, only to discover that the eight of diamonds was missing in each deck.*

skunking range A deficit of 30 points or more

squamping A dramatic come-from-behind move, bringing a player who had been behind by at least 20 points into the lead. *This is sometimes also referred to as **storming into contention**.*

nits and lice Two very low pairs

notch To beat someone by one card

nubbin A very small amount of chips or profit

nurse To fondle cards

nut The best possible of a hand, as in a **nut flush** or **nut straight**

nut up To tighten the play of a game

nut-nut A hand in hi-lo that is the best possible hand in both directions

Paper, Glims, Humps, & Ice: Card Cheating

CHEATING AT CARDS, like using loaded dice, is a marvelously ironic sin within a sin where the unwary sinner is punished by the more wary sinner/cheat. While it is impossible to quantify the extent of card cheating either historically or in the present day, based on the fairly extensive language of the card **mechanic**, one would have to assume that cheating at cards is and has been a fairly extensive part of gambling.

The card **mechanic**, or the less commonly used **dukeman**, **mucker**, or **philosopher**, relies on one of several basic techniques—dishonest dealing, the use of a reflecting device while dealing, marking cards (visual or tactile markings), slipping a stacked deck into play, or hiding cards to be played at the opportune moment.

The cheat who is willing to devote long hours of practice can acquire the ability to deal cards from the bottom of the deck (a **base dealer**, **bottom dealer**, **cellar dealer**, or **subway dealer** who deals **bottoms**) or from the middle of the deck (a **middle dealer** who deals a **will-o-the-wisp**). The most difficult trick is to deal the second card from the top, reserving the top card for oneself or a confederate, pulled off by a **second dealer** or **number two man** who relies on **ruffles** or a slight curvature of the edges of cards. All of these techniques require hundreds of hours of tedious practice, with each technique based on a specific position of the hands and fingers known as the **key**.

For a rigged deal to work, the deck has to be arranged, or **stocked**, and the **stocked** deck has to survive a false shuffle (a **Las Vegas riffle**) and a cut of the cards. To survive the cut, the cheating dealer may use a false cut (**butting in**, or a **blind shuffle**, an **elevator**, or a **milch**) after which the dealer **hops the deck** by returning the deck to its original sequence after the false cut, or he or she might use a **bridge** (a card bent enough to be felt by the dealer, used to engineer an arranged cut of the deck) or **break** (arranging the deck with a slight **jog** of a portion of the deck for a confederate to cut). If just part of a deck is arranged, it is a **slug**. If the **dukeman** has arranged for two good hands to be dealt from the arranged deck, it is known as a **double duke**.

Instead of a manipulated deal, some cheating dealers use a mirror-like device placed on the table to see the cards as they are dealt. This practice is known as **glass work**, and the device as a **gaper**, **gleamer**, **glim**, **glimmer**, or **shiner**. A final dealing **gaff** is the **high deal**, a two-player cheating scheme where the cheating dealer

Oh shit! hand A hand on
which a player has bet his
or her last chips, which
he or she portrays as a
poor hand in hopes of
luring bets

one eyes Picture cards
showing only one eye—
the jack of hearts, jack
of spades, and king of
diamonds

one-two-three To play
predictably

on the button In the last
betting position

deals in a manner that permits a cheating confederate to see the cards as they
are dealt.

Marked cards (**cheaters, doped cards,
paper**, or **spooked cards**), used by
painters or **paper players**, range from
the intricately sublime (**readers**, marked
in the printing process itself) to the simply
ridiculous (cards crudely inked by the
card-dauber). Types of **cosmetics, pa-
perwork, shade work**, or simply **work**
include **edge work** (marking on the
edges), **light work** (fine lines on the
backs of the cards), **reflectors** (cards
marked on the back), and **scratch paper**
(cards marked with sandpaper or an abra-
sive).

Some card cheats rely on physical alter-
ation of the cards, which permits them to
identify a card by feel. A **blister** is a small
prick made in a card to identify it; a deck
prepared with **blisters** is **pegged** or
punched by the cheat. Cards that have
been bent (**crimped, warped**, or **waved**)
can be identified by feel, as can an **ear** (a
card slightly bent at the corner) or a **nail**
(a scratch mark made on the card with
one's fingernail). Similarly, cards can be
slightly trimmed for identification; generically known as **shears, strippers**, or
trims, trimmed cards include **briefs**
(cards cut narrower than the rest of the
pack), **humps** (cards cut gradually nar-
rowing from their center to both ends),
and **wedges** (cards cut to narrow from
one end to the other).

A stacked deck introduced into play is
known as a **cold deck, cooler**, or **ice**,
while the introduction into play is **putting
the chill in, putting the cooler in**, or
putting the ice in.

The final method of cheating is the **hold
out**, where the gambler slips cards from
the deck in play and hides them on his person or under the table. The 19th century
saw elaborate cheating devices such as the
bug, placed under the table to hold cards,
the **eagle's claw**, designed for picking up
cards off the table or off the deck, or the
sub, a belt or arm device for holding
cards. Simply **palming** a card is much
neater and much more common, known in
cheating circles as **hand mucking** or **topping the deck**, after which the gambler
must **weave** or conceal the card. Some
professional cheats combine a simple **hold
out** with a special pocket designed for
holding cards, known as a **sleeve** or
silent partner.

One final method of cheating is perhaps
the simplest—work as an **agent** with a
cheating dealer who will **dump off**, or
overpay winning bets or even pay on losing
bets.

on the nose Playing with one's own money

on the sheet Playing with money that is half one's own and half somebody else's

openers Cards that meet the minimum requirements for opening a hand of draw poker

open game A game where newcomers are welcome

outs The unlikely possibilities that would turn a losing hand into a winner

over The higher of two pairs, as in

"jacks over nines"

pack up To withdraw permanently from a game

pass To fold

pat hand A hand played without drawing cards

patsy A hand that needs no cards for completion

pay time To pay the house based on the time at the table rather than a per-centage of the pot

peanut poker A game with low stakes

peanuts and donkey farts Pairs of twos and threes

peeker, peeper A nonplayer who looks at a player's hand

peewees Small (in rank) cards

perfect A perfect low in lowball—5, 4, 3, 2, A

picked off Caught bluffing

pig in the poke A card turned up as the wild denomination

pile A player's money or **chips**

pilgrim A novice

place ticket The second best hand

play behind To play with money that is not on the table

play out of the apron To play on money borrowed from the chip girl

pocket cards Cards dealt facedown

pony up To put one's ante into the pot

pool The pot

post oak bluff A small bet in a no-limit game made in the hope that the bettor will win the pot

Pot A! This is the first pot I have won in this session!

Pot light? It appears to me that somebody has yet to ante up.

Pot right? Has everyone anted up?

pretties Chips of a high denomination

pretzels Low stakes

pushka An arrangement between two or more players to share part of the pots they win

put down To fold

put up To pay money owed the pot

quads Four of a kind

quart A four-card straight flush

rabbit hunting Looking through the undealt deck to see what would have happened if . . .

rack up the game To win so much that wooden racks are needed to carry the tokens

rag A card that does not improve the hand

rail The section of the card room where nonplayers watch

railbird A player who has lost all his money and now just watches others play

railroad hand Pairs of jacks and 6s. *Try saying "jacks and sixes" five* *times fast and you'll hear the railroad association. All aboard!*

rainbow Three or four cards of different suits

rake-off A percentage of the pot that the dealer allocates to the house

ram and jam To bet and raise often and aggressively

rangdoodles A rule permitting an increase in the betting limit after a very good hand

rat-hole To pocket some of one's money or tokens while still playing. *An acceptable practice in casino games but a breach of etiquette in private games.*

read To correctly guess the face-down cards in another's hand

release To fold, or surrender

Rembrandt A game where all face cards are wild

rest farm Where players driven from a game because of heavy losses are said to be

ride along To remain in a pot where no bets are made

ride the pot To borrow money from the pot to make a bet when one is **light**

ring game A game played for money in a card room,

as opposed to tournaments

river The last round of betting in hold 'em

Robin Hood A cheater who cheats for the benefit of other players, often to draw attention away from himself

roll 1. To turn a card face-up 2. A player's bankroll

roll your own To turn your own cards faceup

rope To lure a player into actions through misleading body language or banter

rough Unfavorable in lowball

round-the-corner straight A special hand consisting of five cards in sequence using the ace as both high and low

rover A gambler who cannot join a game because the table is full

rub the spots off To shuffle excessively, as in "Hey, watcha tryin' to do, rub the spots off? So deal already."

runner-runner A hand made on the last two cards

runt A hand of mixed suits and no pairs

sandbag To raise a bet after initially indicating weakness

sandwich To catch a player between two players who are betting and raising heavily

satellite A tournament for

small stakes in which the winner obtains entry into a bigger tournament

school The players in a regular game

schoolboy draw An ill-advised draw

scoop To win a hi-lo hand in both directions

scoot To pass a small amount of money to another player after winning a pot

second fiddle The second best hand in a pot

sell a hand To bet less than the maximum with a strong hand, hoping to lure other players into calling

senate dealer A professional dealer who does not take part in the game

serve To deal, as in "Serve 'em up, Doc."

set Three of a kind

set in To bet as much as an opponent has in front of him

sevens A rule in lowball where every player with seven low or better must bet or forfeit a hand

shill rules The rules established by a house governing the manner in which the players it employs to gamble must play

shoot up the pot To encourage higher betting

short pair A pair of 10s or lower

short stack A stack of chips that is too small to cover the probable betting in a hand

showdown The part of the game where all bets have been made and players lay down their hands

show one, show all A rule in most card rooms requiring a player to show his or her cards to all the players if he or she shows them to one

show play To play a strong hand as if it is not particularly strong to trap others in the pot

show ticket The third best hand

shuck A card that may be discarded and replaced

shy Playing on credit

side arms The lower pair in a two-pair hand

sit down To play poker, as in "Do you boys mind if I sit down with you?"

six tits Three queens. *A tad vulgar.*

sky's the limit A game with no maximum placed on bets

slick Relatively good in lowball

slough, slough up To close a game

slow play To conceal the true value of a high hand by underbetting in an effort to lure players with worse hands into the pot

smoke on the water A raise

smooth Relatively good in lowball

smooth call A call that emphasizes the fact that the player did not raise

snatch To separate money from a pot to show the amount owed by a player who is **light**

snow 1. To mix the cards by continuously stripping off the top and bottom cards 2. To bluff

sock it up To raise

soft play A relaxed, less than fully aggressive playing against a friend

speak To bet, as in "Hey Sleepy—wake up, it's your turn to speak."

speed To play recklessly

spinner A winning streak

spit, spit card A card dealt faceup in the center of the table which may be used by all players

splash the pot To throw your chips into the pot, instead of placing them in front of you

spring To make a sudden large bet

squeeze To bet or raise against another strong hand with the intention of drawing more money into the pot from a third player with a weaker hand

stand pat To play a hand without drawing cards

stay To remain in a hand by calling or raising the bet

steal a pot To make a bet when it appears nobody else has anything worth betting

steal the ante To bet heavily in the first round of betting in an attempt to drive out all other players

step out To place a large bet

still game A regularly scheduled game, such as a Thursday night game

straddle A mandatory raise made by the player two to the dealer's left after an opening **blind** bet

stranger A new card in a hand after the draw, as in "Welcome little stranger!"

street A round in stud poker, as in **fourth street** or **fifth street**

string bet A bet where the player adds chips to the pot in more than one installment, instead of the required single move

stronger than the nuts A very crooked poker game

stud Any form of poker where the first card or cards are dealt faceup

suck To draw cards

suicide king The king of hearts. *So named because the king appears to be stabbing himself in the head.*

sweep To win a hi-lo hand

in both directions

sweeten To increase the size of the pot

swing To win a hi-lo hand in both directions

table All the players in a game

table talk Idle chatter during play, not rising to the level of **coffee-housing**

take-out The minimum number of chips a player may take from the banker at one time

talking chips Winnings

tap To bet all the chips a player has, or if he or she has more chips than his opponent, all the chips that his opponent has

Thirty days, thirty days in the county jail, thirty miles, thirty dirty miles, thirty miles of railroad track, thirty miles of rough road Three 10s

three wise men from the East Three kings

throat shot When a player almost wins, but loses, a big pot

throw, throw away To discard

throw up a hand To fold

tiger A low hand from 2 to 7

time The house collection fee

toad in the hole A card turned up as the wild denomination

toilet flush A missed flush draw

Tom Unfavorable

trips Three of a kind

tupper, tupperware Two pairs

twenty-one days, twenty-one days in the county jail, twenty-one miles, twenty-one miles of railroad track, twenty-one miles of rough road Three 7s

twist A draw in stud poker or an extra draw in draw poker

under the gun The position of the first bettor in a hand

underdog A hand other than the favored hand

unpaid shill A player who is the first to open the game and the last to quit

up **1.** The higher of two pairs, as in "jacks up." **2.** To place one's ante in the pot

up the creek A rule making whiskered kings wild

wait To check

walk To be away from the table long enough to miss at least one hand

walk the table To win a pot automatically with a specified hand

wash To shuffle the cards

Washington Monument Three 5s. *The Washington Monument is 555 feet high.*

weak Likely to fold and reluctant to raise

whack the pack To cut the cards

wheel The low hand 5, 4, 3, 2, A

whipsaw To raise before

and after a player who gets caught **in the middle**

white blackbird A hand so rare as to be beyond one's opponents' consideration

white meat Profit

wild widow A card turned up as the wild denomination

window The card whose face is exposed at the end of a player's hand

window dressing A card intentionally shown other players in one's hand

wired A pair formed by the down card and first up card

You lost me. "I fold."

young Low, as in "I played all night and didn't seem like I was doing anything but nurse a bunch of young clubs."

Z-game The game with the lowest stakes in a casino or card room

zing it in To beat heavily

The Vice of Dice

DICE WE HAVE ALWAYS HAD WITH US. Ancient Egyptian, Greek, Roman, Indian, and Korean civilizations all knew, played, and wagered on dice. The dice game hazard, the direct lineal ancestor of craps, was a big-time pastime in Europe during the Middle Ages, perhaps brought back to Europe from Asia during the Crusades in the 12th century. In 1674, Charles Cotton

Counting in Dice Lingo

WITHIN THE LINGO of dice players is a distinctive way of counting to 12, ranging from the rare American examples of old-fashioned Cockney rhyming slang with 8 and 9, to the puns of 5, to the downright salacious world of 10s. From 1 to 12, the lingo is:

1—**Ace**

2—**Snake eyes**, **cat eyes**, **crabs** (from hazard), **two bad boys from Illinois**, or **Dolly Parton** (all used with two dice), and **deuce** or **duck** (used for one die)

3—**Acey-deucy**, **bad news** (two dice), or **trey** (single die)

4—**Little Joe**, **Little Joe from Baltimore**, **Little Joe from Kokomo**, **Little Dick**, or **Little Dick Fisher**. *For the "little dick" entries, compare and contrast with the number 10.*

5—**Fever, fever in the South, fever in the South and no doctor, Phoebe, Phoebe the preacher's daughter, fee-bee, Little Phoebe, finif, fiver-fiver race car driver**, or inexplicably and obsoletely, **West Kentucky**

6—**Jimmy Hicks, Captain Hicks, Captain Jimmy Hicks of the Horse Marines, Mama's shoes** (two 3s), **Sister Hicks, sixie from Dixie, sixty days**, or **size**

7—**Reno, the magic number, Nell, Nick** (a term from the game of hazard, often applied to the Devil), **Benny Blue, Savannah**, or **Big Red**. *When a 7 is rolled in craps before the point is made, the stickman might shout, "Up jumped the Devil!"*

8—**Eighter, eighter from Decatur, Ada, Ada from Decatur, Ada Ross the**

wrote in the *Compleat Gamester* of the addictive grip of hazard:

Certainly Hazard is the most bewitching game that is played on the Dice; for when a man begins to play he knows not when to leave off; and, having once accustomed himself to play at Hazard, he hardly, ever after, minds anything else.

Hazard was most certainly brought to the New World by European settlers, but the complete passion for playing seems not to have come with it. Whatever the precise origin of craps, it was a game that seized the fancy of African-Americans early in the 19th century. It remained a game that was primarily played by African-Americans until late in the 19th century; the card game faro reigned in gambling halls, with scant attention paid to craps because it was a private game, not a banking game.

In 1907, a dice-maker by the name of John Winn devised the first rules for craps which would turn it into a banking game. He later developed what is known as the Philadelphia Layout, which lets players bet on the dice to lose. With the development of rules making craps a banking game, *jacta alea est*—the die was cast. It probably reached its zenith during World War II—in late 1943, the Army bought 750,000 pairs of dice, vivid testimony to the popularity of craps.

Stable Hoss, square pair (two 4s), or **windows** (two 4s)
9—**Niner, nina, Nine from Carolina, Nina from Pasadena, Nina from Argentina, Nina-Nina-ocean liner, Caroline Nine, ninety days, baseball bum, quinine,** or **strychnine**
10—**Big Dick, Big Dick from Boston, Big Dick the Ladies' Friend, Big Dick from Battle Creek, Big Joe from Boston, puppy paws, Texas sunflowers** (two 5s), or **twin fins** (two 5s). *Thomas L. Clark, the undisputed authority on American gambling slang, speculated that the "dick" in these slang expressions was borrowed from the French "dix." It might just be me and my dirty little mind, but any time that I hear "big dick" and "ten" in the same expression, let alone "Ladies' friend" (and we all know from the erotic verse that "Nine inches will please a lady . . ."), the French "dix" is not what first jumps to mind. Similarly, David Maurer reported, but discounted as apocryphal, a claim that "Big Dick" was a Boston gambler, Richard Mantell, who was shot by one Charles Farris when he fumbled while trying to switch in dice as he shot for a ten.*
11—**Ee-yoh, yoleven, ye old eleven, manna from heaven, nick, Ev-o-leene the Nevada Queen,** or **keno**
12—**Boxcars, hobo's delight on a rainy night, midnight, Gary Cooper,** or **Coop.** *The references to Gary Cooper are to his starring role in* High Noon.

The Lingo of Loaded Dice

THERE'S WORK DOWN! was the traditional argot warning among gamblers in the know that altered dice had been slipped into a dice game. Cheating at dice is another one of those delicious sins within a sin, where the run-of-the-mill sinner is punished by the **barracudas** of the gambling world, the cheaters who are not content to use skill alone and who supplement their natural chances of winning with altered dice—**percentage dice** (so called because they increase the shooter's chances of winning), **sure pops**, or **winners**.

While cheating at dice is more a phenomenon of the past than it is of the present, it is possible to walk into a gambling supply store today and buy altered dice, advertised, of course, as jokes. Suppliers might shy away from the open and notorious endorsements of cheating found earlier in the century, yet it cannot be said that dice cheating is completely a thing of the past. Along with his other admonitions, Nelson Algren might well have added, "Never shoot craps with a stranger on a blanket."

More often encountered in private dice games such as a **floating crap game** than in casinos, the gambler who cheats at dice is known as a **mechanic** (a gambling term applied to card cheats as well as dice cheats) or **mittman**, who might rely on any number of **gaffs**, or cheating techniques. Despised by those on both sides of this issue, the **catalog man** was a dice cheat whose superficial knowledge of the craft was gained from supply house catalogs.

The most common **gaff** is to alter or **hocus** the dice (known in their pristine, unaltered state as **calipers, fronts, hoptoads, levels, perfects, razor edges**, or **square dice**), producing **bricks, cheaters, doctors, fakes, gaffs, goads, honey dice, phonies**, or **pigs**. The dice may be made to favor the shooter (**loaded blocks, passers**, or **peeties**), to favor high rolls (**uphills**), to favor a particular number (a **dead number die**, such as the **dead deuce**, is loaded on the five side, producing a higher than normal number of two rolls), or to favor a certain scenario. (**Misses** or **missouts** are dice that have been altered to roll fewer wins than craps on a first throw, or a seven thereafter; **hits** will not roll a seven; and **six-ace flats** favor the player who has bet against the shooter.)

Dice that have been tampered with must be introduced into a game; the switch is known as **ringing in, topping in** or the **brush, brush-off, rip**, or **run-in**, often accomplished by **capping** or **copping** (palming) the dice, often away from the table toward the pocket (**going south**). Gaffed dice are **busted in** and then **busted out** of a game, giving the cheater the moniker of **bust-out man**. To **clack** the dice during the **rip** is to knock them together, one of several inept moves that can call attention to the switch and earn the warning from a confederate in cheating that **The window's open**. A switch that is done well is known as a **clean move**.

Gaffing dice requires either **inside work** (placing a **fill, load**, or **slug** inside the dice—**plumbing the bones**) or **outside work** (gaffing the dice on the surface). Specific types of altered or **off** dice include **busters** (**blanks**, or unspotted dice that have been misspotted, also known as **brownies** [derived from "Buster Brown"], **tats,** or **dispatchers**); **calendars** (promised to produce more sevens than a month); **cantaloupes** or **snowballs** (designed to roll a 4, 5, or 6); **capped dice** (dice in which one side is more bouncy than the others); **door pops** (dice misspotted to show only sevens and elevens); **first flop** (or **first pop**) **dice** or **settlers** (dice that have been heavily loaded); **flats** (dice whose sides are shaved to favor six or eight); **squeezes** (dice that have been squeezed flatter in a vise); **floats** (dice that are hollowed out at the corner, also known as **gravity dice**); **shapes** (dice that have been shaved out of true); **sucker dice** (dice that have been made concave); **tappers, tap dice,** or **knockers** (dice that have been loaded with mercury or a similar substance that shifts inside when the dice are tapped); **tops** (dice that have been altered so as to have two identical faces, also known as **horses, tops and bottoms, T's,** or **Tonys**); or **trip dice** or **bevels** (dice whose edges have been altered). In the 19th century a cheater who wanted to load the dice in a mild fashion might insert a pig bristle into the center dot of the five face of the die, creating a **bristle,** or he or she might use **heavy paint work** by using zinc in the painted dots on one face.

A more elaborate **gaff** is to load dice with metal and to control their landing with an electric field, creating **electric dice.** This requires a **juice man** to wire and control the table, which turns the establishment into a **bat, battery joint, juice joint,** or **wire joint.** On the opposite end of the technology spectrum, a **mover** cheats by sliding a bet into place after the dice have rolled.

Another cheating technique is to control honest dice with the **flop** (throw of the dice), **spinning them** or **putting the ears on.** Some **mechanics** use a **slick cup** (a dice cup whose polished insides help control the dice), while others rely simply on the throw. **Slick dice** is a toss of the dice in which one die is thrown honestly while the other is slid in a controlled fashion, guaranteeing the results of the roll of that die. To **kill one** is to control one die while giving the other an honest roll.

Cheating or **gaffed** rolls include the **blanket roll** (also known as an **even roll** or **pad roll**), the **bounce shot,** the **English,** the **Greek shot,** and the **whip shot** (known as a **drop shot,** the **hook shot,** the **Hudson,** the **Indian,** and the **Pique** or **Peek**). Before making a controlled shot, the cheat might **cackle** or pick the dice, or make it appear that the dice are being properly shaken by rattling them, while in fact holding them in a special fashion that prevents them from turning over. Another technique is to **coggle the dice** (a practice and term stemming from hazard, the dice game of choice in the 19th century before craps), or rotate them with one's fingers after they have been rolled.

If one is **hawking** the game and through careful observation suspects that the dice being used in a game have been **worked** (altered) or **way off** (very altered)—and one is sure of his self-defense skills—he or she may **burn** or **gate** the dice, or stop them before they have finished rolling to inspect them. After a visual inspection of the dice, if still not satisfied one might **mic the dice,** or measure them with a micrometer.

The game as played in casinos is straightforward—one by one players at the table take turns to act as the **shooter** casting the dice. A roll of a 7 or an 11 on the first roll in a series is a winning roll; a roll of a 2, 3, or 12 is a losing roll; and a roll of any other number establishes that number as the **point**. The **shooter** continues casting the dice until rolling either a 7 (the **shooter** loses) or rolling the number which is the **point** again (the **shooter** wins). The **shooter** continues rolling until he or she loses, either by rolling a 2, 3, or 12 on the first roll in a series or by rolling a 7 after establishing a **point**. In a casino game, it is possible to bet for or against the **shooter**, and to make any number of side bets.

Craps is fast-moving, and has taken its place in the pantheon of American casino gambling as one of the two biggest games in town. It persists in street culture too, with private games still a big part of urban African-American life.

As the stickman would say, though—**All down! All set with a bet!** On to the quite lively language of the vice of dice.

Adjust the stick! A sarcastic cry by gamblers when the dice are not paying

all day Staying in effect until the point is made or a 7 is rolled; not a one-roll bet (said of a bet)

all rooters, no shooters Surrounded by players who do not want to shoot the dice (said of a crap table)

all the tough guys, all the toughies A bet on all the hard **way** numbers

animated cubes, animat-

Bar Dice Games

BAR DICE GAMES ARE IN fact played anywhere, although most often and best in a bar, using a dice cup (sometimes known as the **box**), and without a bank and with no house advantage. There is almost always a wager involved, perhaps for the right to buy the next round of drinks, perhaps for the right to buy lunch, or perhaps for cash. Boss and Liar's Dice are the most popular, but there are dozens of variations on the basic theme.

After the invitation to play is extended (**Wanna wrassle?**), most games begin with the roll of one die to determine who will play first; this one-die roll is known as a **one flop boss, pee wee, piddle, pinkie**, or **tiddle**. Once the game begins in earnest, a roll of the dice is known as a **flop**,

shake, or **throw** (all three terms can also be used as verbs), while a full hand or turn is known as a **horse** or **leg**; by extension, to win a round in a game is to **have a horse** over one's opponent. If all dice do not land flat, they are known as **cocked, stacked**, or as **hotels, apartments**, or **condominiums** (shortened to **condos** and then punned on as **condoms**).

A perfect hand which one's opponent can at best tie is known as a **lock**. A **flop** with no points at all is known as a **5000, Lollapoloosa, Mahoot, sack of garbage, stiff**, or **zip**. In San Francisco, THE hot bed of bar dice, a roll without value is known as an **Alameda** (a city in the East Bay). In the East Bay, a worthless hand is known as a **Milpitas** (an economically strapped city in

ed dominoes, animated ivories Dice

any, any craps A bet that the next number rolled will be 2, 3, or 12

ass-English The actions of a shooter who believes that his or her body movement and incantations can affect dice

babies Dice

back bet An odds bet on the pass line

barefoot A bet on the pass line on which no odds are paid

barker The stickman, who keeps up a near-constant slangy, rhyming patter

bet left and right To bet with the gamblers on one's left and right

big eight A bet that the shooter will roll an 8 before a 7

big six A bet that the shooter will roll a 6 before a 7

big table A craps table with high limits

blocks Dice

boards The raised edge around a crap table against which the dice must be thrown

boat A container that holds the dice not in play

bones Dice

both ways Betting on the shooter and against the shooter at the same time

boxcars A throw of 12

boxman The casino employee at a crap table who changes money

box numbers, off numbers The space where a place bet is made, wagering that a certain number will be thrown before a 7

box them up, box up To mix the dice and offer them to a shooter

buck The marker used to mark the point

buck it To roll the same number on consecutive rolls

---

the South Bay), where a worthless hand is known as an **Alviso** (an even more depressed city in the South Bay). To reshake a hand without value is to **recycle the dice**.

Certain slang terms are used in many bar dice games. A **hammer** is a player who has an advantage because of his playing position, while to be **boxed** is to be in a position where one will lose whatever action one takes. **All day** is a phrase used when a player takes the maximum number of rolls permitted, while **away** means that the specified point (as in "Aces away") does not count. To **bring them back** is to reverse the sequence of passing the dice cup, **Come up** means "I challenge you to beat my hand," **Let's see 'em** means "I call

your hand," a **Klondike** is one role for the high hand, and **wipe out** means that aces nullify a score. **Frozen** dice may not be rerolled within the turn being played.

In the game Red Dog, the **dog setter** is the player who creates the **dog**, the point that the roller must beat to win his bet; to **bet the dog** is to wager the total amount of the pot. In Boss Dice, the player with the best hand after the first roll is known as the **boss**, and **Pick them up!** is the expression used when calling off a boss hand. In Liar's Dice, to **kill the aces** leaves the **aces dead**, meaning that they are no longer wild. In games such as Back Yahtzee or Double Cameroon, a **Big Big** is a roll with all five dice having the same value.

bullfrog A bet resolved on the next roll. *The association is with* **hop.**

bumble and buck Dice playing

burn up To roll consistently well for the shooter (said of dice)

buy bet A 5% commission paid to the house for correct odds on a place bet

c&e A bet on any craps and eleven. *This expression is sometimes spun into "Church of England" or "Chester and Esther."*

cane The stick used by the stickman to retrieve dice after a roll

caster The player rolling the dice in hazard

center bet A wager between the shooter and faders

chopper An operator who charges the shooter when one or more passes are made

cold Making more 7s than points (said of dice)

come bet A bet made after the shooter has established a point

come-out A shooter's first roll

come-out bet A bet that a certain number or group of numbers will be rolled on the next roll of the dice

Coming out! A warning by the stickman to players to get their bets down be-

cause the dice are about to be rolled

crab A losing throw of 2, 3, and sometimes 12 in hazard

crap The numbers 2, 3, 12

crap out To roll a 2, 3, or 12 on the first roll. *Often a term used incorrectly for rolling a 7 after the first roll, properly called* **seven out.**

craps Dice. *See Word History, page 90.*

cubes Dice

cutter A private operator who charges the shooter when one or more passes are made

Devil's bones Dice. *Lest we forget that dice are the work of Satan, there are several expressions that clearly link dice with the Devil.*

Devil's teeth Dice

dice picker A casino employee whose job is to retrieve dice that have fallen from the table

do A bet that the point will be made

do bettor A gambler who wagers on the pass line

don't A bet that the point will not be made

don't come bet A bet that the dice will lose on the next roll

don't pass line A space on the table where gamblers can bet the shooter will roll a 7 before his point

easy way Made without pairs (said of a point)

English Spin applied to dice in an effort to control the roll

e&t A bet on eleven and twelve. *With the movie* E.T., *the expression* **e&t** *often became simply* E.T.

fader A person who places a bet equal to the amount bet by the shooter against the shooter

field A space on the table containing a group of numbers, usually 2, 3, 4, 9, 10, 11, and 12

field bet A bet that the next roll will be on one of the numbers in the field

floating crap game An illegal crap game which moves from location to location to escape scrutiny by the authorities

free bet A true-odds bet allowed after a win on the pass or don't pass line

front line The space on the table where gamblers who want to bet that the shooter will make his point place their bets

full Crowded (said of a crap table)

G.I. marbles Dice

gag, the A roll of an even number made with a pair

galloping dominoes Dice

get behind the stick To open a crap game

hard guys   The numbers 4, 6, 8, and 10 made with a pair

hard way, the   A roll of an even number made with a pair

Harlem cricket   Dice playing. *Because craps was a game played primarily by African-Americans until the late 19th century, many of the slang synonyms for dice and dice playing are racially stereotyped and offensive. Dice playing was also called **Abyssinian polo**, **African golf**, **Congo croquet**, and **Harlem tennis**. In this racist vein, dice themselves were known as **African dominoes**, **African golf balls**, and **African knucklebones**.*

high side   A bet on numbers 8, 9, 10, 11, and 12

hit the boards   To roll the dice so that they hit against the rail

hobo bet   The number 12. *The number 12 is commonly known as **box-cars**, hence the association with hobos.*

hop   The next roll

hop bet   A bet that the next roll will result in one particular combination of the dice, such as a 2-2, known as a "hopping hard way"

horn bet   A bet, made in

multiples of 4, that the next roll will be 2, 3, 11, or 12

hot   Making more passes than 7s (said of dice)

icy cold   Consistently making 7s, not the point (said of dice)

ivories   Dice

ivory cubes   Dice

Jonah   To try to influence the dice by talking to them or making gestures

Label it!   A moderately urgent request that a bet be identified—"Who bet this on what?"

lay the odds   To bet that the dice will lose

live   Capable of being resolved with the next roll of the dice (said of a bet)

long hand   An extended turn by a shooter

loose   Not busy (said of a crap table)

low side   A bet on the numbers 2, 3, 4, 5, and 6

main   The point number in hazard

marbles   Dice

Memphis dominoes   Dice. *Because craps spread up the Mississippi River, several slang names for dice draw on the South.*

miss a pass   To roll a 7 before the point number

Mississippi marbles   Dice

Missouri marbles   Dice

missout   A losing decision on a point

natural   A 7 or 11 rolled on

the come-out roll

nick   An automatic winning roll in hazard, usually an 11

no dice   A roll that does not count

One down!   A stickman's warning that a die is off the table

one mile from home   One point shy of the desired roll

pass   A winning decision on a point

pass line   The space on the table where gamblers who want to bet that the shooter will make his point place their bets

peg   To place a marker on the number established as the point

point   The number first rolled by the shooter. *The shooter wins if that number is rolled again before rolling a 7, but loses if a 7 is rolled first.*

puck   The marker used to mark the point. *Puck is a corruption of poker's*

buck, discussed below.

rail The raised edge around a crap table against which the dice must be thrown

rats and mice Dice. *Rhyming slang which is rarely used in the United States but common in Cockney slang.*

rattle A single roll of the dice

rattlers Dice

red hot Making many more passes than 7s (said of dice)

right bettor A gambler who bets that the shooter will make his point

rollers Dice

rolling bones Dice

rolling ivories Dice

seven out To roll a 7 after a point has been established but before making the point

seven-eleven A fresh start given by gamblers to a fellow gambler who has lost his stake in a private game

shakers Dice

shooter The player rolling the dice

shorthorn A bet, made in multiples of three, on 2, 3, and 12

They hit! An exclamation of victory by a right bettor when the point is made

They miss! An exclamation of victory by a wrong bettor

when a seven is rolled before the point is made

throw-bones Dice

tombstones Dice

tough guys The numbers 4, 6, 8, and 10 made with a pair

trumpet A bet on the numbers 2, 3, 11, or 12—a **horn bet**

two ways A phrase that means that the bet is both for the player and for the dealers

working Capable of being resolved with the next roll of the dice (said of a bet)

world bet A bet that the next roll will be 2, 3, 7, 11, or 12

WORD HISTORIES

BUCK AND CRAPS

THE BUCK STOPS HERE is one of the better known and least understood political slogans of the 20th century. Apparently an original coining by President Truman, **the buck stops here** built on the well-known **pass the buck**, an expression widely understood to mean "to evade or shift responsibility." **Pass the buck** was first used in this sense in 1908, with **buck passer** first appearing in June 1920 in *The New Republic*.

What most don't remember

is that **pass the buck** had a literal meaning that did not involve **buck** in the sense of a dollar. Originally (1865) and literally, the **buck** in **pass the buck** was a marker used to indicate the next player to deal in poker; a knife with a buckhorn handle was often used as the token, probably giving us **buck. To pass the buck** was to decline the opportunity to deal and to pass that responsibility on to another player. Because President Truman was an avid poker player, it is not altogether surprising that he chose a poker metaphor for his presidency.

The buck stops here retains

significance today, 50 years after it was coined. It is a favored political metaphor that surfaces regularly. President Carter went so far as to place a replica of Truman's motto in his office. That the name-recognition of **the buck stops here** is still high is evidenced by an advertising campaign launched in California in 1997 in anticipation of the deregulation of the electric utility industry, with the vendor of an automated meter reading system using "The buck starts here" as an advertising slogan.

Craps, another monosyllabic gambling term, also came into being in the 19th century. The *Oxford English Dictionary* awards the questionable honor of first recording **craps** to Greene "The Reformed Gambler," in 1843. New York lexicographer Barry Popik found an earlier usage of **craps** in the July 9, 1942, *New York Daily Express*. Whenever its first use, **craps** boasts two etymologies—one fascinating and unlikely, the other mundane and probable.

The etymology of doubtful authenticity has a Louisiana rake, Bernard de Marigny, learning the dice game of hazard in London and introducing it to his Creole compatriots in Louisiana. The modified game became known as **craps** because the English-speaking referred to a Creole as "Johnny Crapaud," in honor of *crapaud* as French for "frog." This theory was first advanced by Edward Larocque Tinker in 1993, and it is periodically repeated.

John Scrane, the foremost historian of dice games in America, rejects the *crapaud* theory, arguing instead that in New Orleans, sometime after 1800, African-Americans experimented with the English game of hazard, in which the term **crabbes** or **crabs** was applied to a roll of 2 or 3 at least as early as 1761. The new American devotees of hazard rejected the intricate English and French rules, and a simplified, American version of the game emerged, called **craps** by Creoles mispronouncing **crabs.**

SOURCES AND REFERENCES

A LARGE PART OF MY collection on gambling comes from the Gambler's Book Club of Las Vegas, a wonderful institution with a spirit that mixes the old Vegas of the desert, a love of books, and a love of gambling.

A good overview of the place of gambling in the history of America can be found in *Sucker's Progress: An Informal History of Gambling in America from the Colonies to Canfield* by Herbert Asbury (New York: Dodd, Mead, 1938); *Play the Devil: A History of Gambling in the United States* by Henry Chafetz (New York: Clarkson N. Potter, 1960); *Bookie and Bettors: Two Hundred Years of Gambling* by Richard Sasuly (New York: Holt, Rinehart and Winston, 1982); John Philip Quinn's *Gambling and Gambling Devices* (Canton, Ohio: J. P. Quinn, 1912); and "Easy Money" by Martin Koughan in *Mother Jones* (July/August 1997).

There are three good general studies of gambling language. The least of the three is John S. Salak's *Dictionary of Gambling* (New York: Philosophical Library, 1963). *The Dictionary of Gambling and Gaming* by the late Thomas L. Clark (Cold Spring, N.Y.: Lexik House, 1987) is a first-rate piece of lexicography in which Clark meticulously applied the methodology of historical principles to the subculture of gam-

bling, drawing on a wide range of written and oral sources. The third, *Casino Talk: The Complete Guide to the Secret Language of Dealers and Winners* by S. S. Kuriscak (Stamford, Conn.: Longmeadow, 1993) is a perfect example of what the world needs—an amateur lexicographer with a very good ear, living right in the middle of the culture whose language he is recording. *Casino Talk* is remarkably perceptive in capturing the everyday speech of gamblers and casino workers.

Other interesting works on the language of gambling in general include *The Basics of Winning Slots* by J. Edward Allen (New York: Cardoza, 1984, 1993); *Casino Supervision: A Basic Guide* by Peter G. Demos, Jr. (Egg Harbor, N.J.: CSI, 1983); *How to Become a Casino Cocktail Waitress* by Sally Fowler (self-published, 1983); *Pinochle is the Name of the Game* by Walter Gibson (New York: Harper and Row, 1974); *How to Become a High Paid Las Vegas Casino Dealer* by Bob Kofol and Timothy A. Madden (Las Vegas: Scorpio, 1989); *Gambling Nevada Style* by Maurice Lemmel (Garden City, N.Y.: Doubleday, 1964); *Gambler's Digest,* edited by Clement McQuaid (Northfield, Ill.: DBI, 1981); *Can You Win? The Real Odds for Casino Gambling, Sports Betting and Lotteries* by Mike Orkin (New York: W. H. Freeman, 1991); *Break the One-Armed*

Bandits by Frank Scoblete (Chicago: Bonus, 1994); *Playboy's Book of Games* by Edwin Silberstang (New York: Galahad, 1972); and *Play Gin to Win* by Irwin Steig (New York: Cornerstone Library, 1965, 1971). Ben Chance, a pit boss at the El Dorado Casino in Reno, was a valuable source of information for gambling terms.

The language of poker de-brought a complete and caring understanding of the culture of poker to their work.

Other sources on the language of poker include *Programmed Poker: The Inside System for Winning* by Jim Glenn (New York: Rutledge, 1981); *Poker Faces: The Life and Work of Professional Card Players* by David M. Hayano (Berkeley: University of California

Irv Roddy (New York: Simon and Schuster, 1961); *Scarne's Guide to Modern Poker* by John Scarne (New York: Simon and Schuster, 1979); *Winning Poker for the Serious Player: The Ultimate Money-Making Guide* by Edwin Silberstang (New York: Cardoza, 1992); *Common Sense in Poker* by Irwin Steig (New York: Cornerstone Library, 1963);

serves and in fact owns several full-length treatments. Three excellent efforts by poker partisans are "The Vocabulary of Poker" by Swen A. Larsen in *American Speech*, Volume 26 (May 1951); *The Language of Poker: The Jargon and Slang Spoken Around the Poker Table* by George Percy (self-published, 1988); and *Poker Talk: A Complete Guide to the Vocabulary of Poker,* compiled by Michael Wiesenberg (self-published, 1995). Of the two moderns, Wiesenberg is a bit more thorough, but both have

Press, 1982); *Big Deal: A Year as a Professional Poker Player* by Anthony Holden (New York: Viking, 1991); *Oswald Jacoby on Poker* by Oswald Jacoby (Garden City, N.Y.: Doubleday, 1947); *The Cincinnati Kid* by Richard Jessup (Boston: Little Brown, 1963); "My Son, the Poker Player" in *Adventures of a Verbivore* by Richard Lederer (New York: Pocket, 1995); *The Complete Guide to Winning Poker* by Albert H. Morehead (New York: Simon and Schuster, 1967); *Friday Night Poker: Penny Poker for Millions* by

Thursday Night Poker: How to Understand, Enjoy—and Win by Peter O. Steiner (New York: Random House, 1996); *Poker: Official Rules and Suggestions for Players* (Cincinnati: U.S. Playing Card Company, 1941); and *Poker: A Guaranteed Income for Life* by Frank R. Wallace (Wilmington, Del.: I & O, 1968).

Two very useful references for the slang of craps are "The Argot of the Dice Gambler" by David W. Maurer in the *Annals of the American Academy of Political and Social Science* (May 1950) and the

"Glossary of Dice Terms and Gambler's Argot" in *Scarne on Dice* by John Scarne (Harrisburg: Stackpole, 1945, 1974). Other useful works include *The Winner's Guide to Dice* by John Savage (New York: Grossett and Dunlap, 1974) and "The Language of Craps" in *The Gambling Times Guide to Craps* by N. B. Winkless, Jr. (Secaucus, N.J.: Lyle Stuart, 1981). Relevant articles from the Tamony Collection include an extended discussion of the "Cries of Crap Shooters" in *American Notes and Queries* in 1941 and 1942, and "Legions of Larceny" by Mickey MacDougall in *American Weekly* (June 4, 1944). For the slang of dominoes, I turned to "The Language of Dominoes" in *Dominoes: Popular Games, Rules & Strategy* by Dominic C. Armanino (New York: Cornerstone Library, 1977), as well as various online resources.

I learned most of the keno terms that I include from watching Salim Tamimi, Jack McNally, and the late Larry Foss lose money playing keno. One of the world's most engaging yet dangerous spectacles is Salim Tamimi in search of backers for a sure-winner keno ticket. I supplemented my field gathering with visits to *The Keno Handbook* by Jim Claussen (Las Vegas: Gambler's Book Club, 1982); *The Complete Guide to Winning Keno* by David W. Cowls (New York: Cardoza, 1996); and John Me-

chigian's *Encyclopedia of Keno* (Fresno, Calif.: Funtime Enterprises, 1972). Also helpful, from the Tamony Collection, was "Chinese Gambling" by Henry Rawson Cutter in *The Californian Illustrated Magazine* (February 1894). For the peculiar language of mah jongg, I turned to *Learn to Play Mah Jongg* by Marcia Hammer (New York: David McKay, 1979); *The Ma-Jung Manual* by Henry M. Snyder (Boston: Houghton Mifflin, 1923); and Eleanor Noss Whitney's *Mah Jong Handbook* (Rutland, Vt.: Charles E. Tuttle, 1964, 1991).

My appreciation for the culture of bingo and my language gathering field work began in March 1980, in Milwaukee. I spent a large part of that month at parish hall bingo games, fish fries, and neighborhood bars trying to stay warm during a singularly unsuccessful presidential campaign. Book help came from the *Gambling Times Guide to Bingo* by Roger Snowden (Hollywood: Gambling Times, 1986) and "Bingo Language" in *Hooked on Bingo* by Alice Andrews (St. Louis: Author, 1988). Also useful was "Bingo! And It's On The Side of the Angels Now" in the *San Francisco Examiner* (March 19, 1980).

I picked up most of the roulette terms that are included from conversations with muckers and keepers in Reno and Lake Tahoe, with a little bit of help

from Kuriscak's *Casino Talk*. Jerry Cohen and Ann Smith taught me most of the backgammon terms that I have included when they taught me backgammon in Salinas in 1979. Four books with useful glossaries are *Goren's Modern Backgammon Complete* by Charles Goren (New York: Doubleday, 1974); *The Backgammon Book* by Oswald Jacoby and John R. Crawford (New York: Bantam, 1970); *The New York Times Book of Backgammon* by James and Mary Jacoby (New York: New American Library, 1973); and *Play Backgammon Tonight* by Dave Thompson (Las Vegas: Gambler's Book Club, 1976).

For the slang used by dart players, I referred to *All About Darts* by I. L. Brackin and W. Fitzgerald (Chicago: Contemporary, 1975); *The Book of Darts* by Jack McClintock (New York: Random House, 1977); *Leighton Rees on Darts*, edited by Dave Lanning (New York: Atheneum, 1980); and Keith Turner's *Darts: The Complete Book of the Game* (New York: Harper and Row, 1980).

Many of the terms of sports betting are impossible to avoid in the workplace or sports talk radio, and I simply started paying attention to and recording all that I heard on KNBR in San Francisco or at work at IBEW Local 1245. For backup, I turned to *The Basics of Sports Betting* by Avery Cardoza (New York:

Cardoza, 1991); *The Wise Guy's Bible* by Tony "Sonny" Daniels (Lynnfield, Mass.: North Shore, 1993); *Sports Betting* by Lyle Patrick (Secaucus, N.J.: Lyle Stuart, 1996); *Betting to Win on Sports* by Wayne Alan Root (New York: Bantam, 1989); the "Sports Book Glossary" in the November, 1991 issue of the *Bay Sports Review*; and the "Gambler Glossary" in the *San Francisco Examiner* of January 25, 1995.

While working for the University of Pennsylvania Dining Service between 1969 and 1972, I had daily contact with the joy and vocabulary of the numbers racket. I owe virtually all of the rather slim numbers racket glossary that I include from the men and women with whom I worked; Hilda Moore was my overall mentor and among the many life lessons she taught me came my schooling on numbers. Written sources, all from the Tamony Collection, include "The Truth About Lotteries in America" by W. G. MacLeod in *South Atlantic Quarterly* (April 1936); "The Never-Never Numbers: A True Story Exposing the Lottery Racket" by Tommy Wilson in *G-Men* (August 1937); "The Argot of Number Gambling" by Gustav G. Carlson in *American Speech*, Vol. 24 (October 1949); and "Should Policy Be Legalized" by Samuel J. Battle in *Ebony* (August 1951). Peter Tamony had in his collection a gem of a dream book, *Prof.*

Hitt's Numbers and Dream Guide: The Most Complete and Helpful Number Book Ever Written, distributed by The Arco Agency, Youngstown, Ohio, *circa* 1947.

Golf has never been a passion of mine, but I take pleasure in the witty and cynical slang of golf betting. Mike Connell of Truckee chipped in with many of these terms. Others I found in *Pigeons, Marks, Hustlers and Other Golf Bettors You Can Beat* by Sam Snead and Jerry Tarde (New York: Simon and Schuster, 1986) and *Let's Do Golf* by Ross Farnsworth and Frank Brimhall (Mesa, Ariz.: Golf Fanatics, 1997).

Blackjack, on the other hand, has consumed its share of my time and interest. My father taught us Caddie blackjack and the basic vocabulary; it was Miguel Contreras, however, who first schooled me on the finer points of casino blackjack, and with these lessons came a considerable part of the blackjack vocabulary which I have included. I also fished contributions from the especially complete *Blackjack: A Professional Reference* by Michael Dalton (Merritt Island, Fla.: Spur of the Moment, 1990, 1991); as well as *Winning Casino Blackjack for the Non-Counter* by Avery Cardoza (New York: Cardoza, 1981, 1992); *Scientific Blackjack & Complete Casino Guide* by Donald I. Collyer (New York: Arco, 1966); *Dealing Casino Blackjack* by Thomas F.

Hughes (Las Vegas: Gambler's Book Club, 1982); *Blackjack: A Winner's Handbook* by Jerry L. Patterson (Vorhees, N.J.: Author, 1977, 1978); *Best Blackjack* by Frank Scoblete (Chicago: Best, 1996); *Dummy Up and Deal: The Ups and Downs of 21 Dealers* by Lee Solkey (Las Vegas: Gambler's Book Club, 1980); and *Million Dollar Blackjack* by Ken Uston (Secaucus, N.J.: Gambling Times Books, 1981, 1995). One magazine article that provided a word or two was "Fleecing Las Vegas" by Michael Angeli in *Esquire* (May 1997).

I have been around fighting chickens and lost an old friend, Willie Barientos, to a cockfight injury, but myself have never seen a chicken fight. I picked up many of the words which I included from the farm labor camps of the Coachella and San Joaquin Valleys, and others from articles at the Tamony Collection, including "Pit Your Birds!" by Charles Parmer in *Esquire* (November 1934); "Odd Fight Takes the Main" by Edward Jerome Vogeler in *Esquire* (September 1935); "Origin of Words: High-Flyers" by Peter Tamony in the *San Francisco News Letter and Wasp* (July 28, 1939); "Dead Game" by A. J. Liebling in the *New Yorker* (April 1, 1950); and "The Lingo of Cockfighting" by Charles McCabe in the *San Francisco Chronicle* (July 25, 1962).

I'm not bright enough for bridge. I picked up most of the bridge entries from the *Bridge Players' Dictionary and Quick Reference Guide* by Terence Reese (New York: Barnes and Noble, 1959) and *Adventures in Duplicate Bridge* by Edith McMullin (Memphis: American Contract Bridge League, 1988). Cribbage, however, is one of my sins, and I learned many of these terms as I learned to peg. Two glossaries helped, found in *Cribbage: A New Concept* by John E. Chambers (self-published, 1983, 1993) and *All About Cribbage* by Douglas Anderson (New York: Winchester, 1971). Mike Block, Steve Sattler, and Dan Tweyman all contributed terms by e-mail.

I have little contact with card cheats, other than a memorable few weeks in the fall of 1975 when I was in California's Imperial Valley on a farm worker organizing drive. Every night before the drive really got going we played cards with a group of American basketball players who were playing across the border for a team in Mexicali; the games were all friendly and no money was involved, but there was no small amount of cheating, all of which was explained by the simple "Everybody cheats at cards."

For the language of the card cheat, I went to Frank Bonville's *The Little Secrets*, self-published in 1902, reprinted by the Casino Press of New York (n.d.); *Gam-blers' Crooked Tricks: A Complete Exposure of Their Methods* by Hereward Carrington (Girard, Kans.: Haldeman-Julius, 1928); "Cheating Terms in Cards and Dice" by Thomas L. Clark in *American Speech*, Volume 61 (Spring 1986); *Marked Cards and Loaded Dice* by Frank Garcia (New York: Bramhall House, 1962); "Gambling and Cheating" in *A True Expose of Racketeers and Their Methods* by Emmett Gowen (New York: Popular, 1930); *Koschitz's Manual of Useful Information Concerning Marks and Stamps, Portable and Fixed Devices, Manipulation of Cards, and Other Matters of Interest to Lovers of Draw* (Kansas City, Mo.: Hudson-Kimberly, 1894, reprinted by the Gambler's Book Club of Las Vegas); *Sharps and Flats: A Complete Revelation of the Secrets of Cheating at Games of Chance and Skill* by John Nevil Maskelyne (New York: Longmans, Green, 1894); and *The Phantom of the Card Table* by Eddie McGuire, which originally appeared in *Linking Rings* magazine between November 1953 and January 1954, and then was republished by the Gambler's Book Club of Las Vegas in 1969 and again in 1976. Helpful articles included "Ancient and Dishonorable" by Jerry Kahler in *Town and Country* (June 1936); and "How to Cheat At Cards" in *Life* (August 8, 1949).

Garcia, Maskelyne, Maurer, and Scarne, cited above, treat the practice and language of cheating at dice. In addition, I relied on *Radner on Dice: How to Win, How Gamblers Cheat, Odds and Percentages* (New York: Key, 1957) and "Unholy Rollers" by Jerry Kahler in *Hotel, Resort and Travel Service* (August 1936). The *Handy Pocket Blue Book* published by National Game Supply of Newport Beach, California, (n.d.) is a shocking little catalog of dice made for cheating.

I have passed pleasant hours playing Liar's Dice, and I picked up a bit of the idiom in my lessons from Salim Tamimi and Shawn Berlinn. Published works that provided some terms include "Bar Dice in the San Francisco Bay Area" by Alan Dundes and Carl Pagter in *The Kroeber Anthropological Society Papers Numbers 51 and 52* (Berkeley: University of California, 1978); "How to Play Bull and 35 Other Games with Dice" by Al Giesecke and Jack Fagan (San Francisco: Author, 1960); *Come Up: San Francisco Bar Games* by Gil Jacobs (Cupertino, Calif.: Dixon, 1976); *World's Best Dice Games: How to Play and Win* by Gil Jacobs (Milbrae, Calif.: John N. Hansen, 1981); "On Rolling Dice" by Charles McCabe in the *San Francisco Chronicle* (June 26, 1970); and *Games They Play in San Francisco* by Jester Smith (Sausalito, Calif.: Tri-City Printing, 1971).

Chapter Three:

DRUGS

Check all your razors and your guns
We're gonna be wrastlin' when the wagon comes.

Gimme a pigfoot and bottle o' beer,
Send me, Gate, I don't care.

Gimme a reefer and a gang o' gin
Slay me 'cause I'm in my sin.

—"Gimme a Pigfoot" by Bessie Smith

RUGS WE HAVE NEARLY ALWAYS had with us. Even leaving aside for the moment our national drugs of choice, alcohol and tobacco, as a people we have drugged ourselves for a century and a half. As much as we would like to believe that the crack cocaine epidemic which has devastated urban America for the last 15 years is an aberration from the cultural norm and merely the product of ruthless and godless Colombian smugglers and equally vicious and scary young gangbangers with red or blue kerchiefs, it is impossible for even the casual student of history to deny a long and rich record of drug use in America.

It is impossible not to smell the opium in the air or the sweet smoke of marijuana as you wander through the decades, and impossible not to catch the flash of the needle purchased from the 1897 Sears-Roebuck catalog for morphine injections, the flickering flame cooking the opium or melting the heroin on a spoon or lighting a crack pipe. As you turn the pages you can't ignore the powders and the pills—my God the pills!—caps and tabs, dots and dexies, fast and slow, up and down and far out—red and blue, pink and yellow, black and white. And then there are the bottles, the cocaine-laced Koca Nola, Celery Cola, Wiseola, Rocco Cola, Dope Cola and Coca-Cola ("It enables the entire system to readily cope with the strain of any excessive demands made upon it"), or the cocaine-based Birney's Catarrh Cure, or the opium-rich M'Munn's Elixir, or the advertisements for Mrs. Winslow's Soothing Syrup, suggested use in 1888 being for teething children (no mention though that the active ingredient is mor-phine), or the Lloyd Cocaine Toothache Drops, or the Bayer Pharmaceutical Heroin sold as a cough suppressant. The pictures show the giggling, the idiot grins, the pinned eyes, and the nodding, and then the munchies or the constipation or the vomiting, usually not the overdosing but there is Lenny Bruce dead on the toilet, needle in arm. Look—there—in the 1960s, the drugs that seemed like a good idea at the time, one third of the trinity of drugs, sex, and rock and roll—a philosophy, a religion, organizing principles of life, the drugs creating a music, the music creating a scene with drugs and sex—oh the temptations! And today on the streets of every major city in the country you hear and feel the crunch of empty plastic crack vials that litter the sidewalks as America continues its quest, always looking for an angry fix.

Unlike those special sins where there is an exemption buried somewhere in the theological underpinnings, there is no equivocation in the labeling of drugs as sinful on religious grounds. Undeterred by biblical silence on drug use, Christian theologians construct a series of arguments—drugs have a proven connection with sorcery and witchcraft; drugs have an obvious affiliation with the desires of Satan; drug use will cause others to stumble; biblical warnings on alcohol intoxication serve as an implicit warning against drug intoxication; we are warned not to defile God's temple (the body), and addictions are not pleasing to God. There are no exceptions, no exemptions, and no loopholes.

In secular America, however, we are on far shakier grounds and we send truly mixed signals. We condemn the use of amphetamines, yet we chuckle and wink about truck drivers and their "little white pills," about college students and their "pep pills," and about weight-conscious women and their "diet pills"; we venerate caffeine and its stimulant effect, yet condemn amphetamines and their stimulant effect, horrified that men who 30 years ago were routinely issued amphetamines by the Army while in Vietnam so that they could go three days without sleep now start their working day stirring methamphetamine into their coffee.

We decry the use of heroin, morphine, and opium, yet forget that each was introduced to America as medicine. We denounce those who use cocaine, forgetting Freud's ardor for it, or Sherlock Holmes's devotion to it, or the fact it was touted as the official remedy of the Hay Fever Association at the turn of the century, or that it was once an active ingredient in Coca-Cola, promoted as a Temperance Beverage.

We criticize the use of "downers," yet we are a nation hooked on downers—where would we be without Valium? We glorify alcohol and tobacco, and yet condemn marijuana. We are horrified by LSD, unmindful for the moment that LSD use was launched by government research and that it was praised in its early days by Cary Grant; we praise Timothy Leary and Ken Kesey as subjects of government research, yet vilify and pillory them when they become apostles.

Just as drugs have nearly always been with us, so too have those anxious to warn and alarm us; William Bennett was not the first to make his name and fame by preaching the evils of drug use. In 1856, Dr. George Wood warned us that the use of opiates was yielding to seductive pleasure, moral depravity, and vice. Several hundred silent movies warned us about the dangers of cocaine, while in the 1930s we were treated to Earle Albert Rowell's classic polemic *Reefer Madness* (1939) on the screen, "The Menace of Marijuana" in *American Mercury* (1935), "Marijuana: Assassin of Youth" in *American Magazine* (1937), and so on, as Commissioner Harry J. Anslinger used his pulpit in the Federal Bureau of Narcotics to preach in hyperbolic tones on the evils of drug use and drug users—marijuana was, he cautioned us, "as dangerous as a coiled rattlesnake and twice as deadly. . . . If the hideous monster Frankenstein came face to face with the monster marihuana he would drop dead of fright." Quite an image.

As a nation, we have long been in search of that elusive angry fix, all the while condemning ourselves for doing so. We hate drugs, yet take them; we take drugs, yet hate them.

The Slang of Drugs

THE SLANG OF DRUGS IS NEARLY ENDLESS, and with the exception of LSD slang, it is surprisingly smart. It is richly ironic that drug use, which is almost always destructive both to the individual and to society, spawns an inventive, creative, and bright language. David Maurer, the great student of American criminal argot of the 20th century, believed that the dominant culture's disapproval of drug use "excites increased linguistic activity, usually accompanied by an intensification of internal cohesive forces." Free of inhibitions and immersed in the destructive element of drug use, the user is also freed from the inhibitions of standard language. From the ashes rises an innovative, capricious, and droll language.

Within the family of drug slang, Maurer believed that much was derived from the language of the opium smoker. He openly admired the language of opium smokers, writing that "among the ranks of the opium smokers there are some brilliant minds to whom the carefully turned phrase and the meaningful metaphor are very important." It may be that Maurer was over-glamorizing the linguistic feats of opium users, but their slang certainly has had an impact on drug slang for a century.

The slang of drug users changed radically in the late 1960s. Until then, drug use had been the dominion of several defined subcultures—the underworld, jazz musicians, Bohemian intellectuals, and poor urban blacks. In the 1960s and 1970s, drug use leapt into the middle class. A vast new group of drug users arose; as they shocked their parents with their embrace of sin, they also shocked an otherwise stable argot. Writing in the early 1970s after studying drug language for 40 years, Maurer observed with evident disrespect for the new class of users that "phraseology which, forty years ago, was standard and well stabilized to opium smokers or needle addicts, is now used in all sorts of new and unorthodox ways by the younger generation of addicts." Old terms which had been coined by the relatively conservative and often intelligent opium smoker were corrupted by the brash new wave of drug users, intent on playing havoc with all in sight, including the slang of drug use.

Until the 1960s, very little of the slang of drug users made its way into the standard language of the dominant culture. With the hundreds of thousands of new recruits to the sins of drug use in the 1960s, this changed. As they grew up, those who dabbled or even seriously played with drugs in the 1960s tended to abandon drug use, but they took with them into colloquial American English a small but powerful body of drug words. **Blow your mind, bummer, flashback, flip out, freak, freak out,** and **trip** (see *Word History,* pages 135-36) are all words that began with LSD-specific meanings yet migrated into general usage.

Another contribution to the slang of drug users made by the new generation in the 1960s was a startling degree of imprecision. Until the 1960s, the argot of drug addicts was fixed and precise—**Aunt Hazel** was heroin and **Aunt Nora** was morphine—a name for everything and everything with its name. With the 1960s this precision was lost. Imprecision and vagueness were hallmarks of hippie slang in general; add to that the chemical uncertainty inherent in underground drug production and distribution. Here, want a **dex?** Well, that suggests that it is pharmaceutical dextroamphetamine sulfate, brand-name Dexedrine. There is a statistically significant chance that the pill is in fact Dexedrine, a good chance that it is some sort of central nervous system stimulant, and then always the possibility that it is some nasty poisonous concoction brewed up by the Hells Angels somewhere. Check out this **ace!** Well, if you mean **ace** as in marijuana, perhaps, but if you mean **ace** as in PCP, no thanks. In the land of names based on colors even more uncertainty is present—**blues** might be stimulants or they might be depressants, **black mollies** or **black widows** might be stimulants or they might be depressants, and so on.

As new drugs appear and carve out their market and place in American social history, new drug slang, which is often grown from old drug slang, appears. Or, as old drugs move into new subcultures, new slang emerges. In the last decade, we have seen crack cocaine in the ghetto, ecstasy and ketamine at raves, and Rohypnol, all with new slang, and we have seen marijuana move into hip-hop culture and produce a new crop of words—**blunt, chronic,** and **endo** to name a few. Even crack cocaine, which has devastated the underclass that uses it, has given birth to a sparkling body of language.

Lastly, the dominant culture views drug slang as being almost as dangerous as drugs themselves. In early 1996, National Drug Control Policy Director (a.k.a. "Drug Czar") Lee Brown called on the Adidas company to recall and stop selling a shoe called "The Hemp." Brown was afraid that Adidas was using a "name glorifying the drug culture" and he urged Adidas to "reject any association with the drug culture . . . in order to send the right message to the children of America."

Hey—enough talk already—let's check out the action in the den!

Opium

OPIUM WAS AMERICA'S FIRST recreational drug, coming on the scene in the mid 19th century as its sister morphine was grabbing onto the hearts and minds and bodies of Civil War soldiers. Opium use lingered on into the 20th century, but by 1978 it was distant, exotic, and safe enough to allow introduction of a heavily advertised perfume named Opium. As is the case with most first loves, it holds a special place in our linguistic heart, giving future generations several big-time slang words, such as **dope** (see *Word History,* page 137), **fiend, joint** (see *Word History,* page 141), and **yen.**

Opium use took two forms: abuse of medicinal opium such as M'Munn's Elixir and smoking opium in what the press called opium **dens** and what the sports who frequented them called **joints.** Middle-class white women were specially disposed to medicinal opium; while their addiction was no less tragic than that of opium smokers, it was an addiction enjoyed in solitude without social discourse, and it thus produced no viable slang idiom.

Those who ventured into opium **joints,** however, were deliciously engaged in sin, and a foreign sin at that. Journalists screeched with alarm at the influence of "John Chinaman," noting that while white people were often barred from visiting Chinese opium **dens,** they had places of their own. As reformer George Wood published a treatise in 1856 decrying the use of opiates, enterprising tour guides in San Francisco were busy creating false opium **dens** in the basements of Chinatown, giving tourists daring glimpses of sin in action, whispering in hushed tones that the vice was ever spreading and increasing. Quite some sin!

Because opium smoking was introduced to Americans by Chinese immigrants, a considerable part of the vocabulary of opium smokers was derived from Chinese words and expressions. These borrowings in themselves are not particularly interesting; of greater interest is the Americanization that some underwent—**fun** from the Japanese for a ration of opium (5.79

grains) prepared to be smoked, **pox** from the Chinese *yen-pok* for a ration of opium pre-pared to be smoked, **Yancy** from the Chinese *yen shee* for opium ashes that are gathered and reused, or the crude but evocative **yen-shee baby** for the difficult bowel movement often experienced after using opium. Similarly, to engage in **Chinese needle work** was to sell opium, leading to the use of **embroidery** as a euphemism for opium and smoking supplies.

Terms for the opium itself include **Allah** (see **mash Allah** below), **auntie** (one of the ear-liest personifications of a drug, a naming style found throughout drug slang), **Big O, black shit** or **black stuff** (smoking opium), **brick** (a mass of gum opium and a term used by mar-ijuana users and dealers a century later), **brown stuff, canned stuff** (canned commercial smoking opium), **coolie mud** (inferior grade opium), **cruz** (opium grown in Veracruz, Mexico, a relatively recent term), **dope, dopium** (a term used by journalists but not users), **dreams, dream wax, gee, gow** or **ghow, grease, gum** (gum opium), **hop** or **hops, leaf** (crude opium before it is prepared for smoking), **mash** or **mash Allah** (Arabic for "Gift From God," an expression used by 17th-century Tartars who used opium for themselves and their horses on long trips), **midnight oil** (which casts a curi-ous light on the seemingly tame expression "burn-ing the midnight oil"), **mud, O, op, ope, oz** (a 20th-century allusion to the poppy fields in *The Wizard of Oz*), **P.S.** (from the botanical name *Papaver somniferum*), **pekoe** (high quality opium, borrowing from the tea world), **poppy** (from the flower that produces the opiates), **scours** (crude opium), **skee, tar** (from opium gum's black, sticky appearance), and **toxy.**

Portions of opium include a **bird's eye** (a small opium pill), a **button** (a medium sized opium pill), a **card** (a standard smoking ration, weighed onto a playing card), a **deck** (a small amount of opium wrapped in oiled paper or placed on a common playing card), a **fire plug** (a large pill), a **high hat** (a large pill), a **pill** (a ration of opium prepared for smok-ing), a **tin** (a copper can of opium holding about 6 1/2 ounces), and a **toy** (a small, flat, coin-shaped container full of opium).

Opium smoking is rich with ritual. The entire mechanism needed to smoke opium was known as the **engine, layout,** or **saddle and bridle,** consisting of a lamp to cook the opium (the **fairy lamp**) and the pipe, which has been known as an **altar, bamboo, cha-cha, crock, dipper, dream stick** (from the euphoric, dream-like state achieved from smoking opium), **gee stick, gong** or **gonger** or **gongola, hop stick, joy stick, log, pop stick, saxophone,** or **stem.** The cloth material used to hold a pipe together was a **gee-rag** or **granny,** probably derived from the folk term for scraps of cloth used by rural women in the 19th century.

Terms and expressions which meant "to smoke" included **beat the gong** (the **gong** referring to the pipe), **blow a pill** (referring to opium prepared in pill form for smoking), **hit the
gong, hit the gow, hit the pipe** (an expression used today with users of crack cocaine), **lay**
or **lay down, puff, roll the log** or **suck the bamboo;** a person smoking opium reclined on
his or her hip, and was thus said to be **on the hip,** which is one of at least a dozen credible
explanations for the wildly popular slang term **hip.** An extended, hard inhale was known as a
long draw, producing an opium high or a **load.**

After an opium pill is smoked, the residue is collected and mixed with pure opium for further use, either in a pipe, an injection, or a beverage. Residue slang includes **dog** (weak, non-
addictive residue, often several generations removed from crude opium), **green ashes** or
green mud (residue that has not been cooked long enough for smoking), **rooster brand**
(inferior opium, consisting largely of opium refined from residue), or the Chinese **yen pox** or
yen-shee. The latter gave us **yen-shee boy,** a residue addict, and **yen** gave us the standard
English "yen," or craving.

What journalists liked calling a **den** was known by users and addicts as a **bing den, brewery, joint** (the favored term), or **suey bowl.** To enter a **joint** one paid an admission price,
known as the **bunk fee** or **pad money.** Cooking metaphors prevailed when it came to describe the personnel in the **joint**—one would expect to find a **chef** (the attendant who warms
the pipe and rolls the opium pills) working with **cheffing** (paraphernalia used to roll the
opium pills), or a **cooky** (an attendant) who would **cook** or **cook up a pill** (prepare crude
opium for smoking), asking the patrons if they were ready for another **load** with the quaint,
Mama die? There at the **joint** with no discernible duties might be a **Den John** or **lob**
(derived from the fact that he or she often loitered in the lobby) always willing to run odd
errands to earn enough for a session with the pipe.

Opium is powerfully addictive, leading to **the habit, belly habit** (so named because of the
intense stomach cramps associated with withdrawal), **bunk habit** or **bunk yen** (referring to
the bunks found in many opium dens for users usually overcome by the desire to sleep), or
lamp habit (referring to the lamp used to cook the opium pills). A 20th-century addict—
either the classic **fiend** (and the cognate **pipe fiend**) or the less terrifying **hoppie**—was said
to **chew the gum** in his addiction. Punning on the wholesome Campfire Girls and the gathering around the lamp by opium users, an addict was also known as a **campfire boy.** Mindful of
the atrophying effect of long-term reclining and opium use on an addict's hips, an addict was
also known as **thin hips.**

If addiction were not enough of a problem, the opium user is also often confronted with
extreme constipation. The eventual defecation was known affectionately as a **blockbuster,
giving birth,** or **yen-shee baby,** while the colorful term **rosebud** referred to the swollen
anus produced by the constipated defecation.

Morphine

MORPHINE, AN OPIUM DERIVATIVE, takes its name from Morpheus, the god of dreams. It
relieves suffering which cannot be treated by removing the cause, providing a near-immediate

relief from pain and emotional tension. The drug also imparts a sense of euphoria; it first made its mark as an addictive drug during the Civil War, leading to so much addiction that it became known as **the soldier's drug.**
Much of the slang surrounding morphine came into being in the later 19th and early 20th century, a fact which accounts for the jocular quality to much of it. Take, for example, the sobriquet **God's Medicine**, a slang alias for morphine which is attributed to Sir William Osler, who is said to have said, "Yes, it's God's medicine, for if there were any better, it would be kept in heaven for the angels to use." From this fairly literary coining come the derivative, closer to earth **GOM, good old M,** and **medicine.** Personifications, which are friendly by nature, include **Mary, Miss Emma, Miss Morph, Mr. Blue, (in the arms of) Mr. Morpheus, Sister M** (compare the song "Sister Morphine" by the Rolling Stones), and **White Nurse.**

...the soldier's drug

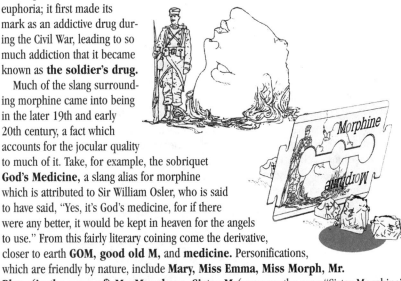

From the word *morphine* come the slang analogues **Big M, em, emsel, M, morph, morpho,** and **morphy. Mojo,** an African loanword primarily used to describe an amulet, also was applied to narcotics in general and morphine specifically; any doubt as to the authenticity of **mojo** as slang for morphine was put to rest on March 26, 1974, when the main character in the television cop show *Kojak,* played by Telly Savalas, referred to morphine as **mojo.**

The drug's somniferous effect produces **dreamer, melter, pins 'n' needles,** and **slumber party.** Other candidates have been **ammunition** (if a syringe is **light artillery,** it makes sense that morphine is **ammunition), gunk, hows, joy powder, junk** (see *Word History,* page 137), **monkey, red cross, Sweet Jesus, sweet stuff, uffi, unkie** (most likely from pig Latin for **junk),** and **white stuff.** Continuing in the happy vein, one who is addicted to morphine is said to be **betting on the horses, booking with Charlie,** or **Ceciled,** with the addict known as **Cecil Jones** (see *Word History,* pages 141-43).

A **block** is a cube of morphine, while a **cube** is a packet of powdered morphine or morphine tablets. To cheat a buyer, the seller of a **block** might **shave** it, or cut it down; from this practice, the term **cut** has come to mean to adulterate a drug to increase profits in selling it. Borrowing directly from opium users' argot, a **can** of morphine is an ounce of the drug. Hipsters learned that morphine was found in the medicine paregoric in the 1950s and 1960s; with a concentration running about 10% in the medicine, it was possible to reduce four ounces of paregoric to 1.2 grams of morphine. The paregoric itself was known as **PG** or **Proctor and**

Gamble, and a user as a **gee-head.** (For a discussion of the use of **head** in various drug contexts, see *Word History,* pages 136-37.)

Marijuana

WE JUST CAN'T DECIDE what we think about marijuana.

Marijuana made its debut in our public consciousness in the 1930s, much later than its 19th-century splash in Europe. On the one hand, during marijuana's first big boom we hummed along with "Sweet Marijuana" sung by Gertrude Michael in *Murder at the Vanities* in 1933 and giggled at "Reefer Man" performed by Cab Calloway and his Orchestra. We weren't sure what to think when Gene Krupa (1943) or Robert Mitchum (1948) were arrested for marijuana possession, but were titillated by Walter Winchell telling us that "reefer smokers" greet each other with "H'ya Jackson" and that they "prefer subdued lights, which they call (no matter what the color is) 'Blue Lights.'"

At the same time, white America was a tad alarmed at the racial overtones of marijuana use, a little unsettled by the image of slick and hip black men seducing previously upstanding and

Marijuana—Equipment & Supplies

YOU'VE GOT YOUR **bag** of **dope** and you're ready to smoke? Not quite. The marijuana must first be **cleaned** or **manicured**, removing the seeds and stems from the dried leaf which will be smoked. Assuming that you are going to roll your marijuana into cigarettes, you will need to roll them in something, no? The papers used to make marijuana cigarettes are known generically as **lick paper, rolling paper,** or **skins;** brand names such as **Zig-Zag, Bambu,** or **EZ Wider** sometimes are used as eponyms.

Once the cigarette is smoked down to a short **roach,** it is finished using a **roach clip** or **R.C.,** also known as a **bridge,** a **crutch,** or a **Jefferson Airplane** (a match split down the middle to hold the cigarette).

Other **heads** prefer a pipe, perhaps a **carburetor, doobie-tubie,** or **steamboat** (all of which build up pressure to force the smoke into the user's lungs); a **bong** or **hookah** that cools the smoke with water; or a no-frills, no-features **j-pipe.** A pipe for hashish is known as a **hash cannon,** in which the user can smoke either **honey oil** (purified oil of hashish) or a flat, circular piece of hashish known by its shape as a **moon** or **quarter moon.**

Not ready to smoke? You can always bake the marijuana into brownies, known as **greenies** or **Alice B. Toklas brownies.** In fact, the original Toklas recipe was for "haschich [sic] fudge" and it contained the admonition—"Should be eaten with care. Two pieces are quite sufficient." Thirsty? You can always brew your marijuana into tea, which would be punningly known as **pot likker.**

virtuous Christian white girls with their "sticks of dynamite." We read with alarm of the "Shocking New Menace to Nation's Youth" in the *San Francisco Chronicle* (January 24, 1937) and sat up in alarm when we learned about "Marijuana: Assassin of Youth" in *American Magazine* (1937), all the more horrified by *Reefer Madness* on the big screen (1939).

Through it all, there were few voices of sanity. Surprisingly, the loudest voice of reason came from a government-sponsored study of marijuana use in New York City, in which the so-called La Guardia Commission reported in 1939 that "the publicity concerning the catastrophic effects of marihuana smoking in New York City is unfounded." How about that?

Beats and hipsters enjoyed marijuana, but as a movement they never attained critical cultural mass and their drug use was only of peripheral concern and interest. Hippies, though, were everywhere, and one of the things that they did everywhere was to smoke marijuana. The late 1960s and early 1970s saw a second boom and a second panic, although the panic was far less hyperbolic than the panic of the 1930s. Spiro Agnew and Merle Haggard got in their shots at marijuana, but the presence of a greater menace in the form of LSD took the wind out of the marijuana panic's sails.

The slang of marijuana thus comes from two eras, the 1930s and the 1960s, with modest neologisms in the 1990s. The marijuana users of the 1960s borrowed a large part of 1930s marijuana slang, but added their own spin and their own crop of words. Seven slang names—**dope, grass, jive, pot, reefer, tea,** and **weed**—have dominated the field of marijuana for 60 years, but they have not driven away competition (for further discussion of **weed, tea, reefer, grass,** and **pot,** see *Word History,* pages 138-41). In fact, competition flourishes, as does the slang vocabulary of marijuana.

Like most drugs, marijuana has built up a considerable body of slang names based on color; unlike other drugs, though, marijuana's color-based names are almost always also linked to a place where the drug was allegedly grown. The major color and/or place names which developed around marijuana and hashish—all in their second wave of popularity/menace—are the following:

Acapulco gold, gold, gold-leaf. *The rarely remembered Rainy Daze took the song "That Acapulco Gold" into the Top 40 in February 1967. A persistent rumor in the late 1960s was that a major tobacco company had registered "Acapulco Gold" as a trademark in anticipation of the eventual legalization of marijuana.*
Acapulco red

African black
Black African finger Dark marijuana, molded in the shape of a fat finger
Black Bombay Hashish
Black mote Marijuana cured in sugar or honey and buried
Black Russian Hashish
Blue de Hue Asian-grown marijuana popular with American soldiers in Vietnam during the war
Blue sage

Breckenridge green Low-grade, roadside marijuana found in central Kentucky; green marijuana has a low resin content and is not very potent
Cambodian red, Cam
Canadian black
Chicago green Marijuana which is said to be popular, not grown, in Chicago
Colombian red, Colombian Colombian red, said to be sweeter and

more potent than most marijuana, was lyrically immortalized by Steely Dan in "Hey Nineteen" where the aging singer enjoys Cuervo Gold and "some fine Colombian" with his 19-year-old girlfriend.

Durban brown Marijuana from the Natal Province, South Africa

Hawaiian

Illinois green

Jersey green

Kentucky bluegrass Any wild, roadside marijuana. The name puns on Kentucky's famous bluegrass.

KGB Killer Green Bud

Manhattan silver, Manhattan white Mythical albino marijuana said to have grown in the sewers of New York City

Maui wowie What a great stoned hippie ring to this one, no?

Mexican brown

Michoacan green

Northern lights High quality marijuana sold in Amsterdam

Pakistani black Hashish

Panama red, P.R. Glorified in a drugs-personified song "Panama Red" by the New Riders of the Purple Sage in the early 1970s, the antihero Panama Red rode into town on his white horse Mescalito.

Quintana roo blue

Zacatecas purple

Speaking of **Panama Red** and personifications of the drug, marijuana enjoys several human names, the most notable of which is **Mary Jane.** Marijuana is almost always a she—as are almost all drugs—be it **Dame Du Paw, Dona Juana, Herb** (from **herb,** in turn from **weed,** leading to **Herb and Al** for marijuana enjoyed with alcohol), **Jane, Juanita, Margarita, Marjorie, Mary and Johnny, Mary Ann, Mary Jonas, Mary Warner,** and **Mary Weaver.**

Marijuana Quantities

EACH DRUG HAS its table of slang measurements, which often are not precise estimations of weight or mass, but rather are user-oriented. Such decidedly is the case with marijuana and its slang measurements. From small to large, they are:

B, bee Enough marijuana to fill a penny matchbox

box Enough marijuana to fill a small matchbox

can An ounce

lid Approximately an ounce

bale A pound

elbow A pound. *From the abbreviation "lb"*

L.B. A pound. *Pronounced "Ell-Bee."*

bar Approximately a kilogram, pressed into a block

key A kilogram

And then there is that most elegant of marijuana quantities, the **bag.** A **bag** of marijuana is a bag of marijuana, plastic sandwich type, precise dimensions or volume neither stated nor consistent. Can you dig it?

The most distinguished male name for marijuana is **Mezz** (or **Mighty Mezz**), in honor of Mezz Mezzrow, a jazz musician who in the 1930s and 1940s was the Johnny Appleseed of marijuana, bringing it to the attention of hundreds of jazz musicians. In the late 1960s and early 1970s poor quality marijuana was known by some as **Nixon**, a tribute to the then president of the United States. Personifications from the 1990s include **Bob** to **bubba** (a Southern corruption of **Bob**) for the drug, and **Marley** for a marijuana cigarette—all obviously drawn from reggae star and marijuana-lover Bob Marley. Hashish is personified only as **Maggie**, derived from **meg**, which in turn was probably derived from "nutmeg," which hashish vaguely resembles.

Leaving personifications, colors, and places behind, there are still dozens of slang designations for marijuana that have enjoyed at least regional popularity—**ashes, baby, bambalacha, banji, bionic, blaze, blonde, bo-bo bush,** the **bomb** (high quality), **boo** or **bu** (a 1960s clipping of the 1930s **jabooby**), **bud** (sometimes referring to the flower of the marijuana plant, other times to marijuana in general, which makes possible the wonderful double entendre out of "This Bud's for you," a beer advertising slogan), **Buddha** (usually Asian marijuana, also called the delightful **funky Buddha,** a term made famous by Del "The Funky Homosapien"), **bull jive** (a 1940s term for marijuana that is very adulterated with catnip or some other alloy), **butter, charge, chicken, chronic** (a third-generation marijuana slang term, coming out of hip-hop culture, usually applied to potent marijuana), **cosa** (Spanish for "thing," and thus evocative of "stuff"), **dagga, dank** (a third-generation term), **Devil weed** (thank God there's at least one "Devil" something here!), **dew, ding, ditch** (referring to roadside marijuana), **doob, doobage, domestic** (locally grown), **draw, ea-tay** (pig Latin), **eed-way** (again), **endo** (another hip-hop entry from the 1990s, also spelled and pronounced as **indo**), **four-twenty** (a late 1990s contribution with a lot of apocryphal etymology; the term lends itself to giggling inside jokes at 4:20 each afternoon), **fu, fuel, gage** or **gauge, gangster, gash, giggle smoke, grunt, gungeon, hay** (a term which plays on **grass** and which led to **India hay** and **hay butts** for marijuana cigarettes), **hemp, herb, herbage, hog** (a word used much by American soldiers in Vietnam), **hooch** (a throwback to the early-20th-century slang name for alcohol), **jingo, joy smoke, killer weed, kitten, kind bud** (high quality), **lambsbread** (large Jamaican buds), **lobo** (Spanish for "wolf"), **loco weed** (a pejorative embraced by users as their own), **lucas, merry** (from the **Mary** family), **MJ, mohasky, moocah, mota** (Spanish slang for "specks," which produces in English **mooster, moota, mooters, mootie, mu,** and **mutah**), **mother nature** (which is clipped to **mother,** which is clipped to **mutha**), **muggles, nugget, nugs, pat, Queen Ann's lace** (like marijuana, a roadside weed), **rope** (usually poor quality marijuana, alluding to one of the primary industrial uses of hemp, and sometimes producing the poetic **rope dope**), **schwag** (poor quality), **scuz, shake, shit** (want some?), **sinsemilla** (the flowering tops of seedless marijuana plants, very potent, known also as **sinse** or **sess**), **skunk** (aromatic sinsemilla), **smoke** (a great noun usage), **square mackerel** (a Florida term, flowing from the appearance of square bricks of marijuana along Florida's coastline), **stash, straw** (like **hay,** from **grass**—spare me these, okay?), **the kind, three-toke killer** (very potent, enough to intoxicate in three inhales), **wacky t'backy** (actually used as slang, a corny mock pejorative),

wacky weed, wheat, and **yerba** (Spanish for "herb").

Joint and **reefer** are powerful candidates when it comes to describing a marijuana cigarette, which is virtually never referred to as a "marijuana cigarette." While heroin users will at times call heroin by its standard English name, the marijuana user will very seldom, if ever, use the standard English description of what is being smoked.

Surviving in the face of the two dominant terms for a marijuana cigarette have been **ace** (a single cigarette), **blunt** or **Phillies blunt** (marijuana rolled in the tobacco leaf wrapper of a Phillies Blunt cigar), **bomb** or **bomber** (a fat cigarette), **booster stick, Buddha stick** (a cigarette made with Thai marijuana), **cheroot** (a large cigarette), **creeper, cripple** (a term that evolved backwards from the term **crutch** to hold the butt of the cigarette; a crutch supports a cripple—see?), **deck** (a large number of cigarettes), **deuce** (two cigarettes), a **doobie** (perhaps derived from the *Romper Room* admonition—"Be good do-bes"; also reported as **dubbe, duby,** and **dubie**), **dog leg, dynasty** (a cigarette made with third generation marijuana which has survived two smokings), **fatty** (a fat cigarette), **first generation** (a cigarette made with all never-smoked marijuana), **gasper, goober, goof-butt, greeter, hooter** (a large cigarette), **J** or **jay** (drawn from **joint**), **jive stick** (definitely a 1940s feel to this term), **killer, LBJ** (a pound of cigarettes—an *lb.* of **j**—get it?), **number, pin** (a thin, tightly rolled cigarette), **rainy day woman, rocket, root, second generation** (a cigarette made with marijuana leftover from a first smoking), **snop, specials** (more powerful than normal), **spliff** (a large, cone-shaped cigarette), **stick** (a thin cigarette), **Thai stick** (a cigarette made with Thai-grown marijuana, sometimes wrapped around thin bamboo slivers), **thumb** (a fat cigarette), and **twist.** The La Guardia Report included three terms said to have been in use in New York in the 1930s, **sass-fras** for the least expensive cigarettes, **panatella** for the mid-range, and **gungeon** for the top of the line.

The short butt of a marijuana cigarette has been known as a **roach** for at least 60 years, but has known several modest aliases—a **cocktail** (when placed in the end of a tobacco cigarette), a **nose burner** or **nose warmer** (I get it!), and **snipe.**

Ready to smoke? Don't "smoke," though—**bake** (which produces the lovely **wake and bake** for an early morning session), **be on the beam, blast, blow, do up, get efficient,** scratch the dragon (a heroin term recently imported into marijuana lingo), **torch, turn on,** or **vipe.** As you inhale or take a **hit** or **toke,** don't hog the marijuana cigarette—**don't Bogart that joint.** After a few **tokes** or **pokes** on the cigarette, the user (**grasshopper, head** [see *Word History*, page 136], **muggle head, pothead, stoner, sweethead, tea head, weed head,** or—coolest of all—**viper**) should be well on the way to being **annihilated, baked, blasted, bombed, boxed, buzzed, floating, foxy, high, irie, ripped, sailing, smashed, stoned,** and **wrecked,** which often produces a prodigious hunger, known cutely as **the munchies** or not so cutely as an **eating rib.** When the marijuana or hashish is all smoked, it is said to be **cashed.**

Heroin

WITH THE VIVID IMAGES OF NEEDLES and death, heroin is the poster child of big bad drugs, the scariest of the **nocks** or **'cotics,** the biggest and baddest of the **Cotton Brothers** (heroin, morphine, and cocaine, all of which require cotton for straining when cooked for injection). It was developed in 1898 as a substitute for morphine and codeine, and it was marketed as a cure for morphine addiction. Good idea! It has drawn its disciples from two groups—the largely black, largely urban under-class, and exceptionally gifted musicians.

Either because heroin has enjoyed a longer history of abuse than most drugs or because it seems to appeal, among others, to the gifted and creative—or both—the slang idiom of heroin is extensive and in large part resourceful and poetic.

Slang analogues for the drug itself are abundant. The most widely used and best known are **horse** (see *Word History,* page 138) or **hoss, junk, smack** (from the Yiddish and German schmeck, which is used at times itself), and—best of all—**shit.** Also-rans include **anti-**

Heroin—Doctor script me please

IN THE FIRST SEVERAL DECADES of this century, narcotic users were able at times to **sail,** or obtain legitimate prescriptions (known as a **dog tag, reader,** or **script**) for morphine or heroin from sympathetic or gullible physicians (known affectionately as **croakers**). To convince the physician of their plight they might take a **bug,** an injection of an irritant, to gain sympathy from the physician, or they might fake a spasm—a **Brodie, circus,** or **Duffy. Brodie** has a special place in American English; in 1886, Steve Brodie claimed to have survived a jump off the Brooklyn Bridge; he had no witnesses and his claim was widely doubted, but he gave the language his name as an expression with several meanings, including this one.

Convinced of the medical need, the **croaker** or **ice tong doctor** then **writes a script** and the addict has his drugs, known as his **McCoy.** To this day, federal prosecutors occasionally will charge a doctor or pharmacist in what they call a **scrip case** where drugs have been illegally prescribed or dispensed.

freeze, Aries, Aunt Hazel or Aunt Helen (with a letter from Aunt Helen meaning a package of heroin), Baretta, the beast, big-time (as in problems, no doubt), black, black gold, black pearl, black tar (all four "black" entries referring to distilled and concentrated heroin, as does the simple tar), blanco (Spanish for "white," the color of most heroin), blue sky, boat, bone, boy, brother, brown, caballo (Spanish for "horse"), carga (Spanish for "load"), cat, chick, chicle (Spanish for "gum," also appearing in English since 1889 or so), chiva (Spanish for "goat"), 'cotics, crap, dirt, dojie (with many variant spellings, such as dogie, doojee, and duji), dooley, dope, eight, golden girl, good and plenty, H, Harry or the derivative hairy, happy dust, Hazel, heavy, Helen, Henry, hero, him (from *her* from *heroin*), hop (a nice little holdover from opium), jazz, jive (more often applied to marijuana but at times to heroin), joy dust (used in the Steve Canyon comic strip on March 21, 1954), liquid sky, mahoska, Mexican brown, mooca or moocah, mortal combat (potent heroin), muzzle, nice and easy, nod, noise, Old Steve, pack, p-dope (20% to 30% pure), peg, Racehorse Charlie, red chicken, scat, skag, smoke, stuff, Sweet

Veins in Vain

BECAUSE HEROIN IS MOST OFTEN consumed by intravenous injection, there is a chilling body of slang used to describe veins and vein conditions. Displaying in general a marked lack of respect for the body as a temple, the heroin addict refers to the median cephalic vein as the **channel** (a term which produces **channel swimmer** as a brave synonym for a heroin user), the **gate**, the **gutter**, **home**, the **main line** (leading to the verb form), the **pipe**, or the **sewer**. To **blow a shot** is to miss the vein completely, while to **blow the vein** is to ruin it for future use. A **sharp shooter** rarely misses the vein.

Conditions of veins are of great interest to the addict, who has a smart and descriptive lexicon at his disposal to describe them:

burned out Collapsed
cave An abscess at the site of the injection
cement arm Sclerotic tissue over the veins of the arm
crater An ulcer in the skin from repeated injections
embroidery Puncture wounds from past injections
raspberry An abscess at the site of the injection
roller A vein that will not stay still for an injection
service stripes Puncture wounds from past injections
tracks Puncture wounds from past injections

Saving the best for last, the truly committed heroin user who either has **burned out** other available veins or wishes to avoid detection will **tough**—inject heroin into the underside of his or her tongue. Where does one sign up?

Methadone & The Slang of a Cure

DESPITE EARLY MEDICAL OPINION to the contrary, we have learned that heroin is in fact addictive. Addicts who want to break their addiction—to **kick** the habit—have several choices.

They may, for one, go **cold turkey** (see *Word History*, page 143), or withdraw from heroin use suddenly and without pharmaceutical support, which makes one a **babe**. If in jail or prison, this is often the only choice and is known as the **iron cure, quarry cure** (when combined with forced hard labor), or **steel and concrete cure;** even in a hospital, **cold turkey** is difficult for the **winder**, or voluntary patient. The addict will have a tremendous craving for heroin, a **bogue** or **yenning** (an opium word), and will feel **gaping, sick,** or **twisted;** as the addict detoxifies or **dries out**, the withdrawal symptoms are cheerfully described as the **agonies, heaves and squirts, whips and jangles,** or **whips and jingles**. When the addict is completely withdrawn, he or she is said to be **around the corner**. The hospitalized addict who breaks down is often assigned to a special ward, the **flight deck**, for treatment.

The second choice for breaking the heroin addiction is to use methadone, an addictive drug itself that was introduced as treatment for heroin addiction in the mid-1960s, the thinking being that withdrawal from methadone addiction was more easily managed than withdrawal from heroin. Although the problem almost always produces a more vital slang than the cure, methadone has its own modest vocabulary. It is known as **biscuits, dolls, dolly, dollies,** or **dolo** (from Dolophine, a brand of methadone). Addicts are typically given a glass vial containing one day's dose of methadone, known as an **amp**. The trusted addict who is faithful to the methadone treatment program will at times be given **take-homes**, two or three doses of methadone for use over a weekend.

Jesus (Dear God!), **Tootsie roll** (distilled and concentrated), **white god, white stuff**, or **witch Hazel**.

Poor-quality heroin is **beat stuff, blank, bonita** (adulterated with milk sugar), **brown sugar** (grainy), **ca-ca** (from Latin via Spanish for "shit"), **flea powder, lemonade, red rock** (grainy), or **sugar**, while high quality product is known as **bomb, China cat** or **China white** (the Cadillac of heroin, or sometimes applied to fentanyl, a synthetic narcotic), **dyno, P** (for pure), and **pinch**. In a pinch, a heroin user might use codeine, known as **schoolboy** or **cement**.

Heroin is quantified by such slang terms and expressions as **balloon** (a small packet), a **bird's eye** (a small amount, borrowed from the language of opium users), a **Cadillac** (one dose), a **cap** (a capsule filled with heroin, also known as an **h-cap**), **deck** (a packet), a **dip** (a dose), a **dram** (a teaspoon, or about 20 grains), **fix** (a dose), a **G** (one grain), a **load** (a dose, again an opium word), a **piece** (an ounce), a **short go** or **short order** (a smaller dose than normal), a **sixteenth** (1/16 of an ounce of the drug), a **taste** (a small dose), or **things** (capsules of heroin).

Injection being the preferred method of administering heroin, the slang glossary centered around syringes and the equipment associated with injections is considerable and graphic. Slang synonyms for a syringe include **artillery, banger, Bay State** (a standard medical syringe), **bayonet, B&D** (a manufacturer), **blow dart, clean works** (a new, sterilized syringe), **factory, feeder, glass, gun** (shortened from the quaint **dope gun** or **hop gun**), **harpoon, hype** or **hypo, hypestick, jabber, Luer** (a commercial medical syringe), **machinery, monkey drill** or **monkey pump** (an addict has a **monkey on his back,** thus the ape reference), **Mr. Twenty-Six, nail, point, rocket** (by extension, a **rocket man** is a person who sells syringes to addicts), **sharps** (medical jargon), **silver bike** (usually referring to a syringe with chrome fittings), **silver girl** or **silver lady, spike** (happily called an **ikespay** by those happy pig-Latin-using addicts), or **Yale** (a commercial syringe). The entire collection of equipment needed to prepare heroin for injection and to inject is known as the **biz** or **business, gear, gimmicks, horse and buggy** (punning on **horse** as heroin, and evocative of **saddle and bridle** from opium days), **Jim Johnson, joint, kit, layout** (a borrowing from the lexicon of the opium user), **outfit, rig, set, tools, the workers,** or **the works.**

Moving to an improvised injection, there is the **dingus** (or **Deazingus** from carny slang meaning a "thingamabob"), the **emergency gun,** a **fake,** or a **fakus** (a combination of **fake** and **dingus**)—all made with a dropper and needle, using a **collar** or a strip of paper around the dropper to make a tight fit with the needle; there is also the **tomcat,** an improvised mechanism using a needle from a sewing machine.

With the **works** ready and in need of a **fix,** the user melts or **cooks** the powdered heroin, usually in a spoon. The liquid result is **hocus,** ready to inject. The user **ties off,** fastening a tourniquet around his or her arm, and is ready for the injection.

The terminology of injection—a **bang** (or **angbay**), a **bing,** a **jab,** a **jolt**—is explicit and extensive, covering a range of methodologies:

boot To draw blood back into the syringe, to mix the blood with the drug, and to inject the mixture back into the vein

constitutional An addict's first injection of the day

cotton fever A dangerous condition that arises when the cotton used in cooking the heroin is shot into the vein

douche To inject. *Nice talk!*

eye opener The first injection of the day

fire, fire up To inject the drug

flag, red flag Blood visible in the syringe, showing that the vein has been hit

give wings To inject someone else

gravy The mixture of blood and drug in the syringe

hit, hit the sewer, hit up To reach the vein

jack a fix To prolong an injection deliberately, controlling the initial euphoria or **rush**

jack off To draw blood back into the syringe, to mix the blood with the drug, and to inject the mixture back into the vein

job To inject

kick To draw blood back into the syringe

main, mainline To inject into the median cephalic vein

make up To inject

milk a rush To prolong an injection deliberately, controlling the initial euphoria or **rush**

morning glory   The first injection of the day. *This expression is also used in horse racing with a quite different meaning—a horse that performs well in pre-race workouts but not in races.*

oil   To inject

pop   To inject heroin into a muscle

rifle range   A place where addicts congregate to inject heroin

session   A gathering where several addicts inject heroin together

shoot gravy   To reheat and inject a mixture of blood, water, and the liquid heroin after missing the vein on the first try

shoot up   To inject

shooting gallery   A place where addicts gather to inject heroin

shooting party   A gather-

ing where several addicts inject heroin together

skin, skin pop   An injection into the skin

straighten out   To give a free shot of heroin to another user

take off   To inject

turn on   To give a fellow traveler a shot of heroin. *An early use and sense in this very important part of the drug vocabulary of the 1960s.*

What now? The initial euphoric flooding is most commonly known as the **rush,** and less commonly known as the **burn, call, flash,** and **jab-off;** the intoxicated user is now **behind** the heroin, **feeling the kick, goofing, high, loaded, petrified,** and/or **stoned.** Some users vomit or **flash** after injecting, while others (**grocery boys**) get the **chucks** and crave sweets. After the initial **rush,** the user enters a dream-like state known as **coasting, going on the nod, goofing off,** or **nodding off.**

Once the effect of the drug wears off, the user feels **beat** or **low** and begins the process again if he or she has heroin, or begins to **chase the bag** and search for heroin if he or she doesn't, asking his **paper boy** or **man,** "**Are you anywhere? Are you holding?**"

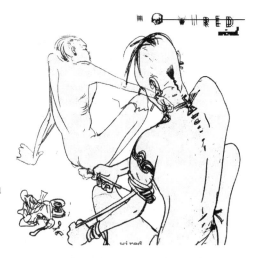

And then there is addiction, which has its own lexicon, with the addict known as an **attic** (say it—get it?), a **cadet** (a new recruit), an **H-man,** a **hog** (an addict who uses more than you do), a **horsehead,** a **hype** (leading to **hype tank** as a jail cell that houses addicts), a **junkie** or **junker,** a **main-liner,** or a **schmecker;** the addicted known as **hooked, on the stuff, strung out,** or **up against it;** and the addiction known as a **bee** or **bee that stings,** a **burning down habit** (a heavy addiction), **Dr. White, faith,** a **jones** (see *Word History,* page 141), a **King Kong habit** (a heavy addiction, punning on **monkey**), a **monkey,** or an **oil burner** (a heavy habit, borrowed from the argot of opium users). Some users can dabble without developing an addiction; they **chip, joy bang,** or **joy**

pop, and have what is known as an **ice cream habit.**

For the needle-shy, there are other routes of administration, most notably smoking it (to **chase the dragon** or **chase the tiger** by inhaling the fumes of heroin as it is cooked), by **firing the ack-ack gun** (dipping a cigarette into heroin and smoking it), and by inhaling powdered heroin through the nose (to **sniff** or **snort**). In Vietnam, American soldiers called tobacco cigarettes dipped into heroin as **loud** because it was not "**as loud**" (aromatic) as smoking marijuana. For the needle-shy and heroin-deprived, there might be temporary relief found in codeine, known in slang as **the nods** or **schoolboy.**

Downers

CENTRAL NERVOUS SYSTEM DEPRESSANTS, and most especially barbiturates, are our most common drugs of abuse after alcohol and tobacco. Every decade or so we look around and are alarmed by all those pills we are taking. In 1953, the American Medical Association gently warned us that barbiturates, a useful drug, "can be dangerous." In 1963, *Good Housekeeping* warned its readers about barbiturate abuse, and then came *Valley of the Dolls* by Jacqueline Susanne and its startling portrait of bored American housewives hooked on pills. This theme was repeated by the Rolling Stones later in the decade in their song "Mother's Little Helper" ("Doctor please / Some more of these / Outside the door / She took four more"). In 1972 and 1973, the Drug Enforcement Agency battled what it termed an "epidemic" of barbiturate abuse; Elvis Presley, a genuine icon of the American 20th century, joined in the DEA's public efforts, only to die himself before the end of the decade, caught in the web of barbiturate abuse.

The stupefying, anticreative effect which **downers** have on users would predict a linguistic sloth, yet there is an extensive and poetic slang lexicon for central nervous system depressants.

Starting with the term "barbiturates," slang spins off to **barbs,** and from there to **Barbie dolls** and **Barts;** from "tranquilizer" come **trank, tranks,** and **tranx.** The protected trade name "Nembutal" for a pentobarbital leads to **nemish, nebbies, nembies, nemmies, and nimbies.** From "phenobarbital" comes **feenies** or **phennies,** and from "Seconal" come **seccy, seggy, sekkie,** and **sekky.**

Colors play a critical role in the slang naming of nervous system depressants, introducing a linguistic and pharmaceutical imprecision and ambiguity. For the most part, color-driven slang terms originated from specific drugs but soon migrated into vaguer and more general use. All **blues** were originally amobarbital sodium sold as Amytal, **pearls and grays** were Darvon, all **pinks** were Eli Lilly Seconal, **purple hearts** were phenobarbital sold under the trade name of Luminal, all **reds** were secobarbital sodium sold under the Eli Lilly trade name of Seconal, and **yellows** were pentobarbital sold under the Abbott trade name Nembutal. The precision suggested by the names does not exist on the street though, and anybody's guess is as good as anybody else's when it comes to colors:

black mollies	*dots, blue heavens,* and	*purple hearts*
blues, blue angels, blue	*blue tips*	*reds, Mexican reds, red*
birds, blue bullets, blue	*green hornets*	*birds, red bulls, red dev-*
devils, blue dolls, blue	*pinks, pink ladies*	*ils, red dogs, red dolls, red*

lilies, red smacks, and *roll of reds* (ten Seconals)

yellows, yellow bullets, yellow dolls, yellow jack-

ets, yellow submarines, and *high yallers*

Mixing colors, a **Christmas roll** or **rainbow roll** is an assortment of barbiturates, while a **Christmas tree, rainbow,** or **red-and-blue** is a Tuinal, a combination of amobarbital and secobarbital manufactured by Eli Lilly and packaged in a red and blue capsule.

Moving away from colors, the slang used to describe depressants is varied and inventive:

Abbotts Nembutal. *From the manufacturer.*

apple

backwards

blockbuster

bullet Originally Seconal

busters

canary Originally Nembutal

candy

damps *Punning on amps and its association with amphetamines.*

dees Dilaudid

demis Demerol

devils Would that be a **blue devil** or a **red devil?** *Do you care?*

dids Dilaudid

dies or *dyes* Valium. *From diazepam, the generic name of the drug.*

dillies Dilaudid

dolls Any central nervous system depressant. *A popular term coined by Jacqueline Susanne, as in "Valley of."*

dors, doors, or *dories* Doriden

double trouble Tuinal

F-40's Seconal. *From the Identi-Code symbol "40."*

fours Empirin with codeine

G.B. Nembutal. *From goof ball.*

goof ball Nembutal

goofers Glutheimide

gorilla pills

green dragons

happy pills

hog

idiot pills

jellies

King Kong pills

little D Dilaudid

lullaby pills

M&M's Seconal

marbles

Mighty Joe Young

peanuts

punkies

RD's Seconal. *Derived from* **red devils.**

sleepers

slows

softballs

splits

stumblers

tammies Tamazepam, a sleeping pill

t-birds Tuinal

tooies, tooties, or *tootsies* Tuinal

trees Tuinal

vals Valium

Impressive, no?

Cough medicine with the central nervous system depressant dextromethorphan or DXM has a small but devoted group of users who love their **drink, hooch, juice,** and **syrup.** Robitussen is the favorite, and its name has produced **robe, robo, rojo,** and **sky;** to be intoxicated with the syrup is to **tuss,** while a drug store employee who is vigilant against excessive purchases of the product is a **robo cop.** For some reason, riding elevators while under the influence intensifies the feelings—to do so is to **jolly.** Also-rans in the cough syrup department are codeine (**nods**), Drixoral (**drix**), and elixir of terpin hydrate with codeine (**G.I. gin** or **turps**), high in alcohol and codeine content and a favorite of soldiers.

One of the latest additions to the depressant game is Rohypnol, a brand name for flunitrazepam, a tranquilizer that is several times more potent than Valium. Inexpensive and powerful, it is very popular among high school and college students. Because it loosens inhibitions and induces amnesia, it is used as and known in journalese as the **date rape drug.** Slang synonyms include **rib, roach, robies, Roche, rochies, roofers** (a term with some questionable legend involving roofers in Florida after a hurricane), **roofies, rope, rophies, R-2, ruffies, rufinol,** or **rupees.**

Also new on the scene and also associated with date rape is gamma hydroxy butrate, the abuse of which was first reported in the *Arkansas Democrat Gazette* on January 20, 1986, and the abuse of which was widely associated with the death of actor River Phoenix in October 1993. Its slang aliases include **cherry menth, cherry meth, easy lay, fantasy, Georgia home boy, gook, great hormones at bedtime, grievous bodily harm, GBH, G-Riffick, liquid E, liquid ecstasy, liquid X, salty water, scoop,** and **soap.**

Uppers

AMPHETAMINES HAVE marched through the latter half of 20th-century America, making their mark in every decade. Here, watch the highlights:

In 1946, Harry "The Hipster" Gibson recorded "Who Put the Benzedrine in Mrs. Murphy's Ovaltine." We laughed. A milkman was arrested at San Quentin Prison in California, caught smuggling Benzedrine inhalers to inmates. We were shocked.

In 1947, California made it a felony to transport Benzedrine inhalers into prisons. We applauded. The newspapers reported that the "Benzedrine Trio" had circled the world in three days, four hours, and 55 minutes. We chuckled.

In 1948, persistent rumors had Bob Mathias using amphetamines before the 1500 meter race, the final event in the decathlon. We did not know what to think.

In 1949, Benzedrine was removed from inhalers. We sighed with relief.

In 1953, the American Medical Association reported on amphetamine use by student athletes at Harvard. We were worried.

In 1954, the *San Francisco News* warned us in headlines that "Goofballs and Bennies Mean Misery, Disgrace, Death." We were afraid. We learned of amphetamine use in the Canadian Football League. We were self-righteous.

In 1957, the American Medical Association stepped up its claims of regular amphetamine use by some college athletes. We didn't want to believe it. Pearl Bailey blamed her bizarre behavior during the live television broadcast of "Sunday Night at the Palladium" on a "pep pill" that somebody gave her before the show. She told us she did not know what the pill was. We believed her.

In 1960, amphetamines dominated the news from the summer Olympics. The death of a Danish cyclist was blamed on amphetamine use, and the parent of a member of the United States women's swim team, Weikoo "Finn" Ruuska, alleged that three swimming clubs had used amphetamines to qualify their swimmers for the Olympics. We were not happy. *Today's Health* warned us late in the year about "The Pep Pill Menace—Wake Up and Die." We worried.

In 1961, the *American Weekly* magazine in Sunday newspapers warned us about truck drivers with the bold headline "Pep-Pill Driving: New Menace on Our Highways." We were afraid to drive near trucks.

In 1963, *Good Housekeeping* joined the fray—"Sleeping Pills, Pep Pills—Handle with Extreme Caution." We thought that we would.

In 1964, the State of California Education Board approved a *Teacher's Guide to Narcotics* that focused on two fads, glue sniffing and Benzedrine. We took note.

And so on. Amphetamine abuse has only picked up steam in the last 30 years.

The most common slang names for stimulants are **beans, dexies, speed, uppers,** and **whites,** all of which spawn an inspiring family of variants.

Beans evolved from Benzedrine. There are several other sound-driven analogues—**A** (amphetamines, used by **A-heads**), **B** (Benzedrine), **B-bombs** (Benzedrine inhalers, formerly manufactured by Smith, Kline and French), **bennies, benz,** and **dexes** or **dexies** (from Dexedrine, a protected trade name for a dextroamphetamine sulfate).

Speed and **upper** convey the sense of stimulation. Other stimulating terms and expressions used to describe amphetamines include **AAA** (like the automobile club, amphetamines help you travel long distances), **accelerator, arrows, Billy Whizz, boosters** (a slangy euphemism used regularly during the discussions about the 1960 Olympic women's swimming team), **bumble bees** (that buzz—get it?), **co-pilots** (a trucker term), **coast-to-coast** (another trucker term, suggesting that the amphetamines will permit a trucker to drive from one coast to the other without sleeping), **drivers, eye-openers, forwards, go-fasters, go pills, helpers, jack ups, L.A. turnabouts** (another trucker term, again suggesting coast-to-coast powers), **lid proppers, lightning, marathons, rippers, snap, thrusters, truck drivers, turnabouts** (as in Los Angeles), **United Parcel Service** (UPS—get it?), **ups, wake-amine, wake-ups, whizz, zingers,** and **zoom.** To **spin** or to be **spun** is to achieve amphetamine intoxication, while a person who is **on a run** is using continuously.

Many prescription amphetamines are white, giving us **whites** as a common term, glorified by Lowell George and Little Feat in the song "Willin'," where the truck-driving narrator sings in each refrain—"Give me weed, whites and wine, and give me a sign." Other color-driven synonyms which originated from specific pharmaceutical amphetamines but now used with frightening ambiguity are **black beauties** (sometimes used to mean a biphetamine or a barbiturate), **black birds** (like all black pills, originally an allusion to Durophet), **black bombers, black Cadillacs, black hollies, black mollies, blues** (originally Drinamyl), **blue and clear, blue boys, French blues, browns, green dragons, oranges** (originally applied to Smith, Kline and French's Dexedrine), **peaches** (originally applied to Smith, Kline and French's Benzedrine), **roses** (also originally Benzedrine), and **yellow bam** or **peanut butter** (poor quality amphetamine; a term from the 1940s when users extracted a usable product from Benzedrine inhalers).

Other slang terms for amphetamines are based on the physical appearance of the drug other than its color; with the advent of generics most identifying marks don't apply anymore though the names still persist. **Cartwheels, Catholic aspirin, cross-tops,** and **double cross** all attest to the cross marking on the top of the white Benzedrine pills. Diphetamine is oval-shaped, leading to the names **bird eggs** (sometimes shortened to **birds**) and **footballs;** Smith, Kline and French's Dexedrine was at times heart-shaped, producing **hearts** or **horse**

hearts. Because of their resemblance to jelly beans, amphetamine pills are also sometimes known as **jelly babies** or **jolly beans.**

Many of the other entries in the idiom of amphetamines display the full-throttle linguistic creativity invoked by stimulating the central nervous system:

A-head A user of amphetamines

amped, amped up Under the influence of or addicted to amphetamines

amp head An amphetamine user

amp palace A house or apartment where amphetamines are used

B-20's Biphetamine. *Taken from the trade name.*

B-52's Amphetamine. *An obvious allusion to bombing.*

bam Amphetamine. *Probably a sound-effect slang tag.*

Bentley Etorphine, a synthetic morphine

blue haze The sense of well-being produced by Xanax, a tranquilizer

bombitas Amphetamine

cat Methcathinone, a dangerous low-grade stimulant made at home from drain-cleaner, Epsom salts, and battery acid. *Also known as* **battery acid,** **goop,** *and* **morning star.** *This is one that is definitely not to be missed.*

cheese A user

chicken powder Amphetamine in powder form

crossroads Amphetamine

dominoes Durophret

fives Amphetamines. *Other numbers referring to amphetamines are* **13** *and* **357.** *Go figure.*

glow The effect of amphetamine

grads Amphetamine. *From what?*

greenie, green bomb Amphetamine

hi-ball Benzedrine

jag Amphetamine intoxication

jug An injectable amphetamine

legs The duration of an amphetamine intoxication. *A strong amphetamine is said to have* **good legs.**

macka Amphetamine

nugget Amphetamine. *This is more commonly a word associated with crack cocaine, but it has been used to refer to amphetamines as well.*

pill head, pill popper, pilly A regular abuser of amphetamine, an addict

pixies Amphetamine. *A special little word, no?*

popcorn Amphetamine. *Used in Vietnam (the word and the pills).*

railroad To move one's

jaw side to side compulsively while withdrawing from amphetamine use

rhythms Amphetamines. *Downers are often* **blues,** *leading to this musical pun.*

rinse Traces of amphetamine rinsed out of a plastic bag that has held amphetamine. *The traces are then used by a truly desperate A-head.*

snot The residue left after smoking amphetamines. *Pretty picture!*

sparklers or **sparkle plenty** Amphetamine. *The original* **Sparkle Plenty** *comes from a character in the Dick Tracy comic strip.*

special forces Amphetamine. *A very special expression from Vietnam.*

speed bumps Bumps on a user's arms from injecting amphetamine

speed freak A regular abuser of amphetamines

speed willy The shrunken penis of a **speed freak**

spun, spun out Under the influence of amphetamines or methamphetamines

squirrel To engage in compulsive efforts to buy and use amphetamine

strip *The Benzedrine-drenched paper inside the tube of a Benzedrine inhaler was folded eight times into eight **strips**,* with two **strips** *making a dose.*

strung out Exhausted from excessive amphetamine use

sweets Amphetamine

tops Amphetamines. *An acronym from* **Take Off**

Pounds Sensibly.

tube A Benzedrine inhaler

tweaked Under the influence of amphetamines or methamphetamines

wired Under the influence of amphetamines

Like amphetamines, methamphetamine has a stimulating effect on the central nervous system. Soldiers discovered the joys of methamphetamine in the 1940s, and then in the 1950s students, truckers, and athletes all dabbled. **Pep shots** were most often methamphetamine. In the 1970s, methamphetamine abuse took off. It is almost exclusively manufactured illegally; until recently, motorcycle gangs in California dominated production. In the last decade, organized crime in Mexico has stepped in with a high quality, low price product that has taken over the market.

Methamphetamine, best known as **crank**, is also known as **chalk, crink, crystal** (and the variants **cris, Cristina,** and **criss-cross** as well as the derivative **crystal palace** referring to a place where methamphetamine is either sold or used), **dice** (originally applied to Desoxyn-brand methamphetamine), **gank, glass** (freebased methamphetamine), **go, go-fast, go-go, ice** (high grade methamphetamine which is smoked), **jet fuel, met, meth, motherfucker, rocket fuel, shards, splash, tweak,** and **water.** With a tip of the helmet to motorcycle gangs, **biker's coffee** is methamphetamine stirred into coffee.

Methamphetamine users are a strange breed with a thoroughly stimulated vocabulary. Extended use of methamphetamine can produce in the **meth monster** near-constant hallucinations; insects known as **crank bugs** are often imagined. The abnormal behavior of a heavy methamphetamine user is known as **geeking, schitzing,** or most commonly, as **tweaking.** A **tweaker** (sometimes **tweak** or **tweakster**), or heavy user, tends to **tweak and geek** or come to believe that worthless objects (**rootage**) are in fact priceless; an **amped** user who **digs for diamonds** is obsessively convinced that the glitter in concrete sidewalks is in fact precious diamonds.

Cocaine

FOR THE FIRST 40 YEARS of its life, cocaine enjoyed a remarkable degree of respectability for its powers as a local anesthetic and stimulant. Cocaine was isolated from the coca leaf sometime between 1850 and 1860, depending on which of several competing claims one accepts. Its first giant leap into our lives came in about 1863 when Corsican chemist Angelo Mariani developed and began to market a wine laced with cocaine; known as Vin Mariani, it was a favorite beverage of many of the great names of the late 19th century, including notorious dopers such as Pope Leo XIII, President William McKinley, and Thomas Edison. Cocaine was the primary ingredient in a wide range of quasi-medicinal products in the late 19th century; most notable of these products was Coca-Cola, launched in 1886 by John Styth Pemberton of Atlanta, Georgia, after an earlier product patterned after Mariani's wine failed to penetrate the market.

Meanwhile, cocaine in its pure form was making its mark. In late 1883, Dr. Theodor Aschenbrandt published a study reporting that soldiers in the Bavarian army responded positively to cocaine-dosed water. A young Sigmund Freud took note, tried cocaine, and in 1884 sang its praises in *Über Coca*. Conan Doyle's fictional alter ego Sherlock Holmes was a heavy cocaine user who found the drug "transcendingly clarifying to the mind."

Early in the 20th century cocaine started to take some pretty serious hits as an addicting drug of abuse. In 1903, Coca-Cola changed its formula and removed cocaine as an ingredient in response to public pressure exemplified by a 1903 letter to the editor of the *New York Tribune* written by one Col. J. W. Watson of Georgia, who blamed cocaine for "horrible crimes committed in the Southern states by colored people."

Banned completely by 1922, cocaine carved out its own special niche in the community of drug users—an esoteric, elitist drug enjoyed only by those who could afford its high cost and short-lived effect. Three of its nicknames—**downtown, pimp,** and **rich man**—suggest its elitist nature.

Musicians kept us aware that cocaine was still around, as in the Memphis Jug Band's "Cocaine Habit" (1930), Leadbelly's "Take a Whiff on Me" (1934), and "I Get a Kick Out of You" by Cole Porter in his Broadway show *Anything Goes* (1934):

> *I get no kick from cocaine.*
> *I'm sure that if*
> *I took even one sniff*
> *It would bore me terrifically too*
>
> *But I get a kick out of you.*

In later years, Dave Van Ronk gave us "Cocaine Blues," Sammy Hagar sang "The Ice Man," Eric Clapton gave us J. J. Cale's "Cocaine," and the Grateful Dead gave us "Casey Jones" with its grating "Ridin' that train / high on cocaine / Casey Jones, you better / watch your speed." Richard Pryor's terrible 1980 accident while freebasing cocaine, the scandal involving Tim Kraft of the Carter administration in 1980, and the widespread allegations of cocaine use in professional football in the early 1980s, all let us know that cocaine was present and accounted for. Until the appearance of crack cocaine on the scene in the 1980s, though, cocaine was a drug of the elite.

While Sherlock Holmes chose to inject his cocaine, it is most commonly ingested through the nose. The user pours powdered cocaine onto a hard surface such as a mirror or **foil**, and using a razor blade chops (**wacks**) the cocaine into a very fine powder that is then measured into two **lines**—**one and one**—which together constitute a **hit**. Using a folded matchbook cover (a **quill**, originally a moonshining term) or some other device (a **tooter**), the user then inhales one **line** into each nostril. After **sniffing, snorting,** or **tooting** the **lines**, the user feels an immediate sense of power and energy, a **buzz** or **rush**.

When it comes to slang surrogates for the drug itself, **coke** (see *Word History*, page 137), **snow,** and **flake** are the big names. A sizable slice of the slang synonym pie for cocaine is based on winter images, inspired by the widely used **snow** which is evocative of cocaine's white appearance. Other winter metaphors include **Arctic explorer** (a cocaine user), **caught in a snow storm** (intoxicated by cocaine), **Florida snow** (acknowledging the crucial role played by Florida in the importation of cocaine from South America), **freeze, icing, nieve** ("snow" in Spanish), **reindeer dust, sleigh ride** (a cocaine spree), **snow bird** (a user), **snow-caine, snow-cone, snow shed** (a place where cocaine is hidden), **snow slide** (a shot of cocaine), and **snow white.** Slang tags for cocaine based on its white color include **dama blanca** ("white lady" in Spanish), **Dr. White, pearl, white cross, white lady, white mosquitoes**, and **white tornado** (freebase form).

Personifications of cocaine abound in the body of slang synonyms—**Angie** (derived from **angel**), **Aunt Nora, Billie Hoke** (a little piece of rhyming slang, as is **big bloke**, from which is derived **bloker** for a user), **Carrie, Carrie Nation, Cecil, Charley** and the variant **cholly, Corine** or **Corrine, girl** (and the Cockneyed **goal**), **HMC** (Her Majesty Cocaine), **lady** or the Spanish **mujer, Mama Coca, Old Madge, Peruvian Lady**, and **she.** Names drawn from the sound and spelling include **Big C, blowcaine, C, caine, candycaine** (a fabulous pun as puns go, based on **candy** as cocaine), **Cecil, Cee, coat, coconut, coco-puff, coke, coke party** (a cocaine party), **cokie** (a cocaine addict or user), **cokomo** or **Kokomo** (a user), **cola, Kokomo Joe** (a user), and **Vitamin C.** The fact that Birney's Catarrh Cure at the turn of the century contained 5% cocaine led to **Bernies, Bernice, Birney, Birney blower** (a user), **blow the Birney** (to use), and **Burnese.**

Several dozen other cocaine slang terms have enjoyed at least moderate popularity over the decades:

bindle or **bing** A package of cocaine. *A direct borrowing from opium argot.*

blasts Cocaine

blam Cocaine

blo or **blow** Cocaine

bounce powder Cocaine. *From its mood-elevating effect.*

candy or **nose candy** Cocaine

candyman A cocaine dealer

chanel Cocaine. *Punning on the name of fashion designer Coco Chanel.*

charge Cocaine. *From its invigorating effect.*

chick Cocaine

cookie Cocaine

cooler A cigarette laced with cocaine.

dust Cocaine. *From its form as powder. Gold dust (as in the Fleetwood Mac song "Gold Dust Woman"), happy dust, heaven dust, and star dust are variations on the dust theme.*

dynamite Cocaine. *From its energizing effect.*

fillet Cocaine

flake Cocaine. *From its powder form.*

frisky Cocaine. *From its stimulating effect.*

gin Cocaine

happy trails Cocaine

hooter Cocaine. *From the*

association with the nose.

horn To snort

leaf Cocaine. *From the raw form—the coca leaf.*

leaper A cocaine user.

lola Cocaine

merk Cocaine. *From Merck Pharmaceutical, one of the earliest manufacturers of medicinal cocaine.*

mosquitoes Cocaine

pasta Coca paste, midway in the refining process

pimp Cocaine

powder Cocaine

powdered Under the influence of cocaine

railers Cocaine

ringer Cocaine

sleep Cocaine. *Hardly.*

sniff Cocaine. *From the fact that it is most often ingested through the nose.*

snoot Cocaine. *Again—the nose.*

soda Cocaine. *Perhaps from its resemblance to baking soda.*

stay awake Cocaine. *A whole lot truer than* **sleep.**

thinking man's Dristan Cocaine. *Thinking what?*

train Cocaine. *Again, rhyming slang, making the Grateful Dead's lyrics "Ridin' that train / high on cocaine" poetic redundancy.*

wings Cocaine.

zee An ounce of cocaine

In the song "Truckin'," the Grateful Dead asked "What in the world ever became of Sweet Jane / She lost her sparkle, you know, she isn't the same / Living on reds, Vitamin C and cocaine / All a friend can say is 'Ain't it a shame?'" If you think that cocaine was rough, fellows, hold on for a few years and take a look at crack cocaine.

Inhalants

THOSE WHO STUDY DRUG ABUSE speak of "inhalants"as a class of drugs. The substances that are lumped together and called "inhalants" are all breathable chemical vapors that produce a psychoactive effect, but this loose definition is all that they have in common.

Of all the inhalants which are "recreationally" abused, only nitrous oxide is intended to be inhaled. We have had it with us as a drug of abuse since the 1840s, which saw "Ether Follies" and **laughing gas** demonstrations. Coleridge, Peter Mark Roget, Samuel Colt, William James, and Winston Churchill all at least dabbled in nitrous oxide. Within the argot of nitrous oxide users, the nitrous oxide itself is known as **blue bottle, deadhead air** (because of heavy use by fans of the Grateful Dead), **laughing gas,** simply **gas, mind sweeper, nice balloon, rave breeze,** or **sweet air.** A **buzz bomb** or **whippet** is an 8-gram metal cylinder of nitrous oxide, originally designed as a propellant for canned whipped cream; a special tool, known as a **cracker,** is needed to open a **whippet.** To use nitrous oxide is to **shoot the breeze.**

An inhalant with a strong niche market is amyl nitrite and its sister butyl nitrite. The two, known as volatile nitrites, are inhaled; they lower inhibitions, provide a sudden intensification of positive emotions, relax muscles, and in general act as a sex intensifier. Abuse of nitrites blossomed and peaked in the wild and loose gay sex of the 1970s, but it did not start there. On April 8, 1953, Walter Winchell broke the story of nitrite abuse in his daily column—"The Hep Set now gets its kicks from ampules of amyll nitrate (*sic*), which can be had sans prescription . . . knocks you higher than taxes for about two minutes." Herb Caen, a fixture in San Francisco newspapers for decades, picked up on nitrites in 1969, writing on February 13 that they were "very big with those looking for sexy kicks." Amyl nitrite was an integral part of the gay sex scene of the 1970s and early 1980s, but use dropped off when it was thought to be a chemical cause of Kaposi's sarcoma, which was later understood to be the most common cancer found in AIDS patients.

Often carried in small canisters worn around the neck (a **bullet**), **amps** of amyl or butyl nitrite are most widely known as **poppers** or **snappers**; they also travel under the name of

Amy, Aimless Amy, aimies, ames, banana splits (from the ripe banana odor they emit), **bang, crackers, joy juice, lightning bolts, oz, popsies, posies, quicksilver, Rice Crispies** (from the "snack, crackle and pop" slogan—cle-ver!), **sniff** (which produces **sniff queen** as a heavy user), **Uncle Emils,** and **whiteout.** Butyl nitrite is marketed under a number of manly names, which sometimes serve as eponymous labels—**Locker Room, Ram, Thrust,** and so on.

Okay—let's get industrial, let's hit those volatile hydrocarbons and their depressing effect on the central nervous system. Someone somewhere has tried to get a **buzz** off of everything under the kitchen sink. Even lowly ammonia has the slang alias of **scrubwoman's kick.**

Abuse of volatile hydrocarbons probably peaked in the early 1960s. *Time* magazine warned us on February 16, 1962, that glue sniffing was "the new kick," while *This Week* magazine screamed out on January 20, 1963, "Danger! A New Kids' Fad: Glue Sniffing."

Glue sniffing and its cousins never attracted the sharpest knives in the drawer, and the slang associated with it is on the sparse side. To inhale glue or other industrial products is to **blow a bag, flash, gas,** or **huff,** which makes the user of industrial inhalants a **huffer** as well as an **Elmer** (as in the glue) or a **gluey.** Rather than admit what it is that they are inhaling, the inhalant abuser will refer to the product as **gunk,** the **rush,** a **glad rag, heart-on, oz,** a **spray, tolley** (toluene, a paint solvent), or a **wad.**

LSD

THE 1960S SAW A WHOLE NEW wave of recruits to drug use and a whole new drug to use— D-lysergic acid diethylamide tartrate 25, shortened to LSD-25, more commonly further shortened to LSD. Dr. Albert Hofmann of the Sandoz Laboratories in Switzerland developed LSD in the late 1930s and came to understand its powerful psychoactive effects as a hallucinogenic drug in the early 1940s. Word of LSD's powers began reaching the world in the late 1950s. The *San Francisco Chronicle*'s intrepid Herb Caen reported rumors of experiments involving LSD at the Psychology Department of the University of California at Berkeley in his column on April 24, 1958. Three months later, a University of California radio and television production explored LSD use in a show entitled "A Journey Within."

The LSD story went national in February 1960, when Cary Grant told the *American Weekly* Sunday newspaper insert that he had used LSD and that it was "almost like a miracle." On May 15, 1960, the *Chronicle* explored the possible medical use of LSD as treatment for alcoholism in an article by Franz E. Winkler headlined "LSD: A Cure or a New Sickness: Beware of LSD!"

In 1962, two books which touched upon LSD use were published, *My Self and I* by Constance Newland and *The Joyous Cosmology* by Alan Watts. A year later, LSD use was spreading enough in San Francisco that it became something of a fixture in the local media—"Hallucination Drug Research" in the *Chronicle* (July 3, 1963); "The Unhappy Story of LSD" in the *San Francisco Examiner* (July 23, 1963); "The Other Side of Reality" on television station KRON (September 23, 1963); the companion "The Toxic Side of Reality" by Merla Zellerbach in the *Chronicle* (September 27, 1963); and "LSD Mystery in Attorney's Weird Death" in the *Chronicle* (December 29, 1963).

Ken Kesey in California, Dr. Timothy Leary at Harvard, Richard Alpert (now Baba Ram Dass) at Harvard, and several other early LSD zealots were responsible for the rapid spread of LSD use in the mid-1960s. LSD was well-established in the hippie counterculture by 1965 and within young America by the late 1960s.

The Lesser Hallucinogens

LSD WAS THE MAIN EVENT IN the main arena of hallucinogenic drugs in the 1960s, but it was not the only event. There were a number of other hallucinogens available and used, although in the brave new world of brave new drugs it was impossible to know exactly what was in a pill. More often than not the pills marketed as hallucinogens other than LSD were in fact low doses of LSD, perhaps enhanced by some vile amphetamine concoction.

Morning glory seeds, which contain a lysergic acid derivative, enjoyed a brief fling with fame thanks to their mildly hallucinogenic powers. The *San Francisco Examiner* headlines shouted "Morning Glory Madness" on March 13, 1964. Five years later, the dean of the University of California at Berkeley canceled an advertisement which had been placed in the campus newspaper for morning glory seeds ($1 for 150 seeds). The colorful names given the flowers by seed companies provided the terminology used by seed-eaters, who referred to the seeds as **flying saucers**, **heavenly blues**, **pearly gates**, and **wedding bells**.

From the American southwest came peyote, known as **buttons, full moon, nubs, topi** or **tops,** and personified as **Mescalito**. Mescaline, peyote's main alkaloid, was known as **beans, big chief, mesc, mezc,** and **moon.** Synthetic mescaline pills were known on the street as **pumpkin seeds** or **yellow footballs.**

And then there was psylocibin, a hallucinogen derived from mushrooms and known as **boomers, musk, Simple Simon** (punning on the nursery rhyme), **magic mushrooms**, the quintessential dude-speak **'shrooms, silly putty,** or **tweezies.** Hallucinogenic mushrooms first arrived on the national scene in *Life* magazine on May 13, 1957, in an article entitled "Seeking the Magic Mushroom" by Robert Gordon Wasson, but mainstream tolerance was short-lived.

Dimethyltryptamine had its fans; a fast-acting, short-lived hallucinogen, it was known as **DMT** and **the businessman's special** or **lunchtime special** (it could be experienced during a lunch break). **STP** was a hallucinogenic chemical produced by the Dow Chemical Company, and hippies seized upon the acronym to build **Serenity, Tranquillity, and Peace.**

Saving the best for last, one comes to **mellow yellow.** Thanks in large part to an all-in-all insipid song by Donovan Leitch, scraped, dried banana peels ("Electrical bananas, gonna be the very next craze . . .") were rumored to have a psychedelic effect when smoked. A crack team of UCLA psychiatrists determined in 1967 that "there are no known hallucinogens in bananadine"; the entire **mellow yellow** craze was a ruse from the start.

As LSD use spread, a vocabulary sprang up around it. Given the undeniably creative character of the hippie subculture and the hallucinogenic powers of LSD, one would expect linguistic creativity in the argot of LSD users. Such decidedly was not the case. For the most part, the vocabulary of LSD use was bland and unimaginative, a stark contrast to the inventiveness and even elegance of most drug argot. Perhaps this can be explained by the demographics of LSD users; while up to this point in the 20th century most drug use in America was found in the underclass or artistic subcultures, LSD was used by millions of middle-class white youth. Linguistic creativity is not a hallmark of the middle class of a dominant culture, and it is thus not particularly surprising that the slang of LSD users was so flat and lifeless.

In any event, LSD was best known as **acid** (see *Word History*, page 134), an appropriately frightening sobriquet. From the simple **acid** came several extensions—the clipped **'cid** or **sid**, **acidhead** for a frequent user, **acid rock** for music played by and for those under the influence of psychedelics, and **acid test** (for further discussion of **acidhead** and **acid test**, see *Word History*, pages 134, 137).

LSD is ingested orally, referred to nearly universally as **eating, dropping**, or taking a **hit,** the **eating** providing the wonderfully scary-sounding **eat acid**. The vehicle by which the LSD is ingested makes a tedious contribution to the slang surrounding LSD. When dissolved in liquid it is known as—hold on—**liquid;** when absorbed into blotter paper it is known as **blots, blotter, sheets** (100 doses on perforated blotter paper), **dots,** or **microdots** (the "micro" coming from the fact that LSD is measured in micrograms, aka **mikes** or **gammons**); when absorbed into tiny transparent gelatin chips it is known as a **contact lens** or **windowpane** (sometimes shortened to simply **pane**—half clever, no?); when absorbed into a sugar cube it is known as—yes—**cube** or—yes again—**sugar;** when placed in a capsule it is known as—good guess!—a **cap,** or a **barrel, pellet,** or **tab;** and when absorbed into a domed tablet it is known as—of course!—**dome** or **double dome.** Anything can be laced (**dosed**) with LSD, and it is then **electric,** as in **electric Kool Aid.** At least in the San Francisco Bay area, a bowl of **dosed** fruit punch would be known as **fucko punch.**

If the **blots** and **caps** and **cubes** were not tiring enough, there are the colors. With the exception of **purple haze** which is interesting only because of the Jimi Hendrix song and **brown acid** (the LSD that was "not specifically good" at Woodstock), there is not much to be said for the litany of LSD slang color names. They can't be ignored, but then again they can't be praised either

You be the judge, though; check these out:

Black star, black sunshine	*domes,* or *green wedge*	*pink witch*
Blue bar, blue cheer, blue heaven, blue mist, blue moons, or *blue star*	*Orange barrel, orange cube, orange haze, orange sunshine,* or *orange wedge*	*Purple barrel, purple flat,* or *purple haze*
Golden dragon	*Pink blotters, pink panther, pink robot, pink swirl, pink wedge,* or	*Red dragon*
Gray shields		*White lightning*
Green dragon, green		*Yellow dimples, yellow sunshine,* or *mellow yellow*

Quickly leaving the color-based names, slang aliases include **A**, **Alice** (probably related to Lewis Carroll's *Alice in Wonderland*), **animal**, **Big D** (from the "d" in D-lysergic acid etc.), **California sunshine, the chief, chocolate chips, coffee** (a term coined in Cambridge, Massachusetts, where LSD was often sold in coffee houses), **crackers** (another Cambridge phrase, derived from the fact that LSD was sold on animal crackers), **cupcakes**, **deeda** (a term used in Harlem, where it is difficult to imagine that much LSD was consumed), **devine, fields** (from the **trippy** song "Strawberry Fields Forever" by the Beatles), **flash, the ghost, the hawk, haze, headlights, hits, instant Zen, one-way, Owsley** (named after a prolific pioneer in LSD manufacture), **potato, pure love, sacrament** (one of the few religious metaphors one finds in the slang of drugs, fitting to the LSD-is-religion mentality of many early users who spoke of seeing the **great white light** during the intoxication), **Sandoz** (from the Swiss laboratory), **smears, sunshine, ticket** (in keeping with the travel theme discussed below), **trip** or **trips**, **25** (from the 25 in D-lysergic acid diethylamide tartrate 25), **wafer** (a term used when a cookie is **dosed** with LSD), **wedge**, and **zen**. The LSD of the 1990s is known as **cocktail acid**, alluding to the fact that the typical dose is far smaller than the typical dose of the 1960s.

To ingest LSD is to **turn on**, or to **bust a cap, drop a cap, drop acid, eat acid**, or **trip**, which brings up the element of LSD slang that is of greatest linguistic interest—the repeating theme of travel. **Trip** was a pervasive word in the 1960s; it originally referred to an LSD **experience** (which gave us **experienced** as an adjective to describe those who have used LSD and a great record album from Jimi Hendrix), with a bad experience known as a **bad trip, bummer**, or **bum trip**. **Bummer** moved into mainstream slang with a broader meaning, and then into mainstream American English.

The travel theme is ubiquitous. The place where one took LSD was known as the **launching pad** (a nice little pun on **pad** as it had been used in the past—**pad fee** with opium users in the 19th century and **tea pads** with marijuana users in the 1930s). Those who took LSD often chose to be accompanied on their experience by someone not taking LSD—**ground-man/ ground control** ("Ground Control to Major Tom!") or a **guide** (**baby-sitter, sitter,** or **gatekeeper** if one digresses from the travel motif). A group of users could be referred to as an **explorers' club**. After-the-fact hallucinations, known most broadly as a **flashback**, were also known as a **return trip**.

A person under the influence of LSD was said to be **flying, tripping,** or **turned on**; even if one had not personally ingested, it was possible to get a **contact high** from those who were. At least in San Francisco, some users used an old heroin term from the 1930s and spoke of being **behind acid** when under the influence. In the 1990s, someone under the influence of LSD is said to be **mad spun**.

PCP

AFTER TRYING ALL KNOWN drugs of abuse and still searching for uncharted territory, some turned in the 1970s to animal tranquilizers, chiefly phencyclidine or **PCP**. Originally developed as an anesthetic for humans in 1959, its use with humans was discontinued in the early 1960s

because of its extreme side effects, such as delirium and confusion. When it reappeared as a veterinary anesthetic, some latched onto it and its combination of effects produced by depressants, stimulants, and hallucinogens. Blank stare, loss of memory, disorientation, muscle rigidity, sensory distortions—what were they thinking?

In spite of its destructive character—or perhaps because of it—PCP is prolific in generating slang synonyms. **Angel dust** is by far the most popular. The earliest recorded use that I have found is in an article in which a reporter for the *San Francisco Examiner* quoted a PCP user on August 12, 1970, claiming that smoking **angels** (*sic*) **dust** "really gets you whacked in a surrealistic way."

Angelic offspring include **angel hair**, **angel mist**, **angel puke**, and **dust of angels**. On the flip side of the coin, the lethal nature of PCP is recognized in the slang monikers of **dead on arrival**, **death wish**, **DOA**, **embalming fluid**, **keys to St. E's** (alluding to St. Elizabeth's, a psychiatric hospital), **killer weed**, **mad man**, and **yellow fever**. Capturing both the angelic and the lethal is **heaven 'n hell**. Showing that even PCP users have a sense of humor, the drug is glorified in the slang names **love boat** and the clipped **boat** (which produce **take a cruise** as an expression meaning to use PCP), the derivative **lovely**, **magic**, **magic dust**, **paz**, **peace pill** (and the clever **PeaCe Pill**—get it?), or **Peter Pan**. The fact that PCP is an animal tranquilizer is acknowledged in **elephant**, **hog**, **mad dog**, **monkey dust**, **pig killer**, **porker**, and **wolf**.

P$_a$
C
P

Other slang analogues for PCP are **ace**, **ameoba** (the state of one's mind after using PCP), **aurora borealis**, **bad grass**, **bad pizza**, **black whack**, **busy bee**, **butt naked**, **Cadillac** (a dangerous ambiguity, for **Cadillac** is more commonly used to describe cocaine), **CJ**, **cozmo**, **crazy Eddy** (high quality PCP), **crazies**, **crystal** (another tiny ambiguity, for **crystal** most often refers to methamphetamine), **cyclone** (describing the effect on the nervous system), **Detroit pink**, **dummy dust** (no pulling the punches here!), **energizer**, **fairy dust** (based on reputed use by gays), **goon** (good shot!), **green snow**, **green tea**, **Hercules** (high quality PCP), **Hinckley** (referring to the nice young man from Texas who attempted to murder President Ronald Reagan in 1981), **hot cakes**, **jet fuel**, **KJ**, **kools**, **log**, **mean green**, **mint leaf** or **mint weed** (because the PCP is often sprinkled on mint and smoked), **mist** (again pertaining to the user's mental condition), **more** (Want some? Some what? Who's on first?), **ozone**, **P**, **parsley** (another vehicle for smoking—PCP-laced parsley), **peanut butter** (PCP mixed into peanut butter), **peep**, **pit**, **puffy**, **rocket fuel**, **scaffle** or **scuffle**, **Shermans** or **Sherms** (an allusion to a cigarette brand), **super**, **surfer**, **T-buzz**, **THC** (the drug marketed on the street as "THC" was often PCP, not a marijuana derivative), **tic tac** (applied to PCP in white tablet form, resembling the breath mints), **tish**, **wack** (or **wac** or **whack**), **worm**, **zombie weed**, **zoom**, and **zoot**. What a set of slangonyms!

Quaaludes

ONE OF THE MOST POPULAR RECREATIONAL drugs abused in the 1970s was methaqualone, a powerful sedative/hypnotic compound. In low doses it produces calmness and relaxation, in moderate doses euphoria and sexual arousal, and in high doses general numbness and weakness. Combined with alcohol—**luding out**—it produces a mind-numbing stupor so powerful that a **luded out** youngster could find comfort curled up on the floor during a quite loud and quite busy Grateful Dead concert at the Fillmore. It was a brilliant little addition to the arsenal of post-60s drugs enjoyed by the young in the 1970s. Fittingly, it played a prominent role in that of-the-time classic *Tales of the City* by Armistead Maupin in 1976.

Most of the prominent slang names for methaqualone are obvious evolutions of protected brand names—from the William H. Rorer brand name "Quaalude" came **Q**, **quas**, **quaas**, **quacks**, **quads**, **luds**, and **ludes** (the predominant slang name); from the British Roussel Laboratories brand name "Mandrax" came **mandies** and **mandrakes**; while from "Sopors" (itself a borrowing from the adjective "soporific") came **soaps** and **sopes**. Rorer Pharmaceutical's product was marked with a "714," giving the pill the slang nickname of **714's**; when Lemmon bought Rorer, the "714" stayed on the pill, leading to the new **Lemmon 714**.

Leaving the realm of protected trade names, Quaaludes also answered to **breakfast of losers** (punning on the "Breakfast of Champions" slogan for the breakfast cereal Wheaties), **disco biscuits** (alluding to the widespread use of Quaaludes in the 1970s disco scene), **Dr. Jekyll and Mr. Hyde**, the **love drug** (recognizing the affectionate, tingling, and sexual feelings often produced by the pill), **pillows** (with a nod to the drug's soporific qualities), **stumble biscuits**, and **wall-bangers** (both acknowledging the drug's effect on motor skills).

Raves: Ecstasy and Ketamine

IN THE LATE 1980s, the world came to know the **rave**, an all-night party event open to the paying public, usually in a large venue, based on the premise that sensory overload orchestrated by a deejay can and will elevate participants into an altered, **luvdup**, group-feeling state. While a **rave** is open to the public, a **party** is open only to invitees—full-time **ravers** only, no part-time **plassies**.

Dance drugs are an integral part of the rave experience, and in the lead role one finds

MDMA, a synthetic **designer drug** (a substance that appears in the illicit drug market and is a chemical analog or variation of another psychoactive drug) with hallucinogenic and amphetamine-like properties. Banned by the Drug Enforcement Agency using its emergency powers in 1985, MDMA is best known as **ecstasy** and also known as **Adam, doves, E** or **e** (which produces the quite clever **riding the E-train** for using MDMA), **essence, Eve, kleenex, M** or **Double M, presence, X, XTC** (get it?), and, borrowing from LSD, **Zen**. To be under the influence of ecstasy is to be **cabbaged, faced, rolling,** and/or **sledgied.**

Also in the illegal department and definitely back again in the whatever-could-they-be-thinking department, young people in the 1990s discovered ketamine hydrochloride, an anesthetic used primarily for veterinary purposes, and it quickly became a rave drug. Chemically related to PCP, it also boasts psychedelic properties and it creates a powerful sense of dissociation.

Ketamine has a modest portfolio of slang names. It is most commonly known as **K** or **Special K**, a fun allusion at the expense of a popular breakfast cereal. Other slang handles for ketamine include **2CB, cat valium** (recognizing its veterinary heritage), **cloud 9, green, honey oil, jet, kitkat** (playing with the "k"), **nexxus, purple, super C** (good spelling!), **Vitamin K** (ha!) or the clipped **vit K,** and **zenith. To ket** is to use ketamine. A regular dose is a **bump,** while a **line dose** takes the user to dissociation and into the ketamine-induced confusion of the **K-hole** or into the **K-state** where the user sometimes is so removed from his or her body that he or she forgets to breathe. What a great idea!

The legal substance of choice at raves is the **smart drink,** a blender drink made with nutrients that are claimed to supply precursors and cofactors that the body uses to manufacture neurotransmitters. Say what?

Sensual touch that is not overtly sexual is common at raves, especially in a **feely-feely room** where **ravers** might join in **puppy piles** (piles of people on the ground, affectionate like puppies) or in **snake slithering** (touching with hands like snakes slithering). Once the sensory overload of **techno music,** strobe lights, and Tiger balm massages actually produces an overload, the **raver** heads to the **chill-out room** to—yes—chill out, or relax and recover.

Crack

AS WE LEARNED EARLIER, cocaine was long the drug of the elite. The demographics of cocaine use shifted dramatically in the 1980s, though, with the introduction of crack cocaine.

The first step towards crack cocaine was **freebase,** cocaine that by a user-generated heating process (**chasing** or **ghost-busting**) is reduced to its basic, alkaloid psychoactive level; the result is smoked, producing a much more potent intoxication—**double bubble. Freebase** gave us a series of **base** slang—**base** or **baseball** as the actual freebase cocaine, **base** as "to smoke," and **base gallery** or **base house** as a place where one pays a fee to enter and use freebase.

In the early 1980s, the bright minds of the drug trade developed crack cocaine, precooked cocaine that is mixed with other, cheaper chemicals such as baking soda. Crack was sold in vials for as little as $2, creating a whole new market for the drug. The distribution and street sales of crack became a major form of employment for some of the urban young;

vials are color-coded by dealers, who stake out territory that is theirs. The effects of crack addiction and the constant battles over territory by competing dealers have all but brought down what little remained of a social fabric in American inner cities as the 1980s progressed.

Despite its thoroughly devastating effect on urban black America, crack cocaine has spawned an admirable slang that is every bit as vibrant as its users are desperate. The *Oxford English Dictionary* cites a first usage of **crack** in the *San Francisco Chronicle* of December 6, 1985; a Nexis search produces two slightly earlier usages, the *New York Times* of November 17, 1985, and again in the *Times* on November 29, 1985. **Crack** is known as **rock** on the West Coast and **crack** on the East Coast, **crack** coming from the crackling sound it makes when smoked and **rock** from its appearance. Not content with a simple **crack** or **rock**, users have coined a series of synonyms based on the appearance of the drug—**applejacks** (the pieces of crack cocaine resemble breakfast cereal), **crumbs** (tiny pieces of crack), **crunch and munch, golf ball, gravel, grit, hail, ice cube, kibbles and bits** (small pieces of crack), **nuggets, pebbles, ready rocks, Rox** or **Roxanne** (an obvious personification of **rocks**), **sleet, stones,** or **white girl.**

Aside from these image-based names, crack is also known as **7-Up** (a sweet little pun on **coke**), **Atari, Baby T, bad** (and how!), **ball, bee-bee** (from the Spanish **bebe**, for "baby"), **beemers, berry** (a great connection to the 1920s, when something that was very good was "the berries"), **bings, BJ's, blast, blizzard** (alluding to the thick white cloud of smoke or **mist** that emits from a crack pipe), **bolo, bomb, bump, cake** (a round disk of crack cocaine), **Casper the Ghost, chemical, chewies, cloud** or **cloud 9, cookies** (round, flat pieces of cocaine residue from the bottom of the jar used to cook the product), **demolish, devil's dust, devil's smoke, dip, Eastside player, egg, famous dimes, fan, fat bags, flavor** (high quality), **French fries** or simply **fries** (three-inch sticks of crack with ridged edges), **fry** or **fry daddy, glo, groceries, half track, hamburger helper, hubbas, jelly beans, Johnson, kangaroo, lightem, megablast** (a dose of crack), **one-fifty-one, p-funk, parlay, paste, pee-wee, perp** (fake crack, made of wax and baking soda), **piles, pony, press, raw, ringer** (a good hit of crack), **rooster, Scotty, scramble, scruples, Sherms** (a crossover from PCP), **slab** (highly adulterated crack), **sleet, stones, teardrops** (a dose, packaged in corners of plastic bags), **teeth, tension, top gun, troop, ultimate, wave, work, Yale,** and **yahoo.**

With the product in hand, the user is ready for the pipe, known as a **demo** (a lab pipette used for smoking), **the devil's dick** (quite a metaphor!), **horn, Lamborghini** (or **Kabuki** or **Maserati**, a pipe made from a plastic rum bottle and a spark plug cover), **space ship** (a glass pipe), **stem,** or **Uzi.** The oily residue left in the pipe after smoking goes by the names of **Bazooka, con-con, due,** or **res.**

Pipe in hand and crack in pipe, it's time finally to **beam up, play handball,** or **play hardball.** Those wide eyes after use? **High beams.** Hallucinating? Well, we say **buggin'.**

Who is the user, this person who will walk down the one-way highway of crack cocaine addiction? He or she answers by **beamer** (as in "Beam me up, Scotty," a reference to *Star Trek*), **chaser, cluck** (I'll say), a **cracker jack, jar head, nickelonian, piper, puffer,**

rockette (a female user), and **tweaker** (a word used to describe both methamphetamine addicts and crack addicts).

Crack is often smoked in a house, apartment, or building dedicated to that purpose and known as a **crack house** or **rock house**. To enter, one pays the owner or proprietor either in cash (a **house fee** or a **tax**) or in kind with crack (a **house piece**). With large numbers of users in one place, it is always possible that there are small pieces of crack, or even entire vials, on the floor of the often dark room. Those truly desperate souls on their hands and knees looking for crack remnants are **on carpet patrol, ghost-busting, pianoing**, or **searching for crumbs**. When your body tells you that it is time for some more crack and it means NOW, you are **fiendin'**, **thirsty**, or having a **crack attack**. If nobody will **pass** or **pimp their pipe** (share with you) or there is nothing more to share, somebody leaves on a **mission, interplanetary mission**, or **tweak mission** to buy more crack.

Crack cocaine dealers have developed a vocabulary of their own, a definite deviation from the basic dealing vocabulary used in other drug deals.

The **crew, bomb squad** (a group of young people selling crack), or **shower posse** (from the image of showering the street with automatic weapon fire) efficiently divides tasks, under the direction of the dealer (the **pitcher** or **server**) and **pumps** or **slangs** the crack.

The manufacture of crack cocaine is under the direction of a **cooker**, who using **comeback** or **swell** (a street chemical used to increase the yield) and a **can of gas** (butane torch), processes the cocaine in a **shaker**, or small bottle. At the end of the process the residue is known as **caviar**.

Next is the crew **behind the scale**, dividing the finished product into vials or **bottles**; rows of vials heat-sealed together are **clips** or **trays**. The colored, dome-shaped caps on the vials are **rocket caps**. If the police raid the building where this or any other step in the process is taking place, there is usually a designated **stash catcher**, a younger child whose job is to catch the **stash** thrown out the window and run very fast. For the larger customer there is the **Big 8**, 1/8 of a kilogram of the product.

Out in the **cop zone** or **crack spot** where the actual selling takes place, the **steerer** or **tout** directs prospective buyers to the dealer. After cash passes hands, a **runner** delivers the drug to the buyer; the dealer must be vigilant, for some runners **dip out** or remove some crack from the vials that they are delivering, either for personal use or personal sale. In addition to the standard drug dealing terms of **nickel** ($5 worth of drugs, also called a **pee-wee**) and **dime** ($10 worth of drugs) are the **twennies** (larger vials with $20 worth of the drug). **To front** is to sell on credit; failure to pay for sales made on credit is one of the major causes of drive-by shootings, a sad by-product of crack.

Combinations

THE TRULY INTREPID DRUG USER is sometimes not satisfied with the rush, risks, kicks, and dangers of using one drug at a time. Why stop with a single set of physiological effects when you can experience the interaction of different drugs? Why stop with the chance that one drug is not exactly what it is claimed to be when you can combine drugs and combine ambiguities?

Why not mix and match? It's not unlike a mixed drink or cocktail when you come to think of it, isn't it?

In the world of drug combinations (called **mixers**), the linguistic creativity that one finds with individual drugs is present and accounted for. Here, try these:

A-bomb A marijuana cigarette laced with an opiate or with heroin

B-40 A cigar laced with marijuana and then dipped in malt liquor

back-to-back Crack cocaine and heroin, or heroin and crack cocaine

bam A pill that combines barbiturates and amphetamines

black and tan A pill that combines stimulants and depressants

black beauty A pill that combines stimulants and depressants

black widow A pill that combines stimulants and depressants

blue velvet Paregoric and an antihistamine

boys and girls Heroin and cocaine

candy flip LSD and ecstasy

cannon ball Morphine and cocaine

clicker PCP and crack cocaine

cold and hot Cocaine and heroin

crack cooler Crack cocaine soaked in a wine cooler

croak Crack cocaine and speed

dust To combine marijuana and heroin for smoking

duster A marijuana cigarette laced with PCP

eight-ball Crack cocaine and heroin

fours and dors Codeine and Doriden

flamethrower A cigarette with cocaine and heroin

French blue A pill that combines stimulants and depressants

Frisco speedball Heroin, cocaine, and LSD

fruit salad A bowl filled with various pills—*Here, grab a handful and take 'em!*

Geronimo Alcohol and barbiturates

gremmie Marijuana and crack cocaine

HMC Heroin, morphine, and cocaine

load Codeine and Doriden

loveboat A marijuana cigarette dipped in formaldehyde. *What twisted person first thought of this?*

lovely A marijuana cigarette laced with PCP

M and C Morphine and cocaine

Marmon and Cadillac Morphine and cocaine

Monroe in a Cadillac Morphine and cocaine

moonrock Crack cocaine and heroin

Murder One Heroin and cocaine

new Jack swing Heroin and morphine

overs-and-unders A pill that combines stimulants and depressants

pancake syrup Glutethimide and codeine cough syrup

p-funk Crack cocaine and PCP

primo Marijuana and crack cocaine

sheet rock LSD and crack cocaine

space base PCP and crack cocaine

space dust PCP and crack cocaine

speedball 1. Morphine and cocaine 2. Heroin and cocaine 3. Alcohol (wine) and barbiturates (Seconal)

star speed PCP and crack cocaine

supergrass Marijuana laced with PCP

sweet Lucy A marijuana cigarette that has been dipped in wine

torpedo A marijuana cigarette laced with crack

tragic magic PCP and crack cocaine
turbo A marijuana cigarette laced with crack cocaine
twister Heroin and cocaine

unforgettable Heroin, Valium, and cocaine
whiz-bang Morphine and cocaine
wildcat Methcathinone and

cocaine
woolah, wollie A cigar filled with marijuana and crack cocaine

Dealing

ARE YOU ANYWHERE? Are ya layin' down the hustle? Are ya stickin'? Do you have any illegal drugs to sell me? Drug dealing is capitalism pure and simple, a market and a demand, a buyer and a seller, goods for cash. With the economics, comes a slang.

Here come the drugs from a foreign country, brought in by a courier known as a **mule** or **puller.** He, or sometimes she, who sells the drug is the **bagman, banker** (sometimes a separate function of holding cash for the seller), **connection, dealer, my man, peddler** (for the most part a scare word used by journalists in the 1930s, but at times mockingly embraced by sellers), **pusher** (again a term used more by outsiders than buyers or sellers), or a **shooter** (sometimes a separate function of holding drugs—**in pocket**—to be turned over to the buyer after cash has passed hands). In the 1950s, a **bottle dealer** or **jar dealer** sold pills in 1000-pill units. In New York, a **Barnes man** came to mean a big-time drug dealer thanks to one Nicky Barnes of Harlem. To buy is to **cop, serve,** or **score, to take care of** is to sell, to **get a wife** is to introduce a buyer to a seller, while a **meet** is a meeting between a buyer and a seller.

Raves produce a few dealing words of their own—the person who steers customers to dealers is a **snarler,** the seller is a **Joey,** and the heavies who provide muscle are **minders.**

Both **brewery** and **factory** are used to describe a place where drugs are manufactured or measured and put in capsules (**capped up**) or bags (**bagged up**). The temptation is always present to dilute the drug to be sold, or to **cut** it (drawn from **shaving** cubes of morphine), **step on it,** or **sugar down.** At times a product without any drug at all is passed off as a drug, especially if there is a shortage of the drug available for sale (with heroin, called a **panic** as in *Panic in Needle Park* with Al Pacino and Kitty Winn in 1971); if powdered milk or some other non-narcotic is sold as heroin, it is known as **lemon** or **snidey drug.** With cocaine, it is possible to **beige** the drug, which makes it appear to be better quality than it is.

Several quantities for selling are universal—a **dime bag** being $10 worth of drug and a **nickel bag** being $5 worth of drug. An **O.Z.** or **pamphlet** is an ounce, and, fittingly, **two books** are a kilogram. A **teenager** is 1/6 of a gram, a **Henry IV** is four grams, and **Henry VIII** is 8 grams.

LSD WORD HISTORIES

ACID, TRIP, AND HEAD

THE RUSH TO psychedelic drugs—especially LSD—in the late 1960s and early 1970s was a middle-class rush to drug use unparalleled in American history. Long the province of the underclass and criminal subcultures, drug use took on a whole new dimension as upper-class and middle-class youth rallied around LSD. Although LSD had been used experimentally for several decades, it was new to public consumption and it required a vocabulary.

The leading slang term for LSD was clearly **acid**, a simple shortening of LSD's full name of "lysergic acid diethylamide." It had an appropriately, even deliciously, dangerous sound to it, especially when "to take LSD" was translated into to **eat acid**. The first use of **acid** as LSD recorded by the *Oxford English Dictionary* was in 1966, in the inside cover of Richard Alpert and Sidney Cohen's book *lsd*. **Acid** was certainly used regularly by the relatively small but getting bigger circle of LSD users in 1965, as reflected in the use of **acid test** by Ken Kesey and his Merry Pranksters late that year (see below). By early 1966, the mainstream press had started picking up on **acid**—the *New York Times* on March 21 ("Students call it acid"); *Life* on March 25; the *New Republic* on April 16 (comparing LSD use with "surfing, frugging, and digging Bob Dylan songs"); and *Newsweek* on May 9 ("the drug is called 'acid'").

Acid gave us the offspring of **acidhead** for a user of LSD; **acid rock** for music played while under the influence of, or for the purpose of enhancing the experience of those under the influence of LSD; and the punning **acid test**. When coined in 1892, **acid test** referred to the use of nitric acid to test for gold. In 1908, the term was applied in

Chorus Lady by James Forbes as a metaphor referring to a severe test of a person's or people's true character and competence; Woodrow Wilson breathed colloquial life into the expression in 1918, giving it a popularity that had not faded when **acid** took on its new 1960s meaning.

In 1965, Ken Kesey and friends—the Merry Pranksters—staged three events in the San Francisco area which they called **acid tests**—the first in Soquel, and later efforts in San Jose and Muir Beach. The Merry Prankster brand of an **acid test** was a sensory experience designed to enhance the effects of LSD. If one could survive an entire night that alternated between the intensely interesting and the intensely boring, one passed the **acid test.**

Enough **acid.** The experience when under the influence of LSD was most commonly known as a **trip**, a word which came into the popular vocabulary in 1966. Norman Mailer, an unlikely source for the coining of drug slang, is credited by the *Oxford English Dictionary* with the first recorded use of **trip** in a drug sense. In an essay written between 1952 and 1954 and published in *Advertisements for Myself* in 1959, Mailer wrote of his drug use at the time that he was writing *The Deer Park*— amphetamines, barbiturates, marijuana, and mescaline:

A few weeks later we came back to the city, and I took some mescaline. Maybe one dies a little with the poison of mescaline in the blood. At the end of a long and private trip which no quick remarks should try to describe, the book of The Deer Park *floated into mind, and I sat up, reached through a pleasure garden of velveted light to find the tree of a pencil and the bed of a notebook and brought them to union together.*

Peter Tamony argued in "Tripping Out From San Francisco" in *American Speech*, Volume 56 (1981), that the first use of **trip** in reference to drugs was two years earlier than Mailer, in *The Connection*, a play by Jack Gelber that was copyrighted in 1957, staged in New York in 1959, and published by Grove Press in 1960. Gelber used **trip** twice in that play. "Steady boys, we have a long **trip**. Our other actors are off in the real world procuring heroin," says Jim Dunn, the producer of the play-within-a-play, and then, a few lines later—"All right, junkies. During our **trip** we will incorporate an allied art—the motion picture." Tamony theorized that Gelber used **trip** in this sense as an outgrowth of prison language, citing a 1962 California prison glossary that defined **trip** as "fantasy, daydream, fable, factual or fictional." My sense is that Tamony jumped the gun on Gelber and **trip.** In a March 24, 1966, note to *San Francisco Chronicle* jazz critic Ralph Gleason, Tamony confessed his own reservations with respect to Gelber and **trip:**

> *Do you recall when to take a trip began to come in? Seems to me that it was used in connection with H in the middle or earlier 1950s. Attached is the earliest printed example—from* The Connection. *This is not directly "out-and-out" but points to an understood colloquial usage.*

Tamony was thus himself equivocal. His theory of **trip** coming from prison argot is undermined by the common uses of **trip** in prison speech. **Trip** was commonly used in pre-1960 prison argot to refer to an arrest (especially a third arrest and conviction) or a transfer from one prison to another; both these meanings are more commanding than the daydream sense reported in one glossary. Lastly, as Jonathan Lighter pointed out in a letter on the subject, the uses of **trip** in *The Connection* are hardly clear evidence that the "drug fantasy sense was familiar to Gelber in 1957." With the first **trip,** Lighter argues, Gelber may "simply be speaking figuratively"; although the second **trip** "does begin to sound more like

recent usage," Lighter wrote, "as it merely adverts to the first trip …it is not very good evidence either."

If Gelber's *Connection* **trip** is discounted, one is left with Mailer's coining, which has a sound more of a literary metaphor than of slang. Travel metaphors abound in the early literature of mind-altering drugs, beginning with Aldous Huxley in the 1930s. Huxley was as eloquent a spokesman as a mind-altering drug could want. In *Brave New World* (1932), Huxley invented the "euphoric, narcotic, pleasantly hallucinant" drug *soma.* Huxley used "holiday" for what we would later know was a **trip,** in contexts that would later be familiar to **trip:**

> *Take a holiday from reality whenever you like, and come back without so much as a headache or a mythology ….*
>
> *… the infinitely friendly world of soma-holiday ….*
>
> *… taking holiday after holiday, without ever having to come back to a headache or a fit of vomiting, without ever being made to feel as you always felt after peyotl. … Soma never played any of these unpleasant tricks. The holiday it gave was perfect … Linda, his M–, remains permanently on holiday.*
>
> *And if ever, by some unlucky*

chance, anything unpleasant should somehow happen, why, there's always soma to give you a holiday from the facts.

Huxley got real about hallucinatory drugs in *The Doors of Perception* and *Heaven and Hell* (1954, 1956), describing his experiences with mescaline and discussing the use of LSD, which he referred to as lysergic-acid. In both books, Huxley used the standard English term **experience,** writing of "the mescaline experience," "the typical mescaline experience," and "mescaline or lysergic-acid experience." Huxley's choice of **experience** would be echoed in the late 1960s by Jimi Hendrix, whose rhetorical "Are you experienced?" gave a new slang spin to **experience.**

Returning to early travel metaphors, one finds the use of "journey" in the title given a radio and television program on LSD aired by the University of California on October 19, 1958. In late 1959 and early 1960, soon-to-be famous health food advocate Adelle Davis took LSD several times under the supervision of psychotherapists, and writing under the name of "Jane Dunlap" in *Exploring Inner Space: Personal Experiences Under LSD-25* (New York: Harcourt, Brace and World, 1961), Davis was lavish in her praise for the drug. Davis relied most heavily on a curtain metaphor (lifting the curtain, dropping the curtain, behind the curtain, pulling back the curtain), but she did write that using LSD was "the best traveling I've ever done, and certainly the cheapest." In a private note to a friend in the early 1960s, Davis lapsed into colloquial speech if not slang, saying that she was then "going on" mushrooms, which she found "the best ever …marvelous."

Similarly, in *Myself and I* (New York: Coward-McCann, 1962), Constance Newland (another *nom de plume*) touched lightly on the voyage image, writing of her "travels and travails under LSD therapy." A number of travel metaphors may be found in *LSD: The Consciousness-Expanding Drug,* edited by David Solomon (New York: Putnam, 1964). An article by Dan Wakefield about Timothy Leary's early use of LSD uses "flight,""voyage," and "journey." In an article that originally appeared in *Playboy* in 1963, Alan Harrington wrote of an "LSD voyage" and an "LSD journey" before hitting pay dirt:

*You may be able to take off on other, much more easy, inward journeys. Unlike the first **trip**, these can be programmed to orbit you around a given life problem.*

As LSD moved from psychiatric and medicinal to nonmedicinal experiments, and finally to

agent of inebriation, the literary tone of **trip** began to take on a slangy air. Yet, no newspaper article about LSD before 1966 used **trip,** a fact which further suggests that Mailer's use may have been literary metaphor, not drug slang. All that said, there is a slightly earlier recorded use of the adjective **trippy,** and one would think that where there's **trippy,** there's a **trip.** On September 25, 1965, the *San Francisco Chronicle* reported the closing of the Blue Unicorn, a Beat intellectual coffee house. Quoting a Blue Unicorn customer, the *Chronicle* used **trippy,** explaining, "that means good, great."

In January 1966, San Francisco saw the Trips Festival, a spiritual descendant of Kesey's **acid tests,** produced by Stewart Brand and others at the Longshoreman's Hall; the ephemera from and newspaper articles describing the Trips Festival provide the first recorded, clearly LSD-related uses of **trip.**

With the gates breached, the mainstream media quickly picked up **trip,** and it is found in newspaper and periodical sources regularly starting in February 1966. Even with widespread media use of **trip,** it did not reach all quarters, even in San Francisco. In an April 12, 1967 article in the *Chronicle* ("Kesey Gives Judge the Word") about Ken Kesey's trial for mari-

juana possession, one finds this interchange between Kesey and the judge:

Judge Karesh then asked the much-traveled defendant to teach him what the word "trip" really meant. Kesey said it was a happening "out of the ordinary" when induced by a psychedelic drug (such as LSD or mescaline).

Despite its roots in LSD usage, **trip** soon branched out into general purpose hippie use, meaning an obsession, an interest, an attitude, state of mind, or a catchall explanation of odd behavior— "That's his trip, man."

He or she who used LSD? Most commonly, the LSD-user was known as a **head.** Standing alone, **head** first appears in 1952, applied to marijuana smokers, in *H is for Heroin* (New York: Doubleday, 1952) by David Hulburd ("But some were **heads**—you know, blowing up a joint, that means smoking those cigarettes") and in *Time* on July 7, 1952. ("Being a 'head,' Marti feels, is being part of a whole new culture.…There are lots of blowing cats [musicians] who have been smoking for years.") In a more general sense, meaning a drug addict, **head** is found in a glossary in *The Traffic in Narcotics* by H. J. Anslinger and William F. Tompkins (New York: Funk and Wagnalls, 1953).

The stand-alone **head** soon

produced a number of combinations—**pothead** (1959), **marijuana head** (1959), and **acidhead** (1966). In fact, the combination was an earlier form than the stand-alone, for that prolific early-20th-century slangster Thomas "TAD" Dorgan used **hophead** on February 24, 1901; **dopehead** (1903), **cokehead** (1927), **lushhead** (1938), and **juicehead** (1955) all followed. In the ebb and flow of slang, the combination **acidhead** proved too cumbersome and the "acid" was dropped, leaving **head** as a clearly understood slang term for an LSD-using hippie.

In this sense, **head** was roughly akin to **freak;** like **freak, head** soon left the confines of LSD usage and, joined with defining nouns, it came to mean a devotee. New combinations abounded—**stamp-head** (1969), **film-head** (1970), **chili-head** (1975), **food-head** (1976), **vodka-head** (1978), **flower-head** (1993), **java-head** (1995), and **dish-head** (1997) are only a few of the many spawnings.

In a hopelessly unlinear fashion, **head** as devotee had some earlier usage. The most noted example is by Lord Buckley, a tremendously important conduit of jive from the 1920s to the 1960s. In his 1960 *Hiparama of the Classics*, which was transcribed from earlier recordings, Buckley wrote of "Reed Heads,

the Lute Heads, and the Flute Heads."

WORD HISTORIES

COKE, DOPE, HORSE, JUNK

COKE AS A CLIPPED and then slightly corrupted *cocaine* is first found in the Supplement to the Funk and Wagnalls *Standard Dictionary* in 1903, which identified **coke** as slang from the southern United States. Ten years later, **coke** began to appear in earnest. As a side story, **coke** for cocaine appeared six years before the first recording of **Coke** as a clipped *Coca-Cola;* the earliest recorded use of **Coke** for Coca-Cola was, according to the *Dictionary of Americanisms* (1951), on November 17, 1909, in a trade publication, the *Coca-Cola Bottler*. The Coca-Cola Company has fought hard and long to protect its name, including the term **Coke.** Coca-Cola began to use **Coke** in its advertisements on January 10, 1942, in the *Saturday Evening Post*, explaining that **Coke** was "the friendly abbreviation for the trademark Coca-Cola." **Coke** remains a closely protected trade name—if a customer asks for a **Coke** and the vendor does not sell Coca-Cola, the vendor must tell the customer and obtain the customer's consent for a substitution.

Like **coke, dope** has several meanings, one involving the

soda fountain. **Dope** came from the Dutch *doop* for sauce, and it originally (1807) meant a thick liquid sauce or a gravy. From sauce, **dope** went to mean a preparation of opium (December 24, 1872, in the *Chicago Tribune)*, and from there it ventured into the broader field, signifying drugs in general. After a detour into horse racing, **dope** came to mean a thick, sweet syrup (1904), and then a sweet, carbonated drink (1914). Like **coke,** then, **dope** could mean either a drug or a soft drink.

Junk as a slang synonym for heroin came onto the scene in the July 5, 1924 issue of *Liberty,* and on August 8, 1925 in *Colliers: The National Weekly*, from which we learned that **junk** is any kind of narcotic drug. An earlier use is likely, for one finds **junk** defined simply as "drugs" in "A Prison Dictionary (Expurgated)" by Hi Simons. Although the Simons word list was not published until October 1933 *(American Speech*, Vol. 8), it was compiled by Simons while he was incarcerated at the Fort Leavenworth military prison during World War I. In *The Trail of the Poppy* (1966), Charles Siragusa suggested that **junk** originally applied to opium, that opium was largely smoked by Chinese, and that the Chinese who sold the opium often used **junk** boats. Richard Lingeman wrote in *Drugs from A to Z: A Dictionary* that **junk** came from

junker, a peddler, or perhaps it came from the fact that heroin was considered inferior to opium—nothing but **junk.** With the drug itself **junk,** the user was a **junker,** then a **junkhog,** and then finally a **junkie.**

Horse came to mean heroin in the 1950s. Although the usual sources all cite a *Time* magazine article of August 28, 1950, as the

Why **horse?** Partridge and his cohort Ramsey Spencer theorized that **horse** came about because heroin has "more kick than the softer drugs." With all due respect to the great slang lexicographer, this is not particularly convincing. Richard Lingeman's suggestion that **horse** is drawn from "the initial *h* sound" is a bit timid. The most plausible explanation is from the world of

dreaded opium derivative is a powerful stimulant of horses."

MARIJUANA WORD HISTORIES

WEED, TEA, REEFER, GRASS, POT, AND JOINT

JUST AS THE ROMAN Army dedicated considerable resources to the construction of roads (the

Reefer showed up on Broadway the next year....

first recorded use of **horse** as heroin, Richard R. Lingeman wrote that **horse** had been used "since around 1940," while Eric Partridge dated **horse** to *circa* 1945.

horse racing. Articulated by Tom Ainslie in *Ainslie's Complete Guide to Thoroughbred Racing* (1968), it is as follows: "Heroin is known as 'horse' because trainers used to dose race-horses with it. The

better to conquer you with), so too does a drug subculture dedicate resources to constructing a slang vocabulary to describe all aspects of drug use.

With the first wave of the

marijuana epidemic came the first wave of slang terms to describe marijuana, all of which were in place well before the hippies of the 1960s discovered the joys of marijuana and marijuana slang. First out of the chute was **weed,** which can be found in the *Chicago Tribune* of July 1, 1928, in an article about jazz and the tendency to "emit sour notes after smoking **weed.**" In using

weed, marijuana users turned to a venerable piece of slang, for according to William Craigie's *Dictionary of American English*, **weed** (usually **the weed**) had been used to mean tobacco since 1606, with a strong series of cited American use in the 19th century.

Arriving at roughly the same time was **tea,** found on the scene by Ernest Abel at least as early as 1930 with the song "Tee Roller's Rub," recorded by one Freddie Nicholson. In "Marihuana as a Developer of Criminals" by E. Stanley in the *American Journal of Police Science* (1931), we learned of one possible etymology—**tea** "is the cheapest and weakest of all the preparations of hashish and is taken as 'tea.'" And when Benny Goodman recorded "Texas Tea Party" in 1933, he was not talking about Earl Grey or Darjeeling. **Tea** really came into its own in the late 1930s and 1940s, with its outgrowth of **tea pad** (1938), **tea hound** (1942), **tead up** (1944), **tea party** (1945), and **tea head** (1948).

Reefer, the most common slang term for marijuana in the initial wave of marijuana use of the 1930s, also made its first appearance in a popular song, "Reefer Man," recorded by Don Redman in 1931:

Have you ever met that funny reefer man?
Have you ever met that funny reefer man?
If says he's goin' to China
Or to sell you South Carolina
Then you know you're talking
To that funny reefer man.

Have you ever met that funny reefer man?
Have you ever met that funny reefer man?

If he trades you dimes for nickels
And calls watermelons pickles
Then you know you're talking
To that funny reefer man.

Have you ever met that funny reefer man?
Have you ever met that funny reefer man?
If you hear him slip and jiggle
And he starts to squirm and wiggle
Ha, ha—that's that dog,
That's that reefer man.

The song was also recorded by Harlan Lattimore and his Connie Inn Orchestra, Baron Lee and his Blue Rhythm Band, and Cab Calloway and His Orchestra: The Missourians. **Reefer** showed up on Broadway the next year in the song "Smokin' Reefers" in the 1932 show *Flying Colors*, and from there there was no turning back.

There are two major theories on the etymology of **reefer** and several esoteric ones. The most commonly accepted conjecture is that **reefer** was Anglicized from the Spanish *grifa* (variously spelled *greefa, greefo, grefa, greifo, grifa, grieffa,* and *grifo*), used by Mexicans in America to refer to marijuana, which was often described in hyperbolic terms as a "poisonous Mexican weed." The Spanish word appeared on the scene in the Southwest at roughly the same time that **reefer** did, leading to speculation that **reefer** sprang from the Mexican slang.

The second significant theory was articulated by David Maurer, the eminent lexicographer of American underworld slang, in correspondence dated February 7, 1944. Pointing to the earlier use of **twist** as slang for a marijuana cigarette from the association of rolling the loose marijuana into a cigarette, Maurer wrote that it "would be natural to select *reef* meaning to roll (or roll up)."

Maurer was quick to avoid certainty in this etymology, writing that it was "entirely speculative on my part and I can give no philological guarantee." Had Maurer taken things a step further, he would have come tantalizingly near to a complete circle, for the root of *grifa* in Spanish is the verb *engrifarse*, which means to twist or to kink. From the Spanish "to twist" came the Spanish for marijuana cigarette, and from the English "to twist" came the English for marijuana cigarette. Too neat a package? Perhaps.

Esoteric theories include Peter Tamony's private musings about **reefer** as a refrigerator in 1933 ("Are 'reefers' so called because crimes involving bloodshed are so 'cold blooded' when committed under the influence of mari-

juana? Reefers are said to 'coldcock' smokers—they remember nothing after the effects wear off"), and the implausible explanation offered by Arthur "Bugs" Baer in his "One Word Led To Another" column published in the *San Francisco Examiner* on March 28, 1945:

The word reefer was originally griefer. It stems from the southwest near the Merry Anna fields. They called it griefer because anybody contemplating rough action stoked up on the dizzy salad. And it always brought him grief.

Richard Spears claims in his *Slang and Jargon of Drugs and Drink* that there is a 1938 use of **grass,** but he gives no citation. Without a 1938 citation, the familiar references all acknowledge an article in *Time* on July 19, 1943 as the first written use of **grass.** Use of the term soared in the 1950s, and **grass** was probably the most commonly used slang synonym for marijuana during the 1960s. The term was probably coined in deference to the greenish appearance of marijuana prepared for smoking; the suggestion that **grass** was "a *calque* [loan translation] of the semantic range of *hashish* ... (literally grass)" is found in *Notes and Queries* (January 1974, New Series, Vol. 21, No. 1).

Pot, the slang word of choice

for marijuana in the 1950s, was first recorded in the pages of— yes—*Time* on June 13, 1951. While the first recorded use is not in dispute, explanations of its etymology abound. David Maurer first believed that **pot** came from the Portuguese *potaguaya*, used to describe marijuana pods after the leaves had been removed. Maurer eventually changed his mind, and in a "deluxe version" of his etymology of **pot** contained in a July 3, 1972, letter to Philip Gove of Merriam-Webster, he wrote of his work in the Lecumberría Prison outside of Mexico City, where he

encountered the technique among old-timers of collecting the ripe seed-pods from the female cannibis indica and stuffing them into a bottle, which was then filled with wine or pulque or other alcoholic drink and allowed to stand for a couple of weeks or more while the gum dissolved, after which the liquid was sipped. ... The drink was called potiguaya, an old caló word, also used to indicate very strong marijuana, and sometimes shortened to pot. Potiguaya, I assume, is a normally telescoped word made from potación de guaya— drink of grief.

Ernest Abel discounted even the Mexican connection, arguing that had "pot originated from the

Mexican it would have appeared during the 1920s or 1930s, along with words such as *griefa* and *muta*."

Several have theorized that **pot** derived from the association with **tea.** For example, in the article "Life and Love Among the Beatniks" in the *San Francisco Chronicle* on June 15, 1958, Allen Brown explained that **tea** led to puns on **teapot,** which was then shortened to simply **pot.** I've got the **tea,** who has the **pot?**

Robert S. Gold, whose *Jazz Lexicon* (New York: Knopf, 1964) is usually a startlingly reliable and clear source for understanding slang, was a bit whimsical when it came to **pot,** suggesting that it was possibly "because [it was] frequently grown in windowsill flower pots." *Playboy's Book of Forbidden Words* (Chicago: Playboy Press, 1972) contains two possible explanations, neither of which has been widely accepted—"probably from the southern use of *pot* to mean bootleg whiskey made at home" (a claim not particularly well supported by word lists from the South), or from *shitpot,* with the recognition that *shit* was used to described marijuana, as well as other drugs.

Merriam-Webster's files contain a number of letters suggesting other etymologies for **pot.** Theories in these letters include the following:

Opium users referred to

opium as "pot." Very likely the term was retained when the intoxicant was changed. (Harry George Parke, November 28, 1973)

Negroes did often speak of a "smoking pot," referring probably to the big, black tripod-based iron pots they used out of doors to do laundry in. To me, it's an obvious etymology. (Mrs. J. R. McDavid, January 8, 1974)

A person smoking marijuana took a puff of smoke into his mouth, blew it out into a "pot" formed of his cupped hands, then reinhaled the smoke from the pot through his nose and into his lungs. Eventually, the term for the cupped hands became the term for the marijuana itself. (Arthur Widder, November 29, 1973)

Another obviously apocryphal derivation was printed in the syndicated "Glad You Asked That!" column by Hy Gardner on December 24, 1970: "A group of jazz musicians had dinner at the home of a socialite jazz buff. For dessert, she served rum cakes in small crockery pots. A guitarist dug a small hole in one side of the pot and another across from it, then inserted a marijuana cigarette in one hole—turned the pot around and drew smoke into his lungs."

Time was also first to record

joint as a marijuana cigarette. **Joint** had been used by opium smokers in the 19th century to refer to what the mainstream press called an **opium den,** and drug addicts in the 1930s used **joint** to refer to a hypodermic needle, but on June 9, 1952, it made the leap to marijuana:

From Jocelyn, a 19-year old senior, Amy learned to play hooky when high school opened; she also learned that "blowing up a joint" means smoking marijuana.

From its birth with Amy and Jocelyn, **joint** quickly joined the ranks of major drug slang, and it is still the preferred slang to describe a marijuana cigarette almost 50 years later.

WORD HISTORIES

JONES AND COLD TURKEY

ONE OF THE MOST common surnames in American English, Jones, has in its spare time developed two drug-related slang meanings. In 1962, David Maurer picked up **jones** meaning a drug habit. In this sense, it can stand alone, or it can be modified by the drug to which the user is addicted, as in a **scag jones** (the *New York Times Magazine,* December 16, 1973) or a **heroin jones** (*Newsweek,* February 7, 1977).

Three years later, Claude Brown in *Manchild in the Promised Land* (1965) used **jones** in a slightly different sense, as a collective noun describing the horrible symptoms associated with withdrawal from heroin addiction.

Jones first appeared in black vernacular English, but its semantic roots have never been definitively identified. It is on its face a personification, and it is used in a personal sense, as shown in this article from the *San Francisco Examiner* of July 5, 1971:

> *"If I could get my kids back, I would stop taking heroin."*
> *But Sue makes that pledge frequently—whenever, as she says, "jones isn't coming down," an expression that means she needs a fix.*
> *And heroin is easy to buy in her neighborhood when Jones does come down.*

Jones as personified here is clearly not a friend; pure speculation and conjecture suggest that **Mr. Jones** somewhere became the moral equivalent of **The Man,** and that drug addiction was seen as an oppression roughly equivalent to blatant racial oppression.

As is the case with many drug slang terms, **jones** soon left the ghetto of drug users and came to mean any sort of habit or strong need. An example of the new

jones, which Jonathan Lighter found first recorded in 1970, is found in the November 1973 issue of *Ms.* magazine; in an article about rock singer Janis Joplin, David Getz and Susan Lydon wrote that Joplin had "a Jones for love and reinforcement as strong as her physical craving for smack

or alcohol." Popular culture historian John Pontell uncovered 16 songs with the titles "Love Jones" in the 1970s and 1980s, beginning with a version written and performed by The Brighter Side of Darkness (who?) in 1972. Pontell was not at all convinced that he had found all possible

"Love Jones," but he found eight songs with the title "Mr. Jones," not to mention "Don't Jones Me" by Neil Haggerty, "I've Got A Jones on You Baby" by J. Simon, "Basketball Jones" by Cheech and Chong, "Don't Let the Joneses Get You Down" by the Temptations, "Jones Crusher" by Frank Zappa,

and "Janie Jones" by The Clash. As Pontell has found, **jones** has turned into a verb of sorts, with the craving person said to be **jonesing** for the object craved; a young man in a monogamous relationship might quip to a buddy, "I'm **jonesing** for some strange," suggesting that a change of partners might be welcome.

Although **jones** is sometimes used to describe the symptoms experienced as a result of the sudden withdrawal of an addictive drug, the most common expression is **cold turkey**, which is also used to described the

actual sudden withdrawal. The expression first appears in the *Daily Colonist* in British Columbia on October 13, 1921: "Perhaps the most pitiful figures who have appeared before Dr. Carleton Simon ... are those who voluntarily surrender themselves. When they go before him, they

are given what is called the 'cold turkey' treatment."

Several theories on the expression's etymology assume that it first arose in the context of drug addiction. The dominant theory in that vein was repeated by Herb Caen of the *San Francisco Examiner and Chronicle* in his column of May 28, 1978: "It derives from the hideous combination of goosepimples and what William Burroughs calls 'the cold burn' that addicts suffer as they kick the habit." Tom Philbin in *Cop Lingo* recites a second theory, that "the term may derive from the cold, clammy feel of the skin

during withdrawal, like a turkey that has been refrigerated."

The problem with both these theories is that they ignore the uses of **cold turkey** before its application to drug addiction. In a cartoon that appeared in newspapers on November 12, 1920, ace slangman Thomas "TAD" Dorgan used **cold turkey**—"Now tell me on the square—can I get by with this for the wedding—don't string me—tell me **cold turkey.**" Jonathan Lighter found an even earlier citation in the *Historical Dictionary of American Slang*: a 1910 usage where the speaker lost $5,000 "cold turkey," thus in the sense of "outright." As we learned a little later in the *London Daily Express* of January 4, 1928, "'Cold turkey' means plain truth in America." Even earlier than these **cold turkeys** is **talk turkey**, to speak frankly and without reserve, found in *Dialect Notes* in 1903.

Given the earlier, pre-drug uses of **turkey** and **cold turkey** with meanings of "direct," "frank," and "outright," it is hardly surprising that the direct and outright cessation of drug use might be called **cold turkey**. Like **jones, cold turkey** soon left the confines of drug addiction and came to be used in a jocular sense in any number of contexts suggesting a habit— "I went cold turkey off of cigarettes" or "He went cold turkey on watching football after she threw that huge fit." **Cold turkey** is still understood in its original drug addiction sense, but any association with "direct," "frank," and "outright" (the pre-drug meanings) is all but lost.

SOURCES AND REFERENCES

IN MY YOUTH, drug use was a fact of life for many young Americans, and drug slang was a fact of language. Since 1986, in my real-life day job as a lawyer I have spent an inordinate amount of time battling random urine testing in the workplace; in the course of fighting urine testing, I regularly come into contact with drug slang. Dr. Vina Spiehler, Dr. Martha Harkey, Dr. Gary Henderson, Stuart Lake, Jim Crotty, and Jon Neary all helped with the vocabulary of drug use.

For an overview of the history of drug use in America, I have relied on *Hep-Cats, Narcs and Pipe Dreams: A History of America's Romance with Illegal Drugs* by Jill Jonnes (New York: Scribner, 1996) and to a lesser extent *The Barbary Coast: An Informal History of the San Francisco Underworld* by Herbert Asbury (Garden City, N.Y.: Garden City, 1933).

I began my work in written references with the literature of drugs and drug abuse, rather than the slang of drugs. The works which I consulted were *Isd* by Richard Alpert and Sidney

Cohen (New York: New American Library, 1966); *The Traffic in Narcotics* by H. F. Anslinger and William Tompkins (New York: Funk and Wagnalls, 1953); *Cocaine: Its History, Uses and Effects* by Richard Asley (New York: Warner, 1975, 1976); *Kids and Drugs* by Jason D. Baron (New York: Perigree, 1981, 1983); *Marijuana* by E. R. Bloomquist, M.D. (Beverly Hills: Glencoe, 1968); *Marijuana: The Second Trip,* Revised Edition, by Edward R. Bloomquist, M.D. (Beverly Hills: Glencoe, 1971); *Vice Exposures* by Virginia Hudson Brightman (New York: Better, 1930); *Junkie* by William Burroughs (New York: Ace, 1953); *The College Drug Scene* by James T. Carey (Englewood Cliffs, N.J.: Prentice-Hall, 1968); *Methaqualone: The Quest for Oblivion* by Marilyn Carroll and Gary Gallo (London: Burke, 1985); *Employee Drug Abuse: A Manager's Guide for Action* by Carl D. Chambers and Richard D. Heckman (Boston: Cahners, 1972); *Crack: What You Should Know About the Cocaine Epidemic* by Calun Chatlos (New York: Perigree, 1987); *The Drug Dilemma* by Sidney Cohen, M.D. (New York: McGraw-Hill, 1969); *The Scene* by Clarence L. Cooper, Jr. (Greenwich, Conn.: Fawcett, 1960); *Addicts Who Survived* by David Courtwright, Herman Joseph, and Don des Jarlais (Knoxville: University of Tennessee Press, 1989); *Kick Heroin*

by Liz Cutland (London: *Sky,* 1985); *The Golden Spike* by Hal Ellson (New York: Ballantine, 1952); *Ecstasy: The MDMA Story* by Bruce Eisner (Berkeley: Ronin, 1989); *Portraits from a Shooting Gallery: Life Styles from the Drug Addict World* by Seymour Fiddle (New York: Harper and Row, 1967); *Drugs and the Young* by John Garabedian (New York: Tower, 1970); *The Coke Book: The Complete Reference to the Uses and Abuses of Cocaine* by R. C. Garrett, U. G. Waldmeyer, and Vivienne Sernaque (New York: Berkley, 1984); *800-Cocaine* by Mark S. Gold (New York: Bantam, 1984); *What You Should Know About Drugs* by Dr. Charles W. Gorodetzky and Dr. Samuel T. Christian (New York: Harcourt, Brace and Jovanovich, 1970); *Barbiturates: Sleeping Potion or Intoxicant* by Jack E. Henningfield (London: Burke, 1986); *Drug Awareness,* edited by Richard E. Horman and Allan M. Fox (New York: Discus, 1970); *Drugs: Facts on Their Use and Abuse* by Norman W. Houser (Scott, Foresman, 1969); *Marijuana: Time for a Closer Look* by Curtis L. Janeczek (Columbus, Ohio: Healthstar, 1980, 1981); *Minute Police Talks* by Captain Thomas S. J. Kavanagh (Boston: Williams Book Store, 1938); *PCP: The Devil's Dust* by Ronald L. Linder, Steven E. Lerner, and R. Stanley Burns (Belmont, Calif.: Wadsworth, 1981); *Nightmare Drugs* by Donald

Louria, M.D. (New York: Pocket, 1966); *The Drug Scene* by Donald B. Louria, M.D. (New York: Corgi, 1968, 1971); *Boom! Talkin' About Our Generation* by Joel Makower (Chicago, Contemporary, 1985); *Narcotics and Narcotic Addiction, Fourth Edition*, by David W. Maurer and Victor H. Vogel (Springfield, Ill.: Charles C. Thomas, 1954, 1973); *Understanding the Weed* by Michael Keith McBride (Matteson, Ill.: Greatlakes Living, 1977); *High on the Campus: Student Drug Abuse—Is There an Answer?* by Gordon R. McLean and Haskell Bowen (Wheaton, Ill.: Tyndale House, 1970); *Keep Off the Grass: A Scientific Enquiry into the Biological Effects of Marijuana* by Gabriel G. Nahas (Oxford: Pergamon, 1979); *Ecstasy: The Clinical, Pharmacological and Neurotoxological Effects of the Drug MDMA,* edited by Stephen J. Peroutka (Boston: Kluwer Academic, 1990); *Cocaine: The Mystique and the Reality* by Joel L. Phillips and Ronald D. Wynne (New York: Avon, 1980); *Marihuana: Myths and Realities,* edited by J. L. Simmons, Ph.D. (North Hollywood: Brandon House, 1967); *The White Stuff: The Bottom Line on Cocaine* by B. J. Plaskett and Ed Quillen (New York: Dell, 1985); *Pimp: The Story of My Life* by Ice Slim (Edinburgh: Payback, 1967, 1996); *Pot: A Handbook of Marijuana* by John Rosevear (New York: University, 1967); *Snowblind: A Brief Career

in the Cocaine Trade* by Robert Sabbag (New York: Vintage, 1976, 1990); *The Trail of the Poppy* by Charles Tiragusa (Englewood Cliffs, N.J.: Prentice-Hall, 1966); *Barbiturates: Their Use, Misuse and Abuse* by David E. Smith and Donald R. Wesson (New York: Human Sciences, 1977); *The Marihuana Papers,* edited by David Solomon (New York: New American Library, 1966); *Close Pursuit* by Carsten Stroud (New York: Bantam, 1987); *What Works: Workplaces Without Drugs* (Washington, D.C.: U.S. Department of Labor, n.d.); *Marihuana: America's New Drug Problem* by Robert P. Walton (Philadelphia: Lippincott, 1938); *The Drug Scene: Help or Hang-up?* by Walter L. Way, M.D. (Englewood Cliffs, N.J.: Prentice-Hall, 1970, 1977); *Chocolate to Morphine: Understanding Mind-Active Drugs* by Andrew Weil and Winifred Rosen (Boston: Houghton-Mifflin, 1983); *Use and Misuse of Drugs Subject to Abuse* by Melvin H. Weinswig (New York: Pegasus, 1973); *Narcotics and Hallucinogens—A Handbook,* Revised Edition, edited by John B. Williams (Beverly Hills: Glencoe, 1963, 1967); *Crackhouse: Notes from the End of the Line* by Terry Williams (Reading, Mass.: Addison-Wesley, 1992); and *Youth and Drugs: Prevention, Detection and Cure* by Dr. Francis H. Wise (New York: Association, 1971).

Industry and government materials which I consulted include *The Marihuana Problem in the City of New York* by the Mayor's Committee on Marihuana (1939); "The Slang of Drug Addicts" within the unpublished *Lexicon of the Trades Jargon* by the Federal Writers' Project (1939); *The Narcotic Problem: A Brief Study* by the Bureau of Narcotic Enforcement, State of California, Department of Justice (no date, early 1960s); *Men and Chemical Comforts* (Toronto: Alcoholism and Drug Addiction Research Foundation,1964); *Drug Abuse: Escape to Nowhere* (Philadelphia: Smith, Kline and French, 1967); *Stimulants: Some Questions and Answers* and *Sedatives: Some Questions and Answers* (Washington, D.C.: U.S. Department of Health, Education and Welfare, 1970); "Expressions Used with Dangerous Drugs" in the *Congressional Record* (May 6, 1970); a *Glossary of Drug Terms,* published by the National Institute on Drug Abuse (1979); a *Glossary of Drugs and Drug Language* published by the Sacramento Municipal Utility District (1986); *Guide to Abused Drugs,* published by Abbott Diagnostics (October 1993); *Street Terms: Drugs and the Drug Trade,* published by the Drugs and Crime Data Center and Clearinghouse, United States Department of Justice (October 1994; regularly updated electronically); NARCANON's *Glossary of Drug Terms* (1996); a *Narcotics Identification Guide* published by the Amsterdam Company (no date); and *McGruff's Guide to Drugs* (no date).

And then there were the newspaper and magazine articles. The following are the most important of the many articles that I drew upon, most of which I found in the Tamony Collection at the University of Missouri: "What Shall They Do to Be Saved" in *Harper's* (August 1867); "San Francisco Opium Joints" in the *Review of Reviews* (June 1892); "The Raw Opium Industry in America" by C. F. Holder in *Scientific American* (1898); "The Warfare Against Opium-Smoking in America" in *Outdoor* (February 6, 1909); "Words Used in the Drug Traffic" by Whitney Hasting Wells in *Dialect Notes,* Vol. 5, Part 5 (1922); "Drug Addict's Cant" by Whitney Hastings Wells in *Dialect Notes,* Vol. 5, Part 6 (1923); "Girl Addict, 22, Defies Cure" in the *San Francisco Call* (April 28, 1930); "Junk Jungles: The First Hand Story of the City's Drug Traffic" by Edward McQuade in the *San Francisco News* (May 9, 1932); "Addenda to Junker Lingo" by Victor Folke Nelson in *American Speech,* Vol. 8 (October 1933); "Facts and Fancies About Marihuana" in the *Literary Digest* (October 24, 1936); "Shocking New Menace to Nation's Youth"

in the *San Francisco Chronicle* (January 24, 1937); "Reefers" Jam-Jive Hotters, U.S. Judge Told" in the *San Francisco Call-Bulletin* (November 10, 1939); "Sailor Held in Reefer Riot" in the *San Francisco Examiner* (January 11, 1943); "The Weed" in *Time* (July 19, 1943); "Cons Get High on Benzedrine" in the *News* (March 22, 1946); "Benzedrine for Barbiturates" in *Time* (July 1, 1946); "Reefer Ring" in *Time* (October 14, 1946); "The Coca Leaf Chewer" in the *Examiner* (September 26, 1947); "Pair Trapped Smoking Reefers With Actress" in the *News* (September 1, 1948); "Ballet Ballads" in *Life* (June 7, 1948); "Opium Argot: New Orleans 1887" by R. M. Lumiansky in *American Speech,* Vol. 23 (October and December 1948); "Farewell to Benzedrine Benders" by Hannah Lees in *Colliers* (August 13, 1949); "This Dark Evil" in the *Chronicle* (February 19, 1950); "Reefers for Sale: The Story of a T-Man" as told to Warren Gardner in *Our World* (September 1950); "Teen-Age Hophead Jargon" by William C. de Lannoy and Elizabeth Masterson in *American Speech,* Vol. 27 (February 1952); "Coca"in *Life* (May 19, 1952); "Useful Drug Can Be Dangerous" by W. W. Bauer, M.D. in the *Examiner* (May 19, 1953); "SF Girl Tells How She Got Dope Habit" in the *Call-Bulletin* (August 18,. 1953); "Canadian Football Stars Use Bennys" in the

Call-Bulletin (February 17, 1954); "Goofballs and Bennies Mean Misery, Disgrace, Death" in the *News* (September 8, 1954); "Narcotic Argot Along the Mexican Border" by Haldeen Braddy in *American Speech,* Vol. 30 (May 1955); "Hint Reds Back Big Dope Ring in Peru" in the *Call-Bulletin* (August 10, 1955); "Pearl Blames Pill for TV Hi-Jinks" in the *Examiner* (March 18, 1957); "Pep Pill for Pearl—TV Blues" in the *Chronicle* (March 18, 1957); "Milers Don't Win on Pep-Up Pills" in the *Chronicle* (June 12, 1957); "U.S. Olympians to Disqualify all Pep Pill Users" in the *Chronicle* (December 4, 1957); "Blame Pep Pill for Death of S.F. Woman" in the *Call-Bulletin* (April 10, 1958); "Four Face Court on Pep Pills" in the *Examiner* (April 21, 1958); "Life and Love Among the Beatniks"by Allen Brown in the *Chronicle* (June 15, 1958); "No Pep Pills, Coach" in the *News* (October 25, 1958); "Pep Pills Can Help" in the *Call-Bulletin* (May 27, 1959); "Will Pep Pills Improve Athletic Performance?" in the *Examiner* (September 6, 1959); "LSD: A Cure or a New Sickness: Beware of LSD!" by Franz E. Winkler in the *Chronicle* (May 15, 1960); "Wake Up and Die—The Pep-Pill Menace" in *Today's Health* (October 1960); "Juvenile Dope Warning" in the *Examiner* (June 30, 1961); "Pep-Pill Driving: New Menace on Our Highways" in *American Weekly*

(July 30, 1961);"The New Kick" in *Time* (February 16, 1962);"State Board Hears About Glue Sniffing" in the *San Francisco News Call-Bulletin* (October 25, 1962); "Danger! A New Kids' Fad: Glue Sniffing" in *This Week* (January 20, 1963);"Hallucination Drug Research" in the *Chronicle* (July 3, 1963);"The Unhappy Story of LSD" in the *Examiner* (July 23, 1963);"The Big Switch—From Marijuana to Pep Pills" in the *News Call-Bulletin* (July 31, 1963);"Sleeping Pills, Pep Pills—Handle with Extreme Caution" in *Good Housekeeping* (September 1963);"A People Fights the Coca Habit" in the *Chronicle* (September 8, 1963); "The Toxic Side of Reality" by Merla Zellerbach in the *Chronicle* (September 27, 1963);"How to Stop Glue Jags" in the *Examiner* (October 26, 1962);"LSD Mystery in Attorney's Weird Death" in the *Chronicle* (December 29, 1963); "Morning Glory Madness" in the *Examiner* (March 13, 1964); "Morning Glory Madness" in the *Chronicle* (May 15, 1966);"The Story of Eve—A Mother on LSD" in *Life* (May 31, 1966);"Drugs and Factory Workers" in the *Chronicle* (October 11, 1966); "Drugs: The Mounting Menace of Abuse" in *Look* (August 8, 1967); "Your Health: The Drug Name Game" by Dr. L. L. Coleman in the *Examiner* (June 18, 1968);"Drugs and the Young" in *Time* (September 20, 1969);"War Vet Arrested

on Drug Charge" in the *Examiner* (March 13, 1971);"National Barbiturate Epidemic" by James A. Finetrock in the *Examiner* (November 27, 1972);"Huffing Can Be Fatal or Crippling" in the *Examiner* (November 19, 1974); "Poppers: The Pros and Cons of Amyl Nitrite" by Joseph Rochia in the *Examiner* (December 15, 1976);"Cocaine: Middle Class High" in *Time* (July 6, 1981);"Ex-Player Says NFL Covered by Cloud of Cocaine" in the *Examiner* (June 9, 1982);"Catch a Rave" by Tom McKusick in *Utne Reader* (September/October 1992);"The New View From On High" by Patrick Rogers in *Newsweek* (December 6, 1993);"A Rose by Any Other Name Would Smell as Sweet" by Ross G. Winter in *High Times* (August 1995);"Built for Speed" by Todd C. Roberts in *URB* (October 1995);"Drug Alert: Date Rape Danger" by Wendi Hale in *Sassy* (June 1996); and "Ecstasy: The New Drug of Choice" by Mark Narron in the McGill University *Daily* (August 12, 1996).

In addition to the primary materials on drugs, I turned to seven drug-specific slang dictionaries. They were the pleasant and scholarly *A Marihuana Dictionary* by Ernest L. Abel (Westport, Conn.: Greenwood, 1982); the largely derivative *Drug Abuse A-Z* by Gilda and Melvin Berger (Hillside, N.J.: Enslow, 1990); the little gem *Digging for Diamonds: A Lexicon

of Street Slang for Drugs and Sex* by Geoffrey Froner (self-published, 1989); the meticulous and sweeping *Dictionary of Street Alcohol and Drug Terms,* Fourth Edition, edited by N. Peter Johnson (Columbia, S.C. Author, 1993); the first-rate *Drugs from A to Z: A Dictionary* by Richard R. Lingeman (New York: McGraw-Hill, 1969); the quirky *Narcotics Lingo and Lore* by J. E. Schmidt (Springfield, Ill.: Charles C. Thomas, 1959); and the thorough *Slang and Jargon of Drugs and Drink* by Richard A. Spears (Metuchen, N.J.: Scarecrow, 1986). *Signs of Drug Use: An Introduction to Drug and Alcohol Vocabulary in American Sign Language* by James Woodward (Silver Springs, Md.: T.J., 1980, 1996) was a thought-provoking, admirable addition.

Jin Emerson-Cobb, a graduate student at the University of Memphis, generously shared her research into marijuana slang; her 1997 paper, *Scratching the Dragon: Marijuana-Related Terms and Attitudes* is the best drug slang field work done since David Maurer, bar none.

Lastly, I consulted *The American Thesaurus of Slang* by Lester V. Berrey and Melvin Van den Bark (New York: Thomas Y. Crowell, 1942, 1947) and *The Underground Dictionary* by Eugene E. Landy (New York: Simon and Schuster, 1971), largely for dating purposes.

Chapter Four:
HORSE RACING

I got the horse right here
The name is Paul Revere.
And here's a guy that says
If the weather's clear
Can do, Can do.
This guy says the horse can do.
—"Fugue for Tinhorns," *Guys and Dolls,* by Frank Loesser (1950)

T HEY'RE OFF! FROM HOLLYWOOD PARK TO Saratoga Springs, New York, from the Solano County Fair in Fairfield, California, to the Union County Fair in Union, Maine, horse racing is as lively, colorful and bright a spectacle as can be found in modern America. The atmosphere is electric and hopelessly attractive to the romantic sensualist—the immaculate track and looming grandstands, the glorious horses nervously snorting and prancing to the starting gate as the bugler in red jacket sounds "Boots and Saddles," the high-strung, fiercely athletic and intense jockeys in their bright-colored silks, the cigar-chomping old-timers prying secrets from the *Daily Racing Form*, handicapping in scribbled notes on the margins of the paper, their coded conversations with each other mixing with a dozen languages of immigrants drawn by the rags-to-riches/no-English-needed world of the track, the initial roar from the crowd as the race starts and then the palpable surge towards the track as the horses round the far turn and burst into the homestretch with the incantations of the announcer as he or she calls the race, the exotic horse names rolling off his tongue with excitement and irony, the roar building as the horses streak for the wire, winning betting tickets then clutched in hands raised in triumph over heads and the many more losing tickets fluttering down from loosened fingers, discarded into the sea of losing tickets and plastic beer cups that cover the ground as the horses—almost forgotten now—walk off and cool down after the race, blanketed, led back to the mysterious world of sheds and stables and barns and trailers and apartments over stables—Shed Row—with only 20 minutes until post time for the next race . . .

Horse racing has been a fixture of American popular culture since the earliest days of European immigrants. The first race conducted in what would become the United States was held in Hempstead Plain, New York, in 1665. New York, Virginia, and Kentucky were the hotbeds of Colonial horse racing, with racing stock imported from Great Britain in the name of "improving the breed." The Revolution dealt horse racing a blow, but it found its feet again by the early 19th century and became a focus for a strong regional rivalry between Northern and Southern sportsmen.

The Civil War interrupted horse racing almost entirely. At the outbreak of the war, horse racing was suspended throughout the United States except in Kentucky, which understood its priorities well; although distinctly Southern in character, Kentucky did not secede from the Union and only suspended racing once and then briefly, in the fall of 1862 when General Kirby Smith's army encamped on the track in Lexington. Racing resumed in the North when it became apparent that battles would be waged for the large part below the Mason-Dixon line, but it did not resume in the South until well after Appomattox.

The latter half of the 19th century saw a boom in **pool rooms**, gambling establishments focused on horse racing; a large **pool board** served as a model of the racetrack, with model horses moved around the track based on telegraphic **calls** of position from the racetrack.

Horse racing—and gambling at the racetrack—have been well-established elements of sporting life in America. The Kentucky Derby is one of the major pageants of American sports, as we as a nation remember our agrarian roots for a day, lulled by the images of Kentucky bluegrass horse farms, linen suits and straw hats, and mint juleps to sip.

But—WAIT—do not forget! Because of the gambling component inherent in horse racing, it is a vice and a sin. Beware of its charms—it is evil and it will enslave us. The *Clinton Reader*, a popular textbook in the early 19th century, was explicit in its warnings about the depravity of horse racing:

> *Who loves a horse race? Are not too many fond of it? Does it not lead to many evils, and to frequent ruin? Never go to a horse race. Mr. Nix had one child, whom he called Irene; he also had a good farm, and some money. He went to the races with his child, dressed in black crepe for the loss of her mother. Here Mr. Nix drank freely, and bet largely, and lost all he was worth. At night he went home a beggar; took a dose of brandy, and died before morning, leaving his child a pennyless (sic) orphan. Never go to a horse race.*

Either we never learned our lesson or we forgot it, for John Philip Quinn included the evils of horse racing within his reform umbrella early in the 20th century, explaining to us in no uncertain terms that horse racing is evil, evil, and evil. He insisted on

> *tearing away the mask of harmless sport from the death's-head that grins behind it, and exposing, in all its hideous nakedness, not the moral wrong that there is in the vice of gam-*

bling by betting, but the personal rascality toward the individual, the plain and evident object of robbery that is involved in all the schemes of the book-maker, the pool-seller, and every other person who makes either a profession or a systematic practice of offering bets upon the results of the race-track.

Despite warnings from the pious and prudent among us, we seem enthralled with what Quinn saw as "one of the most dangerous and pernicious of all that threatens the interests, the welfare and even the safety of society." Save your sermon buddy, I've got ten bucks riding on High Heeled Hope in the fifth!

The Language of Horse Racing

SLANG IS FORMED IN MANY DIFFERENT WAYS. Closed institutions, such as the military or a prison or a boarding school, often produce a vivid slang lingo. Inversely, a confluence of cultures can generate a flourishing slang lexicon, and such is the case with horse racing. In "The Argot of the Racetrack," David Maurer identified four major sources of racetrack language—professional gamblers (jaded, cynical, and hardened), breeders and trainers (horse-oriented, decidedly rural), jockeys and stable hands (race-oriented, performance-oriented, competitive, and intense), and writers (from the slangy jargon of the chroniclers of past performance to the skeptical-one-minute-fervent-and-ardent-the-next prose of the newspaper writers).

The slang indigenous to horse racing and gambling thereon is nothing if not picturesque. One need not know much about horse racing to understand it or to appreciate its inventive and descriptive power. A number of horse racing slang terms and expressions have become regular parts of mainstream American speech—**across-the-board, all out, also-ran, country mile, dark horse, deadweight, homestretch, in the money, long shot, odds-on favorite, out of the running,** and **smart money** are all racetrack loans to American English.

A Horse Racing Wordlist

acey-deucey Uneven stirrups, with the left side lower than the right to achieve better balance on turns. *Popularized by the legendary jockey Eddie Arcaro in the 1940s, it is unrelated to the backgammon sense (see page 42).*

across-the-board Placed on a horse to win, place, and show (said of a bet). *See Word History, page 170.*

airing A workout

alive Bet on (said of a horse)

all alone Ahead in a race by several lengths

all out Driven by a jockey to the limit to win (said of a horse)

all-the-way win A victory where the horse led the race from start to finish

also-ran A horse that finishes below third place. *See Word History, page 170.*

apron The paved area between the grandstand and the track

armchair ride An easy victory without urging by the jockey

around the park Consisting of an entire lap around the racetrack (said of either a workout or a race)

at home in the going Running on a track exactly suited to a horse

baby A two-year-old horse

backstretch The straightaway on the far side of the track from the stand

back up To slow down noticeably

back wheel A bet on two races with a bet on one horse in the first race and three horses in the second race

bad actor A poorly behaved horse

badger An inexpensive horse that does little more than qualify the owner for track privileges

bad post actor A horse whose temperament leads to problems in the starting gate

ball A composite of different cathartics given a horse. *As was seen in the Word History of "highball" in Chapter 1, this sense of ball may have contributed to the formation of that term.*

bangtail 1. A tail that has been bobbed or tied short

Sulkies, Swedges, and Scalpers: The Slang

HARNESS RACING, THE YOUNGER and less popular sibling of horse racing, sports its own enthusiastic supporters, its own etiquette and culture, and to some extent its own slang dialect. While much of the body of horse racing slang is applied without modification to harness racing, there is a core of slang words peculiar to harness racing.

Start with the contraption which carries the driver and which the horse pulls—the **bike**, **cart**, **gig**, or **sulky**. The **jog cart** or **training bike** is used in training and is slightly longer and heavier than the **racing bike** actually used in races.

Next is the person, a **driver** or perhaps a **reinsman**, but not a jockey. The driver who is hired on race day as a replacement or simply at the last minute is a **catch driver.**

And then there's the **gear**, the equipment carried by trotters and pacers. The trotting stride required for harness racing is known as the **gait**; some horses use **hopples** or **hobbles** to keep on **gait**, leather straps worn around the legs. **Hobbles** are kept in place with **hobble hangers** or **suspenders**, a strap that runs over the horse's back; a horse that can keep gait without **hobbles** is **free-legged**. Because trotters have a tendency to **cross fire** or strike a hind foot with a front leg, they are fitted with **Indiana pants** (boots that cover the top of the front leg) and **scalpers** (boots that protect the rear hoof from being cut by the front shoe). For added traction a horseshoe known as a **swedge** is used, and a **spreader** made from hose is looped around the horse's upper front legs to prevent the knees from hitting each other.

Are you ready for the race? Over there in the **birdcage** the horses are being paraded and inspected by the judges. Check out the starting gate—those several horses that are starting behind the first row of horses be-

2. A racehorse

barn money A substantial amount wagered by insiders

baseball A bet on two races with a bet on one horse in the first race and three horses in the second race

bat A jockey's whip

battle the iron men To bet using pari-mutuel machines

beagle A racehorse

bear out To veer wide on the turns

beat An unfortunate defeat. *Very close to the "bad beat" of poker players.*

beat the bushes To race a horse in the minor circuits

bellows to mend Horse's lungs that are in need of treatment

bet down A horse whose odds are dropping

betting tool A horse that wins bets for owners and insiders

Big Apple A major racing circuit

big boy A jockey

big train A great horse

black type A horse that has won or placed in a stakes race. *The expression comes from the use of boldface type in sales catalogues when listing*

# of Harness Racing

cause there are more horses in the race than starting places are known as **trailers.** During the race, a **well-gaited** horse will rarely **break**, or deviate from the trotting gait; the **rough-gaited** horse, on the other hand, can be expected to **break.**

As is the case with all races, position is critically important. The horse and driver who have been forced to the outside of the track during a race are said to be **parked out**; when they regain a rail position, they are said to be **tucked.** Wind resistance is a significant factor in harness racing, so horses tend to **sit** or **trail**— race immediately behind another horse which it is using as a windbreak. This at times leaves the horses running in **Indian file**, one after another, until the final straightaway.

A horse that is not racing behind another horse is **uncovered**, **without cover**, or **has no cover.** Trapped behind another driver and horse, a driver will try to **flush out** the lead horse, enticing it to leave the

rail and give the trailing driver an opening. When trying to slow a horse down to conserve energy, a driver must be careful not to **choke it down** (cut off its breathing); in the same vein, a driver does his best to avoid being **tipped out**, or spilled from the **sulky.**

Several special terms are reserved for the horse immediately outside the leader, one horse off the inner rail—**the Death**, **the death seat**, or **facing the breeze.** This horse is forced to travel farther on turns and is dragged down by wind resistance, so it's in a difficult position. The **one-one** is one horse off the rail and one horse off the lead, giving it more protection from the wind and still able to make a move.

After the race is won using traditional horse racing terms, the drivers and horses are taken to a **tow ring**, a small circle around which the trotters are walked to cool off.

horses that have won or placed in a stakes, or **black type**, race.

blanket finish   An extremely close finish

bleeder   A horse that bleeds at the nose when working out or racing

blind switch   A situation during the race where a jockey is sandwiched between other horses and must either find an opening or drop back and go around the pack

blinkers   A hood that blocks a horse's peripheral vision and thus prevents it from indulging in bad habits such as nearing the rail

blister   To treat an injury on a horse's leg by raising a blister on it which increases the blood flow to damaged tissue

blowout   A brief, final drill several days before a race

blow up   To breathe hard after a race because of poor conditioning

board horse   A horse whose odds are dropping

bobble   To break stride awkwardly, especially stepping away from the starting gate

bold eye   A prominent eye

bolt   To duck suddenly to the outside rail and thus be eliminated from contention

bomb, bomber   A winning horse quoted at extremely high odds

book   1. A jockey's schedule of riding assignments 2. The group of mares being bred to a stallion in a given year. *A stallion who is bred with the maximum number of mares allowed by his farm manager has a **full** book.*

boot   To urge a horse with spurs or heels

bottom   Stamina

bounce   A poorly run race following a very well-run race

boxcar mutuels   Very long odds. *In dice games, the expression "boxcars" usually refers to a roll of two 6s, or 12. Odds of 12:1 would generally be considered long, perhaps explaining the origin of this expression. Another possible explanation for this expression is the traditionally high numbers that were stenciled on the sides of boxcars.*

boy   A jockey

brace   Horse liniment

break   The start of a horse race

breakage, breakcents   The odd change left after paying off each winning bet to the nickel, dime, or $1 unit

break cherry   To win a first race (said of a horse or jockey)

break in the air   To leap upward rather than surge forward at the start of a race

break maiden   To win a first race (said of a horse or jockey)

breather   The portion of the race before the stretch drive where the jockey will retrain it

breeze   To exercise a horse moderately

breeze in   To win a race without great exertion

bridge-jumper   A gambler who only bets on favorites. *The racetrack belief is that a gambler who makes only safe bets that consistently pay off will most likely jump off a bridge at the first big loss.*

broken wind   A breakdown of the air vesicles of the lungs (said of a horse)

bug, bug boy   An apprentice jockey. *Apprentice jockeys are sometimes allowed to weigh less than the weight required of other jockeys in the program. This name comes from the asterisk, or "bug," denoting how much of a **weight allowance** is given to an apprentice. One-bug* is a five-pound **weight allowance**, two-bug is a seven-pound allowance, and three-bug is a ten-pound allowance.

build up   To bet on several horses at a track to increase the payoff on another horse away from the track

bulldog   To claim that one predicted the winner of the last race when one did not do so. *The word is used to describe a* **tout** *practice.*

bullet   The most favorable time to work out for a given distance on a given day at a given track

bullring   A small track with sharp turns

burned   Run-down, as in "burned heels" (said of a horse)

bushes   Small-time racing

buy the rack   To purchase every possible combination of the daily double

by   Sired by

calculator   A pari-mutuel clerk who computes pari-mutuel odds

calks, caulks   Metal grips affixed to the front shoes of horses to help on muddy tracks

call   The position of a horse at various stages of a race

caller   A person who calls the positions of the horses during a race for the

chartmaker

campaign   To operate a racing stable

campaigner   A horse that is raced all year

can't miss   A horse that appears likely to win

capped   Swollen (said of a horse's legs)

card   A racing program

carry the target   To run last the entire race

cast   Prostrate and unable to regain its feet (said of a horse)

cast in the box   Down in the stable, injured, and unable to get up (said of a horse)

chalk   A horse favored to win

chalk player, chalk eater   A gambler who only bets on favorites

chart   A table showing the results of a race together with the position of each horse at different stages of the race

chase   A race over jumps

check   To slow a horse because others are in the way

cherry   A horse that has not yet won a race

Chinese   Blurred numbers on the tote board. *This is just one of many slang terms derogatory to the Chinese.*

choice   The favored horse in a race

choked down   Experiencing difficulty breathing during a race

chop   To shorten the stride

city block   A wide margin

claimer, claiming race   A race in which any horse may be bought by another owner. *Before the race, the owner establishes a* **claiming price** *for the horse; anyone who's willing to pay the price may buy or* **claim** *the horse.*

cleverly   Easily (said of a horse winning a race)

click   To win a race

climb   To have difficulty getting a foothold

clocker   A person who times horses during workouts

clothes   A horse blanket

clover   Money

cold   Not expected to win

cold-blooded   Not a Thoroughbred

cold dope   Statistics on past performance

collar   To win by a neck

colors   An owner's identifying racing colors worn by his jockeys

comeback money   Money to be bet at a mutuel track sent by out-of-town bookies

come on   The call of the starter as a race starts

condition book   A publication issued by the secretary of the meet before the meet opens, listing the races to be run and the qualifications for each race

connections The owner, trainer, and his associates

cooler 1. A horse that is not expected to win 2. A cotton blanket used to cover a horse after a workout

cool out To walk a horse after a race or workout

cop To win a race

country mile A wide margin

coupled Wagered on two or more horses with the same owner or same trainer. *If either horse wins, the wager wins.*

crab To belittle a horse's performance

cracking down Determined to win (said of a horse)

crawl down on To urge a horse to its maximum effort

cresty Thick-necked and probably slow (said of a horse)

cribber A horse that chews on the wood of its stall

cropper A spill, usually during a **steeplechase**

cross The spot where a jockey joins the reins

cuff a bet To accept bets that are guaranteed to produce a loss for the bookie

cull A poor quality horse

cast off by a big stable

cup horse A horse that performs well in longer races

cuppy Likely to break out under a horse's hooves (said of track topsoil)

cushion The surface of the track

dark No racing scheduled

dark horse An underrated horse that wins or has the potential of winning. *It is said that this expression had its roots in a coal-black stallion "Dusky Pete" owned by one Sam Flynn. Looking at the field of horses before a race, a spectator was said to have said that he thought that the "dark horse" would win.*

dead heat An exact tie. *An expression clearly part of mainstream English but first used in 1796 in a horse racing context.*

dead to the pan Likely to win (said of a horse)

dead track A racing surface that is not resilient

deadweight Lead weights carried under the saddle when the jockey's weight is less than the horse is required to carry

declare To withdraw a horse from a race. *More commonly referred to as scratch.*

deep Recently harrowed

and thus with increased holding qualities (said of a track)

delicatessen book A betting operation where the prices are always being cut

distance The point 240 yards from the winning post where race-watchers begin to pay serious attention. *Usually used in the phrase "at the distance."*

distanced Beat by more than 25 lengths

doer A horse that enjoys eating

dog A cheap horse

dogs Temporary guard rails set up to keep horses from going to the inside during workouts, protecting the inside rail's condition for a race

dope 1. Information about a horse, including its past performances 2. Any illegal drug given to horses to improve their race performance

double-bug rider An apprentice jockey who is given a **weight allowance** of seven pounds in claiming races

draw away, draw out To pull away from the field

drawback A bet that is refunded if a horse does not start a race

drench To give a horse liquid medicine

Boat Races, Businessmen, & Buzzers: Cheating at the Racetrack

MARKED CARDS—OH DEAR! Loaded dice—oh my! Cheating at the race-track—oh no! Oh yes! We tend to think of cheating at the racetrack as a thing of the past, but it is happily ensconced in the here and now. Look no further than Bay Meadows racetrack just south of San Francisco—check out the 1994 murder of top jockey Ron Hansen and the scandal swirling around him concerning fixed races.

Want to fix a race? First, find yourself a **businessman**, a jockey or stable employee who might be persuaded to participate in a cheating scheme. To pay a bribe is, quaintly enough, to **do business**, resulting in a **boat race**, one in which the results have been preordained.

Performance-enhancing drugs probably constitute the single greatest area of cheating at the racetrack; much of the drug testing technology used to analyze the urine of American workers was developed to counter cheating by drugs in the horse racing industry. The stimulants themselves are referred to as **dope**, **fast pills**, or **tea**, a curious borrowing from the human drug slang lexicon but given a general, non-marijuana-specific meaning with horses. With the offending pill in hand, one proceeds to **dust** or **wake up** the horse, which is then said to be **hot**. If the drugs are to be injected by hypodermic needle, the horse is **needled** or **nobbled**, which makes the person who administers the drug a **nobbler**. A **hop horse** or **hophead** requires stimulants to run well, and a **drugstore handicap** or **drugstore race** is one made up largely of horses that are running under the influence of stimulants. After a race, horses are taken to the **spit box**, a barn where they are tested for illegal drugs. A drug-free racing horse is **on his oats**.

The other major mode for stimulating a horse during a race is the use of an illegal electrical device, known affectionately as a **battery**, **buzzer**, **Edison** (hats off to Thomas), **joint**, **prod**, **spark**, or **sting**.

Another way of **doing business** is to hamper a horse, preventing it from running well or winning. This can be accomplished several ways—by **sponging** the horse (inserting a sponge in its nose making breathing during the race difficult), by **watering** the horse (giving it water just before the race, thus slowing it down), by engaging a **night rider** (someone who secretly rides the horse the night before the race to tire it), or simply by **pulling** the horse (reining it in to slow it down and prevent it from winning).

A final cheating technique seems too simple not to be detected, which is not to say that it is not tried—the use of a **ringer**, a horse disguised to resemble another.

drive To win a race under strong urging (said of a horse)

drop A cash-handling error by a track clerk favoring the clerk

drop-down A horse moving down in class or claiming price

dump To bet heavily at the last possible minute

Dutch book Odds that show the bookie no percentage in his or her favor

on a horse as soon as the betting windows open

educated currency Money bet on what is perceived to be intelligent analysis and good inside information. *Pretty much the same thing as smart money.*

exotic wager A bet other than a win, place, or show bet, involving

tered in a race **2.** All the horses with position 12 and up; if any one wins, the bettor on the field collects

figure To have a decent chance of winning

figure horse A horse strongly favored to win a race

film patrol The crew responsible for taking the films of the

dwell To start a race slowly

dynamite Money that one bookie bets with another bookie to cover bets that he or she does not want to keep

each way Placed on a horse to win and place (said of a bet)

eaglebird A long shot winner that has not been bet on with a bookie

early foot Speed in the initial stages of a race

early money Heavy betting

more than one entry and/or more than one race

factor A contender

fade To tire and drop out of contention

false favorite A horse mistakenly picked as the favorite by the public

fast closer A horse that finishes fast in the stretch run

feather An extremely lightweight jockey

field **1.** All the horses en-

race reviewed by the judges to determine if a horse should be disqualified

finger horse A horse favored to win

finish on the chinstrap To finish a race under restraint, winning easily

fire **1.** To accelerate in a burst of speed **2.** To use an electric needle or hot iron to treat a horse's leg

first today and last tomorrow Erratic in

performance, doing well one day and poorly the next

flag down To wave at a rider during a workout to indicate that the horse is exercising too hard

flak jacket A jacket worn by jockeys designed to protect against injuries to the ribs, kidneys, and back

flash A change of information on odds on the tote board

flatcatcher A horse that looks the part but fails to perform well

float 1. To level off a horse's teeth to improve his chewing 2. A piece of equipment dragged over the surface of the course to push off surface water

force the pace To stay right behind the leader of a race

fresh money The amount of money brought to the track on a given day. *This is not the same as the* **handle,** *which includes bets made with money*

won at the track.

freshen To rest a horse that has become jaded after too much training or racing

from flag fall to finish Over the course of an entire race

full book The maximum number of mares with which a stallion is permitted by an owner or manager to breed in a year

full of run Physically fit and enjoying racing (said of a horse)

fuzzy A horse that is certain to win. *For more discussion, see the Word History on "fuzz" in Chapter 7, page 273.*

gad A jockey's whip

Garrison finish A win by a horse that finishes very fast after trailing most of the race. *The expression comes from Snapper Garrison, a famous jockey who used this tactic.*

gee gee A racehorse

gentleman jockey An amateur, usually in a steeplechase

getaway day The last day of a racing meet

get into To whip a horse

gimmick A wager won by combining two or more horses

give him his head To allow a horse to run at full speed

go ahead man A tout's assistant

goat A poor racing horse

goggles Blinkers

goo A muddy track

good doer A horse that eats all its feed

good feeler A horse showing promise

good thing A horse that wins with moderately long odds

go on To win at a new, longer distance (said of a horse)

goose-rumped Possessing high hindquarters (said of a horse)

go overboard To fail to pay a gambling debt

go to bat To use a whip on a horse

grab To win a purse with a horse quoted at long odds

grab a quarter, grab himself To injure the back of the foot or hoof, usually when a horse has stepped on itself

graduate To win one's first race (said of a horse)

grass slip Permission to exercise a horse on the turf course

green Never raced or raced only a few times (said of a horse)

groceries Feed

Guinea A rubdown man or groom for horses. *The term is said to date back to the custom of reward-*

ing the groom with a golden guinea in England.

gumbo Heavy mud

gun An all-out effort by a jockey

gun from the gate A horse that starts quickly

guts A combative and competitive spirit

gyp, gypsy An owner with only a few horses or just one horse

hair-trunk An ugly horse that performs poorly

halter To claim a horse

halterman A person who claims a horse out of a **claiming race.** *The winnings in that race belong to the original owner, although ownership passes to the new owner as soon as the horse steps on to the track.*

handbook Illegal offtrack betting, not always at the track odds

handily In an easy manner when not under pressure (said of the way a horse wins)

handle The total money bet by all players on one race or meet or for the entire season

hand ride A workout or race in which the jockey does not use the whip; also used as a verb

handy Nimble, easily guided (said of horse)

hard boot One who is well-traveled and old-fashioned, as in "He's a good Kentucky hard boot!" (said of a trainer)

hat trick The winning of three races in a single day. *This phrase originally applied to the feat of dismissing three consecutive batsmen in cricket; the bowler who accomplished this received a hat as a reward.* **Hat trick** *was later extended to similar feats in such sports as horse racing and hockey.*

have a bucketful To have been fed before a race to decrease the chances of winning

have one in the boot To ride a horse whose owner or trainer has placed a wager for the rider

hayburner A horse that does not win enough to pay its keep

heaves Emphysema

heavy Drying out but still damp (said of a track)

He likes to hear his feet rattle. This horse likes a firm turf racecourse.

herd To change the course of a horse during a race to block another horse from improving its position

hide A racehorse

high school horse A horse that seems able to read the tote board and wins when the odds on him are high

home free Easily and with a comfortable margin. *A horse who finishes a race with a good margin is said to "come in* **home free.***"*

homestretch The straightaway leading to the finish line. *See Word History, page 170.*

honest Gentle and reliable (said of a horse)

hopeful A horse showing promise

hoss A horse

hot 1. Expected to win 2. Stimulated by drugs

hot and cold Erratic

hot walker A stable employee who walks horses to cool them after a workout or race

hunt An amateur race, usually on grass and over jumps

if bet A wager that is conditioned on winning an earlier wager. *If the player wins money on one race, that money is then bet on a specified horse in a subsequent race.*

in high At top speed

inside 1. The portion of the track closest to the inner rail 2. The position closest to the inner rail 3. To the horse's left

in the can Finishing below third place

in the crapper Finishing below third place

in the money Finishing first, second, or third

in the rut In a position during the race from which the horse has little or no chance to finish **in the money**

Irish rail A movable rail

iron men Mutuel betting equipment

irons Stirrups

jail The 30 days after a horse has been claimed, during which the horse must run for a claiming price 25% higher than it was claimed for. *The horse is said to be "in jail."*

jam A crowd of horses during a race

JBM Not likely to win. *JBM stands for "just beaten maiden"; a horse with only one victory is given little chance against more experienced horses.*

jobbie A racehorse

jock A jockey. *The athlete as "jock" is a shortening of "jockstrap," taken from the English slang "jock" for "penis." This horse racing jock is a shortening of "jockey," a Scottish nickname for "John."*

jogging A slow warm-up of several miles with the horse going the wrong direction on the track

jump The start of a race

jumper A **steeplechase** horse

jumping race A **steeplechase**

jump up To win with an unexpected reversal of form

key horse A single horse used in different combinations in an **exotic wager**

kick in the ass, kick in the pants A horse seen as likely to win

kidney sweat Foamy lather on the legs of a nervous horse

killing A big betting win, usually based on inside information

kiss the eighth pole To finish far behind. *The eighth pole is exactly one furlong—220 yards—from the finish.*

kitchen A restaurant for jockeys and stable employees in the backstretch area

kitty The amount of money taken by the track as its share of the wagered money

knocking at the door Close to winning

late money Heavy betting just before the betting cut-off before a race

layer A bookie

lay off To bet part or all of the money taken in (by a bookie) with another

bookie to hedge the bet

leaky roof circuit Minor tracks

leaper A horse that competes in **steeplechase** races

leather The jockey's whip

left at the post Prevented from starting a race

let out a wrap To loosen the grip on a horse which has been running under restraint

lick Speed

light over the kidney Slender-loined (said of a horse)

live in the double Still eligible to win a daily double wager after the first of the two races that form the daily double

loaded shoulder Thick shoulders

lob A horse entered in a race with no expectation by its owner that it will win

lock A nearly certain winner

long shot A horse quoted at high odds. *See Word History, page 171.*

look for a hole in the fence To act as if one would rather return to the barn than continue the race (said of a horse)

look of eagles A proud look

loose mount A horse that continues running after the jockey has fallen off

lose one's maiden To win

a race for the first time (said of a horse)

lug in To pull towards the inner rail

lug out To pull towards the outer rail

machines The pari-mutuel betting machines

maiden A horse that has never won a race

man in Kokomo An anonymous source of inside information

meant Meant to win (said of a horse)

meatball A cathartic pill

minus pool A payoff price of less than 10 cents per $2.00

money from home Easy money

See the Dogs Run

GREYHOUND TRACK RACING imports a large part of its racing and betting slang-stock from horse racing, but there is a modest little body of dog-specific slang.

Greyhound racing as it exists today was made possible when Owen Patrick Smith invented a mechanical **lure** around 1912. Before that, greyhounds had **coursed**, or chased hares in the wild. The dogs, which hunt by sight, chase the **lure**; shaped like a rabbit or a bone, it is operated around the inside of the track. A **lure** kept close in front of the pursuing pack of dogs is a **short rabbit**, while one that is kept some distance ahead of the dogs is a **long rabbit**. Each track names its lure, and in a tone reminiscent of a bingo caller at the beginning of the race the public address announcer proclaims, "Here comes Lucky!" or "Here comes Sparky!" or "Here comes Hollywood!"

The dogs are highly trained purebred greyhounds. A **spook** is extremely timid and nervous, but its fears do not affect its racing abilities. A **fighter** tends to nip other dogs during the race, which will earn it **strikes**; enough **strikes** and a dog is suspended from racing. Dogs are meticulously weighed before races; some, known as a **WL** or **weight-loser**, are so nervous that they regularly lose a great deal of weight just before a race.

For two hours before the race, the dogs are kept in a track-run kennel, the **lockup** or **ginny pit**, where they are examined and cleared to run in the race. Their starting position is chosen by **draw**, and they are then given a **blanket**, a covering with a color and number corresponding to the starting position. A **leadout** or **leadout boy** will eventually take the dogs from the **lockup** out to the track, or **strip**, and parade them before leading them to the starting gate or **trap**. A race made up of the best dogs at the track is a **hotbox**.

Once the race is under way, dogs have different running styles. The dog who **clears** by reaching the first turn ahead of the other dogs is likely to win the entire race, but there are **slashers** (dogs who perhaps **fly the turn** by taking it wide and then cut to the inner rail after the first turn), and there are **pacers** (dogs who like to run behind the lead dog, often finishing in the money but rarely winning a race).

money rider A jockey who does well in high-stake races

monkey crouch, monkey on a stick A riding style in which the jockey bends forward over the horse's withers

morning glory A horse that works out well in the morning but races poorly in the afternoon

morning line The earliest odds quoted before actual betting begins

mortal lock A nearly certain winner

mud lark A horse that races well on mud

mud mark A horse's rating in Past Performance charts on muddy tracks

mudder, mud-runner A horse which races best on a muddy track. *In the "Fugue for Tinhorns," the tout cautions that Paul Revere is a good bet, but that "it all depends if it rained last night / Likes mud, likes mud / This X means the horse likes mud." In other words, Paul Revere was a mudder.*

mug A player who bets randomly, without handicapping the race

mute A pari-mutuel betting machine

near side The left side of the horse, which faces the inner rail during a race

nickel Inferior. *An all-purpose racetrack pejorative.*

niggle To urge a horse to greater effort with hands and rein

night eyes Irregular growths on the inside of a horse's legs, used to identify a horse much as fingerprints are used to identify humans

nightcap The last race on a program

nine of hearts A horse that has no chance of winning a race

nod 1. Permission given a jockey to dismount after a race 2. A noselength, as in "won by a nod"

no go A horse that fails to leave the starting gate

nostril A very small margin between horses

not a boy's horse A horse that's too large or unwieldy for an apprentice to handle

now and thener A horse whose effort is erratic

nursery race A race of **babies,** two-year-olds

nut The tax on betting levied at the track

oatburner A horse that does not win enough to pay its keep

odds-on A horse that is quoted at better than even odds

off Made slow by rain (said of a track)

offside The right side of the horse, which faces the outer railing during a race

off the board Quoted at odds that exceed 99 to 1

oil-burner A fast horse

oil in the can Seen to be a sure winner (said of a horse)

one for the boy A bet placed in the name of the jockey

on the beak Placed to win (said of a bet)

on the Bill Daly Well out in front, leading the field. *A legendary trainer, "Father Bill" Daly used to urge jockeys to "get on top right away and improve your position." It is the opposite of a Garrison finish.*

on the engine Leading

on the limb Forced to an outside position in a race

on the nose Placed to win only (said of a bet)

on the paint, on the rail, on the wood Running close to the inner railing

ouchy Sore (said of horse)

ouija board The official odds board at the track

out of the running Definitely not a factor in a race

outrider A horseman employed by the track to lead a racing horse to the starting gate

outside 1. The portion of the track nearest the outer railing 2. The position closest to the outer railing 3. To a horse's right

outsider A horse not favored to win

out ticket A winning ticket not presented for payment on the day of the race

overlay A horse quoted at odds that are too high

overnight race A race in which the entries close 72 hours before the first race of the day

pad the ring To improve the odds of a horse by placing smaller bets on the competition at the track and a large bet on the original horse away from the track

pagoda czars The official judges

pal A stable pet (dog, pony, goat) to which a horse has become attached

panel A furlong, or 220 yards

parlay A series of two or more bets so arranged that if the first bet wins, the bet plus the winnings are risked in successive wagers

parrot mouth A horse with a pronounced overbite

part wheel A type of bet using the **key horse** in some, but not all, combinations of an **exotic wager**

pasteboard A fast track

past post To place a bet on a race that has already been run

pay or play Fixed even if a horse is dropped from the race (said of a bet)

pay to the dime, pay to the 20 cents Round off the winning wager. *This practice, known as breakage, produces considerable revenue for tracks.*

peacocky Prone to hold its head high and act skittish (said of a horse)

peep To finish in third place

photo finish A very close finish of a race the results of which are determined by a picture taken of the horses as they cross the finish line

pickup weight To carry more weight than was carried in a horse's last race

picture A photo finish

pig A horse that gives up

pig eye A small eye, perceived as a sign of meanness

pigeon An invalid, nonwinning ticket that someone tries to cash in place of the proper one

pill A small numbered ball that is drawn to determine post position

pilot A jockey

pinch To ride a horse in front of another horse, or to squeeze another horse into the rails

pinched back Caught in a jam

pinhooker Somebody who buys a horse for the sole purpose of reselling it

pink A uniformed track policeman. *The Pinkerton Detective Agency was established by Allan Pinkerton in 1850, leading to the use of "Pinkerton" for a private detective; this was soon shortened to pink.*

pit To enter a horse in a race

place To finish second

plant A racetrack

plater 1. A horse that competes in small-purse races.

In 19th-century England, winners in small-purse races were given silver plates rather than cash purses, leading to this term. **2.** A blacksmith

play A horse that one has bet on

player A bettor

play the mutes To bet using pari-mutuel machines

play the nuts To bet according to the advice given in racing publications

plodder A horse that is steady but not especially fast

pocket A situation in which the horse is surrounded by other horses and not given an opening

policeman A horse with no chance of winning a race, entered in a **claiming race** to permit the owner to claim another horse

pony 1. To send a horse out with a stable pony to limber up 2. A racehorse

pool The total amount wagered for win, place, show, and **exotic wagers**

poor doer A horse that does not eat all its feed

pop a splint To suffer inflammation of the tissue over the splint bone

post The starting gate. *To be "at the post" is to have*

reached the starting gate.

postage stamp Extremely lightweight

prep A workout or race used to ready a horse for a future race

price line Odds on all the horses in a race

prop To stop suddenly, digging the front feet into the ground

puller A horse that is straining to spring throughout the race

pull the plugs To remove plugs from a horse's ears, stimulating it through noise

punk A mediocre jockey

punter A small-time bettor who regularly loses

purse The total amount paid after the race to the owners of horses that finish in the top four or five places

quitter A horse given to tiring and stopping in the final stages of a race

rabbit A speed horse that sets a fast pace, usually entered in a race with a come-from-behind stablemate whose chances are improved by the initial fast pace of the race

rack up To get in the way of or otherwise interfere with other horses such that they must slow down

rail-lugger A horse that bears to the left, towards

the inner fence of the racecourse

rank Unreceptive to a jockey's guidance on pace (said of a horse)

rate 1. To restrain a horse during a race until it has a chance to go all out and challenge 2. To slow down while leading to save endurance

ride the rail To ride close to the inner rail during a race

ride with To bet on a horse

right money A bet placed by someone with influence over the outcome of the race

right numbers, right price Good odds

rogue A horse with a bad disposition

rogue's badge Blinkers. *Usually worn by rogues.*

romp An easy race

route A race of a mile or more

router A horse that can keep up speed for more than a mile

rug A heavy horse blanket

Sssssss...sleeper

red board 1. The official sign that announces that the results of the race stand 2. Someone who after the race claims that he picked—but failed to bet on—the winner

refuse To fail to start in a race (said of a horse)

repeater A horse that wins at least two consecutive races

right spot A situation which is advantageous to the astute bettor, usually arising from quoted odds that are too high

roarer A horse that develops a deep coughing attack when galloping. *The horse is sometimes said to have bellows to mend. Usually a roarer does not perform well.*

rug up To cover a horse after a race or workout

run out To run wide on a turn, losing time

run up an alley To fail to win money in a race

salute To raise the whip to stewards after a race, seeking permission to dismount. *The permission is given with a nod.*

sanitary ride A race performance in which the horse did not try its utmost or in which the jockey stayed wide to avoid tight spots

savage To try to bite another horse during a race

scenic route Far from the inner rail

school To accustom a

horse to racing practices

scratch To withdraw a horse from a race

seagull A bettor who eavesdrops on heavy bettors and then makes small bets based on what has been overheard

send To enter a horse in a race

set A group of horses exercised together

set down To suspend a jockey because of a foul

shadow roll A roll worn below the horse's eyes to cut off the horse's view of the track

shank A rope, strap, or chain used to lead a horse

shed row The barns behind the racetrack

sheet A horse racing publication

ship-in A horse that is racing for the first time after arriving at the track

shoe board A sign that reports what kind of shoes each horse wears

shoo-in 1. A sure bet 2. A guaranteed winner in a fixed race

shop around To visit different bookies in search of the best odds

short Not conditioned enough to run the complete race at its fastest (said of a horse)

show To finish third

shuffle To hand-ride, pumping one's hands and moving one's feet

shut out Prevented from betting because the betting windows have closed

shy feeder A horse that does not eat all its feed

silks Racing togs and colors worn by jockeys

Silky Sullivan A come-from-behind horse. *An eponym based on a horse who once came from 41 lengths behind to win a race.*

skin To roll and harden the track surface, making it easier and faster

sleeper An underrated horse that has the potential to perform surprisingly well or does perform surprisingly well

sloppy Covered with puddles but not yet muddy (said of a track)

slot A horse's post position

smart money Bets from allegedly knowledgeable players

snatch Any sudden action with reins

sophomore A three-year-old horse

soup-plate feet Large feet

Spa The racetrack in Saratoga Springs, New York

spasm A single race

spill A fall of one or more horses and jockeys

spit the bit To tire and run less aggressively

spot To concede an advantage on the **weight allowance** to another horse

spot play Betting only on relatively worthwhile risks

springer A horse that becomes the favorite or a second after betting starts although it was not so considered before the race

stake, stakes The highest paying type of race in which the winners are paid both by the track and a pool of entrance fees paid by the horse owners

stale Overworked, jaded (said of a horse)

stall-walker A restless horse that won't sleep and paces in its stall. *This term is at times applied to nervous jockeys who pace.*

stanza A single race

stargazer A horse that carries its head too high

stayer A horse that performs well in longer distance races

steeplechase A race over jumps

stick 1. The jockey's whip 2. To whip

stick horse A horse that runs faster when whipped

stickers Metal grips affixed to the front shoes of horses to help on muddy tracks

stiff 1. A horse entered in a race with no expectation by its owner that it will win 2. To restrain a horse and prevent it from winning

stooper A person who picks up discarded mutuel tickets in hopes of finding a winning ticket

stop To tire abruptly

straight Placed to win (said of a bet)

straight as a string Going all out

straggler A winning ticket that is not cashed before the next race but which is cashed before the end of the day

strapper A groom. *An Australian slang term, rarely used in the United States.*

stretch, stretch drive *See Word History, page 170.*

strip The portion of the track closest to the rail

stroke A betting coup or scam

suicide club Jockeys who ride in **steeplechases**

sulk To refuse to run or obey a jockey's guidance

sure thing A horse seen as certain to win a race

swamp fever Infectious equine anemia

sweat the brass To overwork a horse

sweeper A horse that races at the rear and then swings wide and makes its move in the homestretch

swipe A stable employee who rubs down horses after a race or workout

tag The claiming price

tail off To fall out of contention

take the numbers down To disqualify a horse from a race and declare a new winner

take the overland route To go wide because it is the horse's tendency or to go around a pack to pass it

talent A race fan who is presumed to be a shrewd bettor

teaser A male horse used in breeding farms to test a mare's readiness for breeding

telephone numbers A winning bet at big odds

tenderfoot A horse that

performs well on a muddy or otherwise soft track

thief A horse that runs worst when its chances seem best

tiffany A stopwatch. *Inspired by the famed jeweler Tiffany and Company.*

tight Fit and ready to race (said of a horse)

tightener A race which is entered with the goal of bringing a horse to its peak

timber An obstacle in a jumping race

timber rider A steeplechase jockey

tip boss A horse that is touted to win

tong A noose placed around a horse's nose and upper lip to quiet it in the starting gate

tote The pari-mutuel betting machine. *Short for "totalizator."*

tout A person who sells information about a race

track lawyer An owner or trainer who is always complaining and citing perceived rule infractions

track take The amount of money taken by the track as its share of the wagered money

trailer A horse that performs poorly

trappy Nimble, gentle (said of a Thoroughbred)

travel in straw To travel with the horses in trailer vans

trip The course followed from starting gate to finish line

tub To soak a horse's leg in water to treat an injury

tube To insert a nasogastric tube through a horse's nose into its stomach to administer medicine

turf consultant A person who sells information about a race

turn out To send a horse to a farm for a rest

twitch 1. A nose leash used to quiet a horse in the starting gate 2. To pinch a horse

underlay A horse quoted at odds that are too low

under wraps Showing less than its best (said of a horse)

up Assigned to ride, as in "Pride of Spokane, Sandberg Up!" (said of a jockey)

used up Exhausted

valet A jockey's attendant

vice A bad habit of a horse

walking on eggs Sore (said of a horse)

walkover A race with only one horse entered

washed out Sweating profusely, due to nervousness (said of a horse)

washy Likely to break out in a nervous sweat before

a race (said of a horse)

webfoot A horse that performs well in the mud

weed An undersized Thoroughbred

weigh-in The weighing of the jockey and equipment after the race

weigh-out The weighing of the jockey and equipment half an hour before the race

weight allowance The amount of weight each horse must carry in a race determined by the racetrack

wet hair Perspiration on a horse

wheel 1. To veer suddenly to the right or left after leaving the starting gate 2. A bet using a **key horse** in all possible combinations of an **exotic wager** 3. To make a wheel bet

whipsaw To pick the winner and second-place horse in a race

whistler A horse that emits a whistling sound because of a strain on the lungs

whoop-de-doo A racing tactic involving an all-out effort from start to finish, with no pacing of the horse. *A rider using this tactic is known as a "whoop rider," epitomized in the 1940s by Johnny Longden.*

wildcat To race on unlicensed rural tracks

wind sucker   A horse with
a defective windpipe

wing   To sprint to the front
of the field and to remain
there, winning easily

wire   The finish line

work a horse by lantern
To exercise a horse before
the normal starting time of
5 a.m. to keep its condi-
tion secret

worry   To ride a horse

wrinkleneck   An older,
experienced horse trainer
or handler

WORD HISTORIES

HORSE WORDS

HORSE RACING slang has, to a
startling degree, permeated mainstream American English, providing colorful metaphors for everyday speech.

Across-the-board, used as an
adjective meaning that the modified noun embraces or affects all
classes or categories, got its start
at the racetrack. An **across-the-
board** bet is a wager that includes win (first place), place (second place), and show (third
place); if the horse finishes first,
second, or third, the bettor wins.

In the 1930s, the expression
also appeared in radio, but probably in an unrelated sense. The
glossary appended to M. Lowell's
Listen In (New York: Dodge, 1937)
defines **across-the-board** as "a
program scheduled five days a
week at the same time." The
expression was prevalent in the
first decade of commercial television, the 1950s; in both radio and
television it seems to have been a
literal reference to a program
board on the station's wall, not a
borrowing from horse racing.

The earliest metaphorical use
of **across-the-board** which I
have found is in Merriam-
Webster's files, from *Time* of
December 10, 1945: "without
hope of across-the-board success
until the U.K. and the U.S. came to
terms in their Washington deal."
The most frequent uses of **across-
the-board** are in the field of
industrial relations (such as "an
across-the-board increase of 7 1/2
cents an hour" in the *Wall Street
Journal*, June 14, 1948) and politics (such as a "proposed 20-per-
cent across-the-board tax cut" in
The New Republic, December 9,
1946).

An **also-ran** as a contestant
who does not win would not be
an **also-ran** if there had been no
horse racing and no horse racing
slang, which uses **also-ran** to
refer to a horse finishing in fourth
place or worse. **Also-ran** crossed
over into everyday speech at least
as early as 1899, when William
Archer wrote in his "The American
Language" column in the October
issue of *Pall Mall* magazine,

*When Artie has cut out all
rivals in the good graces of his
Mamie, he puts it thus: "There
ain't nobody else in the one-*

*two-sevens. They ain't even in
the also rans."*

When we reach the final stage
of a project or trip, we often say
that we are now in the **homestretch,** borrowing a slang term
from horse racing that in that context refers to the part of the racecourse between the last turn
and the winning post. Mitford
Mathews identified an article in
the *New Orleans Picayune* of
January 10, 1841, as the first written use of **homestretch.** By 1864
the usefulness of **homestretch**
had taken it from the world of
horse racing; Richard Thorton
found **homestretch** outside of
horse racing on March 12, 1864:
"Already we see the slave States of
Maryland and Missouri, Arkansas
and Louisiana, and others, on the
home-stretch to become free."
Homestretch is commonly used
in political campaigns (in 1968,
Hubert Humphrey engaged in a
"furious home-stretch spurt,"
according to the *London Daily
Telegraph* of November 4) and
baseball, where **homestretch** is
shortened to **stretch,** and then
built up to **stretch drive** for a
team's final effort to win a division championship.

Lastly, there is the **long shot,** a bet in which the chances of winning are slight but the possible winnings are great. The **long** is easily understood, but just what is the **shot** that is long?

The phrase may have been derived from the simple thought of a long-distance shot with a rifle. By the 19th century, a **long shot** was a venture involving great risk. From 1869 on, one sees it emerging as a handy racetrack term. In horse racing, a **long shot** is a horse with odds that are 10 to 1 or higher. Clearly, it is a horse with little chance of winning.

SOURCES AND REFERENCES

A STUDY OF THE LANGUAGE of horse racing should—and my study of the language of horse racing did—begin with David Maurer's incomparable "Argot of the Race," *Publications of the American Dialect Society No. 16* (November 1951). While Maurer's glossary is dated, his fieldwork and analysis were thorough and insightful.

Other written references included *Ainslie's Complete Guide to Thoroughbred Racing,* Third Edition, by Thomas Ainslie (New York: Simon and Schuster, 1976); *Off to the Races* by Ernest E. Blanche (New York: A. S. Barnes, 1947); *Let's Go Racing* by Rita Cannon (London: Daily Mail, 1948); *Payday at the Races* by Les Conklin (North Hollywood:

Wilshire, 1974); *Playing the Races: A Guide to the American Tracks* by Robert Saunders Dowst and Jay Craig (New York: Dodd, Mead, 1960); *Wanta Bet? A Study of the Pari-Mutuels System in the United States,* by Barbara Free-man and Robert Freeman with Jim McKinley (self-published, 1982); *Inside Racing* by Mel Heimer (New York: Van Nostrand, 1967); *Railbird Handbook,* published by Hollywood (Calif.) Park (probably early 1960s); *Beat the Track!* by Ada Kulleck (Grand Rapids: Gollehon, 1988, 1990); *The ABC of Horse Racing* by Dan Parker (New York: Bantam, 1947); *How to Win Money at the Races* by Nate Perlmutter (New York: Collier, 1964); *Horse Racing* by George King (Las Vegas: Gambling International, 1965); *How to Win at Horse Racing* by Robert V. Rowe (New York: Cardoza, 1994); *Horse Racing* by Walter Steigleman (New York: Prentice-Hall, 1947); and Dean Alfange's *The Horse Racing Industry* (New York: Kensington, 1976).

From the world of magazines and newspapers collected by Peter Tamony and found in the Western Historical Manuscript Collection came "Turf Slang-uage" in *Writer's Review* (September 1933); "Martyr to the Scales: Story of Jockey Maher" in *American Weekly* (February 2, 1947); "Baseball

Poor Second in Slang" in the *San Francisco Call-Bulletin* (April 2, 1947); "Groom Claims He Needled 2 Howard Colts" in the *San Francisco Examiner* (August 15, 1948); "Four Horses Needled" in the *Examiner* (September 1, 1948); "The Language of Horse Racing" by G. Clark Cummings in *American Speech,* Vol. 30 (February 1955); "Horse Racing Accounts in the Spirit of the Times" by Barbara Lynette McClung in *American Speech,* Vol. 40 (Feb-ruary 1965); "Americanisms from Horse Racing" also by McClung in *American Speech,* Vol. 40 (October 1965); "Boning Up On Horses" by Jack McDonald in the *Examiner* (September 13, 1966); and "Turfmen Have Own Mysterious Lingo" in the *San Francisco Chronicle* (April 21, 1971).

For the language of harness racing, I relied primarily on *The Gambling Times Guide to Harness Racing* by Igor Kusyshyn, Al Stanley, and Sam Dragich (Secaucus, N.J.: Lyle Stuart, 1994) and *Harness Racing* by George Sullivan (New York: Fleet, 1964). My references for greyhound racing included *Winner's Guide to Greyhound Racing* by Professor Jones (New York: Cardoza, 1993) and *Greyhound Racing for Fun and Profit* by Thomas A. Walsh (Deerfield Beach, Fla.: Liberty, 1991).

jive

SEDUCTION

Chapter Five:
SEX

Love for sale,
Appetizing young love for sale.

Who's prepared to pay the price
For a trip to paradise?

Love for sale.

—Cole Porter

ARLENE DIETRICH IS SAID TO have said that while sex is a fact in the rest of the world, it is an obsession in the United States. Whether or not sex is merely a fact in the rest of the world, it is difficult to argue with Dietrich's use of the word "obsession" to describe the attitude towards sex in the United States. More so than with most sins and vices, we are driven to and by sex, yet we are equally driven to condemn it, and then when condemned to lie about it.

The Bible, which is probably used to condemn sex more frequently than all other sources combined, is teeming with sex—you can hardly turn a page of the Old Testament without running into Sarah giving a concubine to Abraham, or Rachel giving a concubine to Jacob, or Absalom up on the roof having sex with ten (10!) of his father's concubines, or harlots hired to pleasure Judah, or Lot committing incest with two of his daughters and still walking away from Sodom and Gomorrah unscathed, or virgins seen as therapy for old men, and when it comes to true blue, first-rate erotic writing, you have to search far and wide to better the *Song of Solomon.*

The Bible sends a truly mixed message on sexuality, and so it is probably not surprising to see a checkered history on the issue in America. Not all colonists were Puritans, and for that matter not all Puritans were as self-contained in matters of sex as one might expect. In any event, from the early days of the colonies to the present day, sex has existed as a vice in America, condemned from the pulpit but ubiquitously enjoyed, the Great National Indoor Game. Here, will you take a look at these French postcards and these Tijuana Bibles, check out the *Playboys* and *Hustlers* and *Penthouses*, meet Debbie from Dallas and Marilyn and Linda and Long John, over there Little Egypt doing the hootchy-kootchy and Gypsy Rose Lee with her "Hello honey" to the row of bald heads, the pasties and G-strings and the bumps and grinds as the saxophones grunt, the Mitchell Brothers and the lap dancers, the hookers, the bar girls and the call girls, the short dates and long dates and all-nighters and marathons. Wanna date? Wanna party? Want some company?

Given the intense denunciations of matters sexual by organized religion, it is no accident that our favorite scandals involve sex and the clergy, be it Henry Ward Beecher's affair with one Elizabeth "Lib" Tilton (a strong candidate for greatest news story between the Civil War and World War I, with its whispers of "surrender" and "sexual embrace"), Jim Bakker and Jessica

Hahn (with Tammy Faye, the woman wronged, in the background), or Jimmy Swaggart and his prostitute-without-a-name.

To satisfy all religious imperatives and fulfill God's holy purpose, the only time that sex may be seen as completely sin-free is when the sex is (1) between a man and a woman who are

One-Night Stands—Male

IN MY RESEARCH, I CAME across literally hundreds of terms for masturbation or masturbating that I found recorded only once. Because they are either rare usages or are intentionally coined terms and expressions, I have not included them in the main list of synonyms. Some of the more clever entries in the also-ran category are: **address Congress, adjust your set, apply the hand brake, audition the finger puppets, bash the candle, be your own best friend, beat the bald-headed bandit, beat the dummy, biff off, blast off to Baywatch** (the T and A show of choice today), **bleed the weed, blow the load, blow your own horn, bludgeon the beefsteak, bob your bologna, bop Richard, bop the bish-op, box the bald champ, box the Jesuit, box with Richard, buff the bishop, buff your helmet, burp the baby, burp the worm, butter the corn, call your parents, catch up with Popeye, charm the snake, choke Kojak, choke the bad guy, choke the sheriff and wait for the posse to come, churn your butter, clean out your rope, clean your rifle, clear the snorkel, climb Mount Baldy, cock your shotgun, come to grips with yourself, crank the monkey, crank the shank, crimp the wire, crown the king, dance with Johnny One-Eye, defrost the** fridge, dig for change, do it your way, do the five-finger knuckle shuffle, do the five-knuckle Olympics, do the Han Solo (an allusion to *Star Wars*), crank the love pump, drive the skin bus, dunder the devil, express yourself, fax Jimmy Dean, fax the pope, feed the ducks, fist your mister, five against Willie, five-finger solo, flay the Emperor, flip the bishop, flog the frog, flog the hog, flog your cumber brother, free Willy, frost the pastries, fuck palmala, gallop the old lizard, get a grip on things, get a stiffy, get the German soldier marching, get to know yourself, get your palm read by Mister Softy, give it a one-gun salute, give it a tug, give yourself a low five, go a couple of rounds with Ol' Josh, go on Peewee's little adventure, grease the pipe, grip the gorilla, grip the pencil, handy work, hard labor, have a big date with Rosy Palms, have a little stroke, have a rendezvous with Mrs. Hand, hitchhike to heaven, hitch-hike under the bigtop, hone the cone, hone your bone, hug the hog, hump the hose, iron some wrinkles, jack hammer, jack the beanstalk, jelly roll, jerk Jamby, jerk the turkey, kick sea-men, kill it, knead your dough, launch the hand shuttle, lube the tube, make fist-kabobs, make the bald man puke,

married to each other, (2) at a time that conception is possible, (3) without the use of birth control, (4) with the intention of procreating, (5) in the missionary position, and (6) without pleasure for the woman.

Every other sexual act is a sin to somebody—a fact which, if nothing else, could inflate this

make the scene with a magazine, mangle the midget, man the cockpit, massage your muscle, milk the lizard, molest the mole, oil the glove, pack your palm, paint the ceiling, paint the walls, Pat the Robertson, peel some chilies, peel the banana, phone the czar, play the organ, play tug of war with the Cyclops, play Uno, play with your light saber (an allusion to *Star Wars*), play with your turtle, please your pisser, plunk your twanger, pole vault, polish the pork sword, polish the rocket, polish your helmet, pop a nut, pop the cork, pound the bald-headed moose, pud, pull a pudding, pull rank, pull your own weight, pummel the priest, pump cream, pump the stump, punch the clown, punish the pope, R2 your D2 (an allusion to *Star Wars*), raise the mainsail, ram the ham, read poetry, relieve tension, romance the bone, rope the pope, rough up the suspect, rub the magic lamp, sand wood, secret handshake, shake hands with the governor, shake hands with the unemployed, shake the snake, shift gears, shine your helmet, shoot for the moon, shoot putty at the moon, shoot skeet, shuck the corn, shuffle the palm tree, sing with Rosie, slam the ham, slam the salami, slap pappy, slide the shaft, smack the salami, spank the Frank, spank the wank, spunk, squeeze the cheese, strangle the serpent, strangle Yoda (an allusion to *Star Wars*), stroke it, stroke the bloke, stroke the dog, stroke your poker, strum the ol' banjo, summon the genie, take a nap, take a shake break, take Herman to the circus, take the monster for a one-armed ride, tame the beef weasel, tame the shrew, teach our children to fly, tease the python, tease the weasel, test the testicles, test your batteries, thump the pump, tickle the ivory, tickle the pickle, tickle your fancy, torque the fork, torture the tentacle, toss it, toss the salad, transfer data, tug the slug, tug your tapioca tube, tug your tube snake, tug your tube steak, twang your wire, tweak your twinkie, twist your tool, unstable the stallion, upgrade your hardware, varnish your pole, walk the dog, walk the plank, waltz with Willy, wanker the anchor, wax the dolphin, wax your willy, whip the bologna pony, whip the dripper, white-water wristing, windsurf on Mount Baldy, work a cramp out of your muscle, wrestle the eel, wrestle with your emotions, wrist aerobics, and yank the plank.

One-Night Stands—Female

CONTRIVED OR RARELY recorded synonyms for female masturbation in the noun and verb forms include **air the orchid, a night with the girls, baste the tuna, beat the beaver, beat the bush, brush the beaver, buff the beaver, bury the knuckle, butter the bead, butter the muffin, butter the potato, buzz, caress the kitty, check the foxhole, check your oil, circle the knoll, clap with one hand, clean your fingers, cream the pie, cunt cuddling, dig for your keys, digitize, douse the digits, do your nails, drown the man in the boat, dunk the beaver, dust the end table, erase the problem, explore the deep South, fan the fur, fan the furnace, feed the bearded clam, feed the fish, finger blast, finger dance, finger fun, finger paint, flick the bean, flick the switch, flip the flaps, flip through the pages, flit your clit, floss the cat, fly automatic** (using a vibrator), **fly manually, get a date with slick mittens, get a fat lip, get a lube job, get a stain out of your carpet, get to know yourself, go mining, grab the goatee, grease the skillet, grease your hips, grope the grotto, itch the ditch, juice it up, jump start the river, leglock the pillow, let your fingers do the walking, lube your goob, make bumps, make butter, make soup, make the kitty purr, make waves, man overboard, manual override, mistressbate, null the void, paddle the pink canoe, part the petals, perform for Mr. Swaggart** (the televangelist allegedly would pay prostitutes to masturbate in front of him), **pet Snoopy, pet the bunny, pet the pussy, pitch in the bush league, play fiddle, play piano, play the clitar** (an allusion to the sitar wasted on many who did not come of age in the 1960s), **poke the pucker, poke the pussy, polish the pearl, polish the wedding ring, preheat the oven, push the button, push the petal, read braille, ride slidesaddle, ride the curl, ride the tubespout, ride the unicycle, ride the wild hand, ring for the maid, ring Southern bells** (another reference to the genitals as "down South"), **roll the mink, row the little man in the boat, rub the nubbin, ruff the muff, scratch the patch, scuff the muff, search for Spock, shell the bean, shoot hoops, shoot the rapids, shuck the oyster, silk abuse, skim the cream, slick abuse, soak in Palmolive, sort the oysters, spelunk** (technically, "spelunking" is the hobby of exploring and studying caves), **stiffen your upper lip, stinky pinky, stir it up, stir the cauldron, stir the yogurt, stroke the furnace, strum, stuff the taco, surf at Finger Beach, surf the channel, surf the wet, take a dip, take a finger ride, take a trip South, test the plumbing, the virgin's release, thumb the button, tickle the mustache, tickle the taco, tickle your fancy, tiptoe through the two lips, toggle the bit, touch type, tweak the twig, twit the clit, visit Father Fingers, wake the butterfly, wash your fingers, water the hot spot,** and **work in the garden.**

chapter beyond the bounds which it deserves. For this reason and the fact that a book about slang should not be confused with a treatise from the Morality Squad, the sexual "sins" addressed in this chapter are for the most part sins involving sex and commerce. As tempting as it may be to dally with the slang terms and expressions for the **act of acts** and body parts, I choose not to dally long there; if one is truly interested in the slang of body parts, rent *Real Tickets*, in which porn producer Jim Holliday fits more than 60 synonyms for *penis* into a 60-second film montage. In fact, dispensing with several of the most clever (for clever, how about **offshore drilling** for adultery or **fuckerware party** for a women's party where sex toys are displayed and sold?), I forsake sex per se as a sin.

The slang of sexual sin has at least four different feels to it. First, some clearly has a 19th-century ring, a rejoicing tone of wallowing in vice and venery. Second, burlesque gave us a few good terms and expressions that resound with the wise-guy voice of the 1930s and 1940s. Third, the vibrant character of street English resounds in the speech of pimps, bringing some life to an otherwise dreary place. Finally, the slang of the modern sex industry is a curious blend of veiled euphemism in massage parlors and blunt/crude/half-clever lingo in pornography and sex performances.

As the madam used to say, though—"Company, ladies!"—or in the words of the massage parlor manager—"Customers!" Bring on the broads! Take it off! Down in front!

Masturbation

THOMAS AQUINAS, commonly regarded as one of the greatest Western philosophers and Christian theorists of the Middle Ages, set the stage for the 19th century's thundering condemnation of masturbation as sinful in *Summa Theologiae*, where he wrote that "sins of abuse are more serious than sins of omission. And so among the unnatural sins masturbation holds the lowest [rank] because it omits the involvement of another person."

Although the Bible says nothing about masturbation, the Christian church was fanatic on the subject in the 18th and 19th centuries; rallying to the Church's side was the medical profession, which joined in denouncing masturbation as a great evil. Texts such as *Onania: The Heinous Sin of Self-Pollution* (Anonymous, 1716) and *Onania: A Treatise Upon the Disorders Produced by Masturbation* (Tissot, 1758) had profound effects on medical thought. In 1876, a highly respected medical writer by the name of Pouillet castigated masturbation in the following hyperbolic terms:

> *Of all the vices and of all the misdeeds which may properly be called crimes against nature which devour humanity, menace its physical vitality and tend to destroy its intellectual and moral faculties, one of the greatest and most widespread—no one will deny it—is masturbation.*

Why this intense taboo? Why would the church, the medical profession, and the educational system all equate masturbation with pregnancy and venereal disease? Why describe erotic self-stimulation as **genital pollution**, the **great sin of youth**, the **original sin**, **secret selfish sin**, **secret vice**, **self-abuse**, **self-pollution**, or the **solitary vice**? What's the big worry?

In 19th-century America, passionate crusaders against masturbation included Sylvester Graham of cracker fame ("A masturbator grows up with a body full of disease, and with a mind in ruins, the loathsome habit still tyrannizing over him, with the inexorable imperviousness of a fiend of darkness"), Dr. John Harvey Kellogg of flake fame ("A remedy which is almost always successful in small boys is circumcision. . . The operation should be performed by a surgeon without administering an anesthetic, as the brief pain attending the operation will have a salutary effect upon the mind. . . "), and Sister Ellen White of the Seventh Day Adventists (author in 1864 of *An Appeal to Mothers: The Great Cause of the Physical, Mental and Moral Ruin of Many of the Children of Our Time*).

The 20th century has seen a remarkable if not complete relaxation of the masturbation taboo in America. Even as the Mormon Church advised teenage boys to exercise, take cool showers, and wear restrictive clothing at night, Norman Mailer, Anthony Quinn, Philip Roth, Kurt Vonnegut ("The only person I helped achieve a first orgasm was good old me"), and others began to write freely about masturbation. Masturbation became a common and safe subject for comedy; Woody Allen, Father Guido Sarducci, and Rodney Dangerfield ("They say love thy neighbor as thyself—what am I supposed to do—jerk him off too?") are only three of the many comedians who have helped steer masturbation from the **solitary sin** to the politically correct **self-pleasuring**.

Fear not, though. Conservative Christians still teach that masturbation with illicit sexual fantasies (are there any other kind?) or with the use of pornography is sinful. Let's leave it that way for now, and bring on the slang of autoerotism.

The slang used to describe male masturbation is teeming, a fact which is surprising when one considers the fact that masturbation is in most instances a solitary act (except for the **circle jerk**, a group masturbation session); the surprise lessens, however, when one considers the fact that masturbation is the major sexual outlet for many for whom slang serves to skirt the taboo still associated with **self-pleasure.**

Masturbation is known as an **armswing, bachelor's fare,** a **dishonorable discharge, fist fuck, five against one** or **five-on-one** (a fairly modern American coining that coincides with a 19th-century French expression), **five-fingered Annie, hand gallop, hand game, hand gig, hand jive, hand job, infanticide** (sperm spent in masturbation will never produce a baby), **jerk job, manual exercises, Malthusianism** or **higher Malthusianism** (in honor of Thomas Malthus, a 19th-century advocate of population control), **old lady five fingers,** a **Portuguese pump, soldier's joy,** or **wrist job.**

The major part of masturbation slang though is composed of verb forms as used by males for the act itself. **Jerk off** (see *Word History,* page 212) or **jack off** lead the field, but are not alone. Other recorded slang synonyms for *masturbate* include the following:

ball off
bang the banjo
bang yer wanger
bash the bishop (the first of a few anticlerical allusions)
beat meat (an expression favored by Norman Mailer)
beat off
beat the bishop
beat the dummy
beat the pup
bob
box the Jesuit
bring down by hand
bring off by hand
bring up by hand
choke your chicken
chuff
churn
come your turkey
crank
crank the cream
dash your doodle
do yourself off
drop your load (an expression used by Philip Roth in *Portnoy's Complaint*)

fire your wad (another Roth favorite)
fist it off
flip it off
flog the bishop
flog the dolphin
flog the donkey
flog the lizard
flog the log
flog the meat
flog the mutton
flog the pork
flog the pup
flub
frig
frig off
fuck the fist
gallop the antelope
go on a hand diet
grind off
grip it
haul your own ashes
hot rod it
husk it (a late-19th-century coining, using a corn image)
jerk the gherkin
jerk your jewels (an allusion to **family jewels** as testicles)

keep down the census
knob
lope your mule
make a milk shake
make love with Mother Thumb and her four daughters
make love with Rosy Palm and her five sisters (inspired a song by Jackson Browne)
milk (which makes a masturbator a **milkman**)
mount a corporal and four
nightclub
one-two
paddle the pickle
play pocket pool
play solitaire
play with yourself
pound off
pound pud
pound your pork
pound your pud
prime your pump
pull off
pull putz
pull your pud
pull your wire

pump off
pump your pickle
pump your python
punish Percy in the palm
rub it off
rub your radish
run off by hand
see Madam Thumb and
  her four daughters
sew (a verb derived from the
  expression **sewing circle**
  for a **circle jerk**)
shag
shake hands with the
  wife's best friend
shake hands with the guy
  that stood up when I
  got married
shoot the cat
smash the stake
spank the bishop

spank the monkey
squeeze it off
squirt seed (another term
  used by Roth in *Portnoy*)
stir your stew
strain the vein
strain the main vein
strangle the stogie
sweep off
take matters into your
  own hands
tap-dance
TCB. *The expression "take
  care of business," or
  TCB, is also used on the
  street to mean "to copu-
  late."*
to have a date with a
  handkerchief
toss off
wave the wand

whack off. *A boy who is
  seemingly addicted to
  masturbating is thus said
  to be* **whack silly.**
whank. *This term spawned
  a little family of Cockney
  rhyming slang, including*
  *J. Arthur Rank, Jodrell
  Bank (a famous astro-
  nomical observatory),
  and Levy and Frank.*
whank off
whip it
whip the cat
whip your dummy
whip your wire
work it off
work off
wrench off
yank your doodle
yank your strap

The male masturbator may look at a pornographic magazine while masturbating, or **color in the coloring book**, or he might fantasize about someone he finds sexually attractive, in which case the session is **in honor of** that someone. The hand used by the male to mastur-bate is his **wife.** In the 1950s, an inflatable artificial vagina used for masturbation was known as a **Dutch sea wife,** another example of the seemingly endless string of slurs against the Dutch found in the English language; in French, the inflatable female was known as a *dame de voyage.* In prison, a makeshift masturbation aid consisting of some sort of container filled with some sort of lubricant is a **fifi bag.** Because of the purported frequency of afternoon masturbation, midafternoon is known as **the housewife's hour.**

For reasons which have never been entirely clear to this writer, the vocabulary of female masturbation pales next to its male counterpart. It may be that teenage boys use slang more than teenage girls, or it may be because girls do not discuss masturbation in the slang-using teen years, but the slang is slim, usually deferring to the timid **touch yourself.** While **Jill off** or **Joyce off** are used in the literature of female masturbation, they have a contrived ring to them and do not resonate with the crude, adolescent authenticity of **jack off** and its brothers. Recorded verbs to describe the act of female masturbation include **catch a buzz** (referring to the use of a vibrator), **diddle** (a term from the 1930s), **digitate** (from the 19th century), **do a one-finger exercise, finger, finger fuck, make scissors,** and **rub off.** One of the haz-ards of female masturbation is known in medical slang as a **picket fence injury,** resulting from overly aggressive insertion of a vibrator or dildo.

Birth Control

BIRTH CONTROL IS WIDELY REGARDED as a sin by the Roman Catholic church and by many conservative Protestants, as exemplified by Charles D. Provan's *The Bible and Birth Control* (Monongahela, Penn.: Zimmer, 1989). Characterization of contraceptives as sinful is based in large part on Genesis 1:28, with its fairly general admonition that "God blessed them and said to them, 'Be fruitful and increase in number; fill the earth and subdue it.' "

Whether or not one accepts all birth control as sinful, one has to be impressed with its slang offspring. In general, contraceptives are known as a **lady's friend. Vatican roulette** is a jocular reference to the rhythm method, while a diaphragm might answer to **catcher's mitt.**

The condom, however, stands head and shoulders above its cousins as the birth control that slang users love the most. Rather than have sex **a cappella**, have sex **meat-to-meat** (pretty!), or **ride bareback**, the slang-slinging sinner will put three quarters in a **bubble gum machine**, purchase a condom, and then at the propitious moment will **cloak the captain** and then plunge in and **fight in armor.** The condom itself is best known as a **rubber,** but is also known as an **anti,** a **Bishop** (another one of those pesky clerical images), **cheater** (evocative of the term **pinkie cheater** for a latex glove used during a gynecological examination), **come balloon, cum drum** (love those rhymes!), **diving suit, French letter, glove** (No glove, no love!), **head gasket, jo-bag, latex, nightcap, overcoat, party hat** (a relatively recent, hip-hop generation coining), **Port Said garter** (an expression used by the British military during World War II, named for the port near the Suez Canal), **propho, protection, protective, raincoat, saddle, safe** (an adjective as noun recorded in the 19th century!), **safety, shower cap,** and **washer.**

Sexual Performances

ALTHOUGH PUBLIC DISPLAYS OF sex could be found in sin spots in major American cities well before Little Egypt's **hootchy-kootchy** dance in the 1890s launched the cultural phenomenon that is manifest a century later as **exotic dancing,** it was Little Egypt who put sexual performances on the map. Granted, Salome deserves historical credit for her Dance of the Seven Veils before King Herod, but in America it was Little Egypt all the way.

The artistic zenith of sexual performances was reached during the 1930s and early 1940s when **striptease**—"the great American art" where customers got **an eyeful for a trifle**—reigned. Such cultural lions as Walter Winchell and H. L. Mencken paid tribute to the striptease, with Mencken creating **ecdysiast** from the scientific term *ecdysis* (the act of molting or shedding) as a dressed-up synonym for **stripper.**

In retrospect, the **striptease** of the 1930s seems a bit tame, but doubt not that it was seen as quite sinful, despite the cheerful greetings of the strippers—"Hello, honey!" In 1937, a dozen clergymen in New York made a great display of going to a strip show and an even greater display of their horror afterwards. Dr. Sydney E. Goldstein of the Free Synagogue told the press afterwards that the strip show was "a cesspool of vice." At the same time, when Judge Owen W. Bohan of New York sentenced a strip show producer for indecency, he lambasted him for putting on a show that "undermined moral and religious traditions for a few paltry dollars." Even Hollywood was shocked by burlesque; in September 1941, Samuel Goldwyn changed the working title of a movie then in production from *The Professor and the Burlesque Queen* to *Ball of Fire* after seeing a burlesque show at the Follies Theater in Los Angeles.

The striptease sputtered into the early 1960s, when **topless** dancers, bars, and topless everything else took over. In the 1970s bolder, less "artistic," more shocking forms of sexual dancing were launched, yet even the raunchiest of the sex shows of the 1990s pales in comparison to the open sex found in San Francisco's bars in the days of the Barbary Coast in the late 19th century. The latest addition to the sex performance industry—striptease to go, "Nude Teasing and Girl/Girl Erotica" at any location you choose or in the privacy of a limousine summoned by a simple phone call—is nothing more than a new twist in the same old story.

The slang and vernacular of sexual performances reflect their age. Before striptease hit big in the 1930s, the slang had a naughty edge; as would be expected, the speech of the 1930s stripper was appropriately wise for the era. The slang of today's sex performers reflects the hard edge of life, with the words carrying the echo of sexual exploitation (how about a shoe shine from a naked woman?) and economic exploitation (how about treating exotic dancers as "independent contractors" instead of employees to avoid the protection of labor and employment laws?); the speech of today's sex performers is nothing if not blunt, calling breast implants **fake tits**—no avoiding the truth here.

From the pre-Little Egypt era to the present, the slang of sexual performances includes:

bank Money. *One sex performer might advise another, "There's big bank at table 3." The term produces the variant* **banking** *for earning big tips.*

Bill Watson's beef trust A full-figured stripper, in vogue in the early 20th century. *Named after a 19th-century entertainment entrepreneur.*

bit A skit or routine. *In the 1930s, strippers carefully choreographed and rehearsed their* **bits**. *Moves used by strippers included the Cincinnati, an off-the-log, a snap-back, a buckover, a hitch kick, a Buffalo (in his song "Pasties & a G-String" Tom Waits mentions "a Buffalo squeeze"), an essence, and a toe privilege.*

booth dance A private session with an exotic dancer in a small booth, providing privacy for masturbation or whatever sexual activity might take place. *An innovation of the 1980s and 1990s.*

Boston version A toned-down, cleaned-up version of a striptease show, suitable for Boston's strict censors

bottle dance A novelty dance in which the dancer grips a bottle with her vaginal muscles. *Usually seen at bachelor parties or stag parties.*

bubble dancer A stripteaser who works balloons or soap bubbles into her act

bump To thrust the pelvis forward while stripping. *See Word History, page 211.*

bumper A stripper

cacky Raunchy (said of a routine)

cement mixer A stripper who moves her torso vertically and laterally

circus   Live sex acts displayed to paying customers

coffee grinder   A stripper who grinds her hips and torso

cold   Toned down (said of a strip show brought to a city with strict views on what may and may not happen in a strip show)

come rag   A handkerchief or other cloth used by a customer to clean himself after ejaculating. *Some clubs, particularly in Canada, have instituted a towel dance, in which the dancer places a small towel in the customer's lap and then does a lap dance with the towel in place.*

contact   A skin-to-skin touch between customer and dancer, forbidden in most clubs

cooch, cooch stuff   Very suggestive dancing. *According to* Webster's Third New International Dictionary, **cooch** *is a shortening of **hootchy-kootchy.***

coocher   A stripper or suggestive dancer

couch dance   A **lap dance** performed with the customer seated on a couch

cuddle   To hug a customer

customer   A man who regularly comes to a club to see a particular dancer

daisy chain   A group of women dancers, all on their hands and knees, performing oral sex on the woman in front of them. *The term is used in other group sex situations, but it has this specific meaning in sex clubs.*

d.j.   A bouncer

European atmosphere   Lap dancing in which the dancer faces the customer

exotic   An erotic dancer

fan dancer   A stripper who works an oversized fan into her act

farm   Uninhibited (said of a strip show in a city or town with loose views on what may and may not happen in a strip show, the opposite of **cold**)

feature dancer   A porn star who performs at adult theaters, receiving billing by name (as distinguished from the many **house girls**)

fishbowl dancer   A stripper who strips in a large tank of water on the stage

flash   To expose any part of one's body while dancing

flesh peddler   The manager of a striptease theater

flesh pot   A show featuring live sex acts

floor work   A prone version of **bumps** and **grinds**, performed lying down. *This was at the very suggestive end of the scale*

*and was banned in many theaters and cities. The current term is **floor show**, a **pussy show** performed lying down.*

fuck-me pumps   Very high pump shoes, favored by management

gadget   A G-string. *The term was used in the 1930s and 1940s but is not recognized by dancers today.*

gadget peddler   A salesman of G-strings. *Often a fixture backstage at strip shows.*

gaiety girl   A dancer of the 19th century who strolled on the stage twirling a parasol, perhaps **flashing** an ankle

get nasty   To increase the level of sexual contact with the customer. *A dancer might ask a customer, "Do you want me to get nasty? How about a little present?"*

girlesk   A striptease show

girl-girl   A sexual performance involving only women. *As is the case with pornography, if there is penetration, the show is **hardcore**.*

girly show, girly girly show   A striptease show

give it away   To perform without adequate tipping

grind   To rotate the hips in the shape of the letter "O," simulating intercourse. *This stripper term is also used in modern-day sex clubs, where strippers **lap dance** by grinding their bodies into the laps of the male customers. For further discussion of **bump and grind**, see Word History, page 211.*

grinder A stripper who simulates intercourse by **grinding**

grind house A strip theater that puts on four shows daily, five on holidays

grind stuff Very suggestive dancing

groper A rude customer at a sex show. *The dancers often use the less slangy, colloquial "asshole" or "pig" to describe particularly rude customers.*

G-string A brief patch of cloth that covers a female dancer's genitals. *As strippers used to say, the **G-string** "covers the law." A mystery novel by stripper Gypsy Rose Lee was entitled* The G-String Murders. *For further discussion of **G-string**, see Word History, page 210.*

hardcore A performance involving penetration, almost always with fingers or foreign objects

hen parties Female-only parties featuring male strippers

hootchy-kootchy, hootchie-kootchie, hootchy-kootch, hoochie-coochie, hoochy-koochy A late-19th-century dance popularized by dancer Little Egypt. *It is widely believed that Little Egypt first performed the dance at the World's Columbian Exposition in Chicago in 1893. Sol Bloom, manager of the Midway in Chicago, said, however, that Little Egypt popularized the dance in Coney Island, New York and did not appear at the Exposition at all.*

hot Uninhibited (said of a strip show in a city or town with loose views on what may and may not happen in a strip show)

house girl One of many performers in a sex club who works without billing by name, as opposed to a **feature dancer** who is advertised by name

hump To simulate intercourse sitting on a customer's lap

hustle To solicit money from a customer at a sex show. *Hustling is forbidden. A simpler "Would you like some company?" is acceptable.*

inside-out strip A striptease popularized by Gypsy

Rose Lee, in which the dancer removes her undergarments before her outer garments

jerks The members of the audience at a strip theater

kootch dancer A sexually suggestive dancer

lap dance A one-on-one dance in which a naked female dancer **bumps** and **grinds** on the lap of a male customer who usually masturbates. *Most lap dancing is done with the dancer's back to the customer; **European atmosphere** means that the dancer faces the customer. An anonymous wit on the Internet described a **lap dance** without masturbation as follows: "It is also possible that you might have a lap dance without an erection, in which case you would simply have a woman squirming on your lap."*

leg show A tame striptease, stopping short of nudity

looky-loo A customer at a sex show who watches the dances but neither pays nor plays

lube Any type of personal lubricant, used in **girl-girl** shows involving penetration

money guy The owner of a strip theater

motivate To tip a dancer

nipple cap A small piece of cloth pasted on a dancer's nipples, known informally as a **pastie**

pastie A small piece of cloth pasted on a dancer's nipple. *Immortalized by Tom Waits in the song "Pasties & a G-String."*

peel To strip. *Mae West, who exuded sexuality herself, called Gypsy Rose Lee "Lady Peel." By extension a bar with strippers is a* **peeler bar.**

peep show An exotic dance where the dancer performs for customers who are seated in private booths, each with a one-way window that exposes the dancer but permits masturbation in private. *There are several other meanings of this term, one involving prostitution and one involving pornography (see pages 193 and 207).*

personal show A private performance of an erotic dance for a customer or small group of customers

pink out A collective refusal by the strippers in a club to expose their genitals in routines until a demand is met by management

plastic Plastic surgery, as in "Gina's been away for three weeks—she had a plastic on her nose."

pole tricks Dance routines where dancers slide around a pole, simulating or experiencing genital stimulation

present A tip

princess A dancer with a prima donna attitude

private dance A private performance of an erotic dance for a customer or small group of customers. *In the early 1980s, Tina Turner recorded "Private Dancer" by Mark Knopfler, a powerful portrait of exotic dancing. If a customer requests a private dance or a private show, he also may be asking, "Will you go home with me after your shift?"*

pussy show A routine minimizing dancing and maximizing exposure of the dancer's genitals

quiver A dancing move designed to shake the dancer's breasts

rope trick A dancing move where the dancer rubs her crotch on a rope. *Variations include the French rope trick and the Chicago rope trick.*

rotation The order in which the dancers appear on stage or in a room

scissor fingers To cut a routine short

Separate the palms! Stretch the routine out a little longer! *A cry from the wings of a strip theater if the next act is not ready.*

setup A dancer's figure

sex models Nude women. *In person! On stage!*

shimmy A dancing move designed to shake the dancer's entire body

shower dance A routine in a sex club, where a dancer or several dancers take a shower on stage, washing and simulating masturbation

silhouette routine A striptease routine where the dancer dances in relief

skin game Stripping

slinger A stripper

slow exotic A stripper who teases a great deal as she removes her clothes

smoker An all-male party with pornographic movies and sexual performances

snake type A provocative dancer

spooge To ejaculate. *Dancers use a widely varied vocabulary to describe ejaculation,*

but at least in San Francisco they seem to favor this one.

stag show A striptease. *This is the term used before* **striptease** *came along in 1936.*

strip A stripper. *Battle of the* **strips**! *Fifteen* **strips** *on stage at once!*

striptease A dance in which the dancer, usually female, removes her clothing article by article, accompanied by music and usually involving suggestive body movements. *Variations on the theme include* **strip-cades**, **stripathon**, **striporama**, *and* **stripteuse**. *The first recorded use of* **striptease** *is generally*

considered to have been in 1936. That said, in his 1931 Burleycue: An Underground History of Burlesque Days, *Bernard Sobel uses "strip" as both a noun and verb, as well as the compounds "strip act," "strip dance," "strip dancer," "strip number," and "strip show." Sobel mentions "teasing" in passing, explaining that it is a technical term that means "for every piece [of clothing] they take off . . . they must get applause." Sobel got close, but he did not come up with the compound of* **striptease**.

strippo A stripper

table dancing A routine

performed near or on a customer's table, often on a small portable stage

tassels Ornaments attached to a dancer's nipples, covering the nipples and accentuating the movement of her breasts

t-back, t-bar A brief covering for a dancer's genitals, slightly less skimpy than a **G-string**

teaser A stripper

tech A theater employee who helps run a sex show

tight Cheap. *Said of a customer who does not tip well.*

tights dancer A 19th-century dancer who appeared in tights. *At the time, this was as scandalous as nude dancing once was* *in the 20th century.*

tip out To share one's tips with the bouncer, bartender, and other club employees at the end of a dancer's shift

titty bar A club featuring strippers

topless Wearing nothing above the waist. *The word and craze were developed in the 1960s.*

torso-tosser, tosser A stripper

touch dick To have direct hand contact with a customer's penis. *This is forbidden, but some dancers will* **touch dick**. *Some won't. As about as direct as slang gets, no?*

towel dance A lap dance performed with a small towel in the customer's lap

toy bag A bag of sexual gadgets used by dancers in **girl-girl** shows

trailer The strut across the stage taken by a stripper before she begins to strip

troll An offensive male customer at a sex performance. *Aren't they all?*

two-dollar whore A stripper

uncover girl A stripper. *This term caught the fancy of the industry in the early 1950s.*

up close and personal Very close to the customer

wall dance An erotic dance performed against a wall in the hallway of a sex theater, in the semidarkness, semiprivately

weaver A stripper

white light An unfiltered spotlight. *In most cities, strippers could not legally work in* **white light**; *they commonly used dark blue stage lights and spot lights matching the color of their costume. "No your honor, she never did dance in the white light. We don't allow that . . . "*

yoni The female genitals. *A term from the* Kama Sutra *favored by many dancers.*

Gypsy Rose Lee, the one stripper whose name endures in our collective cultural memory, traditionally ended her shows with an intimate "Now, darlings, I'm so tired," a wonderful closing line.

Pornography

THE LATE 20TH CENTURY HAS seen a taming of several of the sexual sins; in most circles masturbation has been reclassified as something other than a sin, and open and notorious prostitution is less prevalent now than at any time in our nation's history. Pornography, though, has grown raunchier and flourished.

From the early **girlie** magazines denounced in 1952 by Margaret Culkin Banning as "pictorial prostitution," to the introduction of *Playboy* in 1953, to the shocking full female nudity of *The Immortal Mr. Teas* in 1961, to the shocking simulated sex of *I Am Curious Yellow* in the late 1960s, to the shocking and less cultivated *Penthouse* and the shocking and downright smuttier *Hustler*, to the **adult theaters** of the 1970s and the new generation of shocking quite-real-sex classics such as *Behind the Green Door, The Devil in Miss Jones*, and *Deep Throat*, to the shocking sex videos and cable television of the 1980s and 1990s and now the Internet, pornography has come out of the closet. Pornography has always been a fact of life in America, but until the last decade it was safely ensconced in **porn shops**, places where dirty lechers went and that decent people avoided; technological changes have made the distribution, availability, and private enjoyment of hard-core pornography much simpler. Given the chance, it seems that many of us like to watch sex, a shocking fact that flies in the face of our view of ourselves as a prudish, God-fearing nation.

President Nixon and President Reagan both appointed commissions to study pornography; political conservatives have been joined in condemning pornography by religious conservatives on the right (who point to Matthew 5:28 and its admonition that looking at a woman in lust is committing adultery in the heart) and feminist critics on the left (who view pornography as sexual exploitation). The religious and secular criticisms notwithstanding, the sin of pornography continues, unimpeded by the successes of Reagan's Attorney General Edwin Meese in se-

Porn Lingo

ONE FUNCTION OF SLANG in the porn industry is to mask that which is being said. Using the slang lingo of porno, it is possible to have a detailed conversation about a pornographic movie within earshot of dozens of people in a nice L.A. restaurant without them

DIRECTOR: Talked to Diane. She agreed to two commercials, sandwich and a giggler A with Tilly.

PRODUCER: How much?
DIRECTOR: She wanted a dime and seven, but got the package for 12. She'll work no C but still no I, so Sean is out. She actually wants a facial and should go for Southern love.

PRODUCER: Go with Joe, for sure. Will she deal with Scott?
DIRECTOR: Out of the question, after the last rematch. Now a bona fide balsa boy. She wants Bob.

PRODUCER: Too much cake. Get Tim.
DIRECTOR: He's been riding the wave. We'll save time by paying extra. Besides, I can get Freddy for C-light for a buck forty. That'll square it.

PRODUCER: How's Diane's luggage situation?
DIRECTOR: Absolutely excess baggage. Gnarly sniffer and stone cold hodad. But he knows my rules and is still a tourist. He'll no show, figuring she'll P.D., but she already knows she'll get the scalp and the strokes if she doesn't ride the pony.

curing the removal of *Playboy* from the stands of some convenience stores.

There is nothing subtle about pornography, and there is nothing subtle about the slang of pornography:

a Anal sex, currently a major preoccupation of heterosexual porn

air A poor **cum shot**

art photos Classy nude photographs

baby A young newcomer to the porn industry who looks younger than she is

baggage Any male accompanying a female pornography performer to the set

where the film is being made

balsa boy A male pornography performer who cannot be relied upon to achieve and maintain an

understanding the subject matter of the conversation. The following conversation between a director and producer, constructed in large part by porn-lingo-meister Jim Holliday, illustrates the point:

DIRECTOR: *I talked with Diane. She agreed to do two sex scenes, one with simultaneous vaginal and anal intercourse and one with another woman, Tilly, who will use a dildo in her rectum.*

PRODUCER: *How much?*

DIRECTOR: *She wanted $1700 but settled for $1200. She will work without a condom, but will not engage in interracial sex. She actually likes to have the man ejaculate on her face and she should agree to oral contact with a penis directly withdrawn from a rectum.*

PRODUCER: *Hire Joe. Will she perform sex with Scott?*

DIRECTOR: *She won't work with Scott because he was completely unable to attain and maintain an erection the last time he worked with her and on other recent projects. She wants to work with Bob.*

PRODUCER: *Bob is too costly. Hire Tim.*

DIRECTOR: *Tim has not been able to maintain a complete erection in recent outings. I can hire Freddy as a lighting technician for $140 a day so the cost of the scene will even out.*

PRODUCER: *Does Diane have a boyfriend or husband?*

DIRECTOR: *He has been hanging around the set begging for work but he's an absolute pain in the ass even to have around. My reputation will keep the guy off the set. If he thinks that Diane will pull a prima donna number on his behalf as retaliation, the project holds the promise of her photograph on the video box cover. Also, the huge publicity from the major porn magazines will keep Diane in line and not on the rag. In short, she'll behave.*   Who knew?

erection. *This derogatory label is derived from the all-important* **wood.**

bear A male pornography performer with a lot of body hair. *This expression and body type is favored for the most part in homosexual porn.*

beaver A woman's vulva

beefcake An attractive and sexy male pornography performer or model. *A clear play on* **cheesecake.**

big tender A romantic scene that often is the final scene in a pornographic movie

blow book A pornographic magazine

blue Sexually explicit (said of a performance, joke, etc.)

blue movies Pornographic movies. *The expression harkens back to the era when pornographic movies were shown on home projectors.*

bod-comics Male homosexual pornographic magazines

boned Left without a logical transition to the next shot in the editing of a movie

boylies Male pornographic photographs or movies. *An obvious play on* **girlies.**

brown eye, brown eye pie A scene in a porn movie showing anal sex

buddy booths Video booths in a porn store with a glass partition and dual curtains separating two booths, designed to allow people to see each other but not necessarily touch each other

build Dialogue preceding a sex scene in a porn movie

butt book A male homosexual pornographic magazine

cheat To make an adjustment of position during the filming of a scene to improve the quality of the camera shot, as in "Hey, Candy, cheat your ass to the camera!"

cheesecake An attractive and sexy female pornography performer or model

clam dive A scene in a porn movie showing oral sex performed on a woman

c-light A special spotlight used for close-up lighting of a woman's genitals. *The derivation is obvious—a* **cunt-light,** *also known a tad less confrontationally as a* **poon light.**

cock movie A porn movie. *Gets right to the point, doesn't it?*

cocksucker red The brightest possible hue of red lipstick. *One of several clever slang terms*

brought to pornography by makeup artists.

combat zone Originally an area in Boston with sex stores and prostitutes, now applied to any such area in any city

commercial A sex scene in a porn movie. *One purpose of the slang of the porn industry is to mask meaning, permitting industry insiders to discuss in graphic detail the scenes and rates of a movie in a public place without letting even the most adept eavesdropper know what they are talking about.* **Commercial** *is obviously one such term and it was coined for that very reason by Jim South of World Marketing, an agent who is a major player in the porn business.*

cook books Male homosexual pornography

couples booth A video booth in a porn store spacious enough to seat two

cowgirl A shot in a porn movie with a woman having intercourse with a man, above and astride the man. *In the old days, this was known as* **riding St. George** *and is still known in some circles as* **the ride.**

cum Semen. *The porn*

industry heavily favors this spelling, driving the somewhat literary "come" for orgasm into the gutter of body fluids.

cum dodger A pornography performer who tries to avoid semen ejaculated in a **cum shot**

cummy face A close-up shot in a porn movie showing the contortions on a man's face as he ejaculates. *Almost all of these scenes are reaction shots, shot after the actual ejaculation and spliced into the movie. Other endearing terms for the **cummy face** include **rat face**, **chipmunk face**, the **scrunch face**, **weasel face**, etc.*

cum shot A shot in a porn movie showing a male ejaculating outside the body of his sexual partner. *For fascinating psychological reasons, ejaculation outside the body is an important part of all pornographic movies except those produced by overtly feminist pornographers. In the early days of commercial porn movies, the producers insisted on what they called a **proof shot**, a shot showing proof of ejaculation. There are producers of porn videos*

who firmly believe that all you need to make a porn movie is "a title and a **cum shot** every six minutes."

deadwood A flaccid penis on the screen. *Also known as a **dolphin, flounder,** or **softy.***

deliver the load To ejaculate

e-coli pie A scene in a porn movie showing oral stimulation of the anus

facial, face shot A scene in a porn movie showing a man ejaculating on someone else's face

fag mag A male homosexual pornographic magazine

fence painting A shot in a porn movie showing oral sex being performed on a woman from very close to the action

flavor comic A male homosexual pornographic magazine

fluffer A person hired to keep male performers erect during breaks in filming of pornographic movies

French postcard An erotic photograph. *The expression came into vogue after World War I, when American soldiers were exposed to French porn.*

fuck book A pornographic magazine or book. *The magazine* Screw *called its*

book review section "Fuck Book"—*porn humor.*

ghoulies Violent pornographic movies

giggler A scene in a porn movie involving two women. *In the porn industry all males are "boys" and all females are "girls." A scene with two women is a **g-g**, which has evolved to **giggler**.*

girlies Pictures or movies of nude women, usually not engaged in sex. *This term and the magazines it describes were popular in the early 1950s.*

girl things, girl stuff A range of hygiene procedures that women who appear in pornographic movies perform before a sex scene

glory hole A small hole between private video booths in an adult bookstore, about hip high, designed for anonymous sex between men. *This innovation and term originated in men's rooms and migrated to porn stores.*

gonzo A style of shooting pornographic movies in which the cameraman is part of the movie and the camera is shot as his point of view

goods   The external genitals of a man or woman or the female breasts, the primary assets of anyone who appears in a porn movie

grinder   An older commercially produced porn movie with a heavy emphasis on sex, virtually no emphasis on plot or dialogue, and poor production values

gyno shot   A shot in a porn movie showing a woman's genitals from very close quarters

hand books   A pornographic book or magazine. *So called because of the use of a hand to mastur-* *bate while reading the book or looking at the magazine. In the 19th century, the French called this a "one-hand book."*

hard-core   Showing penetration. *Penetration differentiates soft-core porn from hard-core porn, and great care is taken to show clearly the actual penetration, especially the initial penetration.*

het film   A heterosexual porn movie. *A term used to distinguish this product from homosexual porn.*

horn movie   A pornographic movie

hummer   A scene in a porn movie showing oral sex performed on a man. *An old-fashioned term from the early 1960s now very much in vogue in the porn industry. Other terms for the practice used both inside and outside the industry are* **blow job** *and* **head**.

inscrewtable   An Asian female star of a porn movie

jiggly show   A television show like *Charlie's Angels* or *Baywatch* where the jiggling of the breasts of the female stars is a prime draw for the show

jizzer   A shot in a porn movie showing a male ejaculating outside the body of his partner

king triad   A scene in a porn movie including one man and two women

leather film   A porn movie featuring lots of leather fetishes and rougher sex than normal

leg-art magazine   A magazine featuring photographs of scantily clad, but clad, women

lunch   A scene in a porn movie showing oral sex being performed on a woman

lunchmeat   A beautiful and/or sexually appealing

female performer in pornographic movies

m-and-g track The audio tape track containing the moans and groans of the performers

masturbation manuals Pornographic magazines. *This term cuts right to the chase, doesn't it?*

mish To have sex in the missionary position. *This seeming noun or noun-as-adjective is used as a verb in the porn industry—"She gives him a* ***hummer*** *and then they* ***mish*** *for two minutes."*

Mr. Softy A flaccid penis

model A performer in a pornographic movie

money shot A shot in a porn movie showing a male ejaculating outside the body of his sexual partner

monster shot An extreme close-up of genitals in a porn movie, taking up the entire screen

nudie A movie or live show featuring naked women. *This expression was in vogue in the mid-1950s.*

ofer A male pornography performer who has had trouble maintaining an erection and with ejaculation. *The derivation is from the derisive dismissal—"In his last*

shoot, he went 0 for 4."

p&p A close-up shot in a porn movie or photograph, close enough to show pimples and providing an unobstructed view of penetration

Page 3 A British colloquialism referring to pictures of women's breasts. *Since the mid-1970s, the* Sun *has run pictures of breasts on page 3 of every edition.*

peep show A machine in an adult arcade where a semi-pornographic movie could be viewed in coin-by-coin increments. *In its arcade days, this was also known as a* ***peek-arama.*** *Peep show has other meanings, one involving prostitution and one involving sexual performances (see pages 185 and 207).*

pillow book A finely illustrated sex book from Japan

pinch A technique used by male performers in pornographic movies, by which they create the illusion of a full erection by squeezing the base of their penis. *As* Jim Holliday *wrote, this "makes the old pole look harder than it is."*

pink An extreme close-up photograph or shot of a

woman's genitals

pinup A publicity photograph of a movie actress, posed to accentuate the size of her breasts and her sexual appeal. *The pinup came into being in World War II. The New York edition of* Yank *first used the term on April 30, 1943, attached to a photograph of movie actress Doris Merrick.*

plumber A male pornography performer

poon light A special spotlight used for close-up lighting of a woman's genitals

pop To ejaculate

pop shot A scene in a porn movie in which a male ejaculates outside the body of his partner

pornchops A movie that combines pornography and violence

pornzine A pornographic magazine

pricktures Male homosexual pornography

proof shot A scene in a porn movie in which a male ejaculates outside the body of his partner

purple Very smutty or **blue** (said of a joke, performance, etc.)

queen triad A scene in a porn movie involving one woman and two men

reverse anal cowgirl (RAC) A scene in a porn movie or a picture in a magazine in which a woman is astride a male, facing his feet, engaged in anal intercourse

reverse cowgirl (RC) A scene in a porn movie or a picture in a magazine in which a woman is astride a male, facing his feet, engaged in vaginal intercourse

ride the cotton pony To menstruate

riding St. George A shot in a porn movie with a woman having intercourse with a man, above and astride the man. *This is known more nowadays as a cowgirl and in some circles as the ride.*

sandwich A scene in a porn movie showing one woman simultaneously engaging in vaginal sex with one man and anal sex with another

scalp An appearance on a video box cover. *Like the real thing, a trophy and sign of success.*

sex pictures Pornography in the guise of sex education. *These movies were popular in the 1940s and 1950s. In the name of building a stronger marriage, men flocked to movie theaters to see*

early and rather tame mass-production pornography.

sex shop A store selling pornography

shampoo A scene in a porn movie showing a man ejaculating in the hair of another person

Sixty-Ninth Street Bridge A scene in a porn movie in which a woman upon whom oral sex is being performed by one man arches her back and performs oral sex on a second man

skin flick A pornographic movie

smoker 1. A porn movie shown to a group of men 2. A gathering of men at which a pornographic movie is shown

snail tracks, snail trail Traces of vaginal secretion on a woman's leg after a **giggler**

soft-core Sexual but not blatantly so. *This term was coined in the mid-1970s to distinguish a type of movie from hardcore porn. Generally, soft-core will show simulated sex, or will show sex without showing genitals, penetration, or ejaculation.*

solo box A video box cover showing only one female performer, coveted by

most women in porn

Southern love A shot in a porn movie showing (1) the removal of a body part or inanimate object from one person's rectum and (2) the placement of the part or object into another person's mouth (3) without any editing or film trickery. *The porn movie industry loves initialisms. The hip configuration for this type of shot is "a2m."*

splash shot A scene in a porn movie showing a man ejaculating outside the body of his partner

split beaver A photograph showing the spread lips of a woman's vulva

spreader A photograph showing a woman with her legs spread open

stag mag An "adult" magazine for men, featuring photographs of nudity but not sexual activity

stag show A combination of a porn movie and a stripper performing for a group of men

stickspin A scene in a porn movie in which a woman changes her position with the man's penis still inside her

stovepipe A scene in a porn movie showing an extended anus after an anal sex scene

strokes Pornographic magazines

stunt cock, stunt A performer in pornographic movies who stands in for the male star and provides the obligatory ejaculation for the obligatory **cum shot**

suitcase Any male accompanying a female pornography performer to the set—her boyfriend, husband, agent, manager, etc.

the ride A shot in a porn movie with a woman having intercourse with a man, above and astride the man. *Also known as a cowgirl. In the old days, this was known as riding St. George.*

tits and ass Featuring shapely actresses in an attempt to draw male viewers. *This term, often euphemized as T and A, became popular in the late 1970s.*

Tijuana Bible An eight-page or 16-page pornographic comic depicting well-known historical or fictional figures engaged in blatant sex

trade In male homosexual pornography, a man who will only engage as the active participant in anal sex or the passive recipient in oral sex; he will not kiss, and he will not be engaged as the passive recipient in anal sex, or the active participant in oral sex

triple play, triple crown A scene in a porn movie showing a woman engaged in sex with three men simultaneously—oral, vaginal, and anal. *Also known as TP, for triple penetration.*

trunk sales The sale of pornography out of a car trunk

tunnel magazine A pornographic magazine that contains many pictures of female genitals

twink A pretty, young, smooth homosexual male performer in pornographic movies

wallet girl A **pinup girl** before the world knew the term **pinup girl**

wave A penis which is erect but not fully so

western A scene in a porn movie in which a woman is astride a reclining man, facing his head, engaged in vaginal intercourse

wet shot A scene in a porn movie showing a man ejaculating outside the body of his partner

wood An erection. *When the male star of a scene about to be filmed in a porn movie has an erection—full wood—the call of "We've got wood!" signals that filming will now begin. Until then, the crew is "waiting for wood." Porn producer Joey Silvera is thought to have coined this most useful of terms, which was too cool for the confines of pornography and which quickly made the leap to youth slang.*

woodsman A male performer in a porn movie who can be counted on to achieve erection quickly, maintain erection throughout the shooting, and ejaculate in a timely and dramatic fashion.

Prostitution

PROSTITUTION HAS FLOURISHED in every civilization, and America is no exception; the admonitions of Proverbs 9:13-18 have never been fully heeded—we don't care if prostitutes are "loud and brash" or that they bring "lust and shame," we need them! We will follow her down to "death and hell," defying Proverbs 5:3-14. Not all of the early European settlers were Puritans, and it was not long before the buying and selling of venal pleasures became a part of early Colonial life. Every major city in the colonies had its **crimson sisterhood**, its **daughters of joy**, and its **ladies of easy virtue** who were engaged in the **social evil**, prostitution.

Brothels remained illegal but widely tolerated fixtures in American town and city life until early in World War II when municipalities across the country cracked down and managed to close most organized brothels. The demand for commercially available sex did not wane, though, and so prostitution evolved with the changing pattern of law enforcement, onto the streets, into **call girl** operations, into escort services (which themselves evolved from legitimate businesses providing social but not sexual companionship in the late 1930s to thinly disguised **outcall** prostitution operations in the 1980s), into **lap dancing** and other overtly sexual performances, and into massage parlors. Not all massage parlors sell sex, but those that advertise in the sports section tend to, those that keep late evening hours tend to, and most parlors that advertise as "Oriental" tend to sell at least **manual release** or they go out of business rather quickly. The old time madam's cry of "Company, ladies!" has changed to a massage parlor manager's cry of "Customers!," but the beat goes on.

Prostitution and the prostitute are part of our folk heritage, with the whore with a heart of gold, the madam with far-reaching political connections, and the badass pimp with style all playing recurring roles in fiction and song. The Western frontier was a particularly fertile breeding ground for prostitution, and the folklore of the West is laced with prostitution-lore, as is the folklore of mining camps, lumber camps, and railroad camps. The boys-will-be-boys/wink-wink attitude towards organized prostitution was well illustrated by the great success of *The Best Little Whorehouse in Texas* both on stage and screen.

The English language has had centuries to create slang analogues for *prostitute,* and American English has had at least 300 years to develop slang synonyms. The following list is far from exhaustive, and for the most part the terms listed represent only the most common terms for "prostitute" used in the 19th and 20th centuries:

alley cat

amateur   A nonprofessional

baby pro   A young professional prostitute

bachelor's wife

bag bride   A woman who will trade sex for crack cocaine

bangtail

bar girl   *A term from Vietnam, at least as early as 1966; see the Word History of "B-Girl" in Chapter One (page 20).*

basis   The prostitute that a pimp plans to marry when

he "squares up"

bat   *Because the prostitute, like a bat, is a creature of the night. One of many night images used in slang describing prostitutes.*

beast

bed sister

beefsteak   A prostitute who works for one pimp

bim

bint

blister   *Probably a reference—thanks—to venereal disease.*

bottom woman   A pimp's favored prostitute

brothel sprout   A prostitute who is burned out and jaded from a long turn of duty in a brothel

bunter

Burlap sister   *Often used in the phrase, "one of the Burlap sisters."*

business girl

butt peddler

c-girl   A call girl

c-lady   A call girl

camp follower

car whore   A prostitute who

has sex with customers in their cars

cat

charity girl A prostitute who is inclined to have sex and not charge the man

Chileno A South American prostitute brought to the United States (primarily San Francisco) expressly to work as a prostitute

chippy

choker An amateur

college girl

common carrier The lowest form of prostitute

commoner *A term coined and used by Shakespeare for a low prostitute.*

courtesan A high-class prostitute

cow baby A teenage prostitute

deception A transvestite male prostitute who can pass for a woman. *It is estimated that 25% of the street prostitutes in major cities are transvestites, some of whom are in fact deceptions.*

demi-rep A suspected prostitute

doe A young prostitute

dog-lady An unattractive prostitute

dolly

doss

double A pimp's number-two prostitute

doxy *Another Shakespeare*

term.

drab A low prostitute

dress for sale

dress lodger *A term from Britain in the 19th century, when a madam bought clothes for prostitutes who paid her back by working as prostitutes.*

Dutch widow *A 17th-century English slam of the Dutch.*

early door *Rhyming slang.*

endless belt *A term derived from the slang meaning of "belt" as "sex."*

erring sister

fancy, fancy woman

fish

fishmonger

flat floozy A prostitute working on her own out of an apartment

flat-backer A prostitute who has sex with as many men as possible instead of going for fewer, higher paying customers. *To save time, she lies on her back and has sex in the missionary position, one man after another.*

floozy

forty-four *Rhyming slang.*

fresh stock A brothel prostitute who is under 15

frow An unattractive prostitute. *From the Dutch word for "whore."*

Ginger A dishonest prosti-

tute who will rob a customer if the opportunity presents itself

girlfriend *A term used by a pimp to describe a prostitute.*

gong girl A prostitute who has customers drive to a secluded spot to have sex

gook The lowest form of prostitute. *Perhaps coming from "gowk" for "simpleton," this term is unrelated to the highly offensive "gook" applied to Asians and particularly to the Vietnamese during the Vietnam War.*

green goods A very young and inexperienced prostitute

gull A prostitute in a seaport

gypsy A traveling prostitute

hard leg An older, jaded prostitute

harlot *A biblical term.*

harpy

hatrack

heavy cruiser The lowest form of prostitute

hedge whore The lowest form of prostitute

hello-dearie *Greeting as noun—great!*

hen A prostitute who works in a brothel or massage parlor

Hershey Bar An inexpensive prostitute, like those encountered by American troops in World War II

who would sell sex for a candy bar

ho

hole

hooker *See Word History, page 209.*

hoyden A cheap prostitute

hurry whore A prostitute who rushes her customers

hustler A prostitute who seeks customers

jailbait An underage prostitute

Jane Shore *More rhymes.*

Jude

Kate *From the Dutch "Kat" for a wanton woman.*

Kelsey *From carnival slang.*

kid-leather A teenage prostitute

lady *A pimp term, as in "This is Sheila, one of my ladies . . ."*

leather merchant A prostitute who caters to customers with leather fetishes

lingerie lass A prostitute with fancy lingerie

low heel

market dame

mawker

meal ticket *From the pimp's point of view, the prostitute is his meal ticket.*

messer An amateur prostitute who interferes with the professionals' action

model

moll

moonlighter

mouth whore A prostitute who prefers giving oral sex

Mrs. Warren's girl *The expression "one of **Mrs. Warren's girls**" is derived from a play by George Bernard Shaw, "Mrs. Warren's Profession."*

muff merchant

nafka *From the Yiddish, applied to a prostitute who walks the streets.*

nanny *A word that saw the bottom of the barrel and then worked its way bravely back up.*

nighthawk

nightingale

night piece

nightwalker

nymph du pave *Don't the French make it sound romantic? (French "nymphe du pavé" literally means "nymph of the pavement.")*

nymph of darkness

old lady *A term used largely by pimps when they refer to their prostitutes.*

old rip An aging prostitute

old-timer A skilled prostitute. *This is a term of approval used by prostitutes about each other.*

one-way girl A prostitute who will not engage in oral or anal sex

outlaw A prostitute working without a pimp

overnight bag *Early 20th century.*

owl *Another night-oriented term, used in the 19th century.*

painted lady An early-20th-century expression *that is built on a stigma associated with makeup.*

panel worker A prostitute who works in a **panel house**, having sex with customers who do not know that they are being watched by other customers through two-way mirrors

pavement pretty

pavement princess

pickup

pretty girl *From the turn of the century.*

pretty waiter girl *A great euphemism from 19th-century San Francisco.*

pross *Clipped from "prostitute."*

prossy

quiff The lowest form of prostitute

rock whore A woman who will trade sex for crack cocaine

Rory O'More *More rhyming slang.*

saleslady *An early-20th-century acknowledgment of the commercial aspects of prostitution.*

scarlet letter girls *Too literary for widespread use, but recorded.*

scuffer

scupper

shady lady *A nice little rhyme that was very popular during the Civil War.*

sin girl *A term coined in Bangkok during the Vietnam War.*

sister of the night

sitter A part-time prostitute who works in the afternoon and then returns home to her role as housewife in the evening. *The term seems to have originated in Shreveport, Louisiana.*

six-to-four *Even more rhyming slang.*

skeeger, skeezer A woman who will trade sex for crack cocaine

snapper A prostitute who can perform the "Cleopatra" or the "bite," a voluntary contraction of the vaginal muscles around the customer's penis

snatch peddler

sorting girl

stick

stock A young prostitute in a brothel

strawberry A woman who will trade sex for crack cocaine

street girl

streetwalker

tank The lowest type of prostitute

Thatcher's girl *Yes, British, from the 1980s and nicely political.*

thoroughbred

three-penny upright *A British expression for the lowest form of prostitute, having sex outdoors, standing up, for a pittance.*

three-way girl A prostitute who will engage in vaginal, oral, or anal sex

town bike The lowest type of prostitute. *Everybody in town rides her.*

trailer girl A traveling prostitute

tweak *Breaking the ground rules, this is a 16th-century term which became obsolete as a synonym for "prostitute" hundreds of years ago, but one which is of some interest because of its appearance in the lexicon of methamphetamine users in the 1980s.*

two-bit Sadie The lowest type of prostitute. *A term coined in Brooklyn.*

walker

wench

wife *A term used by a pimp to refer to one of his prostitutes.*

working broad

working chick

working girl

zook An old, tired-out prostitute

While prostitution is for the most part a female profession, where there is a demand there is a supply, and there is always a demand for male homosexual prostitutes. That demand drives a supply, and with that supply is a modest slang vocabulary—**angel** (a man who pays a male prostitute to be the passive partner in sex), **aspro** (a professional male prostitute —the pronunciation is the key), **bitch** (a male prostitute), **bunny** (a male prostitute), **call boy** (summoned for sex work by telephone), **chicken** (a young male prostitute), **dilly boy** (19th-century British), **foot soldier** (a prostitute who works the streets), **he-she** (a male transvestite prostitute), **he-whore** (good one!), **iron** (prostitute as metal?), **jag, jag house** (a brothel for men who want men), **Maud** (20th-century British), **midnight cowboy** (hence the movie title), **molly house** (a homosexual brothel), **peg house** (a brothel for men who want men, again), **punk** (a male prostitute), a **rent boy** (usually a runaway selling sex to survive), and a **transformer** (a male transvestite prostitute).

Where? The established brothel is almost a thing of the past, but before it passed from the American scene during World War II, it left us with dozens of slang terms and expressions to use instead of *whorehouse*. Variations on the theme include **bag shanty, barrel house, bawdy house, beauty parlor, birdcage, blind pig** or **blind tiger, boum-boum parlor** (a term used in An Khe during the conflict in Vietnam), **brotel** (a motel that functions as a brothel), **bull pen** (a large brothel), **cab joint** (so called because taxi drivers would deliver customers), **call flat** (an apartment used by a **call girl**), **can house** (a term from the 1930s), **cat flat, cat house, chicken ranch** (a brothel in an isolated, rural location), **chippie joint, clap trap** (a low-class brothel where infection is probable), **common house** (a term coined by Shakespeare), **couple house** or **coupling house, cow yard** (a large brothel with many small rooms), **creep joint** (a brothel or room arranged to facilitate robbing from a customer's clothing), **crib** (a small room or small house where a prostitute has sex with customers), **deadfall, dive, doss house, family hotel, fancy house, flea and louse** (rhyming slang that was too close to the truth for comfort), **flesh market, fleshpot** (the term used by the King James version of the Bible), **fuck house** (not a bit indirect, is it?), **gaff, goat house, gooseberry** or **goosing ranch, heifer den** (a large brothel), **hog ranch** (a term from the Western frontier), **hook joint** or **hook shop** (a crooked brothel), **hotbed** (a motel room used for prostitution, not showing a registered guest), **house of all nations, house of assignation, house of delight, house of ill fame, house of ill repute, house of pleasure, ice palace** (a fancy brothel in the eyes of 20th-century American criminals), **Irish clubhouse** (oh those ethnic slurs—how about **Irish toothache** for pregnancy and **Irish foreplay** for rough, inconsiderate sex as in "Brace yourself Bridget . . ."?), **jab joint, jacksie, joy house** (an expression used by Raymond Chandler in *Farewell, My Lovely*), **juke house, kit kat club** (a bar in a seaport where prostitutes work), **nunnery** (explaining Hamlet's "Get thee to a nunnery" to Ophelia), **old ladies' home** (hobo slang for a dignified, orderly brothel), **panel house** or **panel joint** (either a brothel with two-way mirrors making **peep shows** possible or a brothel with sliding doors that facilitate theft from a customer's clothing), **parlor house, public house, resort, rib joint** (a brothel catering to sexual exhibitions without customer participation), **school of Venus, slaughterhouse, slut hut** (too cute!), **sporting house, stew, telephone house** (a brothel with no prostitutes on the premises, from which telephone calls are made summoning the prostitutes as they are requested), **trick pad** (an apartment where a prostitute takes her customers), **U.N.** (a brothel with prostitutes from many different ethnic and national backgrounds), **vaulting school, working rooms** (rooms where prostitutes take customers), **workshop,** and **zoo.**

Because prostitution is a business as well as a sin, there are supervisors as well as employees, and the supervisor at the brothel had a special place in the business. Like her charges, she was known by a number of slang names, including **abbess, aunt, auntie, bawd, hostess** (the term used today in Nevada's legal brothels), **housekeeper, house mother,** and **Mother Superior** (*another* one of the church jokes!).

If prostitution is the **oldest profession**, then pimping is the **second oldest profession**, a job with a vague job description which might include protecting a prostitute from physical danger, procuring customers for the prostitute, and/or bullying the prostitute into turning over her earnings for no particular service rendered. **Pimp** was first recorded in the early 1600s, and may have been clipped from the old French *pimpreneau,* a knave or rascal. Slangily synonymous with **pimp** are **account executive** (a pimp with either high-class prostitutes and/or high-class customers), **Alphonse** (rhyming slang with *ponce,* a 19th-century British term for "pimp"), **apache** (a French term, from the much romanticized Paris of the early 20th century), **apple squire, ass merchant, ass peddler, B.F.** (short for *boyfriend*), **bludger, bullie** or **bully** (19th-century British), **chili pimp** (a small-time hustler, perhaps with only one prostitute), **chump** (a pimp who earns only enough to support his most basic needs), **coffee and cake pimp** (a small-time pimp), **C.P.** (short for **cunt pensioner**), **easy rider, fancy man,**

fish and shrimp (Cockney rhyming slang), **gagger** (hobo slang of the 1930s), **gentleman of leisure** (a sweet little euphemism, no?), **gorilla pimp** (one who uses violence to control his prostitutes), **hard mack** (a violent pimp), **jelly bean, love broker** (see **love**, defined below), **mack** (a clipped form of the French **maquereau**, borrowed by Americans and especially in the black community), **man, nookie bookie** (too cute for much real usage, but cute), **old man, paddy hustler, pander** (from Pandarus, who procures Cressida for Troilus in Shakespeare), **P.I., player** (a word which came to have strong positive connotations in African-American vernacular English), **popcorn pimp** (a small-time operator), **promoter, stable boss** (one of several horse metaphors used with pimps; the **stable** is the group of prostitutes working for one pimp, who is said to **push ponies** who are **cash on the hoof**), **sugar pimp** (who uses charm and charisma, not violence, to control his prostitutes), **sweet mack** or **sweet man** (a pimp who is not violent).

After an interview with a prostitute (**taking an application**), a pimp will select—**cop**—a prostitute and try to **pull** her, or acquire her services. Many pimps try to maintain a steady number of prostitutes by the **cop and blow** method under which they recruit a new prostitute each time one leaves the group. A pimp and his prostitutes are a **family**, making the prostitutes **sisters-in-law** or **wives-in-law** to each other. A pimp's style is his **flash**, while his **game** is his way of dealing with and controlling his prostitutes, either **gorilla** (violent) or **sweet** (not violent). Back to style, the pimp often drives a Cadillac or other large luxury car, known as a **pimpmobile** or **showboat**, and to be **pimped down** is to be dressed in an exquisitely outrageous style. A **pimp stick** is a cigarette holder, which adds to the fashion statement.

An interesting cultural borrowing has served well in the slang of the hip-hop movement. Because the pimp is often a respected and admired figure in urban neighborhoods, the slang terms **pimp, player**, and **mack** have all crossed over to teenage slang as terms of approval. Some teenagers have then taken at least **mack** one step further, turning the noun into the adjective **mackadocious**, applied to a good-looking and popular boy.

And then there is the vocabulary associated with prostitution that goes beyond the basics, beyond the limits of prostitute, pimp, manager, and place of working—the words that describe the customers, services available, the exchange of money, etc. This vocabulary is at times lewd and at times clever, at times obvious and at times difficult to understand.

Alka-Seltzer A specialty sex act, involving an Alka-Seltzer tablet

all-nighter A session with a prostitute that lasts all night. *The opposite is* **short time**.

ass To have sex with a customer, to **turn a trick**

assisted shower A massage parlor euphemism for masturbation or a **hand job** while the customer takes a shower

baby A customer. *This expression was the most popular in the early 20th century, eventually giving way completely to* **John** *or* **trick**.

badger game A swindle perpetrated by a prostitute and an accomplice who bursts in on the prostitute and customer, pretending to be the prostitute's husband and demanding compensation from the frightened customer

bag A douche

B&D   A specialty sex act, consisting of bondage and dominance or discipline

beat a trick   To rob a customer

beef burger   A customer

bennie   A customer who prefers to perform oral sex on the prostitute

biddy   A bidet

big legs   A customer who is a big spender

Binaca blast   Oral sex performed by a prostitute who has just sprayed her mouth with Binaca mouth spray

birthday party   Sex involving several prostitutes and several customers; an orgy

book   A prostitute's records of her regular customers and their telephone numbers

Boston tea party   A specialty sex act, in which the prostitute urinates or defecates on the customer

break luck   To **turn** the first **trick** of the day

breeder   A passenger in a taxi cab who wants to visit a brothel

bulb   A douche

bull money   The fee paid the prostitute

busy   Having sex with a customer, as in "Gloria can't see you just now, she's busy."

catalog   Photographs of prostitutes shown cus-

tomers who then select the prostitute they want, used in **outcall** operations

circus, circus love   Group sex with prostitutes, usually involving a number of **kinks** and sometimes followed by blackmail by the prostitutes and/or their confederates

cold biscuit   An unappealing customer

cold potato   An unappealing customer

company   Sex. *A common solicitation by a prostitute is "Want some company?"*

cookies   What you want. *To the prostitute, money; to the customer, sex.*

cop a cherry   To have sex with a virginal customer

creeper   A prostitute's accomplice who enters the room stealthily and robs the customer's clothing

curb crawl   To drive through an area frequented by streetwalking prostitutes, looking for a prostitute

dancing lessons   A short-lived cover for prostitution. *Newspaper advertisements in the 1940s offered "strictly private dance lessons to gentlemen only."*

D&S   A specialty sex act—dominance and submission

date   1. A customer 2. Sex with a customer

dig   A sexual exhibition by prostitutes for customers

dis con   Disorderly conduct. *When police cannot catch prostitutes soliciting sex, they will sometimes arrest them and charge them with disorderly conduct.*

dominatrix   A female prostitute who plays the role of a dominator in sadomasochistic sexual games. *Sadomasochism, most commonly referred to as S&M or B&D, exists within and without prostitution. The current term for a female sadist is femdom.*

dowry   The fee paid a prostitute for her services. *Kind of clever.*

English, English culture   A **menu** choice at some brothels, consisting of simulated or real flagellation, which is known as the **English vice**

exhibition   A sexual exhibition by prostitutes for customers

extras   Sexual services in a massage parlor

face man   A customer who prefers to perform oral sex on the prostitute

fish   To steer potential customers to a bar where prostitutes are working

flash man   The bouncer
in a brothel or bar
where prostitutes work

fleshpot   An area where
prostitutes work

fork and spoon   Mutual
oral sex between a pros-
titute and her customer.
*This term was popular
in New Orleans brothels
early in the 20th centu-
ry.*

for love   Offered with no
charge (said of sex with
a prostitute)

forty/five   Forty dollars
for the sex act, five dollars for the room. *The
amounts may vary, but
the construction per-
sists.*

freak trick   A customer
who is a fetishist

freebie   Sex with a prostitute with no charge

French, French culture
Oral sex, as in "For anoth-
er five dollars, she speaks
French."

friend   A man who supports
a prostitute as his mistress

fuck luck   A prostitute chosen by the brothel manag-
er for and not by the customer

full-service   Sexual intercourse. *This is massage
parlor euphemism.*

gaff   A special G-string used
by transvestite prostitutes
to hide their genitals

game, the   The life and

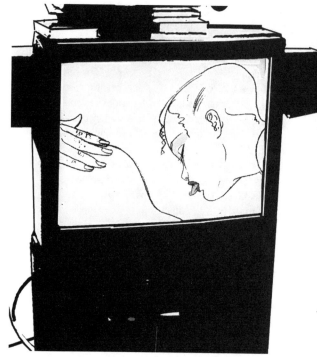

business of prostitution

gangster   A man, often a
pimp, who has sex with a
prostitute and does not
pay for her services

gazupie   A sexual exhibition
for customers. *A term
from the 1930s.*

Georgia   To have sex with a
prostitute and then refuse
to pay for her services. *To
prevent this practice,
most prostitutes accept
the operating premise of
"no snatch before scratch
(money)."*

get-down time   The time of
day when the prostitute is
supposed to start working

go below 14th Street   To
perform oral sex on a
prostitute (said of a customer)

go caso   To become a prostitute

golden shower   Sex involving urination

Greek, Greek culture   A
menu choice at most
brothels, involving anal sex

half-and-half   A specialty
sex act, consisting of oral
sex followed by inter-
course. *The name is per-
haps borrowed from a
traditional English drink
of half beer and half ale.*

hand job   Masturbation of a

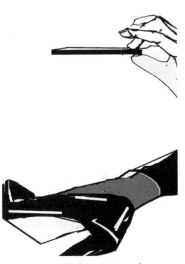

customer by a prostitute

handshaker Masturbation of a customer by a prostitute

hawk, hawk the fork, hawk your mutton To solicit for sex

head date Oral sex with a customer

he-say-she-say Discussions between a prostitute and a third party about her pimp

hide your candy To hide the genitals (said of a male transvestite prostitute)

hip-bath A bidet

house split The share of the fee paid the prostitute

which is given to the brothel, massage parlor, or business sponsoring the prostitution

hustle To seek customers

in-call An arrangement where the customer meets the prostitute at her apartment or **trick pad**

income tax Fines paid the police. *Most prostitutes do not report their earnings and do not pay income taxes, so they view the fines they pay as taxes.*

in the life Working as a prostitute

Italian, Italian culture

A **menu** choice at most brothels, involving anal sex. *D. H. Lawrence used the term the Italian way to mean anal sex in* Lady Chatterley's Lover.

jack shack A massage parlor or lingerie show where the customer is teased but must masturbate if he wants sexual release

jive To feign orgasm

John A prostitute's customer. *In the 1940s, prostitutes began describing their customers as Johns, using the slang term for "toilet" and "condom," both of which were once called a "Johnnie."*

Johnson An African-American man who protects prostitutes, not necessarily a pimp

juice A bribe paid public officials to facilitate prostitution

kiddy freak A customer who prefers young prostitutes

kink, kinkie 1. A customer who is a fetishist of some sort 2. A fetish

lay the note Pay the prostitute

light touch body rub Masturbation of a customer by a prostitute. *This euphemism is used in massage parlors and lingerie modeling.*

lighthouse A person who steers customers to a brothel or bar where prostitutes work

line 1. The area where prostitutes work 2. All prostitutes available at a given moment in a brothel

local Masturbation of a customer by a prostitute. *Used in massage parlors.*

log in To turn the customer's pay over to the brothel management. *This expression is found in Nevada's legal brothels. After the customer pays the prostitute, she leaves the room to log in. When she returns, they have sex.*

long date A prolonged session between prostitute and customer, roughly greater than an hour

look at the ceiling To have sex (from the prostitute's point of view)

love Sex

love booth joint A dancing studio of the 1930s where the male customers and female employees could retire for sexual intimacy

manual release Masturbation of a customer by a prostitute. *Again, used in massage parlors.*

marathon An entire evening spent with a call girl, consisting of dinner, night-

club, and then sex

market prices Prices for different sex acts as quoted by a prostitute

meatball A customer

meat block, meat rack An area where male prostitutes gather to solicit customers

menu A list of different sexual activities and the charge for them posted on walls in Nevada's legal brothels

milk To massage a customer's penis, checking for a discharge which might indicate infection with venereal disease

milk cow A woman in a brothel whose job is to check customers for possible venereal disease

milk route, the Places where prostitutes might find customers very late at night, such as the bus station

Minnesota strip An area where prostitutes work. *The term originated in New York, referring to young women freshly arrived in New York from Minnesota. It is now used in cities other than New York.*

money, moneymaker The orifice(s) by which a prostitute makes his or her living

Murphy game A collabora-

tion in which a prostitute lures a customer to a room where he is then robbed by her confederate or in which the pimp takes the customer's money and then leads him to a room which is empty

no-hands session A display by lingerie models where customers are not permitted to touch the models

old-fashioned Vaginal intercourse

old firm The business of prostitution, as in "I work for an old firm."

old man A rich customer who supports a prostitute

on the bash Engaged in prostitution

on the game Engaged in work as a prostitute

on the line Engaged in prostitution in a **red-light district**

on the turf Engaged in prostitution on the street

oral Oral sex

orbit Oral sex

outcall A prostitution service where the prostitute comes to the customer

papa A rich man who supports a prostitute

party 1. To have sex. *A common solicitation by a prostitute is "Wanna party?"* 2. A session with one customer and two or more prostitutes

patron A customer

pearl necklace Semen on a prostitute's chest

peep show 1. A sexual exhibition by prostitutes 2. A display of a prostitute and her unknowing customer viewed through a two-way mirror in a brothel

peter pan A dish pan used by a prostitute to wash a customer's penis before sex. *What a great pun!*

pin A move or a look that first engages the customer's attention

piper A customer

pony girl A prostitute who arranges to meet customers by telephone

pound the block, pound the pavement Walk the streets, looking for customers

preemie A man who ejaculates prematurely or quickly

price of greens The fee charged by a prostitute. *A 19th-century euphemism.*

prick rag A towel given a customer to clean himself with after ejaculating. *A massage parlor term that gets right to the point.*

professor A piano player in a brothel

public enemy The wife of a prostitute's customer

pucker water An astringent which a prostitute might use to tighten her vaginal muscles

qualified Experienced (said of a prostitute)

quick trick A short session of sex with a customer

rabbit A customer who ejaculates quickly

red-light district An area of a city in which brothels are numerous. *Brothels often had red lights (perhaps as a signal of their business) in their windows.*

relaxation rubdown Sex. *Another euphemism from the world of massage parlors and lingerie modeling.*

relief massage Masturbation of a customer by a prostitute. *Again, from massage parlors.*

Roman A menu choice at some brothels that means an orgy

Rural Route, RR A designation indicating what types of sex a prostitute is willing to perform; **RR 1** is vaginal, **RR 2** adds oral, and **RR 3** adds anal

Russian, Russian culture A **menu** choice at some brothels that involves ejaculation while rubbing the penis between the prostitute's breasts, producing a **pearl necklace**

safe word A preordained word used in bondage and discipline sex that means, "Please stop, this is not working!"

S&M Sadomasochism, a specialty that some prostitutes will perform

sauna club A massage parlor

scene A particular interaction between several people engaged in sadomasochistic sex, usually revolving around a passive customer

session fee The fee paid a lingerie model for her services

78 A customer who has sex quickly. *A reference to the outmoded phonograph record which revolved at **78** rpms (revolutions per minute), considered fast compared to the **33**.*

s-girl A female spy who uses sex to pry loose secrets

shake joint A "dancing studio" of the 1930s where customers and "dancers" would engage in intimate caresses—**shaking**—while fully clothed. *The male customer who ejaculated while **shaking** was said to have reached the "limit."*

shebang Sex involving several prostitutes and several customers

short time A session with a prostitute that lasts until the customer ejaculates. *The opposite is an all-nighter.*

show A sexual exhibition by prostitutes for customers

sightseer A man who drinks at a brothel but leaves without having sex

sit for company To work in a bar, soliciting sex from strangers

sitz-bath A bidet

skunk 1. A small tip 2. To fail to pay

sneak play A surreptitious entry and exit from a brothel

Southern massage Sex. *Another massage parlor euphemism, referring to the genitals as "down South."*

springer A bail bondsman, who can "spring" a prostitute from jail

square up To leave the life of prostitution and live in conventional society

stand-up job Hurried sex while standing up, often performed in an alley

steerer A person who directs customers to a brothel. *Cab drivers, hotel employees, and police were the prime steerers in the days of brothels.*

straight, straight date, straight trick Vaginal intercourse with no frills

stroll The area where prostitutes congregate and work

sucker A customer

switch A massage parlor **extra**, in which the customer massages the masseuse after she has massaged him

talk game To discuss pimping and whoring

tip The fee paid for sex in a massage parlor

33 A customer who has sex slowly. *A reference to the outmoded phonograph record which revolved at 33 1/3 rpms (revolutions per minute), considered slow compared to the 78.*

three p Three persons: two prostitutes and one customer

three-way Vaginal, oral, or anal sex

trade A customer

trade, the Prostitution

trick 1. A prostitute's customer 2. Sex with a customer 3. To have sex with a customer

trick book A prostitute's list of customers and their telephone numbers

trick pad An apartment or house where a prostitute entertains customers

trick suit An outfit that is very revealing and can be easily removed

troll To solicit sex or payment for sex

turkey money Money paid cab drivers or other **steerers** for bringing a customer to a prostitute

turn a date To have sex with a customer

turn a trick To have sex with a customer

turn out To make a girl or woman a prostitute

two-way Vaginal or oral sex

unbetty To unbutton a customer's pants

unslough To unbutton a customer's pants

vanilla sex Conventional sexual intercourse, with no **kinks**

versatile Dominant or submissive (said of a person)

warm up To wash a customer's genitals with soap and warm water

watch and jack The activities permitted in a **no-hands session** at a lingerie modeling show—the customer can watch the women and masturbate, but may not touch the women

water sports Sex involving urination

wet decks A prostitute who has recently had sex. *A crude image, used by John O'Hara in* A Rage to Live.

whore bath, whore's bath Cleaning up by splashing water on one's face, armpits, and genitals

whore stroll An area where prostitutes congregate and solicit sex

window-tapping Solicitation of customers by a prostitute tapping on a window

work To solicit customers for sex

work a crib To work in a low-class whorehouse

work from the book To

work as a call girl, not a streetwalker

work the outs To work as a prostitute on the street

WORD HISTORY

HOOKER

IN A SINFUL SLANG world populated with false etymologies, the undisputed champion must be **hooker.**

The firm popular belief is that the term comes from the name of General Joseph Hooker (1814-79), a United States Army general who is said to have actively recruited prostitutes to serve his troops while encamped in Washington, D.C. during the Civil War. Jokingly known as "Hooker's Division," the "Division" soon was dropped, leaving **hookers.** Takers on this etymology include *Playboy* (May 1968), Herb Caen in the *San Francisco Chronicle* (November 7, 1978), and poet Robert Lowell (on radio station KPFA in Berkeley, California on September 24, 1957).

There is a delightful, sinful air to this etymology, which is flawed only by the fact that the term predates the Civil War and General Hooker's antics. The earliest usage was unearthed by George Thompson of New York University. Thompson antedated the widely accepted earliest date

of 1845 by ten years, finding a use of **hooker** in the *New York Transcript* of September 25, 1835, where a witness explains to a judge that a **hooker** is called a **hooker** because "she allers hangs round the hook [Corlear's Hook in New York City], your honner."

Like General Hooker, Corlear's Hook has been advanced as the origin of **hooker** for a long time with some authority (as in John Bartlett's 1859 *Dictionary of Americanisms* and Stuart Berg Flexner's *Listining to America*), but other theories exist, creating more etymological confusion than clarity:

> The origin is probably from the habit such women have of hooking arms with their prospects. *(Shady Ladies of the West* by Ronald Dean Miller)*

> It is either a reference to one who lives within the district frequented by criminals, or a survival from the 16-18th-century English cant, "hook," to trick, to catch, to take by angling. *(American Tramp and Underworld Slang* by Godfrey Irwin))*

Another version [than the one with General Hooker] ascribes the origin of the word to the Hook, in Baltimore, the town's sailor section, where tarts picked up sea-faring men. (*Washington Confidential* by Jack Lait and Lee Mortimer)

A final possibility is that **hooker** came from the sense of *hooker* found in the *English Dialect Dictionary*—a person who stands outside a merchant's warehouse to invite customers to enter.

Given the apparent American birth of **hooker,** the American theories are the more plausible. It can be said, though, that much like **booze**/bouse/Booz, "Fighting Joe" Hooker gave **hooker** a boost, without which it may have floundered and faded in the 19th century. Thanks to General Hooker, **hooker** has endured marvelously, whatever its precise semantic origins.

WORD HISTORIES

G-STRING, BUMP AND GRIND, AND JERK OFF

IN 1937, AMERICA gave the world a new word to describe a new, decidedly American performance art, the **striptease.** Until the relatively recent past, dancers who stripped retained a shred of modesty, a fig leaf of sorts, a **G-string** or small triangle of cloth passed between the legs and supported by a waist cord.

The *Oxford English Dictionary* (*OED*) lists *Big Money* by John Dos Passos (1936) as containing the first written use of **G-string**—"One of the girls ... wiggled her geestring at him." Within the Tamony Collection, however, one finds a 1931 use in Bernard Sobel's *Burleycue*, which would predate **striptease** by six years:

> *Nevertheless, the improprieties of a Lydia Thompson seem mild indeed, as compared with a modern burlesque show, especially the kind offered nowadays, where girls take off everything but the brassiere and the "G" string—the narrow equivalent to the dancing belt—or sometimes prance down the runway with their breasts bare, making wise cracks to the nearest males.*

Less dramatically perhaps than **hooker, G-string** still boasts a proud false etymology. Articulated by Stan Holden in *Modern Man: The Man's Picture Magazine*

(June 1955), the theory is as follows:

> *The lowest string on a violin is the G-string. When a burlesque comic back in the 20s looked for a way of describing the last item of a stripteaser's costume, the lowest point of her ensemble, the last refuge*

against outright nudity, he hit upon G-string for an apt description. And G-string it has remained through the years.

As inviting as the *Modern Man* thesis is (and incidentally it was embraced in more respectable quarters by Wilfred Granville in

The Theatre Dictionary, 1952), it fails to take into consideration the fact that **gee-string** had been in use to describe loincloths worn by Native Americans at least since 1878. Richard Thorton's *An American Glossary* (1912) cites J. H. Beadle's 1878 *Western Wilds*—"Around each

boy's waist is the tight 'geestring,' from which a single strip of cloth runs between the limbs from front to back." If the spelling detracts from the connection, you'll find a **G-string** from the December 1891 *Harper's* magazine in the *OED*—"Some of the boys wore only 'G-strings' (as, for some reason, the breech-clout is commonly called on the prairie)." The same term was applied to the loincloth worn in the Philippines, and was used in the *Fourth Annual Report of the Philippines Commission, Parts 1 and 3* (1903), and in Australia (*Saturday Evening Post,*

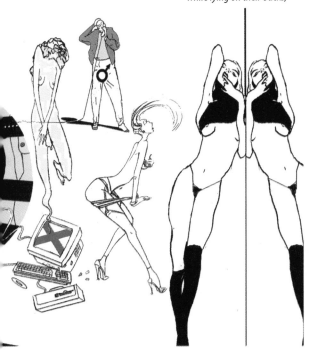

April 10, 1937).

The principal moves in a striptease were the **bump** and the **grind,** often combined into a **bump and grind** routine. The **bump** was a pelvic thrust, and the **grind** (long a slang term for sexual intercourse) a rotation of the hips; both were overtly sexual.

Bump and **grind** came on the written scene at the same time, showing up in Bernard Sobel's 1931 *Burleycue:*

> *At a recent Bill Minsky show some of these girls presented the first time in history, a grind on the floor; that is, while lying on their backs,*

they duplicated all the manoeuvers and gyrations of the belly dance, including the "bumps"—routine term for forward and backward thrusts of the abdomen.

In 1950, actress Sara Allen sued Mae West, claiming that West was interfering with Allen's ability to get work. In a poem attached to the complaint, one finds as charming a use of **bump and grind** as could be hoped for:

> *Can Sara's spinal undulations Be subject to West's regulations?*
> *For buxom Mae now makes the claim*
> *Of introducing sex to fame,*
> *That bumps and grinds were never known*
> *Till in her act they first were shown.*
>
> *Bumps and grinds and flirty song*
> *All to antiquity belong.*
>
> *And sex was known to Eve and Adam*
> *And hips before Mae West e'er had 'em.*
> (*San Francisco News,* November 30, 1950).

Bump and grind has come a long way over the years. In the 1930s, it was smiled at. In the early 1950s, with the resurgence of striptease sweeping America's cities, **bumps** and **grinds** became a threat to decency and the American way. San Francisco Chief of Police Michael Gaffey specifically banned the moves in 1952: "'Bumps and grinds are absolutely out,' said Gaffey. 'Any performers employing these routines will be arrested'" ("Nude Shows OK But Lewd

Ones Out, Chief Says: Gaffey Bans 'Bumps,''Grinds,' Even In Raccoon Coat," *San Francisco Examiner*, August 2, 1952). In the mid-1970s, **bump** had lost enough stigma to become attached to a dance in which the partners bumped hips in beat. By 1996, **bump and grind** was tame enough to be punned upon in an advertisement for Oldsmobile, which offered "a brief respite from the daily bump and grind."

Having been to the striptease and seen the dancers in their G-strings bump and grind—why not a final expression? Just as each generation believes that it is the first to have discovered the guilty pleasures of masturbation, so does each generation of boys believe that it has coined the expression **jerk off**. Neither is true. The *OED* cites a first use of **jerk off** as a transitive verb meaning "to masturbate" in 1937, inexplicably ignoring J. S. Farmer and W. E. Henley, who in 1896 included **jerk off** in *Slang and Its Analogues* as a variant on the then-dominant **jerk one's jelly** or **jerk one's juice.**

Standing alone, **jerk** is a slang old-timer, found in John Cleland's sexual masterpiece *Fanny Hill* (published 1748-49), meaning to procure ejaculation in a man by manual friction, not necessarily self-applied. With the Farmer and Henley citation,

though, we have been **jerking off** now for more than a century.

SOURCES AND REFERENCES

FOR THE ENGAGING interplay between theology and sex, I drew upon *Whatever Became of Sin?* by Karl Menninger (New York: Haw-thorn, 1973);"A Message on Sex-uality: Some Common Convic-tions," as adopted by the Church Council of the Evangelical Luth-eran Church in America on No-vember 9, 1996; and various online resources.

I hit the mother lode in my search for authentic slang from the porn industry in the person of Jim Holliday, the only adult industry historian worth his salt. An industry insider with impec-cable credentials, Holliday has a great ear and he graciously shared his knowledge of porn slang, including a three-part series which he wrote entitled "The Porn Buff Bluffer's Glossary Guide to Inside Industry Lingo" published in *Adult Video News* beginning in August 1995. Mark Cromer and Mark Kulkis were most helpful in this rather raunchy little side-trip.

Later in the process I met Jen-nifer Goldstein, a former exotic dancer with a tremendous sense both of language and justice. Dozens of the words from the world of sex clubs came from Ms. Goldstein.

Sources from the world of books

included *Strip Tease: The Vanished Art of Burlesque* by H. M. Alex-ander (New York: Knight, 1938); *Cop to Call Girl: Why I Left the LAPD to Make an Honest Living as a Beverly Hills Prostitute* by Norma Jean Almodovar (New York: Simon and Schuster, 1993); "Sexual Slang" by Leonard R. N. Ashley in *Maledicta*, Vol. 9 (1986-87); *Little Known Facts About Bundling In the New World* by A. Monroe Aurand, Jr. (Harrisburg, Penn.: Aurand, 1938); *Mayflower Madam* by Sydney Biddle Barrows with William Novak (New York: Ballantine, 1986); "Disturbing Your Seed" by Scott Beach in *Maledicta*, Vol. 5 (Winter 1981); *The X-Rated Book: Sex and Obscenity in the Bible* by J. Ash-leigh Burke (Houston: J.A.B., 1983); *Daughters of Joy, Sisters of Misery: Prostitutes in the American West* by Anne M. Butler (Champaign: University of Illinois Press, 1985); *Sex Work: Writings by Women in the Sex Industry* by Frederique Delacoste and Priscilla Alexander (San Francisco: Cleis, 1987)*; And Adam Knew Eve: A Dictionary of Sex in the Bible* by Ronald L. Ecker (Palatka, Fla.: Hodge and Braddock, 1995); *Harlots, Whores & Hookers: A History of Prostitution* by Hilary Evans (New York: Dorset, 1979); *Working: My Life as a Prostitute* by Dolores French and Linda Lee (New York: Dutton, 1988); *The Language of*

Sex from A to Z by Robert Goldenson and Kenneth Anderson (New York: World Almanac, 1986); *Self-Love* by David Cold Gordon (New York: Verity House, 1968); *Gentlemen of Leisure: A Year in the Life of a Pimp* by Susan Hall (New York: Signet, 1973); *An ABZ of Love* by Inge & Sten Hegeler (New York: Alexicon Corp., 1967); *Her Life as an American Madam* by Nell Kimball (New York: Macmillan, 1970); "Prostitutes and Criminal Argot" by David Maurer in *Language of the Underworld* (Lexington: University Press of Kentucky, 1981; originally published in *American Journal of Sociology,* January 1939); *Gay (S)language* by H. Max (Austin: Banned, 1988); *Shady Ladies of the West* by Ronald Dean Miller (Los Angeles: Westernlore, 1964); *Black Players: The Secret World of Black Pimps* by Christina and Richard Milner (Boston: Little, Brown, 1972); *The Slanguage of Sex: A Dictionary of Modern Sexual Terms* by Bridgid McConville and John Shearlaw (London: Macdonald, 1984); *Final Report of the Attorney General's Commission on Pornography,* with an introduction by Michael J. McManus (Nashville: Rutledge Hill, 1986); *Making Sense of English in Sex* by Lee McOwan (Edinburgh: Chambers Harrap, 1993); *American Encyclopedia of Sex* by Adolph F. Niemoeller (New York:

Panurge, 1935); *Smut: American Sex Slang* by Jim Norris (Los Olivos, Calif.: Olive, 1992); *The Erotic Tongue: A Sexual Lexicon* by Lawrence Paros (New York: Henry Holt, 1984); *A Glossary of Sexual Terms* by Robert Pelligrino (Chicago: Novel, 1965); *A Dictionary of Sexual Slang* by Alan Richter (New York: Wiley, 1993); *Whores in History: Prostitution in Western Society* by Nickie Roberts (London: HarperCollins, 1992); *The Queen's Vernacular: A Gay Lexicon* by Bruce Rodgers (San Francisco: Straight Arrow, 1972); *Literary Foreplay: A Lexicographer's Guide to Sex* by J. E. Schmidt (Washington: Eastern Market, 1983); *The Official Guide to the Best Cat Houses in Nevada* by J. R. Schwartz (Boise, Idaho: Author, 1993); *Free Love and Heavenly Sinners: The Story of the Great Henry Ward Beecher Scandal* by Robert Shaplen (New York: Knopf, 1954); *Pimp: The Story of My Life* by Iceberg Slim (Edinburgh: Payback, 1967, 1996); *Bundling: Its Origin, Progress and Decline in America* by Henry Reed Stiles (New York: Panurge, 1928); *An Intelligent Woman's Guide to Dirty Words: English Words and Phrases Reflecting Sexist Attitudes Toward Women in Patriarchal Society* by Ruth Todasco (Chicago: Loop Center YWCA, 1973); *A History of Courting* by E. S. Turner (New York: Ballantine, 1954); *Sinema*

by Kenneth Turan and Stephen F. Zito (New York: Signet, 1974); *Some Thoughts on the Science of Onanism* by Mark Twain (privately printed "for the trade" in 1879; reprinted 1964); *Whores for Gloria* by William T. Vollman (New York: Penguin, 1991); "Sex and the Single Soldier" by Daniel N. Weitzner in *Maledicta,* Vol. 5 (Winter 1981); *Playboy's Book of Forbidden Words* by Robert A. Wilson (Chicago: Playboy, 1972); *The Lively Commerce: Prostitution in the United States* by Charles Winick and Paul M. Kinsie (Chicago: Quadrangle, 1971); *A Pictorial History of Striptease* by Richard Wortley (Secaucus, N.J.: Chartwell, 1976); and *Eros Defined: Sex in Western Society* by Wayland Young (New York: Grove, 1964).

Almost all of the newspaper and magazine articles that I drew upon were from the Tamony Collection at the University of Missouri. They were as follows: "Grand Juror of '36 Defends Strip Teaser" in the *San Francisco News* (November 30, 1938); "Strip Teaser" in *Vanity Fair* (February 1936); "Strip Girls" in *Easy Money* (June 1936); "The Gentle Art of Strip-Teasing" by Walter Winchell in the *San Francisco Call-Bulletin* (January 19, 1937); "Escorts by the Hour" in *Reader's Digest* (February 1937); "Dancers Face Loss of Bare Subsistence" in the *News* (April 29, 1937); "The History of Burlesk" in *Pic* (August 1937); "G-Men Join

Slave Investigation: Girl's Accusations Lead to Jailing of Man, Woman" in the *News* (January 26, 1938); "Girl's Story in White Slave Trial Scored" in the *San Francisco Examiner* (April 29, 1938); "The Nation's Two Best Undressed Women Here With Bare Facts and Cold Figures" in the *San Francisco Chronicle* (October 19, 1938); "Strip Return Welcome" in the *Call-Bulletin* (October 22, 1938); "City Sleuths Outwit Strip Tease; Seize 4" in the *Examiner* (June 1, 1939); "Disrobing Illegal in Front of Bars" in the *Call-Bulletin* (July 25, 1939); "The B Girl" in the *Examiner* (September 10, 1939); "Los Angeles—America's Wickedest City" in *Look* (September 16, 1939); "True Confessions of a B Girl" in the *National Police Gazette* (November 1939); "Bribes for B-Girls" in the *News* (March 27, 1940); "London to Ban Strip Tease, Nudist Shows" in the *Call-Bulletin* (April 16, 1940); "Strip Teasers Must Go—The Lord Chamberlain Says So" in the *News* (April 16, 1940); "We Take You Backstage at the Burlesque Show" in the *24th Street Progress* (July 18, 1940); "Don't Pity the Pretty Strip-Teasers" in *American Weekly* (October 27, 1940); "More Tease Than Strip" in *Variety* (June 4, 1941); "Dance Boss Denies B Girls Employees" in the *Examiner* (July 17, 1941); "Glorified B-Girls Barred" in the

Call-Bulletin (May 7, 1942); "State Warns 50 Taverns They Must Oust B Girls" in the *Examiner* (May 9, 1942); "Impure Show Brings Jail: Judge Denounces Immoral Productions" in the *News* (December 18, 1942); "Social Disease Drive Gains: Red Light Districts Now Almost Eliminated, Says Report" in the *Examiner* (December 27, 1942); "Girl, 14, Says She Worked As Third Street 'B' Girl" in the *Examiner* (March 31, 1943); "Leesville Against Syphilis" in *Collier's* (April 10, 1943); "'Call Girl's' Best Customers Latin" in the *News* (June 23, 1943); "Rumba Dancer Guilty of Entertaining 2 Men" in the *News* (June 25, 1943); "FBI to Continue Drive On Capital Call Houses" in the *News* (June 26, 1943); "Girl Jailed on Call House" in the *Examiner* (July 1, 1943); "Capital Vice Patrons Named in Black Book" in the *Examiner* (April 28, 1944); "Women Guilty in Vice Case" in the *Examiner* (May 3, 1944); "Undies to Overalls" in *Time* (March 19, 1945); "Sally Runs Afoul of the Law" in the *Chronicle* (November 4, 1945); "Playboy Hollywood Hoots at Judge's Fidelity Views" in the *News* (July 6, 1946); "'Call Girls' Face Curb By Cops" in the *Call-Bulletin* (January 26, 1948); "Chief Mitchell To Crack Down on 'Call Girls'" in the *Examiner* (January 26, 1948); "Cabbie Faces Vice Charge: Accused of Procur-

ing 'Call Girl'" in the *Examiner* (February 4, 1948); "Movie Names On 'Call List'" in the *News* (May 6, 1948); "Busy B-Girls" in *Fortnight* (June 18, 1948); "Set 'Call Girl' Sentencing" in the *Call-Bulletin* (July 9, 1948); "Testifies in Call Girl Case" in the *Call-Bulletin* (July 2, 1948); "No Jail Term for 'Call Girl'" in the *Call-Bulletin* (September 13, 1948); "Nancy's Term Suspended in $100 Call Girl Case" in the *News* (September 13, 1948); "Call House Girl Phone Tip Aids Cops' Roundup" in the *News* (October 8, 1949); "Royale Flush" in *Life* (November 28, 1949); "Torrid Art Films Reel In Cash at Dime a Peep" in the *Examiner* (February 14, 1950); "Police to Check Peep Movies" in the *Examiner* (February 15, 1950); "Lady Cop Describes Offer of B-Girl Job" in the *Call-Bulletin* (March 13, 1950); "Tavern Denies B-Girl Charge" in the *Examiner* (March 14, 1950); "New Police Drive Aimed at 'B' Girls And Dice Games" in the *Examiner* (April 7, 1950); "Peepshow Cases To Get Jury Trials" in the *News* (April 4, 1951); "Obscene Peep-Show Operator Convicted" in the *News* (April 19, 1951); "Indecent Picture Displayer Fined" in the *Examiner* (April 28, 1951); "Head of S.F. B-Girl School Gets 6 Months" in the *Call-Bulletin* (May 23, 1951); "B-Girls and Punch-boards Out, Says Reilly" in the *Examiner* (May 24, 1951);

"Male Gold Diggers" in the *News* (June 21, 1950);"Little Egypt Brings the Hootchy Kootchy to Town" in the *Chronicle* (December 8, 1951);"Bar Accused of Using B-Girls to Bilk Marine" in the *Examiner* (April 26, 1952);"Marine Puts a Beef Up to Court: 2 B-Girls Cost Him $350 in 3 Hrs." in the *News* (May 24, 1952);"B-Girls Put 'B' On Marine to Tune of $350" in the *Examiner* (May 25, 1952); "Woman Tells Fleecing of Servicemen at Bar" in the *Examiner* (September 19, 1952); "The Sin Situation" in the *News* (February 3, 1953);"Senate Gets B-Girl Ban Passed By Assembly" in the *News* (April 14, 1953); "Warren Blisters Legislature, Cites Menace of B-Girls" in the *Examiner* (April 18, 1953); "State Board Passes Ban on B-Girls" in the *Examiner* (May 21, 1954); "Stripper Tempest Storm: Maybe It's Mass Love" by Ralph J. Gleason in the *Chronicle* (February 22, 1955);"Can Club's Owner Make Like B-Girl?" in the *News* (March 24, 1955);"Girl, 17, Tells Jury How She Coaxed Drinks" in the *News* (March 24, 1955);"S-Girls" in the *American Weekly* (September 4, 1955); "Sally Stanford Denies She Paid Off Police:'But They Often Called On Me'" in the *News* (October 21, 1955);"Peepshow Raid Here" in the *Examiner* (January 31, 1956);"1st-St Peep Show Raided as Lewd" in the *News*

(January 31, 1956);"'Sex and Steal' Jury Deadlocks" in the *News* (August 30, 1956);"Brown to Scan Girly Magazines" in the *Examiner* (June 11, 1957);"Can B-Girls Survive in the New Alaska?" in the *News* (November 29, 1958);"Mabel Malotte, Callhouse Queen, Dies" in the *Examiner* (December 21, 1958); "The Call Girl Story" in *Scandolls* magazine (New York, 1959); "Meyer Neft and His Undraped Ladies" in the *Examiner* (August 20, 1961);"Masturbatory Insanity: The History of an Idea" by E. H. Hare in the *Journal of Mental Science,* Vol. 108, No. 2 (January 1962);"Night Spot Cleanup Attempt Flops in New Orleans"*New Orleans Times-Picayune* (November 19, 1962);"Nudie Film Producer Unveils His Secrets" in the *Chronicle* (August 6, 1963);"Jean Seberg's Not a Nudie" in the *Examiner* (August 7, 1963);"The B-Girl Did It, Whew!" in the *San Francisco News Call-Bulletin* (October 18, 1963);"More Talk of B-Girls and Lobbyists" in the *Chronicle* (January 16, 1965); "MPs Act in Saigon Bar War" in the *Chronicle* (March 1, 1966); "Saigon—A Tawdry Paris" in the *Chronicle* (May 29, 1966); "Yankee and the Bar Girl" in the *San Francisco Examiner and Chronicle* (October 9, 1966); "Uninhibited Ladies" in the *Chronicle* (November 25, 1966); "Saigon Girls: Some are

Swinging to the American Look" in the *Examiner* (November 26, 1966);"The Girls Behind The War Lines" in the *Chronicle* (January 21, 1967);"Bar Girls Fight For Social Value" in the *Chronicle* (November 21, 1967);"West Berlin's Sin Clubs—Lewd and Little Joy" in the *Chronicle* (January 25, 1967);"Now It's B-Boys" in the *Honolulu Star-Bulletin and Advertiser* (February 26, 1967);"Girls of Saigon Organize To Protect Their Jobs" in the *Chronicle* (November 30, 1967);"Fate Worse Than Death For Girls Lured to Beirut" in the *Chronicle* (April 22, 1971); "Peepshows Are Raided" in the *Examiner* (October 12, 1972); "Saigon's Bar Girls Rue Yank Exit" in the *Examiner* (January 31, 1973);"B-Girl Army—Time Ran Out" in the *Examiner and Chronicle* (February 18, 1973); "Hong Kong Girls Feel the Pinch" in the *Chronicle* (March 7, 1973);"Misadventures in the Skin Trade" by John Jofsers in *Maclean's* (July 1974);"The Woman Behind the Movie About the Scandal" in the *New York Times* (December 14, 1989);"Sex in the 90s" in *New York* (June 8, 1992);"A Smoother Bourbon: Imagination Played a Part When Yesterday's Showgirls Were Stars of the Street" in the *New Orleans Times-Picayune* (May 25, 1996); and "Agent X" in *Los Angeles* (April 1997).

Chapter Six:
DEADLY SINS
AND ALSO-RANS

ERHAPS THE MOST FAMOUS SINS are the seven deadly sins, which have paraded through history with the clarity of figures in a medieval allegory; we may not
always be able to name all seven sins, but we know they are there, waiting to
tempt us. Although the seven deadly sins make up the best known classification
of sins, they are by no means the only ones. There are actual sins, sins against
the Holy Spirit, sins by silence, capital sins, cardinal sins, formal sins, habitual sins, material
sins, mortal sins, sins of another, sins of commission, sins of omission, venial sins, and—my
favorite—sins that cry to heaven for vengeance.

The seven deadly sins draw not only on the theology of sin, but upon the ancient magic
number of seven, which is found in a host of pre-Christian formulations (the seven-day creation of the world, the seven bodies in alchemy, the Heptateuch or the first seven books of the
Old Testament, the seven-branched candelabrum associated with Judaism, the seven divine
names of God in Judaism, the seven hills of ancient Rome, the seven notes in the diatonic
scale, the seven locks of hair which Delilah cut from Samson's head, the seven-day plague of
bloody waters in Egypt, the seven weeks between Passover and the Pentecost, the Seven against
Thebes, the seven sages of ancient Greece, the seven seas, the seven years of plenty and seven
years of famine as articulated by Joseph to the Pharaoh, the seven youths and seven maidens
sacrificed to the Minotaur, the seven days of mourning in Judaism, the seven heavenly bodies,
the seven wonders of the ancient world), Christian applications (the seven gifts of the Holy
Ghost, the seven hours of prayer, the seven Champions of Christendom, Christ's seven utter-
ances on the cross, the seven seasons in the Anglican church year, the Book of the Seven Seals
in Revelation, the seven corporal works of mercy, the seven joys of Mary, the seven loaves of
bread which Jesus used to feed the multitudes, the seven gifts of the Holy Ghost, the seven sor-
rows of Mary), and modern, quite secular applications, such as the lucky seven in craps, the
seventh-inning stretch, the seven-year itch, and—of course—Snow White's seven dwarves.

Thomas Aquinas was not the first to articulate a list of seven deadly sins, but his list from
Summa Theologiae—envy, gluttony, greed, lust, pride, sloth, and wrath—is the list that stuck,
appearing in *The Divine Comedy* by Dante Alighieri, "The Parson's Tale" in Chaucer's *Can-
terbury Tales*, Spenser's *The Faerie Queene*, and two imposing paintings by Hieronymus
Bosch, "The Seven Deadly Sins" and "The Garden of Earthly Delights."

Enough said about theology and the number seven—what of the slang? After all is said and
done, the seven deadly sins are character traits and not actions or activities. As such, there is
no social organization and no sin-oriented culture around them; where there is no culture,
there will not be much slang, and sadly, such is the case with the seven deadly sins. There are
slang synonyms for each of the seven deadly sins, but with the exception of lust no functional
vocabulary surrounds them, and certainly not enough to fill an entire chapter.

In the wings, though, are a host of other slang-rich sins, perhaps never candidates for the main event in the main arena, but sins nevertheless. The book of Leviticus is chock-full of also-ran sins; while many of the also-rans have no slang idiom (the quite vehement prohibitions on eating pork and wearing garments woven with two types of cloth leap to mind as sins without slang), several do. Add to them the never-ending list of sins found by religious and secular sin finders without biblical guidance, and you have a respectable chapter.

The Seven Deadly Sins

AS A RULE, SIN AND VICE COMMAND more synonyms than virtue, and the same goes for the slang of sin and vice. Even in the at-times dormant field of the seven deadly sins, the slang synonyms for the sins far outnumber the entries on the virtuous side of the ledger.

Envy or Jealousy

PROVERBS 27:4 TEACHES THAT "wrath is cruel and anger is outrageous; but who can stand before envy?" As powerful as envy may be, it is not one of the strong seven deadly sins when it comes to a slang vocabulary. There is the halfhearted **jelly** (clipped from "jealous"), the tossed-off catch phrase **Nice work if you can get it!** (denoting some degree of envy), and finally, the heartless retort of **Eat your heart out, sucker!**

But for the most part, the sin belongs to a single expression, the personification of envy as the **green-eyed monster** (not to be confused with the "Green Monster," the wall in left field at Fenway Park in Boston), which produces **green-eyed** as a stand-alone adjective meaning envious. As is the case with so many expressions, we have Shakespeare to thank for **green-eyed**; in *Othello*, Act 3, Scene 3, bad guy Iago says to good guy Othello, "O, beware my lord, of jealousy! / It is the green-ey'd monster which doth mock / The meat it feeds on." Shakespeare had also turned to **green-eyed** in *The Merchant of Venice*, in which Portia speaks in Act 3, Scene 2 of "green-eyed jealousy." Milton and Shelley picked up the image in their poetry, but Shakespeare was the man who started it all, giving us today's **green with envy.**

Gluttony

WE ARE A NATION OF THE OVERWEIGHT, collectively in need of the counsel of Proverbs 23:21, "For the drunkard and the gluttonous shall come to poverty. . . ." Many of the slang terms and expressions associated with gluttony are based on animal metaphors—a glutton is a **chow hound, garbage hound, hog, pelican,** or **pig,** and is said to **pig out, pork out,** or **wolf down** his food. Leaving the animal kingdom, the glutton is known as a **belly god** (with a tip of the hat to Saint Paul, who wrote of those "whose god is the belly"), a **fresser** (a direct borrowing from the Yiddish for someone who eats a great deal), or **greedy-gut,** and that which the glutton does is to **chow down, dive in, feed his face, mac out, put on the feedbag, scarf, shovel it in,** and **stuff his face.** The wit in the room might comment that the gluttonous one **sure plays a mean knife and fork,** but the glutton will be too busy **stowing away the groceries** to reply.

Greed and Avarice

WE ALWAYS HAVE BEEN, ARE, AND probably always will be a nation that worships above all else the dollar. Greed and avarice, the subjects of much biblical warning, are public virtues in America; we admire and want to be that flashy couple with their Lexus, ski vacations in Aspen, season NBA tickets, tennis club membership, top-of-the-line mountain bikes, and so on. We could not have strayed farther from the admonition of Isaiah 56:11, "Yea, they are greedy dogs that can never have enough, they are so wicked that they cannot understand; they have all turned aside to their own way, every one for his own gain and his own advantage."

He who is greedy is said to be a **hog** or **pig**, to have a big dose of **the gimmies**, or to be **grabby** or **piggy**. Where greed and avarice really kick in to make a major contribution to the slang of sin is in the realm of the coin, the laying up of earthly treasures, the root of all evil— money. Among the literally hundreds of slang synonyms for money, the most popular include **ackjay** (see **jack**), **ammunition, ballast, bangers** (coins), **bank, beans, berries, biscuit, blunt, boodle, brass, bread** (along with **dough**, probably the most popular and oldest of the slang synonyms for money), **bullets, cabbage** (the first of quite a few fruit and vegetable references), **casho dinero** (forced, imitation Spanish), **change, cherries, chicken feed, chips** (found in 1840 and again now as a strong contender in hip-hop slang), **coconuts, coin, corn, courage, currency** (the Fats Waller term of choice), **cush, darby, dead presidents** (an expression from the early 1940s that was rediscovered by rappers in the 1990s and is based on the U.S. law prohibiting the depiction of living persons on money), **dibs, dinero** (from the Spanish), **dirt, doots, do-re-mi** (a play on **dough** and the title of a Woody Guthrie song about Dust Bowl refugees barred entry to California), **dots, doubloons** (one of several references to a foreign unit of currency), **dough, ducats, dust** (probably from gold dust), **fews and twos, folding, folding green, folding lettuce, frogskin** (another green reference), **geets, geetus, gelt** (a direct borrowing from Yiddish), **gold, gravy, grease, green** (making its second appearance in the slang of the seven deadly sins, having opened as the star attraction of Envy), **greenbacks, greenie, green stamps** (a play with a brand of trading stamps popular in the 1950s and 1960s), **green stuff, grip** (a recent hip-hop coining), **hay, ice, iron** (coins), **jack** (the single most versatile slang word in the English language, making a guest appearance here in the realm of earthly treasures), **kale, kick** (cool sounding, right up there with **bank**), **laydown, lettuce, liquid assets, long green, mazuma** (from the Yiddish *mezumen*, which means "ready," as in "ready cash"), **mint, mon** (as in a clipped "money"), **moolah, needful, nuggets, paper, rhino, scratch, scrilla** (a word apparently coined by the Luniz, an Oakland rap group, in the early 1990s, with some currency as spoken slang by 1996), **shekel** (from the Hebrew word for a unit equal to half an ounce), **simoleon, smackers, smukes, spondulix, wad, wampum** (from *wampumpeag*, a Native American word for the white string of beads used as currency), and **wherewithal** (a standard English word used in a slangy sense with a slangy attitude to mean money).

A basic rule of money slang in America has been to take a small unit of currency and use the standard term or slang term for that unit to mean a much larger amount. Using this rule produced the following:

nickel ($.05)	$5.00
dime ($.10)	$10.00
bit ($.125)	$12.50
long bit ($.15)	$15.00
two bits, a quarter ($.25)	$25.00
four bits ($.50)	$50.00

Inflation has affected money slang just as it has affected money, and a **dime** today refers either to $100 or $1,000, meaning that you had better check the slang rate of exchange before you start offering to pay a **dime** for something that you probably should not be buying in the first place.

Other terms and expressions that are used for specific denominations include:

<u>One cent</u>: Because the penny has been virtually without value for several decades, the slang terms for it are and sound old-fashioned: a **brown Abe** (because Lincoln is profiled on the penny), a **copper** (a metal allusion that did not enjoy anywhere near the popularity of **nickel**), an **Indian head** (so named because of an obsolete design of the penny), a **meg**, a **peanut**, a **red cent** (an expression that has been around at least since 1839, derived either from the copper color of the penny or as an allusion to the Indian on the face of 19th-century pennies), or a **washer** (an allusion to the penny's relative worthlessness).

<u>Five cents</u>: Gresham's law of economics states that "bad money drives good money out of circulation." The opposite can be said for slang—one good slang word drives weaker words out of circulation. **Nickel** is just that, a good word for a five-cent piece, and one that has dominated the market for decades, although it was first used to describe a nickel-alloy one-cent piece in use between 1857 and 1864. Far back in the field are others: **blip** (a wise-guy term from the 1930s and 1940s), **buffalo head** (from the coin design), **fish scale, flat,** or the catchy triplets **chit** (perhaps derived from its slang use to describe the small end of a cigar, which often cost a **nickel**), **jit** (an early-20th-century slang term, perhaps from the French *jeton*, a token), and **thrip** (originally used to describe the English three-penny piece, **thrip** appears to have slipped into American English in the South).

<u>Ten cents</u>: **Dime** was first used at least as early as 1786, and since the mid-19th century it has taken on all comers and spawned a flock of derivatives—**deemar, deemer, deemon, dimer, dimmer, dimmo,** and **dimo** to name a few, as well as the near-rhyme **shiner**. Because it is the smallest coin, the ten-cent piece picked up the slang names **skinny, thin, thin man,** and **thin one,** and because of its design features, it at times has been known as a **liberty** or **silver Jeff** (a clipped *Jefferson*). **Deece,** another short-lived slang handle for a ten-cent piece, was probably derived from the French *dix* for ten.

<u>Twenty-five cents</u>: **Quarter** has owned the twenty-five-cent piece since the late 18th century; its sound-based slang progeny include **cute, cuter, kuter, kyuter,** and **quetor. Two bits** (as in, "Shave and a haircut / **two bits**") is past its prime but still heard, while **ruff** was only passingly accepted in the 1940s.

<u>One dollar</u>: A dollar has been a **buck** at least since 1856; the derivation is not absolutely agreed upon, but the prevalent theory is that **buck** as a slangy, clipped *buckskin*, which was a

trade currency among Native Americans and used in that sense as early as 1748, evolved from barter to currency. Other $1 players include **ace, berry, bill, boffo, buzzard** (a silver dollar showing an eagle), **case** (from **case dollar**, a gambler's last dollar; this term was also used in the language of the game of faro), **clam, dobe** (an expression coming from Mexico, an **adobe dollar** meaning a Mexican silver dollar, which evolved into a trade union term for working fees, **dobie**), **ducat, frog, frogskin, one, one-spot, peso, potato, single, skin, smacker, smackeroo,** or a **Washington.**

Two dollars: The two-dollar bill is fairly rare, and it has only a couple of viable slang names—a **deuce** (most popular in the 1930s, along with its derivative **deucer** or **deuce spot**) or **two spot.**

Five dollars: From the Yiddish *finif* for five and/or the German *funf*, comes the decidedly American slang **fin** (and the variants **finn, finif, finnif**) for a five-dollar bill; there is a clear Damon Runyon ring to **fin**, and in fact it rang from the lips of his guys and dolls. *Five* figures in several other slang terms—**five, fiver,** or **five-spot.** Berrey and Van den Bark include a list of terms based on the Roman numeral "V"—**V, Vee, V-note,** and **V-spot,** but there is a forced, journalistic ring to them. The previously discussed **nickel** still commands a fair amount of use, especially when describing a quantity of drugs, as in a **nickel bag** (usually of marijuana) or **nickel vial** (of crack cocaine).

Ten dollars: **Sawbuck** (supported by its spin-off **saw** and its proper name **single sawbuck**) is the top seed when it comes to the ten-dollar bill; a sawbuck is an X-shaped brace used for holding a log to be sawed, and the X shape evokes the Roman numeral ten, and hence **sawbuck.** *Ten* figures in **ten, tenner,** and **ten-spot,** while the ten-cent piece contributes **dime** and **dime-note.** One will find an occasional reference to a ten-dollar bill as a **Hamilton,** but that reference requires a little bit more appreciation of history than modern popular culture can sustain.

Twenty dollars: Two ten-dollar bills make $20, so why not **double saw, double sawbuck,** or **twin sawbucks?** The only other contenders are the historically challenging **Jackson** or the so-plain **twenty-spot.**

Fifty dollars: The fifty-dollar bill lacks an identity of its own in slang, described as it is solely in terms of a hundred-dollar bill—**half a C, half a century, half a yard,** or **half yard.**

One hundred dollars: The hundred-dollar bill goes by a couple of cool slang names, most notably a **C note** (and its cousins **one C, C-spot, century,** and **century note**), and **yard.** There is also the clipped **hun** and the jaded **bill,** as in "That suit must have set you back at least five **bills**," and **Benji** in honor of Benjamin Franklin, pictured on the one hundred dollar bill.

Five hundred dollars: Again, the slang terms for five hundred dollars are based either on terms for $100 (**five centuries, five C's,** or **five yards**) or terms for $1,000 (**half a grand** or **half a G**).

One thousand dollars: As the air gets rarer, so do the slang terms. There is the clipped **thou,** the cool **large** (as in, "ten large" for $10,000), the ever-popular **grand** (and its offspring **G** and **G note**), and the very curt **K** (probably from a clipping of "kilo"). Harkening back to $100, both **ten century note** and **ten yards** refer to $1,000.

Moving up, a **big nickel** is five thousand dollars and, even upper, **mil** is one million dollars and **megabucks** is a huge, unspecified amount of money.

Lastly, there is the always fascinating sin within the sin of money, counterfeiting. Counterfeit money is best known simply as **paper**, but also as **backs, bogus, boodle, fronts, funny money, funny paper, phony money, queer, sourdough**, and **wallpaper**. The counterfeiter answers to many names, including **butterfly man, connection, designer, maker, paperhanger** (also someone who floats bad checks), **penciler, penman, pusher** (said of someone who passes counterfeit money), **queer maker, raiser, scratcher, scratch man, script writer** (also used to describe a doctor who will prescribe narcotics to an addict), and **tracer.**

Lust

SAINT PETER URGED US TO "abstain from fleshly lusts, which war against the soul" (Peter 2:11), and Thomas Aquinas seconded the emotion, scorching us with exhortations against excessive sexual desires; we have been thoroughly warned about the Whore of Babylon, yet we rush to her with her scarlet "A." Here is one of the seven deadly sins that commands a huge vocabulary, at least in the manifestations of lust or the **BU** (biological urge). One who is **in lust** is **horny** and is said to **have the hots for** that special someone. They may also be **brimmin', bullin', cocksmitten, cuntstruck, fuckish, fussed up, gamey, goatish, horsing, hot and bothered, in heat, leching, lust proud, mettled, prickstruck, raking, rammy, randy, red in the comb, rutty, sexed up**, or **turned on.** The language of the sins of sex is fully uncovered in Chapter 5.

Pride

PRIDE GOETH BEFORE A FALL, and a haughty spirit before destruction—I heard this mantra directed my way hundreds of times as I grew up. The sin of entertaining an overly high opinion of oneself has produced a small body of slang adjectives, among them **biggity, big-headed** (a mid-19th-century favorite), **cocky, dicty** (big in the late 1920s and the 1930s), **high and mighty** (the name of a melon and lettuce farm in Blythe, California), **highfalutin'** (a 19th-century coining with staying power), **high-hatty, high-toned, hincty, hoity-toity, orgulous, sidity, stuck up, swellheaded, too big for**

his **britches**, **toploftical**, and **uppity**. A person guilty of this sin might be said to be on an **ego trip** or **on his high horse**, while a vain and proud woman might be called, simply, **Miss It.**

Sloth

SLOTHFULNESS, THE DISINCLINATION to work or exert oneself, "casts into a deep sleep" (Proverbs 9:15). Given the sin, you might think that there aren't a lot of slang terms associated with it, but then you might be wrong. That slothful person there could be said to be **bone idle**, a **bum**, a **deadbeat**, a **drag-ass**, a **fuck-off**, a **gold brick**, a **lazy bones**, a **poke-easy**, a **rum-dum**, a **slacker**, or suffering from a big **streak of lack**.

More important from the slang vocabulary point of view, what is it that they are doing when they are doing nothing? The slang terms and expressions which mean "to idle" are plentiful, inasmuch as doing nothing is a major activity of slang-producing youth—**cake**, **chill**, **cold chill**, **cool out**, **dog it**, **do the drag**, **ease**, **fart around**, **fuck off**, **futz around**, **goof off**, **hack off**, **hang**, **hang out**, **jell**, **jell out**, **kick**, **kick back**, **kick it**, **kill time**, **lamp**, **lolly-gag**, **lounge**, **louse around**, **max** (which produces **maxin' an' relaxin'**), **mellow out**, **mess around**, **parlay**, **sluff**, **swing it**, **veg**, **veg out**, and **will**.

Wrath

LAST BUT BY NO MEANS least of the seven deadly sins is wrath, which we are told "is the rottenness of the bones" (Proverbs 14:30). **Pissed off** is probably the leader of the angry pack here at the end of the 20th century, the urination taboo having all but disappeared sometime in the last two decades. If you're not **pissed off**, you might be **p.o.'d**, or then again you might be **ballistic**, **bent** or **bent out of shape**, **bullshit**, **burned**, **cheesed off**, **flipped out**, **fried**, **hot**, **hot under the collar**, **loaded for bear**, **pushed out of shape**, **red-assed**, **sore**, **steamed**, **teed off**, **ticked off**, or **torqued**. As you get angry, your might **blow a fuse**, **blow a gasket**, **blow your cool**, **blow your cork**, **blow your stack**, **blow your top**, **flip your lid**, **fly off the handle**, **foam at the mouth**, **go ape**, **go ape shit**, **go postal**, **have a conniption fit**, **have a cow** (thank you Bart Simpson), **have a hemorrhage**, **have a shit cow attack**, **have a shit fit**, **hit the roof**, **see red**, **shit a brick**, **shit blue**, or **shit nails**.

The Slang of Pool Hall Hustlers

ALTHOUGH THE BIBLE DOES NOT teach on the evils of playing pool, there has been no shortage of secular and religious criticisms of billiards as a dangerous and seditious corrupter of youth, and of pool halls as, in the words of the Rev. John A. Phelan in 1919, "meeting places of underworld mashers, cadets, procurers, gangsters, gunmen, thieves and criminals of all sorts." The ringing condemnation of pool in *The Music Man* ("You've got trouble . . . with a capital T and that rhymes with P and that stands for pool") is more lyrical than most denunciations but no less vehement.

In fact, pool halls—which are not to be confused with the new, upscale "billiard parlors" that market to, cater to, and thrive because of the young, upwardly mobile—*do* reek of vice. It is a male world, and a no-good, still-wearing-hats, always-hustling male world, filled with other sins or at least the near occasion of other sins. Cigar smoke from cheap and stinking stogies, hard liquor, profanity, and constant gambling under the signs that read "Absolutely No Gambling" all provide the setting for the game itself.

The language of pool halls is rich and clever, thanks to the down-and-out and hustling aspects of the culture. There is some jargon, to be sure, but much of it has a slangy tone. Especially when it comes to the words and expressions used to describe the ploys and techniques of the pool hustling **shark**, the slang comes alive, if with a 1930s, wise guy ring to it. A number of pool-hall slang expressions have migrated into colloquial English where they provide colorful metaphors: to **know the angles**, to **get a break**, **dirty pool**, to be **behind the eight ball**, **pocket pool**, to **call the shots**, and to **snooker** all have a birth certificate that says "pool hall" as the place of birth.

Enough talk, though, let's rack up some words!

ace The one ball

action 1. A bet or a game played for money 2. Spin on the ball

action room A pool room where betting is tolerated

air barrel A bet that a player cannot pay off if he or she loses. *This rather risky practice is also known as "shooting the air rifle."*

albino The cue ball

ammunition Betting money

angled Blocked by the corner of a pocket (said of a

ball)

army A large bankroll for betting

around the table Bounced off three or more cushions

back room The practice area in a pool hall

ball-on Direct and unobstructed (said of a shot)

banana A shot for position in snooker, leaving the cue ball near a cushion

banger A clumsy player

barber A narrow miss. *As in a shave.*

barrel A betting unit. *If*

you have $100 and the bet on each game is $25, you are said to have four barrels.

bed The base of the table

bigs Higher-numbered striped balls

Bowery shot **A push shot,** where the cue touches the cue ball more than once

box A pool table

breaker The player who shoots first, breaking the rack

breeze To hit a ball very lightly

bucket A wide pocket that

seems to accept balls easily

bumper   A cushion on the pool table

bumper-to-bumper   A shot that bounces off two cushions

bunch   The object balls

bust   To break up a cluster of balls

call book   A list of places to play pool maintained by a pool hustler

cheat   To impart spin on the object ball, making it rotate towards the center of a pocket

cheese   Luck

cherry   An easy shot

clear the table   To make every shot possible in a single turn

club   A heavy cue stick

coat   To obscure the view of a referee in tournament play, masking an illegal shot

coin-op   A pool table operated by coins

condom   A removable rubber sleeve used as a grip on a cue stick

count   The score. *Although this term has a definite modern sound—and in fact is the slang of choice in playground basketball—it was recorded by George Matsell in 1859 in* The Rogue's Lexicon.

crap   A lucky, unintended shot

cripple   An easy shot

crisp   Well-constructed so that the ball does not roll longer than expected (said of a table)

croak   To miscue

crush   The break shot

crutch   A device used for a cue rest for a shot which a player could not otherwise reach

cut   To hit the object ball intentionally off center

D   A defined area on a snooker table

daylight   A narrow space that permits a ball to be hit or pocketed

dead ball   A cue ball that stops when it strikes an object ball, transferring all of its momentum to the object ball

dead-in   Direct and unobstructed (said of a shot)

deuce   The two ball

diamond   A high-numbered, striped ball

dirty pool   Play that violates rules

dodge   To play a **safety**

dog   1. To miss a shot 2. A poor player

double cheese   A game situation where both players need only one point to win

double door   To win a game quickly

double kiss   A shot in which a ball hits the same ball twice

downtown   Toward the foot of the table

drift   The uneven roll of a ball on a table because of an imperfection in the slate table or cloth

drill   To make a shot in a convincing manner

dump   To lose a game intentionally

dump stroke   A slightly flawed stroke made as part of an effort to lose a game intentionally

egg   A pool ball

even up   A game play with no handicaps allowed

face   A pool hustler who has been recognized

fan   To graze a ball

feather   To hit a ball very lightly

fiddle   To move the cue stick back and forth before shooting

follow   Topspin imparted on the cue ball

freeze-out   A game where one player wins the bet when he or she attains a predetermined lead

frozen   Touching another ball or the rail

full   Direct, on-center (said of contact between a cue ball and object ball)

garbage   A lucky, unintended shot

gardener   A player who wins games and money

Germantowner   A **push shot**

God Bless You A mnemonic device used to recall the placement of colors in snooker—green, brown, and yellow

googan A poor player, a recreational player

go penguin To enter a tournament where the dress code requires tuxedoes

grease Extreme English applied to a ball

greens fee The amount charged by a pool room to play

green thumb The talent to make shots and win games

gully A pool table from which balls automatically return to a collection rack

hanger A ball that is poised at the lip of a pocket

Harrigan A lucky shot

heap The object balls

heavy Good (said of players)

highs Higher-numbered striped balls

hill game A game situation where both players need only one point to win

hitter A cue stick

hooked Blocked (said of a shot)

houseman The best local player in a pool room

hug the rail To stay near a table rail because of spin imparted on the ball

in jail Boxed in by a pack

of balls that leave no real chance of a shot

inning One player's turn at the table

in the drink In a pocket (said of a cue ball)

ivories Pool balls

jam up Lucky

jaw To bang against the sides of a pocket without dropping (said of a ball)

juice Extreme English applied to a ball

junk A lucky, unintended shot

kill To hit the cue ball so that it will stop dead when it strikes the object ball

kiss To deflect one ball off another

kiss-off Unintended contact with a ball that spoils a shot

knock To alert someone that they are playing with a pool hustler

knocker A confederate in a gambling scheme who tries to prevent unfavorable bets from being made

ladies' aid A device used for a cue rest for a shot which a player could not otherwise reach

lag To decide which player will shoot first by shooting from the head of the table; the player whose shot comes to rest closest to the rail at the head of the table after bouncing off the foot of the table breaks

lamb A good player who does not have the character necessary to make a good hustler

leave The position of the balls after your turn

legs The momentum of a ball

lemon To attempt to draw players into a betting game by losing intentionally or winning in a less than forceful manner

lion A good player with strong, aggressive tendencies

littles Lower-numbered solid colored balls

live ball A ball that is in play

locksmith A hustler who takes no chances and plays only when he or she is assured of winning

lockup A shot that is very easy to make

long Wide (said of the angle of a shot)

lows Lower-numbered solid colored balls

man of the cloth A player who shoots and bets well

mark A poor player who is easy to sucker into a betting game

mechanic A person who installs pool tables

merry widow A cue stick made from a single piece of wood, or which appears to have been made from a single piece of wood

mini, minnie An easy shot

money ball The ball that will win a game and bet

mud, mud ball A synthetic, non-ivory pool ball

natural An easy shot

nip A short, light stroke

nudge To hit the cue ball by accident while preparing to shoot

nurse A strategy whereby a player keeps balls in position for successive shots

ocean The center of the pool table

office A signal given by one hustler to another that a game is being intentionally lost

oil Extreme English applied to the ball

orange crush A handicap in which the lesser player is given the five ball (which is orange) and the break

overcoat A player who has mastered a particular table with its idiosyncrasies

pack A cluster of three or more balls

pinch A quick, jerky stroke used when the cue ball lies very close to the object ball

plum The number-four ball, which is purple

po Position

pot A pocket on a pool table

puppy An easy shot

push shot A rule violation that occurs when the cue stick remains in contact with the cue ball after the cue ball begins to move

putting green A large, five-by-ten pool table

rack The triangular form used to arrange the balls at the start of the game

rail bird A spectator

rake A device used for a cue rest for a shot which a player could not otherwise reach

rebel trap A large, five-by-ten pool table. *It is called a rebel trap because Southerners are reputedly not used to large tables.*

safety A defensive shot in which a player elects to make a shot the sole intention of which is to avoid a scratch

saver An arrangement between two or more players in a tournament to share the purse if one wins

saw wood To have a clumsy stroke

scratch To make a shot in which the cue ball falls in a pocket, thus ending the shooter's **inning**

screw Spin placed on the cue ball

Screw Your Buddy A game with three or five players of which the last surviving player wins, which forces temporary alliances as the game progresses

setup The ploy or combination of ploys by which a hustler keeps his victim playing and losing

sewer A pocket that seems to attract balls

shark 1. A pool hustler. *In the 19th century, the pool hustler was known as a sharp, a term also used in gambling circles. His victims were appropriately known as flats.* 2. To distract one's opponent

shark meat The victim of a pool hustler

short Narrow (said of an angle off a cushion)

shortstop A pool hustler who cannot beat the best **shark** but who can beat most other players

silent partner A cue used by hustlers, made to appear like a house cue

sissy stick A device used for a cue rest for a shot which a player could not otherwise reach

sitter An easy shot

sledgehammer A clumsy stroke

slide A delicate shot with slight underspin

slop A lucky, unintended shot

snap The initial shot of a game, the **break**

Sneaky Pete A high-quality cue used by hustlers, made to appear like a house cue

snookered Blocked from any direct shot at an object ball

solids Lower-numbered solid-colored balls

speed Ability

spot To give a lesser player a handicap

spread 1. To break 2. The leave following the break

stack The balls clustered at the foot of the table after the break

stall To lose intentionally or win in a poor fashion so as to entice a lesser player to bet money

stick A cue stick

stone A pool ball

stop shot A shot that stops immediately upon striking an object ball or cushion

stripes Higher-numbered striped balls

stuff Extreme English applied to a ball

sweat To alert someone that he or she is playing with a pool hustler

takedown A hustler's total earnings for a day

tight Narrow and seemingly stingy (said of a pocket)

timberlick A push shot

tool A cue stick

toothpick A light cue stick

top stick The best local player in a pool room

trapper A high-quality cue used by hustlers, made to appear like a house cue

twist Spin imparted on the cue ball

uptown Toward the head rail of a pool table

waggle To take short practice strokes before shooting

wand A cue stick

wastebasket A wide pocket which seems to accept balls easily

weapon A cue stick

weight A handicap given a lesser player. *This concept has been around the block a time or two, and is an integral part of a pool hustle. In the 19th century, the handicap was known as a* **discount.**

wire 1. To alert someone that he or she is playing with a pool hustler 2. The score string

Tats, Tacks, or Tattoos

THE NAME OF THE TATTOO PARLOR on Main Road in North Tiverton, Rhode Island, says it all—"Sin on Skin." They aren't kidding in North Tiverton—Leviticus 19:28 explicitly characterizes a tattoo as a sin. Leaving aside the counsel of Leviticus, tattoos have enjoyed a disreputable standing in the secular world, finding their way with their splashy artistic values and their macho messages of "Born to raise hell," "Too tough to die," or "Defend it or Lose it!" quite nicely into the purview of the outlaw and the down-and-out, the circus freak, the carny, sailors who got **stewed, screwed, and tattooed**, convicts, motorcycle gang members, decadent rock and rollers, and their no-good, badass ilk. A lighthearted appreciation of the tattoo came in the 1939 Marx Brothers movie *At the Circus* with "Lydia, the Tattooed Lady":

Lydia oh! Oh Lydia, say have you met Lydia, Oh!
Lydia the tattooed lady!
She has eyes that folks adore so
And her torso even more so.

Lydia oh Lydia that encyclopedia,
Lydia the queen of tattoo,

On her back is the battle of Waterloo,
Beside it the wreck of the Hesperus too,
And proudly above waves the red, white, and blue.
You can learn a lot from Lydia . . .

Tattoos that themselves depict sin are the most delicious of the skin sins. Of special interest to the student of sin is the tattoo design known as **Man's Ruin,** which depicts a tempting combination of vices and sins, a scantily clad chesty young woman, playing cards, dice, a bottle of whiskey, perhaps drug paraphernalia, perhaps a pistol or knife, and a skull and crossbones.

The language of the **tat parlor** and the **jab artist** is not without its bright moments, although the humor factor is all but completely missing. Fire up the needle, pick your **flash**— here follows a wordlist of **tat** slang:

abomination A tattoo that is poorly drawn and/or executed

armband A tattoo design that encircles the arm

art To tattoo

backroom job A tattoo on a body part which invites modesty and privacy

Battle Royal A traditional tattoo design, a large piece usually on the back, showing an eagle, snake, and dragon in battle

black work A tattoo design in shades of gray and black

blank canvas A person getting his or her first tattoo

bleeder A person who bleeds profusely when being tattooed

blowout A tattoo characterized by blurred, uneven application

bodysuit A tattoo that covers the entire body

canvas The person getting the tattoo

cap A cap from a toothpaste tube or other small container filled with ink used in tattooing. *A prison term.*

carve To tattoo someone. *A great, scary word from carnival slang.*

Celtic Featuring intricate drawings of knots derived from the Celts, usually in black ink (said of a style of tattooing)

clean Technically perfect (said of a tattoo)

cockamamies Fake, stick-on tattoos popular in the 1950s. *A brand name in the 1950s, this has since become an eponym. Fake tattoos are still widely available.*

color To tattoo

cover-up work A new tattoo that masks an old tattoo

devotion A tattoo design that pledges one's love

explosion A blurred, uneven line on a tattoo

fallout Sudden fading of color in a new tattoo

fine line A tattoo design outlined with one needle

flash The sheets of pictures showing tattoo designs displayed in a tattoo parlor

freehand To apply a tattoo without relying on a stencil

FTW A tattoo design that proclaims "Fuck The World," a favorite with motorcycle gang members

fullback A tattoo or tattoos that cover the entire back

full coverage Tattoos that cover the entire body

gun A tattooing instrument used in prisons

hacker An unskilled amateur tattoo artist

high energy Bold and colorful (said of modern tattoo design)

holiday A skip or bare patch in a tattoo design

ink To tattoo

jab To tattoo

jab art A tattoo

jagger An unskilled, untrained tattoo artist. *This is an old-time term, which has been largely replaced by scratcher.*

jailhouse tattoo Any homemade tattoo, usually black and gray. *Inmates gave themselves homemade tattoos in black and gray which was easier to do than color.*

joint style A homemade tattoo, usually black and gray

Lady Luck A popular tattoo during World War II, showing a beautiful woman with other lucky symbols, such as four-leaf clovers, horseshoes, etc.

leg piece A tattoo applied on the leg

liner A tattoo machine geared at a high speed to outline the design

long square one A blunt, painful needle used for tattoos on obnoxious customers or customers seeking political messages that the artist strongly rejects

lose ink To have the color fade from a tattoo

Man's Ruin A popular tattoo design showing vices that cause ruin to men—cards, dice, liquor, and women

mark To tattoo

mural A heavily tattooed person

mush A loss of definition

naked Untattooed

old school The traditional approach to tattoos, including a formal apprenticeship under a master tattoo artist and an adherence to a strict code of conduct

one percent (1%) A tattoo design popular with motorcycle gang members, poking fun at the American Motorcycle Association's claim that only 1% of the country's motorcycle owners were gang members

Oriental Covering the entire body (said of a style of tattooing)

outfit All of the equipment needed to tattoo, including needles, inks, the needle gun, power supply, etc.

outliner A bar holding three to five needles, used to outline the tattoo design unless a **fine line** is used

readable Discernible from a distance (said of a tattoo)

Rock of Ages A tattoo design showing Jesus Christ on the cross on a rock

rub-off A copy of a tattoo design rubbed onto the body

Sailor Jerry A traditional tattoo style, favored by sailors. *Named after the legendary tattoo artist Sailor Jerry Collins.*

scratcher An unskilled amateur tattoo artist. *The aforementioned Sailor Jerry Collins was emphatic—"Good tattoos are not cheap . . . and cheap ones are not good."*

shader A bar holding seven or more needles, used to color inside the outline of a tattoo design

skip A break in the line work or uneven shading

sleeved Covered on both arms with tattoos, a definite commitment to tattoo art

sling ink To tattoo

stewed, screwed, and tattooed The order of battle for many a young soldier or sailor—drink to the point of intoxication, have sex, and get a tattoo

tacked back A heavily tattooed back

tack gun, tat gun A tattooing instrument

tat A tattoo

tat man A tattoo artist

Temptu A temporary tattoo. *This eponym is derived from Temptu Marketing, Inc., a leader in the field*

of temporary tattoos.
thrasher Somebody who moves around when being tattooed
travel marks Tattoos. *This*

expression was used in the 1940s, when sailors were the primary benefi- ciaries of the tattoo artist.

tribal Silhouette designs, sketched in outline and solidly colored in
virgin Someone who is get- ting his or her first tattoo

P.S. Body Piercing

LIKE LOVE AND MARRIAGE, soup and sandwich, horse and carriage, **p 'n' t**—pierce and tat- too—are the "I Am Young!" symbols of the 1990s. Rallying behind the trumpet cry of **modern primitive**, the body pierced begs for society's disapproval and openly defies common sense as well as the explicit forbiddance of piercing found in Leviticus 19:28.

The language of body piercing seems to be mired in authentic, primitive descriptions of the piercings and nearly bereft of any snappy slang at all. To pierce is to **poke holes, stab**, or **stick**, all right-at-ya terms. A person who is being pierced for the first time is a **newbie** or

virgin (a tattoo borrowing); a tough pierce is because of **leather skin**, while an easy pierce is **like butter.**

Any pierce through cartilage is a **cart**, while a pierce through the bridge of the nose is known in Los Angeles as an **Earl**, in honor of Earl Van Aken, the Orange County fitness trainer who was the first to request the pierce in Los Angeles. Male genital piercings include the **ampallang** (from Borneo, a horizontal piercing of the head of the penis), **apadravya** (from the *Kama Sutra*, a vertical piercing of the head of the penis, or along the shaft), **dydoe** (a piercing through the ridge of the head of the penis), **frenum** (a piercing under the underside of the penis, just behind the head), **guiche** (from the South Pacific, a piercing of the flesh between the scrotum and the anus), **hafda** (from the Middle East, a piercing of the outer skin on the side of the scrotal sac), and **Prince Albert** or **P.A.** (a piercing that goes through the urethra and out behind the head, named for a ring allegedly worn by men in Queen Victoria's day to secure the penis when very tight-fitting pants were worn). Names for female genital piercings include the **fourchette** (piercing the flesh near the anus and exiting through the vaginal wall), the **hood** or **Queen Kristina** (piercing of the clitoral hood), and the **Princess Alberta** (the female version of the **Prince Albert**).

The two most common expressions used in body piercing are not even arguably slang—the preliminary question of "Will it hurt?" and the answer, "OUCH!"

Tobacco

TOBACCO IS AS NASTY AND tenacious a sin and vice as we have. Despite widespread and long-standing religious and medical criticism of tobacco use, its profitability for some has helped it to weather storm after storm. Religious leaders urge us not to smoke, citing a straightforward application of biblical principles to a habit that is not specifically addressed in the Bible, while secular and medical leaders from King James I in 1604 to successive surgeons general in the late 20th century urge us not to smoke because of proven links to coronary artery disease and cancer, yet we are a nation of tar and nicotine addicts, huddled outside office buildings grabbing a **smoke** in the cold and rain because we are no longer allowed to smoke inside the office, or smug in a defiantly decadent cigar lounge as we sip expensive whiskeys and eat food that we cannot taste because our tongues are singed with the taste of cigars, or passing the pouch of chewing tobacco down the high school baseball dugout bench from team member to team member, emulating our major league tobacco-chewing heroes.

Endless assaults on tobacco have barely made a dent in the metaphorical walls that surround the industry. Movies continue to glamorize smoking, tobacco companies reach out to the very young (as was done through Joe Camel), tobacco industry apologist doctors continue to deny obvious cause-and-effect relationships, and senators from tobacco-growing states continue to champion the sin and lambaste its critics as un-American.

Unlike most sins, tobacco is legal and it has its outspoken advocates, its unquestioning supporters. For these reasons, it flourishes as a sin, but also for these reasons it has not produced a particularly powerful slang vocabulary. Tobacco's legal status and its widespread use are social factors that drive down the chances of a lively and bright slang; the underground aspects of tobacco (hand-rolled cigarettes in a prison culture being the best example) generate the most vibrant slang. Gathered from the lips of those who partake, here are several hundred words that provide a glimpse into the world of smokers.

backy Tobacco

bale of hay A package of cigarettes

bank To place a **dip** of snuff under the lip so that it does not get wet

bell The pod of the tobacco plant containing the seed

Big Three The American Tobacco Company, Liggett & Myers, and R. J. Reynolds. *In 1941, the Justice Department charged the three companies with antitrust violations.*

binder The wrapper used to bind a cigar before the outside wrapper is put on

birdwood A cigarette

blanket Cigarette paper used in improvised hand-rolling of cigarettes

blankets and freckles Cigarette paper and loose tobacco

bloom White spots on a cigar's wrappers, produced by oils in the tobacco

blunt A trade term for a

slender cigar with a
straight-cut **tuck**
boiler A pipe
boot A cigarette
boro A Marlboro brand cigarette. *Marlboro is the
most popular brand sold
in the United States.*
bowl The receptacle for the
tobacco in a pipe
brain tablet A cigarette
broom A cheap cigar
bug dust Inferior tobacco
Bull Bull Durham tobacco
bum To ask someone for a
cigarette
bunch A cigar before it is
wrapped
bunco A slender cigar
butt **1.** The end of a cigarette leftover after all the
tobacco has been smoked
2. A cigarette
button The tip of the tobacco plant that swells
before blooming
cabbage A cheap cigar
can Half a pound of smoking tobacco
castaway A cigarette stub
catters A grade of tobacco,
used primarily for ciga-
rettes
chain, chain smoke **1.**
To smoke one cigarette
after another, many times
pausing only to light the
new cigarette with the tip
of the last one **2.** To
smoke heavily
chaw Chewing tobacco
cig, ciggie A cigarette

cigarette camp A military
camp in France where
American soldiers waited
for embarkation home to
America at the end of
World War II. *Smoking
was widespread among
soldiers and the camps
were named for cigarette
brands—Camp Philip
Morris, Camp Lucky
Strike, etc.*
clincher The stub of a cigarette
clip a butt To extinguish a
partially smoked cigarette
and save it for future
smoking
coffin nail A cigarette
coffin tack A cigarette
cold turkey *See Word
Histories in Chapter 3,
page 143.*
cornsilk A cigarette made
with a corn-shuck wrapper
crook A cigar molded into a
crooked shape
crumbs The second grade
of leaves. *A North Caro-
lina term.*
cud A chew of tobacco
cull A cigar that is rejected
for being off-color
cut Plug tobacco
dead man, dead soldier
A cigarette stub. *This
expression is more com-
monly used to mean an
empty liquor bottle.*
deck A pack of cigarettes,
as in "a deck of Luckies"
dinch, dincher The stub

of a cigarette
dip **1.** To place a pinch of
snuff behind one's lower
lip or inside one's cheek
and leave it there until the
flavor vanishes **2.** A pinch
of snuff
dope stick A cigarette
drag **1.** To inhale **2.** Inhaling **3.** A puff of another's cigarette, as in "Sure,
I quit smoking but it won't
hurt to have a tiny, itty-
bitty, little drag of your cigarette, will it?"
dream stick A cigarette
drummer A cigar salesman. *This term comes
from the late 19th and
early 20th century and
was also applied to other
types of traveling sales-
men; the drummer dis-
tributed many popular
premiums along with the
cigars.*
dust Pipe tobacco
El Ropo A cheap cigar. *An
imitation of Spanish,
presumably meaning
"the rope."*
fag A cigarette. *This term is
originally British, but is
not without its uses in
American English.*
fast burner A hand-rolled
cigarette in prison that has
been used as currency for
so long that it has dried up
and burns quickly when
smoked
fill a blanket To pour

enough loose tobacco onto a cigarette paper to form a hand-rolled cigarette

filled blanket A rolled cigarette

fillin's Loose tobacco

five-pack A package of five cigars

fix A supply of nicotine to the system provided by smoking a cigarette

flash The brightness of color in flue-cured tobacco

flyings The lowest leaves of the plant

Frenchie A French brand cigarette

French-inhale To exhale smoke through the nose and reinhale it through the mouth

frog's eyes Brown spots that appear on tobacco leaves

fudgeon Chewing tobacco. *This term is from the 18th century, primarily in the Connecticut Valley.*

G's Generic brand cigarettes

gas bomb A cigar

gasper A cigarette

gig To cut a tobacco plant from the side and slit it downwards

goat hair Fine cut Maryland tobacco

good-night nurse The last cigarette smoked at the end of the day

greenie A cigarette made from unaged tobacco

hacker A heavy, longtime smoker who typically coughs a lot

hard Plug tobacco

hard-rolled A manufactured cigarette

Harry rag A hand-rolled cigarette

hay burner A pipe

heifer dust Snuff. *Also a slang euphemism for "bullshit."*

hit A puff from someone else's cigarette

hobo's delight A cigarette stub

Hot lead! A cry from an electric lineman working on a pole to workers on the ground, signifying that he or she is about to spit chewed tobacco

hump A Camel brand cigarette

jack Loose tobacco

jigger A cigarette

jones See Word History in Chapter 3, page 141.

jump stick A cigarette

Lady Nicotine Any kind of smoking tobacco. *This very literary term is best known as the title of a book of essays by J. M. Barrie on smoking.*

light A match or a lighter to light a cigarette. *In the heyday of smoking, many a conversation at the singles bars began with the ever ready, "Do you have a **light**?"*

lip-burner A small short cigarette stub

longies King-size cigarettes. *Now better known as 100s.*

long Tom A long cigar

loosie, Lucy A single cigarette

lump Flavored tobacco leaves molded into a plug

lung duster A cigarette

make a pill To hand-roll a cigarette

makin's Loose tobacco and cigarette papers used for hand-rolling cigarettes

Manila rope A cheap Manila cigar

Match me! Light my cigarette!

Missouri meerschaum A corncob pipe

Navy plug A cheap grade of Burley plug, ordered in large quantities by the Navy

nick fit An attack of withdrawal from nicotine

night nurse A cigarette smoked in the middle of the night by true addicts or insomniac smokers

noodle twister A cigar maker

nose warmer A short pipe

pack To tap repeatedly a cigarette or a pack of cigarettes against a surface to tighten the tobacco. *A cigarette which has been **packed** lasts longer. The tobacco burns slower and* *there are less flyaway ashes.*

pack of humps   A package of Camel brand cigarettes

pack of scrap   A package of chewing tobacco

pimp stick   A cigarette, especially when smoked in a cigarette holder

plain wrappers   Generic brand cigarettes

plug   Pressed chewing tobacco. *The name came from the method of production—tobacco soaked in wild honey was plugged into holes drilled in hickory or maple logs and cured there.*

poison sausage   A cigarette. *Pretty!*

prayer book   A pack of cigarette rolling papers

premiums   Name-brand cigarettes

puff   To smoke

ready-mades   Pre-rolled, hand-rolled cigarettes

rockhound candy   Chewing tobacco. *So named because of its purported popularity with geologists.*

rollie   A hand-rolled cigarette

roll-up   A hand-rolled cigarette

rope   A cheap cigar

rough and ready   Tobacco which is pressed into plugs

sack of Bull   A package of

Bull Durham tobacco

sack of dust   A package of smoking tobacco

Saint-John's-bread   Flavoring ingredients used in cigarettes. *This generally refers to carob but was recorded as "ingredients" by field workers from the Federal Writers' Project in 1938.*

scotch   Dry snuff

scrap   Loose leaf chewing tobacco

scrub   Poor quality tobacco

shorts   The last portion of a cigarette

shuck   A cigarette made with a corn-shuck wrapping, guaranteed to make young boys very sick

skeet   To spit snuff or chewing tobacco. *A brand of tobacco or snuff that makes a long trajectory when spat is known as good **skeeter**.*

skipper   An imperfectly rolled cigar, showing a gap between sections of the wrapper

slow burner   A fresh cigarette, contrasted with a **fast burner**

smoke   A cigarette

smokestack   A pipe

snipe   A discarded cigarette stub

snoose   Snuff. *Probably derived from the Swedish "snus." See also **Swedish dynamite**.*

spit-and-run   Chewing tobacco

spud   1. A tobacco knife   2. A loose cigarette, sold for about a dime in the 1930s

square   A manufactured cigarette

stinker   A cheap cigar

stogie   A cigar. *The term was derived from "Conestoga Wagon"; as the drivers drove their teams with one hand, with the other they rolled rough cigars.*

strips   Tobacco leaves without stems to be used for cigarettes

swab   To take a **dip** of snuff

Swedish dynamite   Chewing tobacco. *This term was coined by American-born loggers who worked alongside Scandinavian loggers who called it "snus."*

tabacky   Tobacco

tailor-made, TM   A machine-manufactured cigarette

toby   A long, cheap cigar

toke   To take a puff from a cigarette. *Also widely used for puffing marijuana.*

tooth   Little spots of oil on a fine quality cigar wrapper

tuck   The end of a cigar that is lighted

tufer   A cheap cigar. *An early play with "two-for," derived from the price of two for a nickel.*

tumblin's   Loose tobacco
twist a dream   To roll a
cigarette
twist one   To roll a cigarette
two-pack hit   A murder-
for-hire in prison, paid

for by two packs of ciga-
rettes
weed   A cigarette. *A weed
was a cigarette and a
pack of cigarettes was a
pack of **weeds** well*

*before **weed** came to
mean "marijuana." For
further discussion, see
Word Histories in Chapter
3, page 139.*
woodbine   A cheap cigar

Pinball Wizard Lingo

IT IS NEARLY IMPOSSIBLE TO understand the fear and condemnation which pinball generated when it was introduced in the 1930s; there was no doubt in the minds of God-fearing flag-loving patriots—pinball was a vice. The game of the 1930s, first known as **pingame** and only in 1936 as **pinball** (and then at times as the **marble machine**), was a game of chance; the **flipper** was not added until the 1940s, leaving the player with little control of the ball. Because it was largely a game of chance, it was condemned as gambling.

In the early 1940s, big city newspapers and politicians lashed into pinball with furious deter-mination. In San Francisco, the *News Letter and Wasp* ran a long series of articles on the "Marble Ball Racket," lambasting pinball in striking hyperbole—"Every day new evidence of the

powerful evil of these machines becomes evi-dent." In New York, Mayor Fiorello La Guardia denounced pinball as "an evil and a menace to young persons because it develops the gambling urge in children." La Guardia's efforts produced an all-out ban on pinball in New York City which lasted from 1942 until 1976, a ban which would not seem to have contributed to an overall de-crease in vice or sin in the city.

The hysteria spawned by pinball continued into the 1950s, with *Better Homes and Gardens* decrying it as a "sucker's game of rigged odds" that could "wreck the civic enterprise and eco-nomic well-being of any village, town, or city," and with the McClellan Senate investigations in 1957 delving into organized crime's role in the pinball business.

It was not until 1969 with the rock opera *Tommy* by The Who that pinball had any vocal support; in *Tommy*, the young, autistic hero of the opera finds meaning and glory in pinball, producing the rock anthem "Pinball Wizard," which is fittingly laced with pinball slang. Now largely replaced in the hearts and minds of teenagers by video arcade games, pinball with its spectacularly garish art, its buzzers and bells and thwacks, seems from a distance to have been an innocent and lively game. But make no mistake about it—in its day, pinball was a formidable vice, and one which produced a fair body of slang and slangy jargon.

action kicker A stretched rebound feature that propels the ball away from a bumper

add-a-ball A game feature in which the player can win extra balls on any turn

air ball A ball that **drains** after scoring no points or the bare minimum

back box The upright portion of the machine, holding the **back glass;** also known as the **head**

back flip To shoot the ball to the same side of the **playfield** as the **flipper** used for the shot

back glass The facing of the upright portion of the game, emblazoned with art and showing the score. *Also known as the **back flash**.*

ball search An internal electronic feature of the game that is activated if the machine's electronic logic determines that a ball may be stuck somewhere on the **playfield**

bang back A somewhat heavy-handed playing technique to save a ball that is traveling down an **out lane;** the player raises the flipper on the side of the machine where the ball is traveling and when it reaches the flipper imparts a generous bit of body movement to the machine,

attempting to drive the ball up to the dormant flipper

bank shot A playing technique in which the ball is bounced off a **playfield** device and hits a target. *On loan from the sinners in the pool hall.*

biff A hard hit to the front of the machine designed to propel a ball heading into the **out hole** back into play

biff rail A thick **wireform** rail below the flippers designed to prevent a ball from being **biffed** back into play

bleed A ball that **drains** after scoring the bare minimum points

bobble bumper A bumper that scores and propels the ball away from it

bounce pass To move a ball from one flipper to the other by letting it bounce off the first flipper

bumper A device on the **playfield** that expels the ball away from it when hit. *Known technically as "scoring illuminated rebounding posts," bumpers were introduced in 1936 with a new scoring feature that deviated from the pins and pockets format in use until then.*

cabinet The body of the machine

captive ball A feature on the **playfield** that holds an extra ball that is released when a target is hit

cellar hole A hole in the **playfield** that leads to a **lane** below the **playfield**

chunk To hit a bumper so hard that it does not respond

collect bonus A hole on the **playfield** that adds accumulated bonus points to the player's overall score

combo A sequence of targets

cross hand Using the right hand to control the left flipper and the left hand to control the right flipper (said of a playing style)

dead catch To stop the ball as it passes the flippers with the flipper in a down position; also known as a **drop catch**

death save A drastic playing technique to save a ball that is traveling down an **out lane,** moving the entire machine forward and to the right to bounce the ball back into play

diverter A feature on the **playfield** that can channel the ball in one of several directions

dolphin ball A ball that passes through the **playfield** without making many points

drain 1. A hole at the end of the **playfield** below the flippers which returns the ball to the inside of the machine, also known as the **out hole** 2. To go down the **out hole** (said of a ball)

drain-o-matic A game whose design features lead to frequent visits to the **drain**

drop catch To stop the ball as it passes the flippers with the flipper in a down position; also known as a **dead catch**

drop target A feature on the playing field that drops out of play when hit

drum unit The scoring mechanism

eject A hole on the **playfield** that expels a ball back into the **playfield**; also known as a **kick-out hole**

English Any body movement imparted to the machine. *Another borrowing from the pool ball.*

flag A scoring feature suspended between two pegs on the **playfield,** that spins around when hit

flipper The major player-driven feature of a pinball game, and activated by buttons on the side of the machine, flippers are used by the player to keep the ball in play. *As is more fully discussed in the* **gunching** *and* **plunger** *entries below, the* **flipper** *was not introduced until 1947.*

floater A machine with so little slant that the ball seems to travel in slow motion

frenzy A situation in which every feature on the **playfield** produces high scores

full Greek To send a ball up and then back down a lane with a **rollover,** scoring in each direction

full rack The maximum number of replays allowed to be accumulated

gap The opening between the bottom flippers

gate A one-way feature on the **playfield,** allowing the ball to pass through in one direction but not the other

gimmick Any feature on the **back glass, cabinet,** or **playfield** that is designed solely to attract attention

gobble hole A hole on the **playfield** that takes the ball out of play, usually accompanied by a big point score; also known as a **sinkhole**

gunching Any body movement imparted to the machine. *This term was most popular before the introduction of the* **flip-** *per in 1947, when a player could influence the course of the ball only by his* **plunger shot** *or by* **gunching,** *slightly moving the machine.*

habitrail Wire paths that guide the ball on the **playfield,** also known as a **wireform**

hat A piece of plastic in the **playfield** that indicates a score value when lit from underneath

head The upright portion of the pinball machine

hopper A ball that hops over a flipper, a rail, or out of a hole

horseshoe A feature on the **playfield** that takes a ball from one side of the **playfield** to the other

house ball A ball that **drains** after scoring no points or the bare minimum

inner shot A projection of the ball by a side flipper

jet bumper, jet An active bumper on the **playfield**

kicker A feature on the **playfield** made out of stretched rubber that forcefully propels the ball in the opposite direction

kick-out hole A hole on the **playfield** that expels a ball back into the **playfield;** also known as an **eject**

knocker The game feature

that produces the loud popping noise that signifies a free game; also known as a **thwacker**

knock-off button A device used to convert a pinball machine from an illegal direct paying mode to a legal free-play mode

lamppost A post that when activated drops into the **playfield**, leaving its top flush with the playing surface

lane A part of the **playfield** that channels the ball, usually towards the **flippers**

Lazarus ball A ball that passes between the flippers but then bounces back into play. *For the sinner who forgets the New Testament, Jesus raised Lazarus from the dead.*

light box The wooden box standing upright at the end of the machine

live catch To stop the ball before it reaches the flippers with the flipper in an extended upwards position

loop A feature on the **playfield** that takes the ball in a semicircular path

low-man-feed An agreement among players that the player with the lowest score will pay for the next game

match A feature on some games that awards a free

game to a player who matches the last two numbers of their score with a randomly generated number

messenger ball A feature on the **playfield** that holds an extra ball that is released when a target is hit

monster A prototype game, wired but made of unpainted white wood

moving target A pendulum-like feature on the **playfield** that scores points for the player when hit

mushroom bumpers Features on the **playfield** that do not have the propelling action of **kickers** but merely serve as obstacles

nudging Any body movement imparted to the machine. *This term was probably derived from a 1947 Bally game named Nudgy, which was designed to let the player move the entire **playfield** forward or backward to control the path of the ball.*

one-ball An early type of pinball game with a payout mechanism and which offered a player one ball per game

operator The owner of a machine

orbit A feature on the **playfield** that takes the ball in a semicircular path

out hole A hole at the end of the **playfield** below the flippers which returns the ball to the inside of the machine; also known as the **drain**

out lane The **lanes** that channel a ball to a **drain**

over the top Exceeding the maximum score that can be shown, returning the score to zero

pass To move the ball from one flipper to the other

Philadelphia shaker A player who is skilled at applying body movement to the machine

pin A pinball machine

pingame A pinball game

pinhead A pinball enthusiast

plastic Artwork in the **playfield**

playfield The area of the machine where the ball is in play

plunger The spring-activated feature that a player uses to propel a ball into play. *Before the **flipper** was introduced in 1947, the player had only two techniques for controlling the course of the ball, one of which was his **plunger shot**, and the other, **gunching.***

pockets Scored holes in old

pingames, before the days of **flippers, bumpers, drains,** and **score reels**

pop bumper A feature on the **playfield** that lights up, makes noise, and propels the ball when struck. *Pinball manufacturer Bally calls this feature a **thumper-bumper.***

post 1. A peg on the **playfield** that serves as an obstacle and as an anchor for **kicking rubbers 2.** A temporary bumper that appears between the flippers, popping up when a specified target is hit and preventing balls from disappearing down the **out hole**

power bumper An active bumper on the **playfield**

push away The action of a bumper, which projects a ball that has hit it with greater force than the ball carried when it struck

rape To exploit a design flaw and accumulate an extraordinary point total

red-eye An illuminated special feature

return lane A **lane** that channels the ball back to the **plunger**

ripper A high-speed shot through a **spinner**

rollover An electronic switch that is activated when the ball rolls over it

roll over To achieve a score that surpasses the game's score-keeping ability

rollunder An electronic switch that is activated when the ball passes under it

roto-targets A series of spinning targets on the **playfield**

roundabout A feature that takes the ball in play from one part of the **playfield** to another

saucer A playfield feature, consisting of a slight concave depression that kicks the ball back out

save To prevent a ball from going down the **out hole**

scab To do well more by luck than by skill

scoop A **playfield** feature that catches and aims a ball towards a target

score reel The wheels of numbers which kept score before the introduction of digital scorekeeping

SDTM **S**traight **D**own **T**he **M**iddle, the path taken by

a ball between the flippers on its way to the **drain.** *This acronym is more than a little evocative of golf's jocular DTFM— "down the fucking middle" (of the fairway)— where you*

want to hit the ball on your tee shot.

shakeout The process of extricating a ball from a channel or gutter by shaking the machine

shark A pinball hustler

sharpie A skilled player

who can play for long periods without paying

shooter The spring-activated feature that a player uses to propel the ball into play, the **plunger**

sinkhole A hole on the **playfield** that takes the ball out of play, usually accompanied by a big point score; also known as a **gobble hole**

skill shot A specific shot at the start of a play that if made produces an extra score

slap save A playing technique to save a ball headed straight down the middle by hitting the flipper button and the side of the machine at the same time

slingshot kicker A feature on the **playfield** that provides a very strong **push away**

special An award, most commonly a free game

spinner A scoring feature suspended between two pegs on the **playfield,** that spins around when hit

stroke The force with which a **flipper** is manipulated

swinging target A pendulum-like feature on the **playfield** that scores points for the player when hit

target A feature on the **playfield** that awards points when struck by the ball

thumb shot A **plunger** shot augmented by the force of the hand and thumb

thumper-bumper A feature on the **playfield** that lights up, makes noise, and propels the ball when struck. *This term is used by pinball manufacturer Bally. Other manufacturers use the term **pop** bumper.*

thwacker The game feature that produces the loud popping noise that signifies a free game; also known as a **knocker**

tilt 1. A feature in the machine that ends the game if the player imparts too much body movement to the machine. 2. To impart too much body movement to the machine thereby ending the game

tour ball A ball that passes through the **playfield** without making many points

trough An area in a machine where balls not in play are stored

wail To score many points in a short amount of time

whiffle ball Pinball. *An article in* American Speech *in 1943 listed* **whiffle ball** *as a synonym for **pinball** at Whitman College. One of*

the earliest coin-operated **pingames** *of the late 1920s was known as* **Whiffle Ball,** *manufactured by the Indoor and Outdoor Games Company in Youngstown, Ohio. It appears that the name for the particular game persisted in a generic sense for at least 15 years.*

whirlpool A **playfield** feature where the ball enters at the top and spins to the exit

wide body Any machine that is more than 22 inches wide

wireform Wire paths that guide the ball on the **playfield,** also known as a **habitrail**

wizard A highly skilled player. *Some games have rewards for extraordinary play built into them, known as **wizard bonuses.***

wood rails Pinball machines made between 1946 and 1959

zip ball A ball that scores no points before **draining**

zipper flipper A short-lived variation with **flippers,** in which a certain sequence of target hits could activate a change in the configuration of the flippers to prevent any ball from **draining**

Java Jive—Coffee Slang

COFFEE IS OUR NATIONAL CENTRAL nervous system stimulant of choice, despite religious teachings and urgings to avoid coffee as a desecration of the temple that is our body. Once considered by the church to be **Satan's drink**, coffee appealed so much to Pope Clement VIII that he exercised his papal authority to baptize coffee—"This Satan's drink is so delicious it would be a pity to let infidels have exclusive use of it. We shall baptize it and make it a Christian beverage." And now, just try to wean us. We love the smell, we love the feel of the mug, we love the ritual, we love the taste, we love the buzz. *Why so tense? He never has a second cup! Times like these were made for Taster's Choice! Wanna cuppa?*

Despite its legal status, coffee has produced some smart slang, thus being the exception that proves the rule that legality or widespread use spoils the chance for a lively slang. Most of the slang synonyms for *coffee* were coined in the 1930s and have a definite cracking-wise, lunch counter ring to them—**alkali** (from the chemical formulation of caffeine, usually a bitter coffee), **barefoot** (black), **battery juice**, **belly warmer**, **belly wash**, **bilge water**, **black and white**, **blackjack** or **blackstrap** (strong black coffee), **blackout** (strong black coffee), **bootleg** (improvised, weak coffee), **Brazilian cocktail**, **brown wash** (weak, thin coffee), **dishwater**, **embalming fluid**, **flowing Mississippi**, **forty weight**, **hobo coffee** (coffee with whole eggs, including broken shells, and salt), **hundred-mile coffee** (strong coffee favored by truckers), **ink**, **iodine**, **jamoka** or **jamoke**, **jangle juice**, **java**, **jo** or **Joe**, **midnight**, **misery** (weak coffee), **mocha** or **moke**, **mud**, **mug of murk**, **one in the dark**, **perk**, **Pittsburgh**, **seconds** (reheated or rebrewed), **smoke**, **suds** (usually in the expression **sinkers and suds** for coffee and donuts), **tar** (black coffee), **warm wet** (weak coffee), and **with socks** (with cream).

And then in the 1980s there was a new crowd, bowing down before huge stainless steel espresso machines, with coffee now "caffe" and lots of high-caffeine-power drinks ending with vowels. On the slang front there is a cute and witty little new Italian-inspired lingo for the new generation of coffee sinners, not without its own wise-guy slacker edge: **Al Pacino** (a cappuccino), **barista** (a worker at a coffee bar), **dope** (a *doppio*, or double espresso), **double** (two 1.5-ounce shots of espresso), **double zero** (a drink that is made with decaffeinated espresso and nonfat milk), **half-caf** (half caffeinated, half decaffeinated), **harmless** (made with decaffeinated espresso), **kiss** (a hot chocolate), **no-fun** (a drink that is made with decaffeinated espresso and nonfat milk), **on a leash** (to go), **on wheels** (to go), **reggae** (regular), **schizo** (half caffeinated, half decaffeinated), **short** (the standard amount of milk or water), **single** (one 1.5-ounce shot of espresso), **skinny** (made with nonfat milk), **sleepy** (decaffeinated), **tall** (extra milk or water), **unleaded** (decaffeinated), **why-bother** (a drink that is made with decaffeinated espresso and nonfat milk), **with legs** (to go), **without** (served without foamed milk), and **with wings** (to go).

Fortune-Telling

THERE ARE SOME SINS that just take themselves too seriously; one manifestation of this tendency towards the serious is a ponderous, obscure language that gives the impression of religion or science or philosophy, anything but sin. Take a look at the language of fortune-telling and astrology—talk about boring! Leviticus 19:26 and 31 clearly delineate divination, sooth-saying, and fortune-telling as sins, and one need look no further than the outrage expressed by many Christians when it was learned that Nancy Reagan regularly consulted astrologers to appreciate the lasting power of the Old Testament admonitions. Despite the undisputed sinful nature of astrology and fortune-telling, their language as reported is bulky, plodding, and of little interest to the student of the language of sin.

It would seem likely that there should be a lively little language to describe the deceptive side of fortune-telling, but if there is I have not yet found it. In the 19th century, a **powwower** was one who conducted seances, while in the 1930s the somewhat generic terms of **spook artist** (the fortune-teller), **sap baiter**, and **shillaber** (the "outside" confederates of the fortune-teller who secured information about the customer) were used to describe alleged psychics and their work.

Of the many branches of fortune-telling, "cartomancy," divination by cards, comes closest to a human voice. When divining with cards, the fortune-teller deals them into a pattern known as a **layout** or **spread**, with the undealt cards known as the **stock**. Like many card games, cartomancy or card **reading** often is built around a card **family** (all the cards of a particular suit) or a **sequence** (a series of cards in ascending value). The first card is known as the **foundation**, and the process of building a **family** or **sequence** is known as **packing**. Cards that cannot be used in the **packing** are placed in the **rubbish heap** and are considered **dead**. If the fortune-teller cannot complete the **family** or **sequence**, the cards are said to be **chockered** or **blocked**. In many **layouts** there is a **surprise card** or **surprise heap**, used to decide ambiguities created in the main arena.

Straying for a moment from the confines of slang, there are several terms and expressions in fortune-telling that are at least mildly interesting to word-lovers. Fortune-tellers will speak of trying to **pierce the veil**, a dandy little metaphor that they use to mean projecting their perceptive powers into the boundless realm of the Unknown. **Scrying** has a nice sound to it, the perfect word to describe the art of interpreting the Unknown by gazing into a crystal ball, candle, bowl of water, or mirror. Other catchy terms are **odyle** (the mysterious force that fills all material objects, including the human body) and **jettator** (someone who possesses "the evil eye"), and **Plain of Mars** (the hollowed-in, central area of the palm). Lastly, there is the incantation **Abracadabra**, a popular sobriquet for amulets during the Great Plague in London.

As dismal as the language of fortune-telling is, the vocabulary of astrology is worse. Even leaving aside the utterly impassable language of Vedic astrology, the idiom of astrology is with several exceptions dull, tedious, and inaccessible. The following short list gives a taste of the flavor of starsspeak:

adept Skilled in astrology. *The term came from alchemy; the **adept** alchemist possessed "the great secret."*

antipathy An unaccountable disharmony, aversion, or antagonism

aura A psychic effluvium that emanates from

humans and animals

critical days "Those which coincide with the formation, by the Moon, directional or transitory, of each successive semi-square or 45-degree aspect, to its position at birth." *That gem of a definition from the* Encyclopedia of Astrology *gives a fair hint of the tone found throughout the language of astrology.*

cusp An imaginary line which separates one astrological sign from another

esoteric Secret, not available to the uninitiated

frustration Intervention by a third planet in a dynamic between two other planets

mansion of the moon One day's average travel of the moon. *It sounds like it is going to be cooler than that, doesn't it?*

philosopher's stone The power by which all minds and all souls achieve kinship. *The metaphorical use is borrowed from an alchemy term—the stone was an imaginary substance used to change base metals into gold.*

querent The person seeking an astrologer's advice

quesified The person or thing that is the subject of

the **querent**'s inquiry

Ruler The planet deemed to be especially potent during a given astrological sign. *During that sign, the planet is said to be "on the throne."*

syzygy Any alignment of celestial bodies. *Not a bad word for Scrabble, either.*

testimony A partial judgment, or analysis, of an astrological chart. *Several testimonies make a judgment.*

throne The period when an astrological sign is the **Ruler**

To its credit, the language of astrology has given us several colloquial expressions. **Dog days**, which refers to the hottest period of the summer, in ancient times began with the helical rising of Sirius, the "Dog Star," and ended 50 days after the summer solstice. **Vibrations**, a huge word in the hippie era, has been used for decades by astrologers and occultists to mean psychic pulsations.

Lying

ALL RELIGIONS ARE ORIENTED in the direction of goodness; like other religious systems, Christianity speaks with disapproval of wicked lips and lying tongues. That said, lying permeates our daily life—personal, social, business, and political. When President Eisenhower calmly denied the overflight of American spy planes with his "What U-2's?" to Soviet leaders in Paris, he signaled the beginning of the era of presidents lying, an era which persists to this day, broken only by the unusually honest Jimmy Carter. Given the near ubiquitous nature of lying, one might expect that it, like tobacco or alcohol, would have its defenders and advocates. True, Oscar Wilde in *The Decay of Lying* argued that lying is a form of art, an "expression of superior imaginative power," but Wilde is long gone and the type of lying that he embraced would hardly apply to Lyndon Johnson and the Gulf of Tonkin, Richard Nixon and Watergate, or Oliver North and Iran/Contra.

Simply put, lying is an integral and irrepressible feature of life in America, and it is fitting that there be a robust body of slang terms and expressions. **I shit you not**—look at these words used to describe terminological inexactitude—**balls, baloney, banger, bloviation** (a word that Davey Crockett loved or would have loved), **bosh, bouncer, BS, bullshit,** bumper, bunk, **cock and bull story, corker, crap, crapola, crock of shit, fib, fish story, garbage, good 'un, hogwash, hokum, hooey, horse manure, horseshit, hot air, howler, jive, likely story, line of bullshit, lollapalooza, malarkey, smoke, stretcher** (a word used beautifully by Mark Twain), **tall tale, terminological inexactitude,** and **whopper.**

Do you doubt me? Well that's my story and I'm sticking to it. What are you going to believe, your lying eyes or these verbs—to **bloviate, blow smoke, bosh, BS, bullshit, cook, jive, lead up the garden path, lie like a rug, phony up, pile it on, salt a mine, shit, shovel the shit, shuck and jive, speak with a forked tongue, spin a windy, string along, talk through one's hat,** or **tell a whopper?**

Gossip

PAUL THE APOSTLE LEFT no doubt in his Epistle to the Romans (1:29-30)—gossips and scandalmongers are wicked, sinful, and deserve death. That said, don't we love to gossip! Don't we love scandal?

When we think of gossip, we might ask—**What's the buzz? What's the 411?** The noun

form of "gossip" is translated as the **breeze, cat chat** (as if women are the only ones who gossip—as if!), **chin music, clothesline** (as in hanging out one's dirty laundry), **dirt, dirty laundry, dirty linen,** the **411, grapevine, lowdown, mudslinging,** or **scuttlebutt.** In the verb form, to gossip is to **bad-mouth, chew the fat, dish, dish the dirt, pass the poison, schmooze** (from Yiddish), or **shoot the shit.**

When it comes to scandal, go the best and forget the rest—the suffix -gate has ruled the coop since 1973. From its humble beginnings on June 17, 1972, **Watergate** in 1973 became the dominant word in American politics until President Nixon's resignation in August 1974. With the coining of **Winegate** to describe a wine vintage scandal in France in 1973, headline writers have not been able to resist the **-gate** construction as, in the word of William Safire, a "scandalizer." Many of the following combinations were one-hit wonders, coined in a column and forgotten, but several, such as **Koreagate, Iran-Contragate,** and the Clinton **-gates** had staying power. Recorded combinations since 1973 include **Applegate** (referring to Mario Cuomo's attacks on Mayor Abe Beame during his campaign to be elected Mayor of New York City), **Beerandbroadsgate** (coined by Jody Powell with no specific scandal in mind in 1978), **Billygate** (scandal-mongering revolving around presidential brother Billy Carter), **Cartergate** (a 1978 coining applied to Carter White House scandals), **Cattlegate** (a cattle feed scandal in Michigan in 1978), **Chinagate** (dubious Chinese connections to Democratic fund-raising under Clinton), **Dallasgate** (a 1975 headline about the assassination of President Kennedy), **Debategate** or **Briefinggate** (a scandal that surfaced in late 1983 regarding the Reagan campaign's acquisition of Carter debate briefing materials in the 1980 presidential campaign), **Drug-gate** (rumors of drug use in the Carter White House in 1978), **Filegate** (a Clinton presidency problem and term, referring to background files that found their way into the Clinton White House), **Floodgate** (allegations against Congressman Daniel Flood in 1978), **Goobergate** (a term used by the *Atlanta Journal-Constitution* to include all Carter scandals), **Greekgate** (a short-lived scandal involving Senator Herman Talmadge and the Greek government in 1978), **Harborgate** (used in a 1977 article belittling the **-gate** construction), **Headachegate** (a term used in 1978 because the Carter presidency was not producing its quota of scandals), **Hollywoodgate** (a label coined by *Newsweek* in 1978 that never got off the ground), **Info-gate** (a South African scandal in 1978), **Iran-Contragate** or **Irangate** (President Reagan's great debacle; **Irangate** was used in an earlier scandal, the 1979 revelation of American involvement in internal Iranian matters), **Iraqgate** (the use of subterfuge to furnish Iraq with rocket technology during the Bush presidency), **Jordangate** (used by Russell Baker in 1978, suggesting that the media was too scandal-thirsty and that it would prey on Hamilton Jordan unfairly), **Koreagate** (the 1976 investigation into the relationship between members of Congress and the government of South Korea), **Laborgate** (crooked southeast Asian unions), **Lancegate** (referring to Bert Lance in the Carter Administration), **Mediagate** (used by Jesse Jackson in 1978 to describe the media cover-up of its failure to treat minorities fairly), **Motorgate** (a Cleveland criminal scheme in 1976 involving false warranty claims), **Muldergate** (a South African scandal in 1978), **Nannygate** (used first in 1977 with respect to Otto and Adrian Langs and then again in 1993 for an early Clinton nomination for Attorney General), **Oilgate** (a British scandal in 1978), **Paperclip-**

gate (a jocular reference to 1979 charges of corruption in the General Services Administration), **Peanutgate** (unsupported charges of criminality in the Carter Administration, used in 1979), **Pearlygate** (unseemly competition between television preachers), **Prisongate** (a pardon-for-pay scandal in Tennessee in 1979), **Rubbergate** (applied to the 1991 House of Representatives banking scandal), **Scalpgate** (a short-lived moniker given to the Clinton haircut on an airport runway in 1993), **Sewergate** (used by NBC television news in 1978),

Travelgate (an early Clinton scandal, the 1993 dismissal of White House travel staff), **Underwatergate** (France's bombing of the Greenpeace ship *Rainbow Warrior* in New Zealand in 1985), **Vietgate** (the proposed pardon of Vietnam deserters and draft-dodgers in 1974), **Volgagate** (1973 rumors of a vast scandal involving the leadership of the Communist Party in the Soviet Union), **Whitehallgate** (a general sense of corruption in England, 1978), **Whitewatergate** (President Clinton's albatross, with the "water" too precious to resist), **Windsorgate** (a 1980 coining looking back at Edward VII and Mrs. Simpson), and **Winegate** (a 1973 French vintage scandal).

The temptation to resort to the **-gate** construction remains irresistible more than 25 years after the burglary at the Watergate complex gave us the first **-gate**. In the first weeks after the Monica Lewinsky story broke, journalists stumbled over each other to invent the **-gate** tag that would stick to the independent counsel investigations of President Clinton. Terms coined early in the scandal include **Fornigate, Interngate, Jailbait-gate, Monicagate, Sexgate** (also the name of a search engine on the Internet), **Zippergate**, and a doubtless many others that have appeared locally.

SOURCES AND REFERENCES

FOR THE INTRODUCTION to this chapter, I read and depended on *Today's Catholic Catechism,* edited by Mary Jo Graham (Dubuque, Iowa: Brown/ROA, 1992); *Whatever Became of Sin?* by Karl Menninger (New York: Hawthorn,

1973); *The Maryknoll Catholic Dictionary,* edited by Albert J. Nevins (Wilkes-Barre, Penn.: Dimension, 1965); *The Seven Deadly Sins: Jewish, Christian, and Classical Reflections on Human Nature* by Solomon Schimmel (New York: Free, 1992); and *Three-Toed Sloths and Seven-*

League Boots by Laurence Urdang (New York: Barnes and Noble, 1986, 1992). My references for the slang synonyms of the seven deadly sins were largely works cited in other chapters or in the overall bibliography. In addition,"Money Slang" in *U.S.: An Index to the United States* by

Malcolm Townsend (Boston: Lothrop, 1890);"Slang Terms for Money" by Manuel Prenner in *American Speech*, Vol. 4 (June 1929); M. Hirsh Goldberg's *The Complete Book of Greed: The Strange and Amazing History of Human Excess* (New York: William Morrow, 1994) was helpful, and for Yiddish background I used Leo Rosten's *The Joys of Yiddish* (New York: McGraw-Hill, 1968). For the *-gate* constructions, I mined the "Miscellany" and "New Words" sections of *American Speech* and turned to William Safire's *Safire's New Political Dictionary* (New York: Random House, 1993).

Other than the terms which I learned during hundreds of sinful and needless hours in pool halls from Mexicali to Yuba City in my twenties, I referred to *The Official Rule Book for All Pocket and Carom Billiard Games* by the Billiard Congress of America (Chicago: Billiard Congress of America, 1968);"Billiards, Pool and Snooker Terms in Everyday Use" by Robert R. Craven in *American Speech*, Vol. 55 (Summer 1980); *"Minnesota Fats" on Pool* by Minnesota Fats (Chicago: Minnesota Fats Enterprises, 1965, 1976); *Pocket Billiards with Cue Tips* by Edward D. Knuchell (South Brunswick, N.J.: A. S. Barnes, 1970); *Willie Mosconi on Pocket Billiards* by Willie Mosconi (New York: Crown, 1948, 1959); the truly fun *Pool Cool* by

Steve Rushin (New York: Pocket, 1990); the excellent *Illustrated Encyclopedia of Billiards* by Mike Shamos (New York: Lyons and Buford, 1993); and *International Tournament Pool* (no publication information other than printing date of 1970).

For the slang of tattoo and body piercing parlors, Marlene Akerblom and Keith Pirtle from Sin on Skin in North Tiverton, Rhode Island were very helpful. I also drew upon *Tattoo: The Exotic Art of Skin Decoration* by Michelle Delio (London: Greenwich Editions, 1994); *Sailor Jerry Collins: American Tattoo Master in His Own Words,* edited by Donald Edward Hardy (Honolulu: Hardy Marks, 1994); *The Total Tattoo Book* by Amy Krakow (New York: Warner, 1994); and "L.A. Speak: Tattoo Parlors" in the *Los Angeles Times Magazine* (July 13, 1997). I garnered most of the words in this section from leafing through back issues of tattoo magazines, including *Skin Art, Skin & Ink, Tattoo Advocate,* and *Tattoo Time.*

I gathered tobacco slang from *Cigarette Confidential: The Unfiltered Truth About the Ultimate Addiction* by John Fahs (New York: Berkley, 1996); *Tobacco and Americans* by Robert K. Heimann (New York: McGraw-Hill, 1960); *Tobacco Dictionary,* edited by Raymond Jahn (New York: Philosophical Library, 1954); and *Cigarette Country: Tobacco in American History and Politics* by

Susan Wagner (New York: Praeger, 1971). I also relied upon the unpublished manuscript of "Tobacco Workers' Slang and Jargon" in *Lexicon of the Trades Jargon* by the Federal Writers' Project (1938) housed in the Library of Congress, as well as a number of articles from the Tamony Collection, including "Cigarette Camps" in *American Notes and Queries* (September 1945);"Coffin Nails" in the *San Francisco News* (March 4, 1947); "Nothing to Sniff At" in the *News* (January 18, 1958);"Coffin-Nail Warnings—Yes and No" in the *San Francisco News Call-Bulletin* (May 27, 1965);"The Snuff Sniffers" in the *San Francisco Chronicle* (January 28, 1967);"The Gentlefolk's Guide to Taking a Pinch" in the *San Francisco Examiner and Chronicle* (June 16, 1968);"Snuff—Nothing to Sneeze With" in the *San Francisco Examiner* (September 2, 1970); "Hot Snuff: Chew It or Sniff It" in the *Examiner and Chronicle* (January 10, 1971); and "The Snuff Revival" in the *Examiner and Chronicle* (July 11, 1971).

For java jive, I pulled words from many regular suspect sources listed in the bibliography at the end of this book, as well as from newspaper, magazine, and journal articles in the Tamony Collection, including "The Argot of the Vagabond" in *American Speech* (June 1927);"Midshipman Jargon" in *American Speech,*

Vol. 3 (August 1928); "Railroad Vernacular" in the *Writer's Monthly* (October 1929); "Slang from the Navy" in *Writer's Digest* (July 1933); "Truckman Talk" in the *Review of Reviews* (June 1937); "My, My! Such Language" in the *Rochester Democrat & Chronicle* (January 16, 1938); "Some Annapolis Slang" in *American Speech*, Vol. 14 (February 1939); "Navy Yard Talk" in *American Speech*, Vol. 17 (December 1942); "Army Slanguage" in the *San Francisco Examiner* (December 17, 1942); "Coffee by 18 Other Names" in *Coronet* (May 1943); "Tokyo Bound" in the *Saturday Evening Post* (July 10, 1943); "Vocabulary of Lakes, Deep Seas and Inland Waters" in *American Speech*, Vol. 19 (April 1944); "Middies Have a Word for It" in the *San Francisco Call-Bulletin* (August 4, 1947); "Cuppa Joe Television Star to Open Unique Snack Bar in Marina" in the *San Francisco Progress* (July 1, 1954); and, not from Tamony, "Java Jive" by Jim Frederick in the *New York Times Magazine* (July 31, 1994). Several entries came from a small "Glossary of Terms" published by the Oliveto Cafe on College Avenue, Oakland, California.

Russ Jensen, a pinball collector, historian, and writer from Camarillo, California, was my greatest guide to the lingo of pinball wizards. Pinball was not a vice of my early youth, although

my college friend Peter Korn did his best to tempt me to join him at The Drug's bank of pinball machines. Peter's early efforts paid off in my twenties when my friend Bill Monning lured me into the Greyhound bus station in Salinas, California, across Gabilan Street from the offices of the legal department of the United Farm Workers, and introduced me to the art and language of pinball. Aside from what I picked up from these two vice crusaders, I relied on *Pinball: An Illustrated History* by Michael Colmer (New York: New American Library, 1976); *Pinball: The Lure of the Silver Ball* by Gary Flower and Bill Kurtz (London: Apple Ltd., 1988); *Pinball Portfolio* by Harry McKeown (Secaucus, N.J.: Chartwell, 1976); *All About Pin Ball* by Bobbye Claire Natkin and Steven Kirk (New York: Grossett and Dunlap, 1978); *Pinball Wizardry: The Theory and Practice of the Art and Science of Pinball* by Robert Polin and Michael Rain (Englewood Cliffs, N.J.: Prentice-Hall, 1979); *Pinball!* by Roger C. Sharpe (New York: Dutton, 1977); *Pinball Art* by Keith Temple (London: Blossom, 1991); *Tilt!* by Jim and Candace Tolbert (Berkeley, Calif.: Creative Arts, 1978); and *Special When Lit: A Visual and Anecdotal History of Pinball* by Edward Trapunski (Garden City, N.Y.: Dolphin, 1979). From the Tamony Collection I drew upon "Pinball Perils" in *Billboard* (July

4, 1936); a series on "The Marble Machine Racket" in the *News Letter* (February 23, March 1, March 15, March 22, March 29, April 26, June 21, and July 12, 1940); "P.-T.A Slaps at Pinballs" in the *San Francisco News* (March 22, 1940); "Pin Ballers Holler TILT" in the *San Francisco Examiner* (August 25, 1940); "City Referendum on Pinball, Claw Machines Sought" in the *Examiner* (April 8, 1941); "Whitman College Slang" in *American Speech*, Vol. 18 (April 1943); and "One-Ball Machines Out" in the *San Francisco Call-Bulletin* (March 8, 1951).

My hearty attempts to find any meager sign of a life within the language of fortune-telling and astrology took me through the *Encyclopedia of Astrology* by Nicholas de Vore (New York: Philosophical Library, 1947); *The Sybil Leek Book of Fortune Telling* by Sybil Leek (New York: Macmillan, 1969); *Gypsy Sorcery and Fortune Telling* by Charles G. Leland (New York: University, 1964); *Fortune Telling* by Agnes M. Miall (New York: Hamlyn, 1973); *The Complete Book of the Occult and Fortune Telling* (New York: Tudor, 1945); *Fortune Telling for Fun and Popularity* by Paul Showers (New York: New Home Library, 1942); and *The Complete Book of Fortune: The Secrets of the Past, Present & Future Revealed* (Exeter, England: Blaketon Hall, 1988).

Chapter Seven:
CRIME

NE NEED PROBE THEOLOGY neither hard nor long to discover the religious bases for labeling as sin most of that which the secular world labels as crime; organized religion, like government, frowns on physical violence and theft. Despite unambiguous religious and governmental restrictions, crime flourishes. Of greater interest is the fact that despite society's unwavering condemnation of crime, as a nation we are endlessly fascinated with and even mesmerized by crime and criminals. The outlaw has always been an important figure in American culture, from the 19th-century legends surrounding Jesse James and Butch Cassidy, to Pretty Boy Floyd ("You say that I'm an outlaw / You say that I'm a thief / Well here's some Christmas dinners / For the families on relief"), to James Cagney in *Public Enemy Number One,* to Warren Beatty and Faye Dunaway as "Bonnie and Clyde," to the keep-it-real, harsh urban edge of gangster rap. Crime's standing as sin is of unquestionable pedigree, and as is the case with most sin, we as a people are compelled to revel in crime even as we condemn it.

Crime has long been a prolific breeding ground for slang, and the slang of crime has been a prolific breeding ground for slang dictionaries. The earliest treatments of English slang in the 17th and 18th centuries focused in large part on the flash and cant of thieves. Leaving aside Benjamin Franklin's 18th-century compilation of synonyms for *drunk,* the first full-fledged dictionary of American slang was *Vocabulum: The Rogue's Lexicon* by George Matsell (1859), which dealt with the language of the "rogue fraternity." Moving to the 20th century, the late David Maurer of the University of Kentucky produced a large body of work studying the slang and argot of criminals; his writings and Hyman Goldin's 1950 *Dictionary of American Underworld Lingo,* compiled by two long-term convicts, a prison chaplain, and a "Board of Underworld Advisers," are as fine examples of slang lexicography based on fieldwork as can be found.

Criminal slang continues to prosper, although it is no longer characterized by the specialization of craft and language found by Maurer and Goldin *et al.* Like other sinful slang, it is driven in part by the creative impulse, by a *joie de parler,* but it has several other functions. For one, to an extent not found in most other slang of sin, criminal slang is at times used to mask the meaning of what is said, if not from police then at least from members of the general public. Secondly, it serves as an occupational jargon for those who have chosen crime as a business; they practice a craft with specialized techniques and tools, and they need a vocabulary to describe those techniques and tools. Lastly, because of the immediate and earthly punishment meted out to those whose sins are also crimes, there is among criminals a deeply developed sense of alienation, of Us vs. Them, a factor which nearly always promotes the fabrication of slang to serve as an adhesive within the subculture.

The only obstacle which I encountered in this chapter was the process of selection. The slang of criminals is well documented; entire books can be, have been, and will be written just about criminal slang. I narrowed my scope to 20th-century American criminals and, to a degree, 20th-century American police (whose language in large part mirrors that of the criminals whom they pursue), and then had the pick of the litter, choosing words which on subjective if not artistic grounds I found pleasing or interesting. For each piece of American criminal slang included in this chapter, ten stand in the wings, awaiting a call to action.

Let's cut short the opening statement—call the words!

accelerator An arsonist

accident An arrest

ace of spades A widow

addict A victim of a confidence game who believes in the con so much that he or she returns to be conned a second time

airmail Rocks or heavy debris thrown from rooftops onto police cars and police. *This is a term from prison, brought out to the streets.*

alligatoring The appearance of burned wood that

has been doused with an accelerant, evidence of arson

apple A victim of a confidence game

around the horn Taking a suspected criminal to each police station in a

Wisecracking Safecrackers

AMONG THE ORGANIZED professional criminal class, there are those who specialize in opening safes and removing their contents. Like their associates the pickpockets and confidence men, those engaged in safecracking have developed a healthy and robust body of slang to de-scribe their work. All crime breeds slang, but the most creative and inventive slang is found among the criminals who rely upon their thinking ability, their understanding of psychology, and highly developed skills, with a minimal reliance on violence. Crim-inals who specialize in robbing safes are decidedly within the linguistically superior subculture.

That which they open and empty is not a safe, but a **box, crate, crib, gopher, locker, pete,** or **peter.** Borrowing on body parts slang, the **keister** (usually the buttocks) is a steel inner compartment

within a safe, separated by an internal door known as a **duster;** still in the realm of the safe, a **bloomer** is a safe which turns out to be empty. Fittingly, a **cannonball** is a safe which is difficult to open. Borrowing a term used to describe the facade of houses, **gingerbread** refers to ornate trimmings on a safe that do not affect the safe's structural strength.

From the slang names for safes come some of the names for those who open the safes—a **boxman, cribman, gopher-man, peteman,** and **peterman.** Other terms and expressions used to describe the professional safecracker include **blacksmith** (the thief who actually opens the safe), **heavy-worker, ironworker, Johnny Yegg, jug heavy, mechanic, muzzler, O'Sullivan,** or **yegg** (a term with many meanings but used at times to denote a safecracker).

city for identification by crime victims and/or in order to subvert his or her right to an attorney

attitude adjustment A police beating

bad bag An oversized shopping bag used by a shoplifter

bait money Money in a bank drawer that triggers an alarm if it is removed

Bates A target of a con game or pickpocketing scheme. *Sometimes called a Mr.* **Bates** *or John* **Bates,** *the mark is usually a middle-aged man who is expected to be carrying more money than younger people or women.*

batter To beg

beat To swindle a victim

beef To inform

belch To inform

belly stick A shill or decoy working at a gambling concession at a carnival, or a **flat joint**

bent Stolen

big con An intricate confidence game involving extensive planning and execution

big end A share of the proceeds of a crime that is larger than an equal share

big noise Anybody important. *In prison, usually the warden.*

binny A large overcoat with big pockets, used for shoplifting

bird dog Someone who

Four basic techniques are used to open a safe—**blow, burn, peel,** or **punch.** A **blow job** is not what one might think; it is one of several ways to describe a safe robbery using explosives. Analogues to the **blow job** include the verbs **blow a pete, blow a peter, get a box, knock a peter,** to be **on the heavy,** or to **shoot it.** The explosive used is known as **dan, dinah, dine, grease, noise** (brilliant!), **oil, picric, power** (very good!), **puff** (again, not bad!), or **sawdust.** To obtain the nitroglycerin, the explosives expert sometimes soaks dynamite in water to leach out the nitroglycerin; the process is known as **cooking up** or **thrashing out,** and the resultant explosive is known as **soup** or **stew.** The explosive is placed on the safe, which is **soaped** to plug the seams in the door frame to prevent the **grease** from seeping out. You then either use a blasting cap (a **bonnet**) or a fuse (**string** or **squib**). If using a fuse, you **torch the squib,** and—BOOM!

Knob-knockers stay away from explosives. Some **burn the box,** using industrial blowtorches to cut through the safe door; the specialist who works on this type of job is known as a **torch man.** Others **peel** it open, using a **drag** to pull the combination lock off the safe. There are also **punch jobs,** where industrial punching tools are used to punch the dials off a safe or a **stem** (drill) is used to drill into the safe, which is then known as a **sieve.** With either the **peel** or **punch job,** the safe is sometimes carted away to a warehouse or some other off-site location where it can be **peeled** or **punched** at leisure; if so, it is a **carry away.**

brings a con man or hustler information about a possible mark

bitch A woman. *Used by*

modern con men to facilitate the axiom based on avoiding housewives as targets—"Never

pitch a bitch."

black To blackmail

black handler An extortionist

Cannon, Dip, & Whiz: Pickpocket Lingo

ONE GROUP OF PROFESSIONAL criminals with an extensive slang vocabulary is the pickpockets. As a whole, they shun violence and despise a crude pickpocket (a **dig**) or purse-snatcher, labeling such unrefined theft as **ball busting** (which sometimes is used literally to describe a technique of immobilizing a victim by grabbing his testicles while robbing him), **clout and lam**, **rip and tear**, **root and toot**, **slam and lam**, or **snatch and grab**. Pickpockets practice their craft, think about their craft, analyze their craft, and—thankfully—talk about their craft.

In a generic sense, the pickpocket was most commonly referred to as a **cannon**, several generations removed from its genesis in the Yiddish *gonif* or "thief," which evolved to "gon," which evolved to "gun," which evolved to "big gun," which evolved to **cannon**. **Dip** has replaced **cannon** as the term of choice; other slang handles for the pickpocket include **angler**, **booster** (a term which is usually applied to shoplifters but which at times has been used to mean a pickpocket), **Catholic**, **grafter** (a word that usually applies in a broader sense but which may apply simply to a pickpocket), **high diver**, **hook**, **jostler**, **shot**, **stripper**, **whiz**, or **whizzer**. Within the species of pickpocket there are specialists—the

frisker who works in crowds, the **home guard** who works in only one area (and uses an expression to describe himself used by railroaders and many other types of workers to distinguish themselves from **boomers** or workers who move from job to job), **jug jobbers** who follow customers from banks and relieve them of their cash withdrawals, **lush workers** who prey on drunks, **thimble-getters** who specialize in watches, **third-rails** who work on trains (**breakers** or **rattlers**), trolleys (**shorts**), or subways (**chutes**), and **whizmolls** who specialize in robbing women.

Except for the **sneak tool** who **muzzles around** (works without an accomplice), pickpockets generally work in a **mob** or **team**; with simple addition, pickpocket (**whiz**) plus team (**mob**) equals **whiz mob**, also known as a **swell mob**. If there is a team, next to the **tool** (the actual picker of the pocket) the most important member of the team is the **stall** who distracts and diverts the victim while the **tool** makes a move. The **stall**, who also answers to **duke man** because he or she obscures the **duke** (hand) of the **tool** or the **front gee**, is known as a **backstop** if he or she works directly behind the victim and is said to **swamp** if he or she uses unsophisticated or awkward diversionary tactics. If there is a

blackjack A hand weapon typically consisting of a piece of leather-enclosed metal with a strap or shaft for a handle

block hustle A confidence game where the con pretends to be selling stolen goods for a low price when actually selling an empty box

blue wall Police solidarity,

third member of the team, he or she is usually the **wire;** after picking the victim's pocket, the **tool** passes the proceeds to the **wire,** who leaves the scene with the proceeds. Even **whiz mobs** sometimes have slackers; the team member who is reluctant to be close to the action is a **center fielder,** a **strap-hanger,** or **sneeze-shy.**

And what might the pickpocket pick when the pickpocket picks from a pocket or a **leather** (purse)? Perhaps he or she picks a **bead rope** (a pearl necklace), a **rock** (a diamond), a **chip** (a small diamond), or a watch (a **kettle** or **souper**), perhaps with a **slang** (an archaic word for a watch chain, but a tough word to resist including, no?). With bad luck, it is **junk** (plated jewelry), and with worse luck the victim is wearing a device that secures the wallet or pocket, an **anchor.**

In the early days of American pickpockets, a pocket was known as a **sky;** this term, however, soon gave ground to the circus word **kick.** Specific pockets carried specific names—the **britch kick** was a trousers pocket, the **butch key** was the hip pocket, the **coat pit** was an inside coat pocket, **outside stuff** was a wallet carried on an outside pocket, and a **pratt poke** was a wallet kept in the hip pocket.

When working a crowd (a **press** or **tip**), the pickpocket tries to dress like the population at large to avoid suspicion, to **ring out.** When a **Bates** (potential victim) is identified, the **stall** goes to work distracting him while the **tool** probes to locate the wallet or item to be picked, by **fanning** the victim's clothing. When the **stall** gets the victim into the right **frame** or **vise,** the **tool** makes his move and picks the pocket or **pulls** the pocket, **reefs** the pocket, or **reefs up** the wallet (to squeeze the pocket lining until it falls out), perhaps using a **stiff** (a newspaper or magazine) to mask the operation. When the wallet or pocket-picking object is under the control of the **tool,** it is said that the wallet **belongs** to him. One last technique expression—to **kiss the dog** is to face the victim as the pocket is picked.

At the end of the day, the **mob** has to dispose of emptied wallets (**dinging the dead ones** or the less lyrical **unloading**) and then divide up the proceeds. If there is no honor among thieves, the pickpocket who does not divide up the proceeds of the day's work fairly is a **burner.**

If spotted by the police in a crowd, a pickpocket is sometimes subjected to **stem court**—he or she is charged, tried, convicted, and fined right there on the **stem** (the street) without the niceties of court, and with the fine paid directly to the apprehending officer.

which at times is manifested in silence with respect to misconduct or criminal conduct by another policeman

bobble To call attention to one's actions while engaged in a **short con**

boiler room A room used for fraudulent telephone sales solicitations

boob A victim of a con

boodle A fake bankroll. *The terms **Michigan bankroll** and **Philadelphia bankroll** are the modern equivalents.*

boost 1. To shoplift 2. An act of theft

booster 1. A shoplifter 2. A career thief

booster bag An oversized shopping bag used by a shoplifter

bracelets Handcuffs

brain The leader of a criminal enterprise

bridge, under the Across an international border. *Obviously a smuggling term.*

bright eyes A lookout, often a female lookout

bugged Wired to a burglar alarm system

bumming A hustle involv-

The Big Store

IN YEARS PAST, confidence men constructed elaborate swindles usually aimed at rich individuals. With these intricate confidence games they also constructed a vocabulary to describe the different games, the stages in a game, and the techniques of the game. David Maurer devoted a considerable amount of his considerable talent to studying confidence men, and in so doing he compiled lengthy glossaries of **big con** lingo. The **big con**, which was also known as a **big store** or simply a **store** because of the set that was often built as part of the game, is largely a thing of the past, and the language that went with it is largely obsolete. Ironically, the closest thing to a **big store** today is found in **stings** by the police, where elaborate ruses such as Abscam approach **big store** complexity. On the other hand, the **short con** or **grift**—petty hustling—is alive and well and it is chronicled with a passion and a poetic voice in Iceberg Slim's *Trick*

Baby. I treat the language of the **short con** in the major wordlist of this chapter.

The confidence men (referred to as **cons** or sometimes, with a tip of the punning hat to "consumption," as **TB's**) who ran **big cons** were a clever and creative breed; most even operated with an ethical underpinning best articulated by "Yellow Kid" Weil—**Never send them to the river**—never drive a victim to suicide. There were dozens of variations of **big store** confidence games, including the **bat** (involving "gold" bricks), the **fight store** (involving a boxing match), the **payoff** (involving horse racing), the **rag** (involving stock), **rock** (involving fake diamonds), and the **wire** (involving horse racing and featured in the movie *The Sting*).

Because of the store motif, the victim of a **big store** confidence game was known as a **customer.** Typically, the **big con** was built around a number of metic-

ing the sale of allegedly stolen merchandise in which nothing is actually sold

bundle The goods or money stolen in a robbery

bust **1.** An arrest **2.** To be arrested **3.** To hustle someone quickly

buster A burglar's tool

butch kid An extortionist

button man A member of an organized crime family who kills as assigned

cadet A person who abducts young girls

calling cards Fingerprints

cap To consummate a **short con** sale

caper A burglary

capper The outside man who brings victims to a gambler or **short con** swindler

car banger Someone who steals out of parked cars

case To conduct preliminary surveillance before a robbery or burglary

caterpillar A smuggler of wool. *Who's busy smuggling wool these days? Not many, but enough were around to give rise to this term in the 19th century.*

---

ulously planned and carefully rehearsed stages; members of the team were assigned parts and lines, which they practiced so as not to **crack out of turn**, or speak their lines at the wrong moment.

First was the **catch**, when the **customer** was lured into the first stage of the **big con** by a **lugger**. His interest in a scheme was then excited in the **buildup**, perhaps with fake newspaper clippings (**blute**), perhaps through glowing recommendations from a member of the **big con** known as a **boost** or a **singer**, or perhaps through intentionally overheard conversation between two members of the team—**crossfire**. If the **customer chilled** (lost interest), there was sometimes a backup scheme in place, a **cap.**

Next, the **customer** was allowed to invest a moderate amount of money and to win, proving the efficacy of the scheme being sold. The money won at this stage of the game was known either as the **convincer** or as **kickback.**

The head confidence man now appeared and put his own money into the scheme, further proof of its worth, and giving this stage of things the name **hurrah.** It seemed too good to be true and it was; the **customer** invested a large sum in the scheme and—surprise of all surprises—the telegraph operator made a mistake in reporting what horse had won a race, the gold was not gold, the diamonds were not diamonds, etc. etc., and the **sting** or **big block** had taken place. Even deducting the **cap** (expenses incurred in **roping** or **guiding** the **customer**), the **big con** often netted tens of thousands of dollars.

When the **customer** and his money had been separated, it was time to get rid of the victim, time for the **blowoff** or the **final.** This was accomplished through a number of dramatic embellishments, including a false arrest (a **button** or **tear-up**), or, as used in *The Sting,* a fake shooting (a **cackle-bladder**).

chester   A child molester.
*Presumably from the
archetypal Chester the
Molester.*
chicken hawk   A child
molester
chill   To kill someone

chisel   To cheat
chiseler   A small-time hustler or petty thief
choirboy   A young apprentice in a pachuco drug
smuggling gang of the
1950s

chop shop   A garage where
stolen cars are dismantled
to be sold as parts
chopper   A machine gunner
clean   Purged of identifying
numbers. *A stolen car is
clean when its serial*

Begging for Sympathy

A S THE 20TH CENTURY COMES to a close, beggars have become a sad fixture on
American streets, a constant reminder of the absence of an economic safety net.
It seems impossible to walk a block in any city without encountering a plea: "You
don't have to be a Rockefeller to help a feller," "The greatest nation in the world is a
do-nation," or a simple "Do you have any spare change?"

Begging is not new in America, and in fact the periods when there has been little
public begging are the exception to the rule. In the early 20th century, begging took
on a slightly criminal and sinful edge, as beggars, many women, **tossed out** or **threw
out**—feigned injuries or afflictions to elicit sympathy and donations. As they devised
injuries, they also devised a language to describe their dramatizations:

army	Pretending to be missing an arm
blinky	Pretending to be blind
blisters	Showing sores from self-inflicted burns
crippy	Pretending to be paralyzed
D&D	Pretending to be deaf and dumb
deafy	Pretending to be deaf
dummy	Pretending to be dumb
flopper	Pretending to be crippled
fritzy	Feigning epileptic fits
ghost	Simulating tuberculosis symptoms
hidden hands	Pretending to be missing a limb
jigger	A sore that is intentionally aggravated
peggy	Pretending to be missing a leg
shaky	Affecting tremors
toss-out	Able to throw a limb out of joint
wingy	Pretending to be missing an arm

At times, the beggars also engaged in petty **grift** or hustles, selling fake merchandise,
such as fur (**skin hustle**), jewelry (the **slum hustle**, with **slum** used in its slang
sense as "fake"), clothing (**weave hustle**), or silk (**worm hustle**).

numbers have been changed or erased by a **numbers changer**. *In the 1930s, the adage "never look an auto bargain under the hood" meant that if a used car was priced below the expected market price, one should not be too inquisitive about the serial numbers.*

cleaner A criminal whose specialty is disposing of bodies and otherwise removing evidence of murders. *The character played by Harvey Keitel in* Pulp Fiction *was the archetype of the **cleaner**. He explained his craft simply: "I solve problems."*

clip To kill

clip joint A bar or club where customers are regularly cheated. *In 1952, the exploitation movie* Clip Joint *had the too-cool advertising slogan of "Sinners and Suckers All Meet at the Clip Joint."*

clout To assault

COD A **short con**, where a Bible or other high-priced item is sent to a recently deceased person COD. *The low-life grifters who work this con are amused by the transformation of COD to Collect On Death.*

collar 1. An arrest 2. To arrest

colored stuff Rubies, emeralds, and other colored gems

cop 1. To steal or take 2. A policeman. *For further discussion of* **cop**, *see Word History, page 271.*

cop the edge To take advantage of a situation

corner A lookout, someone who keeps the neighborhood criminals informed of what is going on without being part of the underworld

crack out To hustle someone quickly

creep To drag the sea bottom for smuggled goods that have been sunk

creepers Soft shoes worn by burglars

crew A street gang

crossfire A quick conversation in argot between two con men to trick the victim of a **short con**

cuff links Handcuffs

cut A share of the proceeds

of a crime. *To divide the proceeds of the crime is thus to* **cut up.**

cuter A prosecuting attorney

damper A cash register

dark A moonless night, good for smuggling

dauber A car painter who will repaint a stolen car

dead Reformed

deadhead An unpromising target of a con game

derrick A shoplifter

DeWolf Hopper's Wedding Rings Brass knuckles. *Hopper, whoever he was, was married five times,*

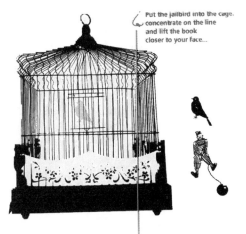

Put the jailbird into the cage. concentrate on the line and lift the book closer to your face...

and brass knuckles have five holes for the fingers and a thumb.

dick A detective. *See Word History, page 272.*

diddler A child molester

dinger A bell alarm outside a bank

dirty dishes Planted evidence

doaker A member of a smuggling team whose job is to divert attention from those actually doing the smuggling as the border is crossed. *A 19th-century term, along with* **caterpillar** *and* **owler.**

doe A kidnapped child

doghouse A small garage rented in a residential neighborhood for short-term storage of stolen cars

drag A burglar's tool

drive call A follow-up telephone call in a phone con where pressure is applied to the potential mark

drop gun, drop A pistol that has been confiscated in a previous arrest and is carried by police to drop near a victim if he or she is involved in a dubious shooting

dropper A paid killer

drop tin To show a police badge

duck soup Any crime or scheme that is easy and profitable

dump To attack, to beat

dye pack A stack of bills that surround an explosive ball of dye, handed to a bank robber and later triggered to explode, coloring the robber with dye

Slang by Runyon

NOBODY HAS CHRONICLED VICE and sin in America with a stronger or more intriguing and colorful voice than Damon Runyon. His portraits of Broadway gangsters, grifters, and grafters of the 1920s and 1930s sparkle today with every bit of the intensity that they enjoyed 50 years ago. Along with his cleverly sculpted underworld characters and the vibrant New York settings, Runyon's use of language stands out.

In telling his tales, Runyon relied on what David Maurer acknowledged to be a solid grasp of underworld lingo, which he supplemented with original coinings. Runyon's coinings included original rhyming slang, words enhanced by decorative and meaningless suffixes, slight twistings of words and expressions in use, double plurals, double past participles, and functional shifts. Representative of Runyon's coinings are the following:

alley-apple	A rock
beesom	Money
blouwzola	A common woman
canneroo	Jail. *From the established "can."*
cat-hop	A party
cupcake	A girl. *From the established "cake."*
darbolas	Handcuffs
face	The mouth, as in "Don't open your face"
Francesca	The buttocks. *Based on "fanny."*
gorgeous	A beautiful woman. *A functional shift, from adjective to noun.*
hamdonny	A bad actor. *An embellished "ham."*
hamola	A swindler. *A meaningless suffix.*

ears People who keep neighborhood criminals informed without being part of the criminal world

egg A mark or sucker

erase To kill

fainter A member of a gang of robbers who distracts the victims

fall An arrest

fall dough, fall money A gang's reserve fund for the legal defense of its members

fall partner A person with whom one is arrested

feero An arsonist

finger To inform

firebug An arsonist

fireproofed Having received the last rites of the church

fixer Someone who acts as a go-between for criminals and law officials

flake False, planted evidence

flash Cheap, gaudy merchandise used to lure suckers to a game

flat joint A gambling operation at a carnival. *Carnivals went to great lengths to avoid gambling; an August 19, 1944 advertisement in* Billboard *was typical— "No Flat Stores or Grifts Allowed at These Fairs." The ads usually failed, and gambling was rampant at carnivals.*

heevus	To leave
honeysuckle	A sweetheart
komoppo	A woman who displays her wealth ostentatiously
meat-house	The morgue
mooley	A dimwit
nasturtium	A sweetheart
Ned	Hell. *Runyon apparently drew on Old* **Ned** *as "the Devil" for this one.*
one-two-seven	Even
ostrich	A boxer who loses a fight on purpose
pancake	A girl. *Taken from "cake."*
paralyzed oath	A strong and binding avowal
pedigree	One's name. *Spun off from the established slang meaning of "police record."*
phonus bolonus	Bad information
pizzolover	A handgun. *A blend of "pistol" and "revolver."*
rooty-toot-toot	A machine gun. *Very possibly from the song "Frankie and Johnny": "rooty-toot-toot that gal did shoot."*
rose geranium	Something that is ultimately excellent
scamus	A situation
sharpshooter	A gold digger
smeller	A play that stinks
smush	The mouth

flink A smuggler's warning light

flipper An accused criminal who quickly and eagerly agrees to testify against his cohorts

floater 1. A traveling thief. *The term floater is or was used by workers in many industries to refer to any worker who travels from job to job, practicing his or her craft.* 2. A corpse floating on the surface of a body of water

flogger An overcoat. *From criminal vocabulary to describe the petty thief or flogger stiff who steals overcoats.*

flop An arrest

flopper Someone who feigns an accident by pretending to be hit by a car

flying game A **short con,** selling an empty carton in the guise of selling allegedly stolen merchandise

fork A pickpocket

forty-some-odd A pistol

Fourth of July A gun battle with police

fresh dough Money earned through a criminal enterprise that has been made to appear to be the product of a legitimate business. *An early term for laundered money.*

front The clothing and impression made by a thief, who sometimes wants to blend with a crowd and sometimes wants to stand out

fuzz The police. *See the Word History on page 273.*

Sharks and Jets: Gangs Part 1

THE FIRST GENERATION OF MODERN American gang members were predominantly white, and then Latin American, urban youth. They frightened us, we called them **hoodlums,** but we were fascinated by their rules for life and morality. When Leonard Bernstein created *West Side Story,* we flocked to Broadway and then to the movie theater, entranced by the images of New York gang members.

To the American gang youth of the 1950s, a gang member was a **bart** or a **citizen,** while a nonmember was a **leaguer** or a **shoe.** Within the gang, the fighting corps were known as **shields,** the top fighters were **ace men,** and the nominal leader of the gang was the **switch.**

The territory which a gang considered its domain was its **turf,** and a violation of its territorial integrity could lead to violence. Other reasons for gang warfare might include **sounding** (insulting through words or looks) or perhaps **roughing** (aggressively shoving or bumping) a rival gang member during a **fall-in** or group entrance to an event.

Once one gang **called it on** (challenged the other gang to a fight), there were three possible outcomes—they could **declare a talk** (meet to settle the disagreement without further fighting), fight with no weapons (a **fair fight** or **fair one**), fight with **blades** (knives) and **pieces** (guns) and other weapons (to **burn, go down, rumble,** or **waste**). Any gang member who refused to fight was a **punk,** an extreme slur but preferable to death, even if death brought Natalie Wood singing "there's a place for us, somewhere a place for us" over your dead body.

gager A person who disposes of stolen goods

gat A gun

gay cat 1. A criminal tramp 2. A saboteur

gee A guy. *At least since the 1930s, gee has been used to mean "guy." A heavy gee is a criminal involved in violent activities, while a c-gee is involved in confidence schemes. A fly-gee is an outsider who understands con games.*

Gentlemen, The Smugglers

get a hard-on To reach for a pistol

get busy To rob someone

get paid To rob someone

ghost A behind-the-scenes criminal lawyer

gig A gigolo

give the finger To cheat

glom To steal

glued Arrested

golfer A Cadillac. *This punny little piece of car thief slang of the late 1920s results from the shortening of "Cadillac" to "caddy" and thus to golfer.*

gone Convicted of a crime

goodfella A mobster. *The Martin Scorcese film* Goodfellas *was based on a Nicholas Pileggi novel synonymously entitled* Wise Guys.

good people An old-timer, especially a retired one

goofer A gangster. *Corrupted from the New York gang the Gophers.*

gorilla A criminal who uses violence

grease the mitt To pay a bribe

grifter A small-time hustler, **short con** artist, change swindler. Billboard's *fair and carnival advertisements in the 1940s and 1950s were peppered with bold warnings—"Positively no grift," "No racket," and "No grift!"*

grounder
A homicide case that can be solved relatively easily and quickly

guide To steer a prospective victim to a gambling operation, brothel, swindle, etc.

gull A victim

gums, gummers Soft shoes worn by sneak thieves

gun A thief

gunmaker An instructor of young thieves

guzzled Arrested

gyp To cheat

hall of fame A police mug book

hand tools Picklocks and screwdrivers

hard way By honest means (said of work)

heat, heater A pistol

heavy Armed

heavy rackets Crimes involving violence

heeled Armed

herring An incorruptible girl. *"Herring" was the name of a safe that defied dynamite.*

hide A place to conceal contraband

hit 1. A sale in a **short con** 2. To murder

hit man A hired murderer

hog eye A large skeleton key for commercial buildings

hoist A burglary

hoister A shoplifter
hooks Keys or picklocks
hoop A ring, usually a stolen jewelry ring
hopscotch To take a confidence game on the road
hot Stolen
hotel worker A thief who specializes in robbing hotel guests
hot short A stolen car
houseman A burglar

hyster A shoplifter
ice Jewelry, or more specifically, diamonds
Italian football A bomb
jabbed Convicted by perjured testimony
jackroll To rob a drunk
Jake A victim of a con man
japper Someone who spoils a **short con**
jay A bank
jiggerman A lookout

jimmy **1.** A short steel crowbar used to force entry **2.** To force entry with a short steel crowbar
jumper A wire used to divert an alarm system
jump the fence To jump bail
jury tax The implicit threat of a longer sentence if an accused does not accept a plea bargain

Biker Lingo: Gangs Part 2

IN THE MID-1960S, WE LOOKED UP and were shocked to see that gangs had changed. Just as we had gotten used to the Jets and Sharks, *gang* took on a whole new, hellish meaning. Motorcycle gangs, primarily the infamous, notorious, and nefarious Hells Angels, were upon us and there was nothing romantic about them, no Broadway musical waiting to be written about them, no chorus of dancers ready to kick their way through a rumble. The Hells Angel was a true outlaw; whether or not a fugitive from justice (**in the wind**), he or she despised all that was **plastic** (less than genuine) and displayed his or her contempt through rough and crude living that terrified even an increasingly jaded America.

Not surprisingly, motorcycle gangs took their motorcycles seriously, very seriously. The motorcycle of virtually unanimous choice was the Harley-Davidson, a **hog;** the degree to which the Harley-Davidson was revered was illustrated by the use of the Harley-Davidson manual, known as an

Angel's Bible or simply the **Bible**, to perform **rebel weddings** of gang members, which could then be annulled simply by ripping up the manual.

Most Angel motorcycles were stripped down to the essentials, and with their high handlebars (**ape-hangers**) they were known as **choppers;** a large, customized **hog** was a **dresser**, while a stock motorcycle was simply a **garbage wagon.** Worst of all were Japanese-manufactured motorcycles—**Jap-scrap** or a **sewing machine.**

A gang-sanctioned outing was a **run;** whoever the gang's leader might be in the clubhouse or bar, the **road captain** was in charge on a **run.** For the **run,** you might **pack** a passenger on your motorcycle, and if you did they would appreciate the backrest known to other bikers as **sissy bars.** Following the gang on a **run** to pick up broken bikes was the **crash truck.**

Central to the image of the motorcycle gang member was his **colors,** the gang insignia on the back of a sleeveless denim

keeper   An arrest that results in the arrestee being
charged
kinky   Stolen. *This term
springs from* **bent** *as
a slang synonym for
"stolen."*
knock   To inform
knockdown   An introduction
lam   **1.** Flight   **2.** To leave
landed   Arrested

lawnmower   A machine
gun
lay down   To sell or dispose of
lay the note   To short-
change a cashier
lead poisoning   Bullet
wounds
leaper   Someone who
jumps bail
lemon pop   A tool that is
used to open the lock on

a car door
lifter   A shoplifter
made   High-ranking and not
subject to intramob vio-
lence without sanction
from mob leaders (said
of a mobster)
make   To recognize
make your bones   To
become a full-fledged
member of an organized
criminal enterprise by

jacket; to **fly colors** was to wear the
denim jacket with the gang insignia, while
one's **originals** were his first **colors**
which were never to be washed, no matter
what vile or nasty substances they absorbed. The **rocker** was the top portion of
the insignia, with the local chapter appearing on the bottom half. The jacket could
also be adorned with patches. Like Boy
Scout patches, some motorcycle gang
patches simply signified achievements;
unlike Boy Scout patches, the achievements that they signified were sexual.
Other patches were based on slangy
acronyms and slogans—**AFFA** (Angels
Forever, Forever Angels), **AFFL** (Angels
Forever, Forever Loaded), **DFFL** (Dope
Forever, Forever Loaded), or **OFFO**
(Outlaws Forever, Forever Outlaws). A
truly dedicated gang member could take
things a step further, getting a **back
pack**—a tattoo of the club insignia on his
back.

The nonmember of the gang, a **citizen**
(a complete reversal of the 1950s gang
terminology in which a **citizen** was a gang
member), was relatively safe from gang
member activity, although gang members
at times took joy in shocking and crude
acts in public (**classing**). Until motorcycle
gangs devolved into little more than
amphetamine-dealing criminals, most of
their unsavory and criminal conduct was
reserved for themselves and the women
who enjoyed, or accepted, their company.
Within the gang, the only woman who was
safe from sexual advances of any member
was a gang member's **old lady**, his steady
girlfriend or wife who called him her **old
man** and who was not available to other
gang members. A female hanger-on who
was available to any gang member was a
mama, **queen**, or **sheep**, while the
female hanger-on who was available for
serial or group sex (a **gang bang** or **gang
splash**) was a **train**. The occasional
stranger who was enticed to an Angels
gathering without fully appreciating the
consequences of attending and who then
was raped was, ironically, a **cutie**.

In the Hood: Gangs Part 3

JUST WHEN WE THINK that things can be no worse, up pops something new that makes us wish for the good old days. So it goes with gangs—when we see what's in store for us in the gang department we start feeling nostalgic for Tiny Terry, the Buzzard, and those rascals in the Hells Angels. America has always had a problem with race-related matters, and here's race right in the face in the 1980s and 1990s, with white America seeming to see a gang member in the face of every inner-city youth it encounters. With reality amplified—if not outright distorted—through the magnifying glass of race-charged hysteria, the new gangs have made us forget the old gangs. Fortunately, though, for our limited purpose here, the slang of **gangbangers** is a tasty blend of traditional African-American vernacular English, gangster slang from the 1930s, slang coined during the conflict in Vietnam, and 1990s neologisms, all mixed and blended in the cauldron of hip-hop and rap.

Within the larger framework of a gang (a **crew**, **posse**, **tribe**, or **troop**), there are **cliques** (a group with a long-range economic plan), **sets** (a neighborhood gang with its own territory, associated with a larger group), and a **tip** (a small group with a specific function). The leader of any unit is known as a **shotcaller**, while **OG** or **Original Gangster** is a term of respect reserved for long-standing, full-fledged, **real deal** gang members. A gang member in general terms is a **gangbanger, gangsta, hardhead, headbanger,** or **roughneck,** one who spends his days **mobbin'** or **hangin', bangin',** and **slangin'** (dealing drugs). Degrees of membership are measured by slang expressions—an **ace kool** is the one fellow gang member whom one can most count on, a **homeboy** is a gang member from one's immediate neighborhood, a **warrior** is a fighter, a **baby gangster** is a young gang member, and a **buster** or **mark** is a young recruit who wants to join the gang.

If fortunate enough to be accepted for gang membership, one must endure a beating as an initiation rite, to be **courted in** or **jumped in.** Once a member of the gang, one is expected to **fly the colors**, to wear gang colors, usually by wearing an appropriately colored **brim** (baseball cap) or **rag** (handkerchief). If one wants to leave the gang (**drop the flag**), **bones out** (quits in fear), **half-steps** (shows some reluctance to commit fully to gang activity), **perpetrates** (brings shame onto the gang), refuses to **put in work** (participate in dangerous activities for the gang), is guilty of a **violation** (of gang rules), or in general is not **down** (living up to gang expectations), they must endure a second, more brutal beating, the **beating out.**

Gangs often resort to slang when they talk of themselves and their rivals. The Jets and Sharks have given way to warring factions such as the Vice Lords and Disciples in Chicago and, most notoriously, the Bloods and Crips in Los Angeles. To the Crip, another Crip (whom one asks "**What it C like?**", with *be* avoided because of its association with Bloods) is a **cuz** or a **BKA** (Blood Killer Always), while a Blood is a **blob, oo-lah, peanut butter, slob,** or **ug.** To the Blood ("**What it B like?**"), the Crip is either a **crab, E-ricket,** or **rooster.**

If one judges a culture by its language, the single most important feature of modern gang life is violence towards other gangs; the slang synonyms for basic words of violence are nearly boundless. A gang has its neighborhood turf (its **hood, N-H,** or **set**) which it must **hold down**. Within that area, they reserve the exclusive right to commit a crime (**make a move** or **manipulate**), and unless you are willing to fight, you would be well-advised to **book** (leave).

Instead of the simple "to fight," there is to **bang, beef, break on, bump titties, bust up, crash, duke, flex, flip, funk up, gank, get busy, jack up, jam, jump, loc on, muff, pug, rag up, reck, riff, roll, rush, set off, step to, style on, squab** (usually to argue rather than to fight), **throw down,** or **wreck.** In a sweet little piece of euphemism, the gang fight that was once known as a **rumble** has become a **demonstration.**

If fighting is not enough, check out that **gangsta** over there—he's **packing** (armed). Generically, a gun is known as a **bis** or **biscuit, burner, chrome, chwop, click, clog, flamer, four-pounder, gak, gat, glock, heat** or **heater, iron, niner, oowop, piece, pump, steel, strap, street sweeper** (usually a semiautomatic weapon), **tech, toast,** or **tootie.** Getting more specific, a **breakdown** is a shotgun, a **double deuce** (a .22-caliber weapon), a **four-five** (a .45-caliber pistol), and a **tray-eight** (a .38-caliber handgun).

Armed with a vocabulary for guns, to shoot someone is to **blast, buck, burn, bust a cap, cap, clip, dent, fade, fry, ice, lead up, light up, peel a cap, pop a cap** (an expression used effectively by the character played by Samuel Jackson in *Pulp Fiction* in the final scene of the movie), **smoke, spray,** or **wet.** To **catch a body, check, do, drop, dust, ice, off, smoke, take out, take out of the box,** and **waste** all mean to kill someone.

Violence is not the only facet of gang life. Drugs and sex have their place, with **mack** or **player** used to describe the man who is more interested in sex than his gang responsibilities. If he has the ability to impress women with his garb, he has **drag** or **rush.** Look at him there—who could resist, **draped** (wearing a lot of jewelry) and **saggin'** (wearing loose pants slung low on the hip), over there with his car (**ride**), posing for the world—with him **everything is everything** (all's well).

engaging in a killing

mark   The target of a con game or other swindle

Mary Ellen   A robbing technique in which a customer in a bar who has been encouraged to get drunk is robbed

mechanic   A criminal skilled in a specialty

meet   A rendezvous before or after a crime

mill's lock   A sure thing

mitt up   To put on gloves

mob   A gang

monicker   One's name

monkey   A victim of a con game

moocher   A small-time thief who works alone

muscle in   To force one's way into a legitimate business

nab   To arrest

nippers   Handcuffs

nuck   A thief

numbers changer   A skilled worker who changes serial numbers on stolen cars

nut   The cost of a crime

one-liner   A **short con**

outsiders   Long-nosed pincers used to turn a key on the inside of a door from the outside

owler   A smuggler of wool. *Another 19th-century smuggling term along with* **caterpillar** *and* **doaker.**

pack   To carry

paperhanger   A forger

payola   Secret payments made especially to a disc jockey by a record company. *See Word History, page 274.*

peach   To inform

penman   A forger

pennyweighter   A thief who robs jewelers by palming jewels

perp   A suspect

persuader   A hand weapon typically consisting of a piece of leather-enclosed metal with a strap or shaft for a handle

Peter-to-Paul   A pyramid scheme, originated in the United States by William Franklin Miller and duplicated by Charles Ponzi, who subsequently lent his name to it. *A pyramid scheme or Ponzi scheme is a confidence game in which investors are promised huge profits in a short time; early investors are paid with deposits of later investors but most of the money is diverted to the con game operator.*

pick   A picklock

piece   1. A gun   2. A share

pig   A policeman. *See Word History, page 273.*

pineapple   A small shrapnel bomb

play, in   Engaged in a con game

pling   To panhandle

plug   To shoot (someone)

punch guff   To discuss past exploits with other criminals

punk licks   Small potatoes, a **short con** with a small payoff

push   One's criminal associates

rap   To inform

rape-O   A rapist

rapper   A prosecuting attorney

rap sheet   A criminal's police record

rep   Reputation

rip   To steal with impunity

rock emporium   A jewelry store

rod   A gun

roll the tab   To leave a restaurant or motel without paying one's bill

root   To steal

rope   To secure a mark for a con game

rosco   A handgun

run   To smuggle

sap   The victim of a confidence game

scare   The extortion racket

scoot   To flee

scratchman   A forger

shag   Worthless

shape   A duplicate key to a newly sold car

sharpshooter   A criminal who meticulously plans and prepares a crime

sheet   A police record

shiner   A diamond

shooting iron A gun

shortcake A share of the proceeds of a crime that is less than expected

short eyes A child molester

sidekick A tool used to break and thus deactivate a steering column lock in a car

sing To inform on other criminals

slow Without anybody at home (said of a house)

slow work Daylight robbery of a house with nobody home

slum Mixed jewelry

slumming A hustle involving the sale of allegedly stolen merchandise in which nothing is actually sold

crime organization who is prepared to kill in a dispute with a rival organization

sour paper Bad checks

spark, sparkler A diamond

spike a job To engage in a **short con** in which a crooked contractor starts work on a house without

Sixteen will get you twenty! Statutory rape is a crime!

skinner A rapist

slap hammer, slap, slam hammer A tool used to yank out the ignition of a stolen car, which is then started with a new ignition

slicker A newly repainted stolen car

slim-jim A tool used to open the lock on a car door

smoke To shoot

smoke iron A gun

smudge A fire set by an arsonist

snatch To kidnap

sneak work Robbery of a house while the occupants are eating

sneeze 1. To arrest 2. To kidnap

soak To place in pawn

soldier 1. An armed lookout on a potentially violent job 2. A member of a

authorization and is then paid to finish the job

spinner A car mechanic who is part of a car theft ring and whose specialty is reversing odometers to decrease the apparent mileage on a stolen car

split To inform

squeal To inform

stall A person who occupies a clerk's attention while his or her confederate shoplifts. *A pickpocket* *term applied in a shop-lifting context.*

stash A meeting place

step in To interfere with a **short con,** intentionally or inadvertently

stick A shill

strap A hand weapon typically consisting of a piece of leather-enclosed metal with a strap or shaft for a handle

swag 1. A burglary 2. Stolen goods other than cash

swamp To arrest

sweet pea An easy victim

swift A quick substitution of something worthless for something valuable in a con game

tail To follow

take 1. Money or goods obtained in a crime 2. To dupe 3. The state of being bribed. *Commonly used in reference to law enforcement officials in the phrase "on the take."*

tap a till To take money from a cash register

target 1. The outside lookout during a crime 2. An easy mark

taw A bankroll

tears Pearls

ten percenter A scout for a gang who locates targets and receives 10 percent of the take

thimble A lookout

throw-down A pistol that has been confiscated in a previous arrest and is carried by police to drop near a victim if he or she is involved in a dubious shooting

ticket A warrant

tinker A novice burglar

tin-mittens A go-between for criminals and law officials; a **fixer.** *He likes to hear coins clank in his open hand.*

tip and toss Any confidence game in which a shill or decoy is used

tocker A murderer

torch, torchy An arsonist

torpedo A gunman, a killer

touch Money taken from a con game victim

touch-off Arson. *From the verb* **touch off,** *"to cause to explode with fire."*

tree-jumper A rapist

trick A burglary

push One's criminal associates

rap To inform

rape-O A rapist

rapper A prosecuting attorney

rap sheet A criminal's police record

rep Reputation

rip To steal with impunity

rock empor... A jew... store

rod A gu...

roll the...

... ...

root To steal

scare The extortion racket

scoot To flee

scratchman A forge...

shag Worthless

shape A duplicate key... newly sold car

sharpshooter A crimina... who meticulously plan... and prepare...

sheet A police reco...

...**iner** A diamond

...**e** A knife

...**ooting iron** A gu...

...**shortcake** ... ... proceeds ...a crime that is ...ess than expected

short eyes A child molester

trip   A woman who steals from men on the street

troops   A gang

turf   Territory

turnip   A gold pocketwatch

typewriter, typer   A machine gun

uncle   A pawnbroker

vag   To arrest for vagrancy

walk the tab   To leave a restaurant without paying the bill

waste   To kill

whack   To kill someone

wheelman   A skilled driver, used for escapes after crimes

whip   Someone who steals from parked cars

white   Silver

winchell   An easy victim of a con game or crime

windows   Spectacles

wire   The actual operator in a crime, who lifts the wallet or seizes the money

wise guy   A mobster

wolf packing   Gang activity. *This is not the first time this metaphor has been used in slang. A "wolf pack" is also a group of submarines that make a coordinated attack on*

shipping.

work   To steal

work blind   To work without protection from bribed officials and/or without a plan

wrong   Somehow against the code of the underworld

yack   1. A telephone sales solicitor   2. A stolen watch

yaffle   1. To arrest   2. To steal

yegg   1. Any variety of criminal   2. A safecracker   3. A bank robber   4. A criminal tramp

WORD HISTORIES

COP, DICK, FUZZ, AND PIG

ON THE OTHER SIDE of the crime-sin coin is the crime-busting, sin-fighting policeman, known over the ages by a number of slang terms, most notably **cop, dick, fuzz,** and **pig.**

Cop has enjoyed a long run as the slang synonym of choice for *policeman;* notwithstanding J. Edgar Hoover's efforts in 1956 to stamp out popular use of the term because he found it offensive, it is in most contexts a neutral designation. The usual sources agree that the first use of **cop** in writing was by George Matsell in *Vocabulum: The Rogue's Lexicon* (1859). Interestingly, Matsell includes definitions for **copped** (arrested), **copped to**

rights (arrested on compelling evidence), and **copbusy** (handing over stolen property to a confederate in anticipation of arrest or search), but not **cop** or **copper.** He does, however, use both **cop** and **copper** in the book. **Copper** is found in an example of the use of **copped:** "The knuck was copped to rights, a sking full of honey was found in his kick's poke by the **copper** when he frisked him." Similarly, **cop** is found in a poem that appears near the end of the volume, "A Hundred Stretches [Years] Hence":

And where the buffer, bruiser, blowen
And all the cops and beaks so knowin'
A hundred stretches hence?

Eric Partridge tracked a use of

copper back to the *National Police Gazette* of February 21, 1846, and Jonathan Lighter provides an 1844 citation of **cop** as a verb meaning "to arrest," which leaves **cop** the noun as the new kid on the block.

As is the case with so many slang terms, there are several competing etymologies for **cop.** Among the less plausible are the following:

John C. Haines, who became chief of police in Chicago in 1858, was well known as a speculator in copper, which bestowed the term **copper** on his police. *(Play the Devil: A History of Gambling in the United States* by Henry Chafetz)

Old-time police badges were made of copper, with no

nickel plating. From this fact arose **copper.** (*Tramp and Underworld Slang* by Godfrey Irwin)

The term comes from the fact that in early times police wore copper toes on their shoes. ("Questions and Answers" in the *San Francisco News,* December 10, 1946)

Cops were called cops because of a chief of police named "Copp." (*Word Study,* Vol. 29, No. 3, February 1954)

Police in England, referred to as constables, signed their reports by name, followed by "Constable on Patrol" or "Constabulary of Police," which was eventually reduced to the initials COP (*Saturday Evening Post,* November 17, 1956). In a June 16, 1964 letter to the editor of the *San Francisco Examiner,* one Alan Dodd of Palo Alto suggested that the original expression was "Custodian of the Peace."

Policemen wore metal helmets, often made from copper, which were made necessary by the fact that bricks or other heavy objects often were dropped on the police from the windows and rooftops in poor neighborhoods. (*The Story of Language* by Mario Pei)

In the mid-19th century,

police wore large copper stars on their uniforms (*Crime Dictionary* by Ralp De Sola). Details are found in the *Buffalo Courier-Express* of September 3, 1959: "In 1845 the star police gave New York a new look. These officers wore an 8-pointed star badge of copper, after the design of the Peel police in England."

The buttons on police uniforms were made of copper, thus **copper,** and then **cop** (*Chicago Tribune,* January 4, 1951). A variant theory traces the copper buttons to uniformed police in New York between 1844 and 1845. (See *Time,* October 16, 1950.)

The term "actually stems from the term 'copper,' an oblique reference to 'copper-stick,' archaic slang for a policeman's truncheon." (*Cop Speak* by Tom Philbin)

Hotten (1859) and Farmer and Henley (1891) combine for the most convincing speculation as to **cop**'s semantic derivation. Hotten surmised that a **copper** was one who **cops** (arrests), and that **cop** as a verb was probably a contraction of the Latin *capere,* to seize or take something. Farmer and Henley took the theory a step further, pointing out the Gypsy Romany *kap* or *cop* (to take), the Scotch *kep,* the Gallic *ceapan,* and the Hebrew *cop* (a

hand, used to refer to snatching something).

Dick, another piece of 19th-century police slang, was first used to refer to a detective in January 1886, almost 30 years after Jacob Hayes, the High Constable of New York, assembled the nation's first detective force. Prior to the creation of a detective force, American police had followed the old maxim and had sent a thief to catch a thief, relying largely on informers to solve crimes. In this regard, one finds **deeker** used in 1821 to mean a thief kept in pay by a constable; with the change in detection methods, the 1891 edition of Hotten defines the related **dee** as a "detective policeman." Also related, one finds **deek** as "to see" in Matsell (1859) and **to keep dick** as "to keep watch" in the *English Dialect Dictionary.*

Dick and its cousins **deeker, dee, deek,** and **keep dick** probably all flow from the Gypsy culture and the Romany language, in which *dick* or *dikk* means "to see" or "to look." This theory was advocated by Barrère and Leland, Farmer and Henley, and Peter Tamony in his "Origin of Words" column in the *San Francisco Wasp and News Letter* (May 12, 1939). The only other half-thoughtful theory (one can safely reject the suggestion by one writer that "the term might have come— negative connotation attached—from Donkey Dick, a term commonly used for a jackass") is that *detective* split into **dee** and **'tec,** and that either could have produced **dick, dee** from the first letter "d" and **'tec** from the sound. The corrupt contraction of *detective* was advanced as the probable source for **dick** by Eric Partridge and Godfrey Irwin.

Fuzz first appeared in 1929 in E. Booth's *Stealing Through Life,* in a context which suggests that it may have been used in 1920. **Fuzz** never drove **cop** from the field, but it enjoyed great popularity in the 1930s. For its origin, Peter Tamony pointed to carnival slang, arguing that **fuzz-tail** or **fuzzy-tail,** a pejorative in the order of **ring-tail** (a lowly coward), was used to refer to police. In their *Dictionary of Word and Phrase Origins* (New York: Harper, 1962), William and Mary Morris suggested that **fuzz** is "most likely ...a corruption of 'Feds,' referring to agents of the Federal Narcotics Bureau"—a corruption which does not rush to the ear. Godfrey Irwin made a case for **fuzz** coming from **fuss,** a person who is hard to please or who is too picky. David Dalby, a scholar of West African languages, suggests a possible West African origin of **fuzz** in an essay "The African Element in American English" that appears in *Rappin' and Styling Out: Communication in Urban Black America,* edited by

Thomas Kochman (Urbana: University of Illinois Press, 1972). Dalby began with the word *fas* (horse) from Wolof, the language of slaves from Senegal, and took that to the English-language **fuzzy tail** for a range horse or a sure bet at a horse race, and from there to a mounted policeman, and from there to **fuzz** as policeman.

Last and least kind is **pig.** In the late 1960s, the Black Panthers introduced **pig** to the country, thinking that they were coining a new term. As Earl Anthony wrote in *A Report on the Black Panthers* (New York: Dial, 1970), "In the newspaper we began to refer to the police as 'pigs.' We were looking for the most despicable name to call the police, and the pig is symbolically the nastiest animal. 'Pig' caught on very naturally, and became a byword used by black people and white radicals." In their zeal, the Panthers almost drove **pig** into the ground. As a single example, in the October 10, 1970 issue of the weekly *Black Panther Community News Service,* six of the nine headlines use the word **pig.**

Black Panther literature defined a **pig** as "a low natured beast that has no regard for law, justice, or the rights of people; a creature that bites the hand that feeds it; a foul, depraved traducer, usually found masquerading as the victim of an unprovoked

attack." The porcine metaphor quickly caught on with both the hippie and political wings of the white youth movement. Linguist and educator S. I. Hayakawa was called as an expert witness in the 1972 trial of a San Francisco anti-war activist; Hayakawa testified in that trial that **pig** was "used to dehumanize the individual," that it was "often used with a pejorative adjective in front of it," and that it was "a very important form of verbal assault." So forceful was the negative association of **pig** with the police that police organizations countered with billboards, creating a **pig** acronym—**P**ride, **I**ntegrity, and **G**uts.

As much as the Black Panthers may have liked to claim **pig** as their own coining, they were more than 150 years too late. Although not found in Grose's 1796 *Classical Dictionary of the Vulgar Tongue,* **pig** is found in the 1811 edition (renamed *Lexicon Balatronicum*), defined as "a policeman." One finds **pig** again in the *National Police Gazette* on February 21, 1846, as well as in George Matsell's 1859 *Rogue's Lexicon.* The 19th century may not have had the chants of "Today's pig, tomorrow's bacon," but it certainly had **pig.**

When a derogatory word is used towards a class of people, they will sometimes appropriate even a highly offensive word and use it as their own as a token of pride. In this vein, the families of police often collect pig artifacts and ephemera, through humor reclaiming pride lost by the public's use of **pig**. In this same vein, many local police departments stage "Pig Bowls"—football games between competing law enforcement agencies.

WORD HISTORY

PAYOLA

IN LATE 1959, America learned about white collar crime in the entertainment industry, and with that lesson came a new word for our vocabulary—**payola**. The term was applied to a new kind of shady business practice in the entertainment industry, most commonly to payments by record companies to disc jockeys who played records issued by the paying company. The scandal stayed with us for several years, ending the careers of many first-generation rock-and-roll disc jockeys, and spawning a large family of words ending with the three letters **-ola.**

Payola seems to have appeared first in the April 1938 issue of *Downbeat* magazine. It appeared in print dozens of times before late 1959, belying its status as neologism in 1959. Examples of pre-1959 uses found in the Tamony Collection, which focuses on San Francisco daily newspapers, include *Variety* on January 8, 1941 ("Fined for Payola"); *Variety* on January 7, 1942 ("Selling Side of Song Plugging"); *Variety* on June 10, 1942 ("Chicago Hears of War Against Payola"); *Variety* on August 2, 1944 ("Payola on a

Sally Slang

THE SALVATION ARMY, KNOWN TO criminals and down-and-outers as the **Sally**, is one of many charitable organizations that aim to improve the lot of the fringe population of very poor. Virtue does not attract or generate slang to the extent that vice does, but the Salvation Army was not immune from military-themed linguistic creativity in the late 1920s and early 1930s. To the Salvation Army faithful, to **fire a volley** was to tell the assembled group of destitute, "Say 'Amen' together." To speak with individuals about their problems during or after a meeting was to **fish**; if they converted to Christianity, they were known as **prisoners** because they were seen as prisoners of war captured in the war with Satan.

Different types of meetings, known collectively as **knee drills**, were given slang names. A **company meeting** was a Sunday meeting where children were taught the Bible in classes known as **companies**, and a **free-and-easy** was a meeting which encouraged freedom and spontaneity. When the guests raised their right hands in affirmation of what was said, there was a military metaphor on hand— what they did was to **fix bayonets**. The praise session at the end of a meeting was an **Hallelujah Wind-Up**, while **grace before meat** was a fund-raising scheme where grace (small contributions) was solicited before meat was served.

Not bad for virtue! However, it should be noted that **free-and-easy** and **fix bayonets** both began with less virtuous meanings. A **free-and-easy** was a tavern or brothel while **fixed bayonets** was military slang for strong liquor.

Rampage"); *Time* on March 5, 1945; *Variety* on January 21, 1953 ("MPCE to Come Out Against Payola in New Pact; Some Say It's Futile"); *Confidential* in June 1954 ("Million Dollar Shakedown in TV"); the *San Francisco News* on March 28, 1957 ("Payola Oils DJ's for R&B Hits"); the *News* again on March 29, 1957 ("Payola Suffers Jolt at Hands of S.F. Radio Station"); the *San Francisco Call-Bulletin* on July 27, 1957 ("Disc Jockeys Are Next In Income Tax Probes" by Dorothy Kilgallen); *Hollywood Diary* on November 3, 1958 ("FCC To Clean Up D.J. Bribery"); and the *San Francisco Chronicle* on December 15, 1958 ("There's Little New About This Payola" by Ralph J. Gleason).

Payola was part of, and contributed to, a frenzy of **-ola** fixations. In some cases, the **-ola** provided an association of bribery, as in **fixola** or **royola;** more often, it was a meaningless affixation which added no substantive value to the word. As such, it was usually purely decorative.

Even before **payola**'s first appearance in *Variety* in 1938, **-ola** was commonly spotted in the names of popular songs and dances (such as the **Cubanola** in 1909, the **Havonola** in 1916, the **Indianola** in 1917, the **Can-Canola** in 1929, the **Swingola** in 1937, and later in the **Carmbola** in 1950 and the **Stomp-**

bola in 1953) and trade names, especially those of radios (such as the **Staticola** in 1926), car radios (**Motorola,** coined in the 1930s as "a new word suggesting sound in motion," according to the electronics company's Web site), phonographs (such as the **Victrola** in 1906 or later the **Phonola** in 1957), other new technologies (such as the **Moviola,** a movie editing machine so named at least as early as 1938), and pianos (as in the **Pianola** in 1909).

When **payola** burst into national vocabulary in late 1959, there were already a number of **ola**-ending improper nouns on the books, largely from the world of show business. Both Damon Runyon (**blouwzola** for a common woman, **darbolas** for handcuffs, **hambola** for a cheater or grifter, and **speakola** for talking) and Walter Winchell (**clinkola** in 1940, **execola** in 1937, **hamola** in 1935, and **heartola** in 1937) were early advocates of **-ola.**

Also predating the first **payola** of 1938 were **bounceola** (meaning "discharged," 1936), **dubinola** (1924), **floppola** (1937), **gringola** (1935), **jazzola** (in a band name, 1927), **lamola** (1949), **pastafoozola** (from Joe Williams, 1939), **pompanola** (1928), **punkola** (used by Nathanael West in *The Day of the Locust,* 1939), and **tankola** (meaning "a drunk act," 1936).

Rising to recorded use after **payola**'s birth in 1938 but before **payola**'s move into the limelight in 1959 were **boffola** (a joke, 1946), **erzola** (coined by Jimmy Hatlo, 1952), **heaterola** (a gun, used in *Scientific Detective,* July 1945), **scramola** (*American Speech,* October 1937), **shaganola** (1938), and **Yockola** (the last name of a comedian, coined by Jimmy Hatlo, 1952).

Once **payola** as a word and scandal made its mark on the national consciousness, headline writers, reporters, and columnists were enchanted with **-ola,** coining new words ending with **-ola** with startling regularity, words which were as quickly forgotten as they were fashioned. Examples of post-**payola -ola**'s include **baloneyola** (*Time,* 1960), **breezola** (the air), **bribeola** (*Detroit Free Press,* 1960), **brickola, brushola** (a brush-off), **bustola** (a flop), **chairola, Clarkola** (coined by Congressman John Moss, 1960, referring to Dick Clark), **crapola, cuffola, cupola, dazzola, dizzola, dreamola, favorola** (coined by Drew Pearson, 1960), **fivola, fixola, flushola** (*Cleveland Plain Dealer,* 1960), **freeola** (*Sports Illustrated,* 1960), **frogola** (coined by Jimmy Hatlo, 1960), **gayola** (shaking down a homosexual bar, 1960), **ghostola** (coined by Senator Wayne Morse, 1960), **G-ola** (one thousand dollars),

grabola (*Life,* 1960), **hayola** (*Variety,* 1960), **hepola, hipola, laundrola** (shaking down a Laundromat, 1960), **linguola** (coined in *American Speech* to describe the **-ola** craze, 1960), **mayola** (mayonnaise), **mickola** (a Mickey Finn), **money-ola** (coined in conjunction with the monitoring of the Teamsters, 1960), **muggola** (a mug), **nayola** (do-nothingism), **peola, plugola** (1960), **porchola, royola** (wedding gifts to Princess Margaret or as undeserved music royalties, 1960), **rubola** (*Detroit Free Press,* 1960), **schnozzola** (the nose), **scrambola, slugola, smackola, snortola** (a short drink of whiskey), **sockola, stinkerola, stinkola, stoolola** (an informer), **torchola,** and **whamola** (a very funny joke).

Payola had a direct semantic descendant in **drugola,** which surfaced in 1973 to refer to "payola in the form of illicit drugs" (Addenda to *Webster's Third New International Dictionary*). In 1973 a scandal arose with particular focus on Columbia Records, and was covered in such outlets as the *New York Times. Rolling Stone* reported on August 16, 1973, "Columbia Records and CBS, on the defensive since the payola and so-called '**drugola**' scandal broke out two months ago, have retreated to the womb position in the face of continuing investigations into the record company's activities."

The **-ola** construction is one of the most popular suffix constructions to make its mark in slang. Other notable examples of the use of suffix formations in slang include Slim Gaillard's **-orenee** coinings of the late 1940s and the 1950s, and the **-atation** inventions of security consultant Bo Dietel, a frequent guest of Don Imus on his syndicated morning radio show "Imus in the Morning." Dietel's fixation with **-atation** is somewhat reminiscent of Damon Runyon, with coinings such as "fryatation" for a legal execution by electrocution, "munchatation situation" for oral sex performed on a woman, and "pumpatation" for sexual relations between a man and a woman.

SOURCES AND REFERENCES

THE BOOKS WHICH proved useful for the slang of criminals and those which proved useful for the slang of prisoners (see Chapter 8) were to a large extent one and the same. Criminals speak of prison, and prisoners speak of crime. Because of this overlap, all of the references for both criminal slang and prison slang are identified here.

In tracking down criminal and prison slang, I consulted *Hillary Clinton's Pen Pal: A Guide to Life and Lingo in Federal Prison* by Reinhold Aman (Santa Rosa, Calif.: Maledicta Press, 1996); *Dictionary of Desperation: An*

Anthology of Expressions Used by Prisoners to Describe the Quality and Events of Their Daily Lives by John R. Armore and Joseph D. Wolfe (Washington: National

Alliance of Businessmen, 1976); *The Gangs of New York: An Informal History of the Underworld* by Herbert Asbury (New York: Knopf, 1928); *Gem of the Prairie: An Informal History of the Chicago Underworld* by Herbert Asbury (New York: Knopf, 1940); *Robbery by Mail: Story of the U.S. Postal Inspectors* by Karl Baarslag (New York: Farrar and Reinhart, 1938); *Let Tomorrow Come* by A. J. Barr (New York: Norton, 1929); *The Joint: Language and Culture in a Maximum Security Prison* by Inez Cardozo-Freeman (Springfield,

III.: Charles C. Thomas, 1984); *Prison Slang* by William K. Bentley and James M. Corbett (Jefferson, N.C.: McFarland, 1992); *Lockstep and Corridor* by

Dimensions, 1992); *Underworld and Prison Slang* by Noel Ersine (Upland, Ind.: A. D. Freese, 1933); *The Compleat Smuggler: A Book About Smuggling in England,*

and Morris Lipsius (New York: Twayne, 1950); *A True Expose of Racketeers and Their Methods* by Emmett Gowen (New York: Popular, 1930); "A Convict's

Charles L. Clark and Earle Edward Eubank (Cincinnati: University of Cincinnati Press, 1927); *The Tongue of the Tirilones: A Linguistic Study of a Criminal Argot* by Lurline Coltharp (University: University of Alabama Press, 1965); *Here's to Crime* by Courtney Ryley Cooper (Boston: Little, Brown, 1938); *Crime Dictionary* by Ralph De Sola (New York: Facts on File, 1982); *Street Signs: An Identification Guide of Symbols of Crime and Violence* by Mark S. Dunston (Powers Lake, Wis.: Performance

America, and Elsewhere, Past and Present by Jefferson Farjeon (Indianapolis: Bobbs-Merrill, 1938); *Beggars and Thieves: Lives of Urban Street Criminals* by Mark S. Fleisher (Madison: University of Wisconsin Press, 1995); *Tramping with Tramps* by Josiah Flynt (New York: Century, 1899); *The World of Graft* by Josiah Flynt (New York: McClure, Phillips, 1901); *The Bunko Book* by Walter B. Gibson (Las Vegas: Gambler's Book Club, 1946, 1976); *Dictionary of American Underworld Lingo* by Hyman E. Goldin, Frank O'Leary,

Dictionary of Words and Phrases," compiled by James Harris in *The Prison Experience* (Rutland, Vt.: Charles E. Tuttle, 1989); *A Booklet of Criminal Argot, Cant and Jargon* by Troy Harris (Somerset, Ohio: Author, 1976); *Keys to Crookdom* by George C. Henderson (New York: Appleton, 1924); *How Con Games Work* by M. Allen Henderson (New York: Citadel, 1994); *Minute Police Talks* by Captain Thomas S. J. Kavanagh (Boston: Williams Book Store, 1938); *Teen-age Gangs: Inside Story of One of

America's Gravest Perils by Dale Kramer and Madeline Karr (New York: Holt, 1953); *Gangster Girl* by Jack Lait (New York: Grosset and Dunlap, 1930); *Put on the Spot* by Jack Lait (New York: Grosset and Dunlap, 1930); *We Who Are About to Die: Prison As Seen By A Condemned Man* by David Lamson (New York: Scribner, 1935); *Life and Death in Sing Sing* by Lewis E. Lawes (Garden City, N.Y.: Garden City, 1928); *Kids and Gangs: What Parents and Educators Need to Know* by Ann Lawson (Minneapolis: Johnson Institute, 1994); *The Big Con: Story of the Confidence Man and the Confidence Game* by David Maurer (Indianapolis: Bobbs-Merrill, 1940); "The Argot of the Underworld," "The Lingo of the Jug-Heavy," "The Lingo of the Good People," "The Argot of Forgery," "The Argot of Pickpockets," and "The Argot of Confidence Men" in *Language of the Underworld* by David Maurer (Lexington: University Press of Kentucky, 1981); *Boy and Girl Tramps of America* by Thomas Minehan (New York: Grosset and Dunlap, 1934); *Criminal Slang: Vernacular of the Underworld Lingo* by Captain Vincent J. Monteleone (Boston: Christopher, 1945, 1949); *Cast the First Stone* by John M. Murtagh and Sara Harris (New York: Pocket, n.d.); *Hustlers and Con Men: An Anecdotal History of the Confidence Man and His Games*

by Jay Robert Nash (New York: M. Evans, 1976); *Dictionary of Crime, Criminal Justice, Criminology and Law Enforcement* (New York: Paragon House, 1992); *Life in Sing Sing* by Number 1500 (Indianapolis: Bobbs-Merrill, 1904); *Broadway Racketeers* by John O'Connor (New York: Liveright, 1928); *Glossary of Terms Used and Insignia and Patches Worn by Outlaw Motorcyle Gangs* (Philadelphia: Citizens Crime Commission of Philadelphia, 1976); *Cop Speak: Lingo of Law Enforcement and Crime* by Tom Philbin (New York: Wiley, 1996); *Road Hustler: Grifting, Magic and the Thief Subculture* by Robert C. Prus and C. R. D. Sharper (n.p.: Richard Kaufman and Alan Greenberg, 1977); *Sister of the Road: Autobiography of Box-Car Bertha* by Ben L. Reitman (New York: Harper Colophon, 1937, 1975); *The Gonif* by Morris (Red) Rudensky and Don Riley (Blue Earth, Minn.: Piper, 1970); *Runyon à la Carte* by Damon Runyon (London: Albatross Library, 1947); *Low Life: Lures and Snares of Old New York* by Luc Sante (New York: Vintage, 1991, 1992); *Chicago May: Her Story* by May Churchill Sharpe (New York: Macaulay, 1928); *Trick Baby: Story of a White Negro* by Iceberg Slim (Edinburgh: Payback, 1967, 1996); *Playing the Field: Autobiography of an All American Racketeer* by Diamond Spike

(Sacramento, Calif.: News, 1944, 1948); *The Milk and Honey Route: A Handbook for Hobos* by Dean Stiff (New York: Vanguard, 1931); *Close Pursuit: A Week in the Life of an NYPD Homicide Cop* by Carsten Stroud (New York: Viking, 1987); *The Professional Thief,* annotated and interpreted by E. H. Sutherland (Chicago: University of Chicago Press, 1937); *The Society of Captives: A Study of a Maximum Security Prison* by Gresham M. Sykes (Princeton: Princeton University Press, 1958); *Lag's Lexicon: A Comprehensive Dictionary and Encyclopaedia of the English Prison Today* by Paul Tempest (London: Routledge and Kegan Paul, 1950); *How To Be A Detective* by F. H. Tillotson (New York: Pratt, 1909); *Fighting the Underworld* by Philip S. Van Cise (Boston: Houghton Mifflin, 1936); *Runyonese: Mind and Craft of Damon Runyon* by Jean Wagner (Paris and New York: Stechert-Hafner, 1965); *The Badge* by Jack Webb (New York: Crest, 1953); *God's Gambler* by R. Frederick West (Englewood Cliffs, N.J.: Prentice-Hall, 1964); and *The Other Half: Autobiography of a Tramp* by John Worby (New York: Lee Furman, 1937).

From periodical literature, I drew on "The Jargon of the Underworld" by Elisha K. Kane in *Dialect Notes,* Vol. 5, Part 10 (1927); "Prison Lingo" by Herbert Yenne in *American Speech,* Vol. 2 (March 1926); "I Wonder Who's

Driving Her Now?" by William G. Shepherd in the *Journal of American Insurance* (February 1929); "The Chatter of Guns" by Colonel Charles G. Givens in the *Saturday Evening Post* (April 13, 1929); "The Argot of the Racketeers" by James P. Burke in *American Mercury* (December 1930); "Convicts' Jargon" by George Milburn in *American Speech*, Vol. 6 (August 1931); "The American Ganguage" in *Literary Digest* (April 9, 1932); "A Prison Dictionary" by Hi Simons in *American Speech*, Vol. 8 (October 1933); "Prison Parlance" by J. Louis Kuethe in *American Speech*, Vol. 9 (February 1934); "American Euphemisms for Dying, Death and Burial" by Louise Pound in *American Speech*, Vol. 11 (October 1936); "My, My, Such Language" by John B. Kenny in *Case and Comment* (March 1938); "The Snitch Squawks: A Glossary of Thieves' Slang" in *Better English* (February 1939); "Underworld Lingo" in *Better English* (April 1939); "Slang, Says You" in *Scientific Detective* (July 1945); "The Language of Delinquent Boys" by Jane W. Arnold in *American Speech*, Vol. 22 (April 1947); "Sex in Prison" by Edward T. Clayton in *Ebony* (July 1951); "Pickpockets Are at Work—On You!" by Jackson Kurtz in *Annual Police Report* (1955); "Smugglers' Argot in the Southwest" by Haldeen Braddy in *American Speech*, Vol.

31 (May 1956); "Payola" by William Randle in *American Speech*, Vol. 36 (May 1961); "Rhyming Slang in a Western Prison" by Inez Cardozo-Freeman in *Western Folklore*, Vol. 42, No. 4 (1978); and *Tennessee Prison Talk* by Carolyn G. Karhu in *American Speech*, Vol. 636u (Summer 1988). Many of these articles were compiled by Peter Tamony and are part of his collection at the Western Historical Manuscript Collection, University of Missouri in Columbia.

Newspaper articles which were helpful included "What The Racket Is and How It Works in Gangland" in the *New York Telegram* (September 6, 1928); "English as It Is Spoken Owes Debt to Racketeer" in the *New York Times* (November 12, 1929); "Underworld's Argo (*sic*) Shifting" in the *New York Times* (April 2, 1930); "Where a Spade is Never a Spade: Underworld Things Don't Go by the Right Names—Have a Jargon of Their Own—And Some of It Is Eminently Apt and Descriptive" in the *New York Times* (January 7, 1931); "A Burglar's Vocabulary" in *New Broadway Brevities* (October 5, 1931); "Salvation Army's Slang Defined: Yearbook Reveals Strange Expressions It Uses" in the *New York Times* (February 4, 1932); "Thieves' Words: A British Visitor Compiles a Record of American Argot" in the *Baltimore Sun* (December 3, 1932); "De-

clares Fair Rates Will Put Skids to Grift" in *Billboard* (March 27, 1937); "Girls Must Mix" in *Variety* (January 5, 1938); "Bunco Men: Police to Curb Crooks at Fair" in the *San Francisco Chronicle* (December 29, 1938); "Ted Cook's Coo Coo Nest" in the *San Francisco Examiner* (June 14, 19, 27, and July 1, 1939); "2 Indicted in Whisky Bunco" in the *San Francisco News* (April 14, 1944); "Glossary of Prison Slanguage" in the *San Quentin News* (September 15, 1944); "French Quarter" by Robert C. Ruark in the *San Francisco News* (March 31, 1948); "Police Nab Ace Bunco Artist" in the *Examiner* (June 11, 1949); "City on Delinquents" in the *New York Times* (May 15, 1955); "Station House Slang" by George Y. Wells in the *New York Times Magazine* (March 16, 1958); "Police (Cops?) Have Slanguage of Own" by David Burnham in the *New York Times* (February 15, 1970); "Prison Argot Changes: Sounds of Slammer-ese Pungent" in the *Washington Post* (September 12, 1970); "Bunco Game to be Topic" in the *Examiner* (November 15, 1973); "Gangs Have Their Own Language" in the *Yuba City* (Calif.) *Appeal Democrat* (September 30, 1991); "New York Con Men's Flying Game" by Barry Bearak in the *Chronicle* (December 29, 1991, reprinted from the *Los Angeles Times*) and "County Jail Jargon" in the *Los Angeles*

Times Magazine (July 28, 1996). Again, all but the last three were found in the Western Historical Manuscript Collection.

Miscellaneous sources included correspondence between Alex Badenoch of Marienville, Pennsylvania and Peter Tamony; Peter Tamony's notes of a conversation with Bill Dealey of the Preston School of Industry in February 1939 (both doing time in the Western Historical Manuscript Collection); a 22-page "Glossary of Underworld Jargon" compiled for and presented to Dr. N.T. Harris in 1932 (found with no further publication information in Merriam-Webster's files); a manuscript entitled *A Simplified Slang Dictionary*, Revised Edition, edited by Richard Croak and Frank Symes (1934), dealing with slang in Ohio prisons; and "Vacaville Vocabulary," collected by Frank E. Prewitt and Francis K. Schaeffer between 1961 and 1962 at the California Medical Facility in Vacaville and privately published by Peter Tamony in San Francisco in 1967.

For the Word History of **payola,** I relied upon "Payola" by William Randle in *American Speech,* Vol. 36 (1961); as well as the following sources in the Tamony Collection: *Downbeat* (April 1938); "Fined for Payola" in *Variety* (January 8, 1941); "Selling Side of Song Plugging" in *Variety* (January 7, 1942); "Chicago Hears of War Against Pay-

ola" in *Variety* (June 10, 1942); "Payola on a Rampage" in *Variety* (August 2, 1944); *Time* (March 5, 1945); "MPCE to Come Out Against Payola in New Pact; Some Say It's Futile" in *Variety* (January 21, 1953); "Million Dollar Shakedown in TV" in *Confidential* (June 1954); "Payola Oils DJ's for R&B Hits" in the *San Francisco News* (March 18, 1957); "Payola Suffers Jolt at Hands of S.F. Radio Station" in the *News* (March 29, 1957); "Disc Jockeys Are Next In Income Tax Probes" by Dorothy Kilgallen in the *San Francisco Call-Bulletin* (July 27, 1957); "FCC To Clean Up D.J. Bribery" in the *Hollywood Diary* (November 3, 1958); "There's Little New About This Payola" by Ralph J. Gleason in the *San Francisco Chronicle* (December 15, 1958); "To Get a Hit Takes More Than Payola" in the *Chronicle* (March 3, 1959); "Is Dick Clark Money Mad?" in *On the QT* (June 1959); "TV Quiz to Sift Hit-Song Payoff" in the *San Francisco News Call-Bulletin* (November 6, 1959); "Disc Jockey Bribery Bared by TV Probers" in the *San Francisco Examiner* (November 7, 1959); "Disc Jockey Talks: 50 Grand per Year in Payola" in the *Examiner* (November 9, 1959); "Television's Dick Clark in Probe?" in the *News Call-Bulletin* (November 17, 1959); "TV Quizzers Seek Payola Van Doren" in the *Examiner* (November 17, 1959); "Clark on Spot" in the *Examiner* (November

18, 1959); "Payola Djs Face Music in 6 Cities" in the *News Call-Bulletin* (November 19, 1959); "Song Plug Payola Inquiry Widens" in the *Examiner* (November 20, 1959); "Payola in Britain?" in the *Examiner* (November 23, 1959); "Will Dick Clark be Payola Star?" in the *Examiner* (November 24, 1959); "Teenage Idol Faces Crisis" in the *Examiner* (November 25, 1959); "Payola and the Jungle-esque World of the Record Business" in the *Chronicle* (November 19, 1959); "A Good Record Will Make It Without Payola" in the *Chronicle* (November 29, 1959); "The Changing Record Business" in the *Chronicle* (November 29, 1959); "Sad Plight of Payola Victim" in the *Examiner* (November 30, 1959); "DJ Asks Immunity in Payola Probe" in the *Examiner* (December 1, 1959); "Some Odd Angles in Payola System" in the *Examiner* (December 1, 1959); "Payola Spans the Atlantic" in the *Examiner* (December 2, 1959); "The Underground Network is Buzzing With Rumors" by Ralph J. Gleason in the *Chronicle* (December 6, 1959); "Churchmen Demand Cleanup of TV, Payola" in the *Examiner* (December 8, 1959); "Payola Satire: Bob Hope Charges NBC Censors Him" in the *News Call-Bulletin* (December 9, 1959); "The Unbeguiled Public" in *Time* (December 14, 1959); "RCA Agrees to Stop Payola for D.J. Plugs" in the *Examiner*

(December 16, 1959); "Legal Payola Status Sought" in the *News Call-Bulletin* (December 17, 1959); "Payola for Inez? Dear CBS—Go Climb an Antenna" by Inez Robb in the *News Call-Bulletin* (December 21, 1959); "D.J. Had That Old Stealing" in the *Examiner* (December 22, 1959); "Rudy the Reindeer Did It …No Payola" in the *Examiner* (December 23, 1959); "Ye Olden Payola" in the *News Call-Bulletin* (December 25, 1959); "Single-Disc Sales Are Way Off" in the *News Call-Bulletin* (December 26, 1959); "Sullivan Asks Probe of Hedda's Fee Plan" in the *Examiner* (December 30, 1959); "Hedda, Ed Wrangle Over TV Payola" in the *News Call-Bulletin* (December 31, 1959); "Key Legislators Split on How to Wipe Out Payola" in the *News Call-Bulletin* (January 1, 1960); "A Swan Song for Top Disc Jockey?" in the *Examiner* (January 6, 1960); "Cool Logic Over Payola" in the *Examiner* (January 17, 1960); "Dick Powell Sad 'Bout Payola Probe" in the *Examiner* (January 19, 1960); "Paar Denies Payola in Real Estate Film" in the *Chronicle* (February 28, 1960); "New FCC Chief Vows War on Payola" in the *News Call-Bulletin* (March 11, 1960); "Lid on Dick Clark Payola?" in the *Examiner* (March 13, 1960); "Rigged TV Shows, Payola Spark Ad Control Warning" in the *Examiner* (March 15, 1960); "The Age of Payola" in *Look* (March 20,

1960); "Payola Probe to Hear Dick Clark's Story" by Drew Pearson in the *Chronicle* (April 27, 1960); "Payola Probe Hints of 11,900 Per Cent Profit" in the *Examiner* (April 28, 1960); "Clark Denies Taking Payola" in the *News Call-Bulletin* (April 29, 1960); "Clark Admits Taking Gifts" in the *Examiner* (April 30, 1960); "Piddling $7000 Got Dick Clark in Trouble" in the *News Call-Bulletin* (May 3, 1960); "Clark Asserts He Got 114 Songs Free" in the *Los Angeles Examiner* (May 3, 1960); "Dick Clark's Fans Rally 'Round" in the *San Francisco Examiner* (May 13, 1960); "Music Biz Goes Round and Round: It Comes out Clark-ola" in *Life* (May 16, 1960); "Say Something Nice About Dick Clark" in the *News Call-Bulletin* (May 18, 1960); "5 DeeJays Held On Payola Charges" in the *Examiner* (May 20, 1960); "Bill OK'd To Outlaw Payola" in the *News Call-Bulletin* (June 9, 1960); "Stiff Payola Curb Mapped" in the *Examiner* (June 10, 1960); "FTC Chief Says Payola Pretty Well Stamped Out" in the *News Call-Bulletin* (August 8, 1960); "Anti Payola Bill Attacked by Senator" in the *Examiner* (August 11, 1960); "Weaker Anti-Payola Bill Passes" in the *Chronicle* (August 31, 1960); "Rep. King Attacks Payola for Nixon" in the *Chronicle* (September 3, 1960); "Payoff to Aid Nixon Charged" in the *Examiner* (September 3, 1960); "The Jockeys Are Asking For—

And Getting—Bread Again" in the *Chronicle* (October 23, 1960); "Rookie Lawmakers Go Slow on Payola" in the *News Call-Bulletin* (February 24, 1961); "Bay Djs, Execs Say No Payola" in the *Examiner* (March 1, 1961); "No Payola, Disc Jockey Testifies" in the *Chronicle* (April 29, 1961); "Laws Won't Cure the Payola Cancer" by Ralph J. Gleason in the *Chronicle* (July 6, 1961); "Peter Tripp Fined $500 in Payola" in the *Examiner* (October 17, 1961); "S.F. Disc Jockey Hits Payola Decision" in the *News Call-Bulletin* (October 18, 1961); "Payola Isn't Dead—It's Underground" by Ralph J. Gleason in the *Chronicle* (January 16, 1962); "New FCC Probe of Payola" in the *Examiner* (Nov-ember 28, 1964); "Senator Eyes FCC Report on Payola" in the *News Call-Bulletin* (December 7, 1964); "Senate Probe on Payola" in the *Examiner* (December 7, 1964); "Probe of Payola in L.A." in the *Examiner* (June 23, 1966); "Girls in Payola Deals" in the *Examiner* (June 15, 1966); "Clark Faces New Payola Charge" in the *News Call-Bulletin* (April 26, 1970); "BBC Probing Sex Payola" in the *Examiner* (February 15, 1971); "Sex Payola" in the *Chronicle* (March 25, 1971); "Drugs Now Linked to Record Payola" by Jack Anderson in the *Chronicle* (April 21, 1972); "How Payola Works in Record Business" by Jack Anderson in the *Chronicle* (August 1, 1972);

"FCC Investigating Record Payola" by Jack Anderson in the *Chronicle* (November 29, 1972); "Music Payola Scandal" in the *Examiner* (June 7, 1973); "Payola Scandal Vastly Overblown" in the *Chronicle* (June 13, 1973); "Payola, Narcotics in Record Business" in the *Chronicle* (July 1, 1973); "Payola for Disc Jockeys" in the *Chronicle* (July 22, 1973); "Payola Probe into Travel" in the *Chronicle* (July 27, 1973); "Rock Star's Charge in Payola Probe" in the *Chronicle* (July 31, 1973); "Soul Music Company Kickbacks Revealed" in the *Chronicle* (August 23, 1973); "Payola Probe— U.S. Denies It" in the *Examiner* (August 31, 1973); "Andy Williams at Payola Probe" in the *Chronicle* (September 6, 1974); "19 Indicted in Probe of Record Industry Payola" in the *Chronicle* (June 25, 1975); "Big Comeback for Payola?" in the *Chronicle* (August 3, 1975); "Pilgrimage Payola" in the *Chronicle* (September 11, 1975); "Payola: Setting Record Straight" in the *Chronicle* (September 17, 1975); "Judge Bars Secret Payola Testimony" in the *Examiner* (February 16, 1977); "Payola? That's What the Other Guys Do" in the *Examiner*

(April 19, 1977); "Getting Airplay is the Name of the Game" in the *Examiner* (April 29, 1977); "Payola Search up to Jaworski" in the *Examiner* (July 21, 1977); and "Payola: Contractors Tell How They Give U.S. the Business" in the *Examiner* (October 25, 1977).

For my look at the word **pig,** I

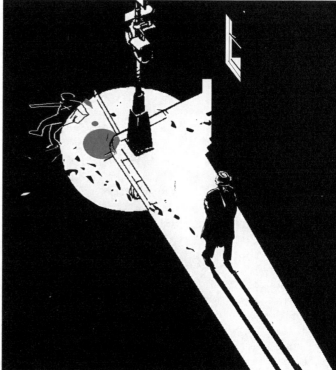

drew on Peter Tamony's files and read the following articles: "Another Day of Panther Protest" in the *Chronicle* (July 17, 1968); "Black Panthers Start 'University of Streets'" in the *Examiner* (July

17, 1968); "Newton Trial Firsts" in the *Examiner* (July 24, 1968); "Sick of Fight Words" by Dick Nolan in the *Chronicle* (July 29, 1968); Herb Caen's column in the *Chronicle* (August 4, 1968); Herb Caen's column in the *Chronicle* (August 14,1968); Herb Caen's column in the *Chronicle* (December 10, 1968); "No Time to Hog the Credit" in the *Examiner* (November 13, 1969); Herb Caen's column in the *Examiner and Chronicle* (February 9, 1969); Herb Caen's column in the *Examiner and Chronicle* (March 2,

1969); "Anti-War Fete Flop At Stanford" in the *Examiner* (May 12, 1969); "The Pig Incident" in the *Chronicle* (May 24, 1969); "A Bill to Fight Police Slurs" in the *Examiner* (September 19, 1969); "Bumper Stopper" in the *Chronicle* (October 22, 1969); "Protest Leader Accused in Chicago Violence" in the *Chronicle* (October 22, 1969); "Police Baiters Sent to Jail" in the *Examiner* (October 28, 1969); "Pig Bowl Winners" in the *Chronicle* (December 8, 1969); "Biblical 'pigs'" by Dick Gregory in the *Daily Illini* (dated by Tamony only as 1970); Herb Caen's column in the *Chronicle* (January 14, 1970); "Panther Office a Fortress" in the *Examiner* (January 21, 1970); "Why Sgt. Oink Was Eliminated" in the *Examiner* (April 23, 1970); "Kansas Student Tension: A 'Pig' They Respect" in the *Chronicle* (July 27, 1970); "Seale Testifies at New Haven Trial" in the *Examiner* (August 21, 1970); "Tate Murders: 'Pig' Spelled in Actress' Blood" in the *Chronicle* (August 17, 1970); "Latino Defendant's View of Policemen" in the *Chronicle* (September 29, 1970); "Los Siete Defendant's View of Cops" in the *Chronicle* (September 29, 1970); "Salinas Speech: Students Berate Reagan" in the *Chronicle* (October 3, 1970); "New Cop Looks Like a Pig" in the *Chronicle* (October 10, 1970); "The Cops Fight Back" in the *Examiner and*

Chronicle (July 11, 1971); "Super Pig's Plea" in the *Chronicle* (March 2, 1972); "Chief's Pig Ploy Annoys" in the *Chronicle* (March 9, 1972); Charles McCabe's column in the *Chronicle* (March 10, 1972); "Court Sees Site of Panther Raid" in the *Chronicle* (July 12, 1972); "Court Asks Hayakawa's Definition of Word 'Pig'" in the *Los Angeles Times* (December 9, 1972); "Cop Wants to Stay Piggy" in the *Chronicle* (April 19, 1975); and "A Cop's No Pig, N.Y. Police Say" in the *Examiner* (March 4, 1978).

Also from the Tamony Collection I used the following articles for the **cop** word history: "Word 'Copper' Traced to 1858 Chicago Slang" in the *Chronicle* (July 7, 1941); "Questions and Answers" in the *News* (April 26, 1945); "Questions and Answers" in the *News* (December 10, 1946); "Question and Answers" in the *News* (December 12, 1946); Jack Rosenbaum's column in the *News* (October 12, 1949); "Don't Call Us Cops" by Roden Garrabrant in *This Week* (February 4, 1951); "Don't Call Me Cop!" by Officer John Carlson in *Pageant* (June 1953); Jack Rosenbaum's column in the *News* (November 3, 1953); Jack Rosenbaum's column in the *News* (January 16, 1956); Jack Rosenbaum's column in the *News* (January 20, 1956); Herb Caen's column in the *Examiner* (March 8, 1956); "Airport Theft Up Since Row

Over Cop Authority" in the *Examiner* (July 30, 1959); "Lets Stop Kidding About Cops" in *This Week* (November 27, 1960); "You Must Be Smart To Be S.F. Cop" in the *News Call-Bulletin* (December 21, 1960); "Why Americans Turn on Police" in the *Chronicle* (November 12, 1961); "Cop Baiting—A Growing Trend" in the *Examiner* (December 11, 1961); "Stupid to Permit Disrespect for Cops" in the *News Call-Bulletin* (January 29, 1962); "Tired of Attacks on Cops, Mayor Wants Commission" in the *News Call-Bulletin* (August 3, 1962); "The Answer Column" in the *News Call-Bulletin* (June 4, 1963); "Cop a Friendly Name?" in the *Examiner* (June 9, 1964); "More on 'Cops'" in the *Examiner* (June 25, 1964); "Side Benefits of the Campaign" by Dick Nolan in the *Examiner* (September 3, 1964); Herb Caen's column in the *Chronicle* (November 18, 1966); "Bogart and the Tough Cop" in the *Examiner and Chronicle* (January 23, 1966); "Why Is a Cop a Cop?" in the *Examiner and Chronicle* (September 29, 1968); Herb Caen's column in the *Chronicle* (January 13, 1970); "Dear Abby" in the *Chronicle* (February 13, 1970); "What's Wrong with 'Cops'?" by Charles McCabe in the *Chronicle* (October 7, 1970); and "The Grab Bag" in the *Examiner and Chronicle* (February 19, 1978).

Chapter Eight:
THE WAGES OF SIN

HOSE WHO TAKE THEIR THEOLOGY from the Bible believe that the wages of sin are death (Romans 6:23), eternal death (II Thessalonians 1:8-9), everlasting punishment (Matthew 25:46), and destruction (Matthew 7:13). There are more immediate wages for most sins, earthly punishments that are either inherent in the sin or imposed upon the sin by external forces, religious, governmental, or otherwise. While the wages of sin cannot claim the same breadth and depth of slang as the sin being punished, they are not without an often ironic, pithy slang vocabulary.

The Wages of Alcohol Sin

THERE ARE SEVERAL PUNISHMENTS inherent in the consumption of too much alcohol. The first wage that one is likely to pay for the sin of excess drinking is the wage of regurgitation— **food escape!** As distasteful as the act may be, the verb "to vomit" has spewed a gorgeous body of slang synonyms, many coined and used by college students in the last 25 years. The choicest include **barf, blow, blow beets, blow breakfast, blow chow, blow chunks** (a favorite of Wayne Campbell in the *Saturday Night Live* sketch "Wayne's World" and two feature films), **blow cookies, blow doughnuts, blow groceries, blow lunch, boot, bow before the porcelain god, call Earl, call Ralph (on the big white telephone), chuck your cookies, chunder, clean house, decorate the pavement, drive the porcelain bus, go to Europe with Ralph and Earl in a Buick, heave, hug the porcelain altar, hurl** (also a big "Wayne's World" verb, as in Garth Algar's trademark line "I think I'm gonna **hurl!**"), **laugh at the carpet (lawn** or **shoes), lose lunch, pray at the porcelain altar** (or **to the porcelain god, goddess,** or **princess), Ralph, spew (chunks), talk to the god** (or **Earl) on the big white telephone, talk to your shoes, technicolor yawn, toss your cookies, upchuck,** or **worship the porcelain god.**

The morning after gives a punishment suffered by almost all drinkers at one point or another in their drinking life, the hangover. Slang descriptions of a hangover include **barrel fever,** the **beezy-weezies, bighead,** the **blues morning after the night before, bottle fatigue,** the **Irish flu** or **Irish toothache** (the Irish being one of the few groups that is still regularly insulted with impunity), a **katzenjammer,** the **Monday,** the **shakes,** being **under the weather,** and the **whoofits** (with the variants **woefits** and **woofits**). When we suggest that our hungover friend drink a little bit to soften the impact of the hangover, we refer to **the hair of the dog that bit you.**

The more serious punishment for the more serious alcohol drinker is delirium tremens, the acute mental and physical disorders that afflict alcoholics while drinking or as the harshest form of alcohol withdrawal. We treat it with a jocular tone, referring to the **DT's** as **pink elephants, snakes,** or **snakes in the boots,** but it is no laughing matter. Other slang analogues for the **DT's** include the **bats**, **black dog** (which can also mean "depression of spirits: blues, dejection" according to *Webster's Third New International Dictionary*), **blue devils**, **blue horrors**, **blues**, **bottle ache**, **bugs**, **dithers**, **drunken horrors**, **heebie-jeebies**, **horrors**, **jerks**, **jim-jams**, **jimmies**, **jingles**, **jumps**, **ork-orks**, **rams**, **rats**, **screaming Abdabs**, **screaming meemies**, **shakes**, **shim-shams**, **staggers**, **trembles**, **uglies**, **wackies**, **wet brain**, **whips and jangles**, and **whoops**.

The Wages of Drug Sins

THERE IS NOTHING AMUSING about the perils inherent in drug use, especially in drug use involving needles and veins. Aside from the dangers associated with addiction, heroin has several thoroughly frightening risks; among them are AIDS (the **monster**, the **plague** or the **virus**, which leaves the infected person **sick**), hepatitis (**hep** or the **yellow peril**), overdose (to **jam** or **o.d.**), and deliberate poisoning by adulterated heroin or a completely foreign substance (a **hot shot** or **ten-cent pistol**). Folk remedies for overdoses abound—the **cold crotch** (placing ice in the user's crotch) or a **salt shot** or **milk shot** (saline or milk solutions which counteract respiratory depression), not to mention the shot of adrenaline into the heart so gracefully depicted in *Pulp Fiction*.

The Wages of Sexual Sins: A Certain Illness

A PAINFUL AND LASTING WAGE OF sexual sins is that **certain illness**, the **gentleman's disease**, the **secret disease**, the **social disease**, and the **vice disease**—venereal disease. As befits a slang-rich sin, there is an inspiring body of slang to describe venereal disease.

Clap is the most common term for gonorrhea, yet it was considered standard English from the 16th century until about 1840 when it went underground and became slang. Beyond **clap**, the first stop is with ethnic slurs, for the slang naming of venereal disease is replete with them, largely at the expense of the amorous French: **African toothache**, the **Christian disease** (from Turkey), **French disease** (so named in a medical poem—yes, a medical poem—of 1530 which gave us the term "syphilis" and the affirmation that it "just took from France his Name"), **French evil**, **French gout**, **French sickness**, **Gallic disease**, **malady of France** (the term favored by Shakespeare), **Neapolitan disease** (in France, from the 16th century), **Polish disease** (in Russia, from the 18th century), **Spanish gout**, and the **Turkish disease** (in Persia). Abandoning the ethnic slur, here come the VD synonyms:

band in the box
big casino   Syphilis.
Gonorrhea is the **little casino**. **Big casino** is also used to refer to the death penalty, to cancer, or to any other fatal illness. It was used in this

last sense in the classic *Rat Pack film* Oceans Eleven, *which takes place in Las Vegas. It has been around for a long time (as in a 1920 O. Henry story), with the specific meaning of the valuable*

ten of diamonds in the card game casino, and other metaphoric uses signifying something or someone important.
bulldog dose   A severe case of venereal disease
coachman in the box

cold in the dong *Runny nose, runny genitals.*

crud

Cupid's itch

curse of Venus

the dog

dose

double event *Dual infections, syphilis and gonorrhea*

the drips

dripsey

forget-me-not *Not bloody likely!*

four-plus *From nurse slang for lab test results*

*which range from a completely negative one-plus to the strongest positive result of **four-plus**.*

full house *Multiple infections*

garden gout

the gift that keeps on giving

gleet

the gleets

haircut

horse and trap *Rhyming slang (**clap**).*

little casino *Gonorrhea*

lobster tails *Not at all a*

pretty visual.

morning drip

nine-day blues *Gonorrhea has an incubation period of nine days.*

old Joe

piss water burns

plague

pox

sauce

siff

six-oh-six *Syphilis*

torch of Venus

wasp *It stings.*

the whites

the yellows

Other slang terms related to venereal disease include to **boil someone's lobster** (to infect a man with venereal disease, again a truly hideous visual), **burnt** (infected), **dirty barrel** (infected), **dosed** (infected), **dripper** (someone who is infected), **fire ship** (a woman with venereal disease), and **Judy-bitten** (infected).

Genital inspections for signs of infection make a cheerful subject for slang inventors. These inspections are made in one of two places—by or of prostitutes and in the military. The military, like other authoritarian institutions, is a most productive breeding ground for slang, and its contributions to the slang of genital inspections is impressive: **chancre mechanic** (the medic who performs the inspection), **cock corpsman** (the medic), **dangle parade** (a group inspection), **dick check** (an individual inspection), **dick doc** (back to the medic), **shanker mechanic** (the medic who checks for chancres—slangified to **shanker**), and **short-arm drill** or **short-arm inspection** (building on **short arm** as a jocular term for penis). An inspection of a prostitute for signs of infection is a **canoe inspection** (derived from the image of a woman's external genitals as a canoe), while her inspection of a customer is **milking it** (massaging the customer's penis as one might milk a cow, checking for any discharge that would suggest infection) or a **pre-check**.

And then there is the cure—**riding the silver steed** (referring to treatment by bismuth subcarbonate and neoarsphenamine), **taking a trip and seeing the world through a porthole** (treatment with tryparsamide for neurosyphilis, which causes tunnel vision), and **taking the bayonet course** (same as the **silver steed**).

The Wages of Crime (It Doesn't Pay)

TO MANY CRIMINALS, crime does pay; if it didn't pay, there would be far fewer criminals. The wages of crime, though, are harsh indeed for the poor sinners who find themselves behind bars in jail or prison. Life in prison is brutal, degrading, dehumanizing, alienating, and for most it is ironically un-rehabilitative. Privacy and dignity are scarce commodities at best; constant noise, bad smells, hideous food, and the immutable near-occasion of violence are the universal facts of prison life that can be fully understood only by those who have experienced incarceration.

Authoritarian institutions such as the military or boarding school nearly invariably give rise to slang, and prison is no exception. Every prison has its culture, its habits, customs, code of

Figures of Authority

IN ANY AUTOCRATIC AND regimented setting or institution, slang kicks into passing gear when it comes time to coin names for those in authority, and such is the case in the autocratic and regimented world of the prison. The warden sits at the top of the authority pyramid in prison, but the slang vocabulary to describe this authority figure is relatively modest because prisoners do not interact with the him or her on a daily basis. The word *warden* is rarely used, except in the graphic and crude dysphemism (opposite of a euphemism) for defecation—to **feed the warden.** In past decades, the warden was known as the **ball of fire**, **big noise**, **head gee**, or **head guy**, and more recently, as **The Man**, the **main man**, the **main squeeze**, or the **old man.**

The prisoner's main authority-bashing-by-slang creativity has always been directed towards the prison guard, whose job is among the most thankless in the country. Over the 20th century, the convict has known his jailer most commonly as a **bull**, **hack**, or **screw** (from the days when **screw** was a slang synonym for "key"), but also as a **badge**, **blue shirt**, **boss**, **chaser**, **cop**, **hacker**, **heat** (like **cop**, a word from the streets originally applied to police), **herder**, **roach** (harsh!), **shack**, **shield**, **six-five** (started as a coded warning that a guard was approaching and then was applied to the guards themselves), **soaker**, **swine**, or **trigger.** If a new prisoner is a **fish**, by extension a new and inexperienced guard is a **fish bull.** A **gun bull** is an armed guard, a **line screw** is a guard who works on the cellblocks, and a **turnkey** is a guard who goes through the motions of doing his job without taking any noticeable interest in prison life. When a group of guards is dispatched to a cell to remove a prisoner by any means necessary, they are known collectively as a **goon squad.**

T h e   S l a n g   o f   S i n : W a g e s   o f   S i n

behavior, and grim realities. As a direct response to the unique culture of prison, inmates speak a slang argot that combines slang of the streets, criminal slang, prison-specific language, and contributions from prison's subcultures, such as prison gangs.

To be sure, one function served by slang in prison is to disguise the meaning of what is being said; guards, however, are with prisoners day in and day out, and the meaning of prison slang does not escape their attention for long. Argot thus is far less useful as a coded language in prison than it is, for example, in a short con where the victim is not a part of the daily life of the grift. Similarly, while slang in prison helps fortify the sense of prisoner identity in the face of prison authorities, one can't help but notice that many guards use the same slang used by prisoners (the sense of "us and them" is undermined if "them" speaks just like "us") and that a strong sense of identity would exist even without a special vocabulary.

Much of prison slang exists simply because society outside prison does not have the same habits, customs, restraints, and codes of conduct that one finds inside prison. New words and new expressions are needed to describe new things, new situations, and new relationships. A large idiom thus exists to describe the basics of prison life—prison sentences, solitary confinement, and guards. The slang vocabulary of prison, built in part on a stable vocabulary of incarceration and in part on an ever-replenishing supply of new coinings, is bitter, grim, and self-effacing. Yet, there is often a spark of defiant humor buried in the dark language, reminders of the resilience of the human spirit.

From **AB** to **zu-zu**, the slang of prison reflects the culture of prison, the culture of walls and fences and bars and locked doors and always guards doing their time too, of fermented catsup or nutmeg for highs or God-knows-what-that-powder-is, of **punks** and **wolves**, of shower rapes and shower stabbings and shower glares, a world where you don't back down, a world where you try to **do your own time**, where there is nothing but time.

AB Aryan Brotherhood, a white prison gang with membership nationwide

ace-deuce A good friend whom you can count on

ad man A prisoner who is too friendly with prison authorities. *Clipped from "administration."*

airmail Trash thrown from upper tiers of cells onto prison guards below

anchor Any temporary legal respite, such as an appeal, a writ, a stay, etc.

angel cake and wine Bread and water served to prisoners in solitary confinement

ankles Ankle shackles

AW An Aryan Warrior, a member of the white Aryan Brotherhood gang

away Incarcerated

back gate exit, back gate commute Death in prison

backup A group of friends and associates who will support you in a difficult situation

bad wire A lie

bag Prison

band A riot squad

band box, band house A county prison

banger A knife

barbecue To burn a prisoner by throwing a Molotov cocktail into his cell

beef A disciplinary charge against a prisoner

BGF Black Guerrilla Family, a black prison gang with members nationwide

Bibleback A religious prisoner

Big A The federal penitentiary at Atlanta

big day Visiting day

big stripes Violent, unmanageable prisoners

Big Top A penitentiary, usually Leavenworth (Kansas) or Atlanta

billy A white prisoner

bingo A riot

birdcage A prison cell

biscuit A black prisoner

blanket party A group assault on a prisoner, started when a blanket is thrown over the prisoner

blind Any area in the prison where guards can't see what is happening

blue sky Prison soup

boat A transfer out of a prison

bomb A handcrafted source of heat made with toilet paper

boob A prison or jail

booby hatch Jail

books The ledger that accounts for a prisoner's credit

boxcar A cell

briar A hacksaw

brick A carton of cigarettes

bricks The outside world

brig A jail

brodie Suicide by jumping off an upper tier. *This term borrows on the legend of Steve Brodie, a New York newsboy who in the late 19th century claimed to have survived a jump off the Brooklyn Bridge. Brodie had no witnesses to his jump, but his name made its way into colloquial American English in several ways, including this.*

bucket A city or county jail

bug A crude electrical

device used to heat water

bug trap A bed

bulldog To engage in hostile harassment

bull pen A common cell or waiting area

bunkie One's cellmate

bunk tank Cells reserved for drug addicts

buried Convicted

burner A knife

bus therapy The practice of transferring a prisoner regularly. *Also known as* **diesel therapy.**

bus ticket A transfer to another prison

butterfly A new, young arrival in prison

button A lookout

Cadillac The best of anything. *For example, a single bunk is a* **Cadillac bunk.**

Over the wall!

BECAUSE WE HAVE WATCHED SO MANY prison movies, we know several things about prison life—riots often start in the dining hall and escape is on the minds of at least some of the prisoners at any given moment. Confined in prison, it is natural to think about escaping, or to **sweat the fence;** some convicts become obsessed with thoughts of escape, and they are said to have **rabbit fever.**

Even if convicts succeed in escaping from prison, they do not escape prison lingo, and they describe their escape in slang terms. No matter what method of escape is used, the expressions **go over the hill, go over the wall,** or **tunnel** all refer to the general act of escape. *Escape* the noun has been substituted by **bush bond** or **bush parole, cornfield clemency, fence parole,** and **jackrabbit parole,** while *escape* the verb has been equated with to **cop a mope, crash a stir, crash out, crush out, make bush,** and to go **out the back door.**

camisole A straitjacket

campus The prison grounds

can 1. Jail 2. A can of loose tobacco

canary A prisoner

cannery A prison

can't hang Unable to survive in the general prison population

car 1. A paperback book tied to a rope made with torn sheets, used to pass articles from one cell to another 2. A group of associates or friends or fellow gang members. *This second sense produces the metaphors of **in the car** and **riding** for being part of a group.*

case A disciplinary charge

cave A cell

cellie One's cellmate

cell 99 A mythical cell where prisoners die

chalk To detain in a cell with a chalk mark on the cell door signifying a rule infraction

check A group beating of a prisoner to test his mettle

check in To enter protective custody

cheese eater An informer. *As in a rat.*

chinaman A prisoner who washes his clothes in his cell sink instead of the prison laundry. *An offensive term based here on a stereotypical Chinese*

laundryman.

chow Food

chronic A chronic offender

citizen A prisoner who is not a lifetime criminal

city A city jail

City College The Tombs, a prison in New York City. *Not to be confused with the City College branch of*

the City University of New York.

clean the books To confess to many crimes

click up To join a gang

clink A jail

coal oil and blue ointment The carbolic bath given newly admitted prisoners

college A prison

color A gang insignia

connection A prison guard who will smuggle contraband for a prisoner

cooler A dark cell

coozie stash A balloon

filled with drugs hidden in a female prisoner's vagina

cop deuces To assume a submissive or apologetic position

Copper John Auburn Prison in upstate New York

count The census of prisoners taken several times each day

country club A federal prison

county A county jail

crab bait A new inmate

crapper A jail or prison

crazy alley An area of a prison reserved for mentally ill prisoners

crossbar hotel A prison

daddy tank A cell reserved for lesbians

dance in the rain room To take a shower

deadline The line near a fence that prisoners may not cross without the threat of being shot

den A cell

diesel therapy The practice of transferring a prisoner regularly. *Also called* **bus therapy.**

dip To show too much interest in another's business

Disneyland A minimum security prison where serving time is relatively easy

dog An offensive guard

doghouse A watchtower on the prison wall

down Incarcerated

down home The Tombs prison in New York City

do your own time To serve one's sentence without complaint

dress in To cloth a prisoner in a prison uniform or, in the case of a prisoner condemned to death, in the special uniform used for the execution. *A newly arrived prisoner is said to be* **dressed in.**

drive on To confront someone

drum A cell

dry cell A special watch when a prisoner is suspected of having eaten drugs or contraband. *Also known as a* **potty watch.**

Words for Sentences

WE KNOW THAT TIME is relative; we vaguely remember Einstein's notions and the speed of light and we halfway remember the cute little joke about time passing in the dentist chair (slowly) used to illustrate the theory. Nowhere in the world does time pass more slowly than in prison, where time is all that there is and **doing your time** is all there is to do. There are, to be sure, other things to talk about, but time is a big topic of discussion and as befits a big topic of discussion there is a substantial idiom of time-related slang.

Words for a sentence in general include **bit** (with **to do a bit** meaning to serve one's sentence), **bounce** ("What's the bounce on the pimp beef?"), **gig** ("After he took the fall for the jewel store job, he did a gig in San Quentin"), **hitch**, **program** ("I'm just doin' my program"), **spot** (which can also mean a year, as in a "three-spot"), **stretch**, **time**, and **trick**. Concurrent sentences are said to be

jammed, while **stacked time** or **time running wild** refers to consecutive sentences.

With most prison sentences, a prisoner can earn a reduction in the sentence through model behavior in prison. The slang vocabulary of sentence reduction is built on images of virtue—**clean time**, **copper** or **copper time**, and **good days** or **good time**. To serve a full, unreduced sentence (a **rosary**) is to **do a flat bit**, **go out max time, jam up**, or **max out**.

Short of a death sentence, life in prison is the ultimate punishment, known in prison slang as **all** (which produces to **do it all** for serving a life sentence and to **get it all** for receiving a life sentence), **all day, all day and night, all day from a quarter** (a sentence of 25 years to life), the **bitch** (a life sentence for a career or habitual criminal, with "habitual" clipped to **bitch**), the **book, no-trump** (without chance of parole; instead of singing "I turned 21 in prison / doing life without

dry run A trip to court where nothing is accomplished

dry snitch To inform indirectly, by speaking loudly in front of prison authorities

ducats Scrip used at the prison store

duck-walk To walk with leg shackles

dump A prison

dump truck A lawyer who opts for expediency at the cost of a vigorous defense for his client

Dutch route, to take the To commit suicide

ends Money

eyes Small, handheld mirrors used to look down the corridor outside a cell

fall partner Someone who was arrested with you

fan To search or frisk. *This is a pickpocket term taken to prison.*

farm A prison

feed the warden To defecate

few Less than 15 days

fido A convict considered trustworthy and allowed special privileges

Fire in the hole! Get rid of your joints, a

parole," Merle Haggard might have sung "I turned 21 in prison / doing a no-trump"), **track thirteen with a washout**, or simply a **washout**. A **yard** (a one-hundred year sentence) might as well be life, and at a certain age if you pull a **telephone number** (a sentence of at least 20 years) or a **quarter** (a sentence of 25 years), you're **buried deep** and you might as well call it life. And then there is the cleverly designated **life on the installment plan**, a series of prison sentences that amount to a life spent incarcerated.

Words for other specific sentences draw on the slang of money:

Three months: A **quarter stretch**
Six months: A **sixer**
One year: A **boffo**, a **bullet** (also used in constructions such as "five bullets"), a **calendar**, **one-spot**, or **valentine**
Three years: A **three-bit**
Five years: A **five-specker**, **fin**, **finif**, or **nickel**

Ten years: A **dime, saw,** or **sawbuck**
Twenty years: A **double saw**

A **pit stop** is a short sentence for a parole violation, while a **sleep, whop,** or **wino time** is a very short sentence.

At this point the slang moves from concrete to conceptual. A **butt** is either the last part of a sentence or a fraction of the sentence that one is describing, as "two years and a **butt**." The second half of a sentence is **down hill; back time** is either time served while awaiting trial or the balance of a sentence that one must serve if parole is revoked (as contrasted to the **front** of a sentence which is the time served before parole); and the **tail** of a sentence is time spent on parole or probation, both known as **paper.** As the release date approaches, one **gets short.** The final night and day spent in jail is a **getup, rollover,** or **wake-up** (a term that was used in Vietnam and brought back to the workplace, where a **wake-up** is one's last day on a job).

guard is coming!

fish A new prisoner

fish line A string that prisoners use to move objects from one cell to another

fish roll The prison uniform, toothbrush, and tobacco issued a prisoner upon arrival at the prison

five in deep A gathering of prisoners that appears dangerous to the guards

five-to-lifers Prison-issued shoes

fix up To beat someone up

flats The bottom tier of a cell block

flavors Brand-name cigarettes

fly a kite To smuggle a letter in or out of prison

flyer A prisoner who commits suicide or attempts

suicide by jumping off the upper tier of a cell block

flying lesson An assault on an inmate in which he or she is thrown off a cell-block tier

fog To delouse a newly arrived prisoner

freeway The walkway outside a row of cells

free world The world outside prison

fresh and sweet Recently released from jail

fresh one A new arrival

front To give or loan something

Gallery 13 A prison graveyard

game, the The unspoken rules that govern life in prison

gapper A lookout

gas To throw liquids on guards from a cell

gate fever The nervous excitement experienced just before release

germ A cigarette

ghost To transfer a prisoner from one prison to another in the middle of the night

gladiator school A prison where young troublemakers are sent

glamour slammer A comfortable, relaxed jail or prison

goldfish Prisoners and decoys in a lineup in which they can be viewed by others whom they cannot see

gorilla A prisoner who takes what he or she wants by force

go to the wall To remain ultimately loyal

GP The general population

green light Preauthorization to attack rival gang members

grill The mesh in front of a cell

ground, on the Released

guest of the city Incarcerated in a city jail

hang on the leg To fraternize with guards

hard candy A prisoner marked for attack

hard time Serving a sentence the hard way, re-

Time Out

WITHIN THE GENERAL PRISON population there occasionally are truly unruly prisoners, those who will no more follow rules inside prison than they would outside prison. One way to punish the truly unruly is to confine them in an individual isolation unit, a segregation unit—you know, solitary confinement, **slammed down**. Known sarcastically by prison authorities as **meditation** or **peace and quiet**, solitary confinement is referred to by convicts as the **back row**, **bing**, the **black hole**, the **blue room**, the **box**, the **bucket**, **chokey**, the **coop**, the **damper**, the **deep freeze**, **digger**, the **hole**, the **icebox**, **on the boards**, the **shelf**, or, with a grim irony, the **Waldorf-Astoria**.

belling against prison authorities and/or the mores of prison life

hardware Weapons

hawk A lookout

heart Loyalty to friends and prison principles

heeled Armed

hen pen A prison for women

hit the bricks To be released from prison

hit the streets To be released. *In Carlito's Way, speaking with one of the great crime novel voices of the 20th century, Edwin Torres wrote of hitting the streets "like Sonny [Liston] hit Floyd [Patterson]"—hard.*

hood The chest. *A weightlifter's term.*

hook A razor

hooks Handcuffs placed on someone behind the back and forced upward so that his or her toes barely touch the floor, as in "Give him the hooks!"

hoosegow A local jail

hospital A prison or jail

house A cell

hut A cell

ice To sentence to prison

ice, on In prison

idiot juice Nutmeg and water, a prison intoxicant

Killing People Who Kill People

ALL CONVICTS IN A PRISON where executions take place are acutely aware of the fact, and a large body of slang has been developed to describe **capun** (capital punishment), the largely cynical slang serving as a defense mechanism to protect against the horror of execution. The slang of the death penalty (the **big casino** or the **works**) is laconic and jaded; a murderer whose execution is in ten days might drawl, "I've got nine more sleeps and then the **long one**." X-row for death row and **DC** for death cell are lifeless, but **dance hall** (meaning death row, the pre-execution cell, the hallway leading to the execution chamber, or the execution chamber), **in back** (the chamber itself), the **last mile** (the walk to the chamber), the **last waltz** (ditto), and **slaughterhouse** (death row) are all half-lively.

Hanging has sired a surprising number of slang synonyms, including the **air jig, air polka, air rumba, dance, dance of death, dance on air, floorless dance, going riding, halter** (the noose), to be **hung up to dry, necktie hanger** (the gallows), to **stretch hemp, to stretch rope, throat trouble, topping,** and **wiping.** Electrocution has generated its own vocabulary—**barbecue,** to **burn** or be **burned, electric cure, flame chair,** to **fry** or be **fried, hot seat, hot squat, Old Sparky** (Florida's oak electric chair, or the chair formerly used at Sing Sing Prison in Ossining, New York), **permanent wave** (electrocution), **ride old smoky,** to **ride the lightning,** the **sizzle seat,** the **state electrician** (the executioner), and to **squat.** The prisoner who commits suicide before being executed is said to **cheat the chair.**

Execution by firing squad gives us just **blindfold act** and the **wall,** while the gas chamber only gives us the **chamber** and **smog** as a verb. After going **up salt creek** (being executed), the prisoner is taken to the **icebox** (the prison morgue) for an autopsy.

inside, inside looking out Incarcerated

iron house A jail

irons Handcuffs

jacket One's prison file

jam A fight

Jasper A lesbian

jewelry Arm and leg shackles

jiggler A thin wire used to manipulate a pay phone to make a call without charge

jointwise Aware of the ways of life in prison

Judas slit A peephole or slit in a solid steel cell door

Judy A meal served in a lockdown area

jug A prison

jupe balls High protein mush served prisoners in isolation cells as punishment. *An old-time word with staying power.*

keep Jail

keister plant A balloon filled with drugs hidden in one's rectum. *Sometimes the balloon is just called a "balloon" and can be hidden in any body cavity.*

kick out To be released

kickup A riot

kindergarten A prison where young troublemakers are sent

kite A clandestine note

knockdown An open cell door

knot A bankroll

knucks Prison-made brass knuckles

lag A prison

lame A newcomer to the prison who doesn't know how to behave

leg ride To curry favor with the prison authorities

lifeboat A reprieve or pardon

lifer Someone serving a life sentence

limbo, in Incarcerated

lip A lawyer

little house A foot locker or wall locker where an inmate's possessions are kept

little school A reformatory

lock To occupy a cell

long chain A group of prisoners being transported from jail to prison

madhouse A rough prison

mainline The general prison population

Man down! A prisoner is sick or injured!

marble orchard A prison graveyard

mark Credit given in prison for good behavior

max end The maximum security section of a prison

merchant A prisoner who sells what should be given

merry-go-round A prisoner's release day, when he or she is shuffled from office to office

minny The minimum security section of a prison

missive A letter

money Anything of value

mug To take a prisoner's picture

mule To smuggle (something) into prison

neck A white prisoner. *Clipped from "redneck."*

Nester A member of Nuestra Familia, a Mexican-American prison gang with members nationwide

new buddy A newly arrived prisoner

old thing A long-term, unmotivated prisoner

On my skin! A sacred oath by white prisoners

Oregon boot A heavy steel manacle attached to one ankle

out of circulation Incarcerated

pad A cell

pads License plates. *In many states, prisoners manufacture the state's license plates.*

passenger A dependable friend who is **in the car**

pen A prison

PG&E Electric shock treatment. *PG&E (Pacific Gas & Electric) is the electric utility in Vacaville, California, where this term was recorded.*

phone's off the hook A guard is listening

pine-box parole Death in prison

play for the gate To conform to prison rules to obtain an early release

playhouse A minimum security prison where it is relatively easy to serve time

pogie A county jail or workhouse

point A lookout

Pops Anyone who is older than you

Pork Dump Clinton Prison in Dannemora, New York

pruno Fermented food scraps. *Pruno is Spanish for "plum," but the prison concoction is a fair piece off the mark if compared with plum wine.*

pull plastic To move to another cell, cell block, or prison. *So called because the prisoner packs his belongings in a plastic garbage bag for the transfer.*

punk **1.** Bread **2.** The kept lover of a prisoner

punk out To inform on another prisoner

quad A prison

Jailhouse Rock

IN 1957, JERRY LEIBER AND MIKE STOLLER'S "Jailhouse Rock" as sung by Elvis Presley seemed cute and innocent. Heard through the filter of prison sex, it takes on a whole new meaning which is neither cute nor innocent:

> *Number forty-seven said to number three*
> *You're the cutest little jailbird I ever did see*
> *I'd sure be delighted if you'd bunk with me*
> *C'mon and do the jailhouse rock with me . . .*

Sex is a fact of life in prison, occasionally involving a truehearted homosexual (a **gump**), but more often involving a brutal display of alpha-wolf power and control. In addition to the words used to describe any new prisoner, there are several with overtly sexual overtones—**canned goods** for an anal virgin and **fresh meat** for any promising, younger prisoner. It is usually not long before a new prisoner who cannot defend himself is raped—**chopped** or **turned out**—often with the crude and blunt invitation to prison sex of **There will be shit on my dick or blood on my blade, which will it be?**

Leaving aside the prisoners who are homosexual by choice and masturbation (perhaps with the aid of a **fifi bag**, or a container filled with some sort of lubricant), the prison world of sex is made up of the predator (the **turk** or **wolf**), the protector who expects sexual favors in return for protection (the **dad**), and the passive prisoner (the **punk**, **chicken**, or **Maytag**, who does laundry as well as sexual favors in return for protection) who is "owned" by a **dad** who protects him from **turks**.

Most of the slang used in prison to describe sex is not prison-specific, although the emphasis is on those expressions that emphasize the aggressive/passive dichotomy in the **dad/punk** relationship, such as **pitch** and **catch**, or the brutality of rape, such as **chop**.

quarter A 25-pound weight used in weightlifting

quiet-side Secret

rack the doors To open or close cell doors

rain check Parole

raise, raise up To be released from prison

raisin jack An intoxicating drink made in prison from fermented raisins

range A tier of cell blocks

rat 1. A prisoner who steals from other prisoners 2. An informer

rattle the tin cup To inform

red-eye Fermented catsup

regulate To beat someone up

rest your neck Be quiet

ride To be part of a group

ride a silent beef To be prosecuted and sentenced harshly for a minor offense when law enforcement officials believe you are guilty of a more serious offense which they cannot prove

riot bait Bad food

road dog A good and dependable friend

rock pile, on the Serving a short sentence in a workhouse

room A cell

roomie One's cellmate

run a shop To deal in contraband

Run, Johnny, Run R. J. Reynolds smoking tobacco

saddle tramp A biker

safe One's rectum or vagina, where drugs are stored and smuggled

sally port The first gate to a prison

salt creek Jail

sand Sugar

satch A piece of paper soaked in a drug, dried, and sent with a letter to an inmate

school of crime A prison

setback A decision denying parole

settled In prison

shakedown A thorough search

shaker wire An alarm wire sensitive to a slight touch on a prison fence

shank 1. A knife 2. To house

shebang A cell

sheets Cigarette papers

shingle A license plate. *Manufactured in prison.*

shiv A knife

short-hair A newly arrived prisoner

six A lookout

sky Prison soup

slam To store a knife inside a tube in one's rectum

slammer Prison. *They throw you in a cell and slam the door behind you, hence the evocative slammer.*

slat A bar of a cell

slow pay To stall someone

smoke A black prisoner. *An offensive racial slur dat-*

ing from at least 1913.

snitcher A metal detector

soda cracker A white prisoner

song and dance A strip search

soup Money or anything worth bartering

spring To be released from prison

spring, at the Confined by a straitjacket

spun out Crazy

square Loose tobacco

stand out To report someone for infractions of a prison rule

stand-up Loyal

state Tobacco furnished prisoners by the prison authorities

stay-out A concerted refusal by prisoners to return to their cells

steel A prison-made knife

stinger A crude electrical device used to heat water

stir A penitentiary

stop ticket A warrant awaiting a convict upon release

suitcase To conceal drugs in a balloon inside a body cavity

tag A license plate

take it to the vent To commit suicide

thirteen and a half percent Twelve jurors, one judge, and a half-assed chance—a convict's view of the criminal justice system

tight Maximum security (said of a prison)

tight, in a In trouble

tip A prison gang

torture chamber A prison where drugs are absolutely not available

trick bunk A bed that is not readily visible to guards where sexual liaisons are scheduled

trolley A wire or string used to pass messages from one cell to another

trusty A convict considered trustworthy and allowed special privileges

turn copper To inform

unfortunate Sent to prison

up the river Incarceration at Sing Sing Prison in Ossining, New York

vacation near Chappaqua Incarceration at Sing Sing Prison

vas Vaseline, used to facilitate the placement of a **keister plant**

vic A convict

visit A visitor

walk To be released from jail or prison

walk-alone A prisoner who cannot exercise in the yard with the general population

War Department One's wife or girlfriend. *An embellishment of the old-fashioned "battle-ax."*

wire 1. A person who has influence with prison authorities 2. The fence around a prison

wood A white inmate. *A clipped "peckerwood."*

woodpile The area in a prison where weightlifters work out. *The area is also referred to more literally* as the *"weight pile."*

writ of God-help-us Any esoteric legal procedure

yard The recreation area of a prison

yard job A contracted murder in prison. *The victim is usually killed in the prison yard.*

young stir A reform school. *Cute pun, no?*

zip A prison-made firearm

zipper A scar

zoo-zoo, zu-zu Something sweet

Sources and References for Chapter 8 are included in the Sources and References for Chapter 7.

The Final Curtain

RETURNING TO ROMANS and all that, death is a wage of sin. While there is a curious near-dearth of slang to describe birth, the breadth of the terms we use to describe death is startling. We dance around the word *death,* shrouding the idea of shuffling off this mortal coil with literary euphemism on the one hand and bravado-laced slang on the other. On the slang hand, we reject the wage of "to die" in favor of to **bite the dust** (thanks to Homer for that one), **buy the farm, cash in your chips, check out, croak, cross the Great Divide, get planted, give up the ghost** (Shakespeare here), **kick the bucket, pull the plug, push up daisies, ring down the curtain,** or **seven out** (a useful craps allusion). Cancer, one wage of tobacco use, is the **Big C** or the **big casino.**

EPILOGUE

LAST CALL FOR ALCOHOL! You don't have to go home, but you can't stay here—any more for anymore? Nightcap anyone? A six-pack to go? We're down to seeds and stems, rinsing the baggie, on carpet patrol in search of crumbs—fiending and jonesing, craving and yenning—it's a panic! It's time to kick the habit, but, *rien ne va plus* though, we're tapped out, busted, over the top and to the farm. We've been pinched and collared, we got buried deep and slammed down but we did our time and now we hit the streets. We've been conned and clipped, Murphyed and badgered, burnt and stung, we learned to blow, punch, peel, and burn a peter, and we've cleaned the books—we've been sounded and roughed and we've rumbled. We've got snakes in our boots—it's time to go over the wall, off onto fence parole, to crash out. We've sevened out—five and two, we're all through. We've been stewed, screwed, and tattooed and it's time to cash in our chips. Outlaws forever, forever outlaws—*adios* my friend . . .

Bibliography

AT THE END OF EACH CHAPTER except Chapter 8, there is a list of sources and references for that chapter. The dictionaries relied upon and referred to throughout the book include the following:

Barrère, Albert, and Charles G. Leland. *A Dictionary of Slang, Jargon, and Cant.* 2 vols. Edinburgh: Ballantyne, 1889-90.

Bartlett, John Russell. *Dictionary of Americanisms.* Boston: Little, Brown, 1859.

"B. E., Gent." *A New Dictionary of the Terms, Ancient and Modern of the Canting Crew.* London, 1696-99.

Cassidy, Frederick G., ed. *Dictionary of American Regional English.* 3 vols. to date. Cambridge, Mass.: Belknap Press of Harvard University Press, 1985–.

Chapman, Robert. *New Dictionary of American Slang.* New York: Harper and Row, 1986.

Farmer, John S. *Americanisms Old and New.* London: Thomas Poulter, 1889.

Farmer, John Stephen, and William Ernest Henley. *Slang and Its Analogues Past and Present.* 7 vols. Printed for subscribers only. London, 1890-1904.

Grose, Captain Francis. *A Classical Dictionary of the Vulgar Tongue.* London, 1785.

[Hotten, John Camden]. *The Slang Dictionary.* London: Author, 1859.

Lighter, J. E., ed. *Random House Historical Dictionary of American Slang.* Vol. 1, *A-G,* and Vol. 2, *H-O.* New York: Random House, 1994, 1997.

Matsell, George. *Vocabulum: A Rogue's Lexicon.* New York: Matsell, 1859.

Matthews, Mitford. *A Dictionary of Americanisms on Historical Principles.* Chicago: University of Chicago Press, 1951.

Mencken, H. L. *The American Language.* 4th ed. New York: Knopf, 1962.

Partridge, Eric. *A Dictionary of Slang and Unconventional English.* 8th ed. Edited by Paul Beale. New York: Macmillan, 1984.

Thorton, Richard H. *An American Glossary.* Philadelphia: Lippincott, 1912.

Wentworth, Harold, and Stuart Berg Flexner. *Dictionary of American Slang.* New York: Thomas Y. Crowell, 1960, 1975.

Weseen, Maurice H. *Dictionary of American Slang.* New York: Thomas Y. Crowell, 1934.

Wright, Joseph, ed. *The English Dialect Dictionary.* 6 vols. New York: Putnam, 1898-1905.

SINDEX

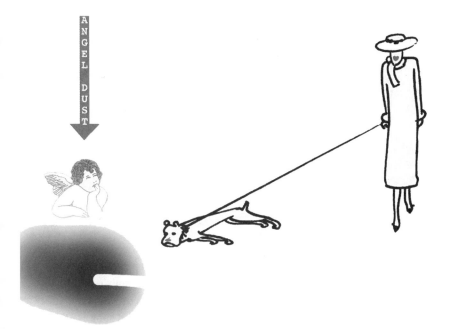

pain killer

queer maker 222
quencher 13
querent 244
quesified 244
Question, The 58
quetor 220
quick aging 18
quick one 13
quick trick 207
quicksilver 123
quiet-side 298
quiff 199
quill 17, 120
quinine 83
quint 63
Quintana roo blue 106
quitter 165
quiver 185
R-2 116
R.C. 104
R2 your D2 175
rabbit 54, 60, 165, 207
rabbit ears 37
rabbit fever 290
rabbit hunting 78
rabbit-footing 17
race 37, 43
Racehorse Charlie 110
racing bike 152
rack 227
rack the doors 298
rack up 165
rack up the game 78
radar Charlie 60
rag 60, 62, 78, 256, 266
rag up 267
rag water 13

rail 42, 78, 90
rail bird 54, 227
rail-lugger 165
railbird 78
railer 121
railroad 118
railroad bible 54
railroad hand 78
rain check 298
rainbow 55, 79, 115
rainbow roll 115
raincoat 181
rainy day woman 108
raise 298
raise the mainsail 175
raise up 298
raiser 222
raisin bread 64
raisin jack 298
rake 55, 227
rake-off 79
raking 222
Ralph 285
Ram 123
ram and jam 79
ram the ham 175
rammer 13
rammy 222
rams 286
randy 222
rangdoodles 79
range 298
rank 166
ransom 50
rap 268
rap sheet 268
rape 240

rape-O 268
rapper 268
Raquel Welch 58
raspberry 110
rat 9, 298
rat face 191
rat-hole 79
rate 166
rats 286
rats and mice 90
rattle 90
rattle the tin cup 298
rattler 90, 254
rave 128
rave breeze 122
raver 128, 129
raw 130
razor edge 84
RD 115
reaches 13
read 79
read braille 176
read poetry 175
readable 230
reader 77, 109
reading 243
ready 36
ready rock 130
ready-made 235
real 13
real deal 266
real McCoy 13
real stuff 13
real thing 13
rebel trap 227
rebel wedding 264
reck 267

About the Author

Tom Dalzell is a man of many talents, and fortunately one of them is gathering slang with a keen eye for the unusual and skillfully drawing a broader cultural picture from the pieces he finds. The author of *Flappers 2 Rappers: American Youth Slang,* published by Merriam-Webster in 1996 as part of the Lighter Side of Language Series, Tom has no trouble getting his hands on slang: his collection of 2,000 books on the subject is one of the country's largest. He came to be a slangmeister by his own road taken. He grew up in suburban Philadelphia and graduated from the University of Pennsylvania in 1971 with a degree in American Civilization. In 1976, he was admitted to the California bar, and since then he has worked as a union lawyer. However, over the years he has also developed a passion for collecting, studying, and writing about slang. Tom Dalzell resides in Berkeley with his two children, and when not maxin' and relaxin' on the home front, he divides his time between the law and the language as it lives outside the pale of received respectability.

About the Illustrator

Born in Hungary, **Istvan Banyai** quickly made his mark in the United States after his arrival in 1981, with his striking and innovative illustrations appearing in such publications as *Atlantic Monthly, Time, The New Yorker, Playboy,* and *Rolling Stone.* Istvan has crafted cover art for Verve, Sony, and Capitol records, and has created an animated short film for Nickelodeon, as well as animation for MTV Europe. His unique vision found ample room to bloom in the children's book *Zoom,* published in 1995. This wordless journey through receding perspectives was hailed as one of the best children's books of the year by the *New York Times* and *Publishers Weekly,* and won a National Children's Choice Award based on the judgments of kids themselves. *Zoom* was succeeded by *Re-Zoom* (1996) and *R.E.M.: Rapid Eye Movement* (1997), which takes one through a dreamscape of changing shapes and subtle connections to an outer world. Istvan Banyai lives in New York and was also an illustrator of Tom Dalzell's *Flappers 2 Rappers: American Youth Slang,* published by Merriam-Webster in 1996.